THE WOOD

OF GREEN

by ALAN LINDGREN

POETRY

The Seeker (1986)
O Days Are Made of Riddles (1987)
The Sun Sings: WORD-PICTURES 1997 (1999)
Winter Hymns (1997-1998)
Pulsing Love and Light Eternal (1998)
Sun and Moon and Stars of Night (1998)
Summer Songs (1998)
Autumn Harvest (1998)
The Diary (1999)
Instrument of the Poetic Word (1999)
A Poet's World (1999)
Ego and Love (1999)
Night-Mysteries 2004–2005 (2005)
Sun, Sparrow, and Star: Sacred and Secular Songs; Selected Poems (2009)
Journeying with the Sun: An Evolving Imagination; A Poetry Chronology (2013)

POETRY with SHORT FICTION and NON-FICTION

Balance is Freedom and Freedom is Love (2002)
By the Sunset there's a Door (2002)
The Courage of the Flame (Two Editions) (2003)
The Magic of the Stars (Two Editions) (2004) (2005)
LOVE- PICTURES 2003–2005 (2005)
The Tides of Evening (Two Editions) (2006)
Love Was All He Vowed (2006)
Imagination: The Final Poems (Two Editions) (2006) (2007)
Imagination and Insight: Selected Poems and Essays (2007)
LIGHT-LICHT: Selected Poems with Three Essays (2007)
The Wood of Green: Poems, Stories, and Studies (2014)

SHORT FICTION, PLAYS, a LIBRETTO, a TREATISE and a NOVEL

Regrouping in Idea and Practice: A Treatise on Mars (2007)
Fiction and Fact: Tales, Stories, and an Essay (2007)
The Folk Tale of the Two Tom-Tom Bird Cousins (2008)
Two Folk Tales 2008 (2008)
Michael and Los Angeles: A Novel (2008)
Oliver and Nancy: A Humorous Story in Ten Chapters (2009)
Two Short Plays by Alan Lindgren (2010) (2011)
Saltiff Shore – Where Love's Requited: A Comedy in Six Acts (2010)
The Property: A Play in Three Acts (2010)
Kings & Commoners, Mouse, Magic and More: Stories and Tales (2011)
Sons and Daughters: An Operetta in Prologue and Five Acts; The Libretto (2012)
I Believe, an Imagination with Tales and Stories by Alan Lindgren (2013)

BIOGRAPHY

Margaret Lindgren: A Biography and Picture of the Human Being (2005)
Alan's Life-Story (Two Editions) (2005)
The Life of Paul Stanley McLester (2006)
Arne Ragnar Lindgren: Man of Heart, Hand and Mind (2006)
Disa Ellen Lindgren: A Biography of a Modern Human Being (2006)

Alan Lindgren

The Wood of Green

Poems, Stories, and Studies

ℰℒ

Sun Sings Publications

Culver City

Alan Lindgren is an expert on the four temperaments and a much-published lyric poet, essayist, and fiction writer. He is the author of By the Sunset there's a Door: Poetry, Prose and Essays Celebrating Nature and Humanity, The Courage of the Flame: Ballads, Sonnets and Other Gardens of Poetry with Prose Writings, The Magic of the Stars: Poems 2003–2004, Sun, Sparrow, and Star: Selected Poems, Journeying with the Sun: A Poetry Chronology, and I Believe: an Imagination with Tales and Stories. His fiction, articles, and poetry have appeared in *Biodynamics*, a publication of the *Bio-Dynamic Farming and Gardening Association, Inc.*, *The Correspondence*, newsletter of the Central Region of the Anthroposophical Society in America, and Highland Hall Waldorf School's newsletter *Rhythms*.

The Wood of Green: Poems, Stories,
and Studies by Alan Lindgren

Sun Sings Publications, Culver City, CA 90232
© 2014 by Alan Lindgren
All rights reserved. Published 2014.
Printed in the United States of America
Book design by Alan Lindgren
10 9 8 7 6 5 4 3 2 1

Library of Congress Control Number: 2014919478

1. Lindgren, Alan David, b. 1962—Poetry, Short Fiction, Non-Fiction.
2. Poetry. 3. English, German, Spanish Poems. 4. Short Stories. 5. German Stories. 6. American Stories. 7. The Four Temperaments. 8. The Soul's Awakening in the Age of Light. 9. Adult Self-Education. 10. The Seven Planetary Types. 11. Paul's Damascus Experience and the Inner Birth of Christ. 12. Practical Wisdom. 13. Knowing by Thinking, Knowing by Imagination. 14. The Face of Our Humanity. 15. Materialism and Technology. 16. Facts and Knowledge. 17. Artificial Sensations and the Children. 18. Viewpoints in Relation to the I. 19. Society and the I. 20. Freedom: On Being 'Different'. 21. Culture Past and Present. 22. Reincarnation and Destiny (Karma). 23. The Dead, the Child, and Us. 24. Identity. 25. Christ Need and Christ Help. I. Title.

Lindgren, Alan David, b. 1962
[Poetry, Stories, Non-Fiction]
The wood of green: poems, stories,
and studies/Alan Lindgren.–1st ed.
p. cm.
ISBN: 978-0-9832053-9-5
2014

Acknowledgements

My deep thanks to my best and dearest friend Dr. Virginia Sease for her abiding friendship, understanding, warmth, love, inwards support, affirmation, appreciation, and esteem expressed in countless cards and letters, telephone calls, and precious personal visits over the many years since our first meeting on February 15, 1986; and to my good and dear friend John Alexandra for his loyal friendship, counsel, good will, and love, shown in phone calls, e-mails, and many wonderful personal visits since October 1978. With deepest gratitude I think on my dearest Christ-brother Gérard Klockenbring† (1921–2004), the great French Christian Community seminary principal and pastor-priest. My warmest gratitude for the unceasing love and support of my good, wonderful, lovely, dearest Mother, Mrs. Margaret Lindgren, and the sustaining reliability of my good, harmonious, even, serene, steadfast, and dependable father, Arne Lindgren† (1918-1994), who have supported me with unending patience and kindness, generosity and understanding, and faithful and loving hearts throughout my 52+ years—full of human goodness and warmth. I owe so much especially to these human beings, and others too numerous to mention, that my heart is very full.

Homecoming—To Christian Morgenstern

When the hand writes,
does not the child or man?
When the home invites,
does not the hearth or stand
the housewife at the door
open welcoming?
She's swept the floor
for this homecoming.

If you see before you
an instrument or a place
Remember those who do
or make a living space
For just as none alone
may stand without a world
So only a stone
reposes like a pearl.

Yet even a pearl
grows in an oyster shell
Thus does each belong
a dwelling place as well
Then welcome on their journey
who come to you in need
Favor those are learning
with books of life to read.

Alan Lindgren
Los Angeles
September 26/28, 2014

Contents

The Poems

Deutsche Gedichte (German Poems: A Review)

Poemas en Español (Spanish Poems: A Review)

The Stories

The Studies

* Studies on/with content on the Four Temperaments

Foreword

"Consciousness in thinking signifies wakeful (thought) perception and (thought) production that flows in a living stream into the thinker."
Preface, the libretto to *Sons and Daughters* (an operetta) by Alan Lindgren (Culver City: Sun Sings Publications, 2012), 12

This is sense-free or autonomous thinking, which lives. Such is the thinking in my poems and essays that is living and creative, as is the imagination of my four German and seven English stories.

For the first time are seven Spanish poems of mine in *The Wood of Green* as I had never composed Spanish poetry before. There are also 11 German poems represented, along with the majority that are (American) English poems (91). I am a poet by vocation. *Destiny* (15 October 2014) appears on page 504. It is as true as it is clear and deep. *Finding Autumn Mountains*, *Tender*, and *Family* (pages 554-556) are the final poems.

The German stories are also my first, the first two written in September 2013 after my 51st birthday anniversary. Entirely different from the other, *The Novelists* (*Die Schriftsteller*) is Juvenalian or dark satire and farcical with a moral lesson, while *Flemsbach* is fairytale-like, a genuine imagination that is living that therefore lives in the spiritual world where soul and spiritual beings experience it. Both stories are translated into English by their author for non-German readers and for those who will benefit from having the original German to compare with the English translation. Likewise I have translated *The Silver Goblet* (*Der silberne Becher*), and *The Little Fairytale of the Old Couple Hühnerfaoth and the Faerie* (*Das kleine Märchen des alten Ehepaar Hühnerfaoth und des Fee*) into English.

The first English-language tale, *Hemdlig, the Three Brothers, and the Three Sisters*, is, in some respects, like a fairy story, even though it is mostly narrative given in speech, and, in content, it draws on Medieval European epic poetry. Certainly not of the caliber of the true great epic poem *Parzival* by the German knight and poet Wolfram von Eschenbach (c. 1170 – c. 1220), which he set in his own day of chivalry and castles in *Mittelhochdeutsch* (Middle High German), it nonetheless compares in

the two reigning lands or kingdoms, in *Parzival* the faerie (sovereign princess) kingdom under Feymorgan (French, Morgan Le Fey, literally "Morgan the Faerie" (she was a half-sister to King Arthur; they are actual historical personalities)) and the knightly (royal kingly) kingdom under the eventual rule of the predestined Parzival. But there mine differs, and in all other ways, for example in audience (*Hemdlig* is ideal for children), *Parzival* is very long (but rich and vivid, capturing the interest and imagination of the reader (it was immensely popular during the two centuries after it was written)), mine is in prose, in my story there are *three* brothers (kings with kingdoms) and *three* sisters (princesses with fiefdoms), and the wise old man Hemdlig plays the central role in my tale.

Every Sun destiny must know the experiences of many of the significant characters in *Parzival*, and thus really *is* these characters along his earthly journey, those who, in this epic, are all in the same bloodline (family). Historically, these were actual human beings, though not blood-relatives, rather intimately connected with one another as initiates and future initiates of the Sun in Christ. Eschenbach cites a certain Meister Kyot in a single location in his epic poem, whom he writes related the entire Parzival history to him, thereby attributing his work to this mysterious Meister Kyot as his source. There may have been a man who *did* relate the real Parzival history to Eschenbach, but then his true name is not revealed to us. Also, historically, the actual human beings portrayed in his great epic verse lived several centuries prior to Eschenbach. But Hemdlig is a character in my tale, albeit the most significant one, neither does the author attribute the story to him, but it is the result of my pen and is purely fiction.

I do not claim to such greatness as we have in the knight, poet, and Minnesinger* Eschenbach in creative invention or historically. However, my modest story is worth reading and of real interest to those who wish to know something of the two great planetary types or destinies in earthly life, Sun and Venus. Together, they have all three aspects of Christ: daylight (Sun), and night with moon and stars (Venus); Holy Week (Good Friday crucifixion, Holy Saturday Land of the Dead, Easter resurrection) (Sun), and the Thirteen Holy Nights of Christmas (Venus). My tale is my own, the result, not only of my knowledge of these two destinies, but of my artistic-poetic creativity. (*see pages 453-456)

The second English story is *Mike and Morris*. It is a humorous tale of twins. The fun multiplies identically, but I will let the reader discover in the narrative the story's unfolding and coming together into every creative and frequently funny detail and say no more here.

My third German story, *The Silver Goblet* (*Der silberne Becher*), was written and translated into English by its author after the first two English-language tales and so in 2014. It makes use of several writing devices, without any planning or forethought on my part. *The Silver Goblet* is mainly narrative, with small but important spoken words and dialogue in places, aside from its opening that is within the mind of the character, who plays a significant role only then. This story, which moves right along, happens in small scenes, with the exception of the beginning that is more a study of a human psyche but in the form of story. After this psychological-fictitious opening is interrupted by a brief scene of poignant humanity, and thereafter the character preoccupied in his mind finishes playing his contrasting part, the entire tale develops, not only in an interesting manner, but in a living way as well, and ends in a setting and a mood earlier in time from the rest of the story, although the reader really doesn't know much more about the little tale were it historical rather than the inventive creative fiction it is. This last part takes place in an old wood house a distance from the rest of the story, the unnamed city (3 km or 1.7 m distant), and this setting is creative of another mood from what precedes it. It closes almost like a folk story with everything related up until then almost forgotten, except for the... silver goblet. Hence this object of the title unifies my tale in a tangible way. There are a few earlier scenes where a child or several children appear and imbue the story with its meaning in these places. Together with the ending of the tale, we have children and old folk, young and old, rich and poor, life and death. Again, though not intentional, I offer it is no chance my story begins and ends this way. The are several other character contrasts in *The Silver Goblet*. It is certainly unlike any other story, as an entire composition with all of these elements present and presented as they are in scenes, not to mention my individuality of expression and unique word-pictures.

The third American (English) story is *Lemon Pie*. It is set in Iowa on a roadside on a summer's afternoon where four men are digging a ditch outside of the small town of Heather, then in town where Sam, one of the men, has just returned home. In his home, while his wife is setting the table, Sam has a deep conversation with his three children about the meaning of death. The story closes with the family sitting down to eat.

There are four further (American) English stories: *Emma the Miser*, *Jakob's Fortune*, *Memories*, and *Frank Mitchell and the Yellow Roses*. *Emma the Miser* is excellent layered writing and could be modern-day. *Jakob's Fortune*, set in the past, can be seen as communicating inner realities in pictures. Then the gambling aspect reflects human nature in some personalities after they have gained profound inwards riches. The brief *Memories* fills the reader's soul with an abundance of rich sensations conveyed in descriptive writing. *Frank Mitchell and the Yellow Roses* is a classic (American) character study with a small cast.

The studies are for the most part first-published and are taken mainly from my planned major work of non-fiction, *Motifs in Human Life*: *Paths of Progress and Contribution*; *Studies in the Content of the World*, written beginning December 2009, with some published in earlier books of mine. They are intended to interest, inform, help, and encourage all those who are on their own, individual path or who want to be.

Like all my written work, much of *The Wood of Green* is for adult self-education. Owing to its creative nature, *The Wood of Green* may be enjoyed by the adult and adolescent reader.

Please read *The Wood of Green* with attentive interest, heart, and love; while enjoying in it what is aesthetic and beautiful.

Alan Lindgren
Culver City/March 20/27–29; April 2/4/18
Los Angeles and Culver City, California
June 10/17; Aug. 16; Sept. 27; October 15/17; Nov. 18/25, 2014

Preface

After my very large poetry anthology, *Journeying with the Sun*, was published in February 2013, I unexpectedly continued to compose poems, some quite lovely and deep, many of real interest. I felt it was too bad they were not included in my anthology, yet at the time I believed my work as a poet was done. Then, I wrote two German stories —short stories—my first in my 51-year life*, which I translated into English. I decided if I were ever able to publish another volume with the new poems, the German stories—with their English translations for non-German readers—would join them. (I also newly composed 11 German poems and seven Spanish poems. As there are 91 first-published English poems there are in total 109 poems, all newly composed and published.) One of the poems is a verse translation I composed on October 27, 2014 from a German poem by Christian Morgenstern. (see page 553)

Later I wrote another German story and a short German fairytale—not fairytale-like, as is *Flemsbach*, but an actual fairytale—that I likewise translated into English, as well as (American) English stories. I also wanted several essays (including some from my planned major volume/s of non-fiction, *Motifs in Human Life: Studies in the Content of the World*) to see publication. Then I selected the title from that of a poem that is also in a line of the same poem, *The Wood of Green*, and this is the result.

As of this writing it is preliminary (I have typed up most of the poems, and the studies are typed but require editing and/or revision), and I cannot know whether it will come to fruition. The e-cover is finished and ready to print in PDF format. A major obstacle, when the work on the interior is done, is the funding. Unless there is a good-sized gift (which I don't expect), getting *The Wood of Green* off the ground is still an uncertainty. Yet it would be such a joy and do much good in poetry with unique word-pictures, beautiful language; profound, didactic, and practical content/insight (in the poems and studies); a German story with a moral lesson (satirical that is droll as it is farcical), and another German story with a fairytale-like quality. Recently, I have written two English stories, so now there are a total of four short stories**. (see foreword, above.)

With these words I preface *The Wood of Green: Poems, Stories, and Studies by Alan Lindgren.*

Alan Lindgren
Los Angeles
November 13, 2013
Culver City, California
February 7
March 20
April 21, 2014 (Easter Monday)
September 20/27
October 15/29
November 1/25, 2014

* On 5 August 2014 I celebrated my 52nd birthday anniversary.

** and now another German story and a little German fairytale, plus five additional (American) English stories, bringing the total number of English stories to seven, and the total number of all stories to eleven.

A Word on the Introductions

Because the writings in this volume are of three larger kinds, and so divided—poetry, stories, studies—each has its own introduction. My foreword was written for the entire volume; it covers all of the materials, and the preface prefaces all three categories. So it is my suggestion the reader first read the foreword, then the preface, and, before embarking on reading the poems, to read their introduction, likewise with the stories and the non-fiction section.

Note: All 109 poems are first-published, likewise the stories. The studies are also first-published, except where noted. Two of the poems are in the non-fiction section: Love (2) (page 396) and Destiny (page 502). One (untitled) is a verse translation I composed from a German poem by Christian Morgenstern (also untitled). It appears at the back with the poem "Wonder" on page 553. "Finding Autumn Mountains" is on page 554, followed by "Tender" on page 555 and "Family", the final poem (on page 556), before "About the Author" (pages 557, 558).

Alan Lindgren

Good Reader

Surrounding me the gift of life
Like gratitude and good housewife
I never once regretted my
Inner journey, low and high

Because I long ago did find
My individual, own path and mind
My place I sought within mankind
Is sun-imbued the way God signed

A poet with his symbols and
Unique word-pictures, pastureland
He led his life so good and grand
His feet on earth, pitchfork in hand

And so, good reader, with this book
Open it and have a look
For you may know good fortune or
Learning new as once before.

Alan Lindgren
Los Angeles
November 14-15, 2014

The Poems

Introduction to the Poems

The poetry published here is a selection of the poems I composed since my large poetry anthology was published (*Journeying with the Sun*), beginning March 21, 2013. The final poem was written November 23, 2014. Numerous (109 poems), those chosen from this time period are very special. The eleven German poems and seven Spanish poems appear for a second time in separate sections after all of the poetry. They are first located with the others according to when they were composed.

****

The poems are only fully experienced spoken as in the art of speech formation. (Google 'speech formation + anthroposophy + art') This art of speech brings them to life with all their rhythms, speech sounds (consonants, vowels, alliteration), and rhymes—which is impossible silently reading the printed text. The speaker must picture/think the imagery/content of the poem as s/he speaks it, else it means nothing. However, in a poem with genuinely poetic language, the pictures are created by the speech sounds, so that the speaker need not give undue attention to/intellectualize the content. This aspect belongs to the miracle of human language. Though speech and thought are distinct, the content (images, thoughts) derives from the sounds of the spoken words. Imagery and later thought has its origin in spoken language. This is apparent in small children; first they learn to speak and then to think.

The deep German Saturnine Goethe is the greatest of the word poets or poetic artists. His death in 1832 marks the end of German Romanticism. (Born in 1749, Goethe may be the greatest mortal. That is not to say his Goethe incarnation was his last. A pantheist, he is the author of the *Fairy Tale of the Green Snake and the Beautiful Lily*. A novelist and great dramatist (*Faust I, II*), Goethe was an equally great scientist. The English bard Shakespeare is also a very great Saturnine. Ludwig Tieck, another German Romanticist, was a poetic musician, one may say.)

There are also conceptual poems that communicate at the level of ideas as in philosophy. Here, too, language is significant. Think of the wondrous Venus destiny Novalis (1772-1801) and his overflowing words in the most beautiful language carrying the conceptual content—

the inexhaustible spiritual perspectives of his novels and poetry (his poems are in hexameter), and the famous Moon destiny Rainer Maria Rilke (1875-1926) with his mastery of complex rhyming schemes and the rhythms which wash over one in his often long poem cycles. The language of both is German, which is the language of the most beautiful poetry. All of 19th century German poetry attests to this. Novalis, with his overflowing flood of words, was the lofty huge gifted German Romanticist, Rilke a gifted Bohemian-Austrian. Both had Christ; Rilke for a time, Novalis eternity. (Novalis wrote the greatest fairy tale directly into his novel *Heinrich von Ofterdingen*. The well-known symbol of Romanticism, *Die blaue Blume* (*The Blue Flower*), is from this novel.)

****

To gain artistic ability in creative speech, practice speaking a poem before a sculpture as though addressing it. Using the lips, the teeth, the roof of the mouth, and the tongue, create an invisible sculpture in the air in front of the mouth from the spoken consonants. To acquire real ability in this art, some study under a speech formationist is necessary. This usually takes place at a seminar or other school where speech formation is taught by a fully trained artist.

There are many speech formationists who dedicate their lives to this difficult art form. Some speak poems while a eurythmy troupe make the poem visible in their art: eurythmy. These speech formationists travel with the eurythmy troupe as they tour. In this way, audiences experience both eurythmy and speech formation to the same poems simultaneously. Other speech formationists teach their art to students of a number of disciplines. Many seminars have their own speech formation instructor. We think of the Christian Community seminaries and the Freies Jugendseminar Stuttgart (Stuttgart Youth Seminar). Of course, those studying to become speech formationists require intensive instruction in this demanding art form. This study takes place in 'schools'. Then there are fully trained speech formationists who speak poems they have practiced for months before audiences. Still others who have the training become special actors and elocutionists. Their speech on the stage goes far beyond clear and understandable enunciation.

At the Goetheanum (whose name honors the man Johann Wolfgang von Goethe and his work), the 'House of the Word' or 'House of Language', the home of anthroposophy in Dornach near Basel, Switzerland, there is a speech formation school. I studied speech formation with the Swiss speech formationist Stefan Allenbach at the Freies Jugendseminar Stuttgart in Stuttgart, Germany, 1984-1985. This intensive practice gave me intimate living artistic 'knowledge' of the spoken German language, which translated into my feeling for spoken English, my Mother tongue. Together with my Waldorf education, where we pupils recited poetry from memory, my intensive study of speech formation at the age of 22 was decisive for my vocation as a poet. Alliteration (repeated same consonant sounds) is frequent in my poems. I have rhythm within. This aspect is in my poetry as well. Thus not the ideas but the words are felt.

As a second semester freshman at Pomona College in Claremont, California, where I majored in German literature, I took a course in 19th century German poetry. I opened my first paper that semester that was on a specific poem by bringing out the poem's rhythmic meter, which is essential to gain a genuine feeling for the poem. (This was before my experiences at the Jugendseminar.) The professor crossed this out and wrote in the margin, 'We don't do it this way', meaning the experience of the meter (poetic rhythms) is excluded from the study of poetry in that course. (My sense for poems' rhythms was untouched.) It would have been singular to experience the spoken elements of poetry at *any* school, *except* a Waldorf School or an anthroposophical seminar or other such training. Yet all genuine artistic poetry, including that of the great poets, is inseparable from living, artistic speech, and especially the rhythms.

Stefan Allenbach was trained in his art at the speech formation school at the Goetheanum. He was a tall, large-boned, very warm, passionate, earnest, hardworking, and original artist. Creative speech is a special experience that shares nothing in common with daily conversation or lectures. The talking we are so accustomed to doing and hearing has none of the sculptural power, richness of sound, artistic life, mobility, forming, shaping, sounds, light and shadows, colors, pictures, rhythms, rising and falling, movement, depths, breadths, heights, elasticity, condensing, quickening—entire worlds—of speech formation.

My poetry is mainly rhythmic with rhyming schemes 'a/b c/b d/e f/e' or 'a/b a/b c/d c/d', or rhyming couplets 'aa bb' or triplets 'aaa bbb ccc', with alliteration a common feature, as mentioned. In order to fully experience my poems, you must enter into the rhythms. Mine is word poetry.

As imagery my poetry is best described as 'word-pictures'. This means I am not literally a poet in the conceptual sense, but a poetic painter. (See Goethe, second paragraph this introduction, above.) I 'paint' pictures in words, which are unique. This fact is essential to my poetry and to understand it (*Homecoming, Beauty, Reveal, Destiny, Finding Autumn Mountains*; then *Views*, all published in this volume, discussed below.) Excepting *Views*, the words are formative of content in all of my poems.

The themes themselves are also of central significance in my poetry, so we must look into this for the poems published in this volume. (A poem without a theme means nothing. It is like a tale with no story.)

It is easy to discover the seasons in the poetry, as a theme entire in some individual poems, and the Easter and Christmas seasons in others, usually composed at those times. Because the poems are arranged chronologically, the reader may go through the pages in the poetry section and locate these poems specifically.

Colors often accompany the four seasons, as well as the Christian Thirteen Holy Nights of Christmas and Holy Week (Passion Week and Easter), so this visual element can often be found in these poems as well. (A Sanguine, I have a deep appreciation for light and color phenomena.) Additionally, some of the poems draw imagery from gardens or Nature, in which (a) color(s) is/are in unison. Take, for example, the poem from which the title to this volume is taken: *The Wood of Green*. In printed ink you can see greens on the book's cover. I am the book designer of this volume. (In my watercolors I have mixed a variety of beautiful greens.)

Nature-phenomena provide the poet with imagery in much of the poetry, especially the Sun and Her clear sunlight. This belongs to the day; we know it is thanks to the Sun (daylight) that our world is colorful. In some of the poems, the Sun is experienced as an inner, heart connection. Here, Sun of Christ is the essence.

Another aspect of Christ is Divine Love. This appears as a candid theme among the poems: by itself (*Love Awakens Us* and *Love (2)*) and in the Holy Nights experience. With the latter we have the mystical-magical faerie race (men, women, and children), whose relationship to Christmas is one of purity and direct understanding. The first man Adam was of faerie, as were the prophet Elijah, Jesus of Nazareth, Maria the Mother, John the Evangelist, Raphael, and Novalis. Christ is the love-God.

There are three poems on words. Many other themes may be discovered in the poetry section: poetry, human being, death, sacrifice, beauty, work, understanding, harmony (see *Harmonious* pages 96, 97) among them.

****

I will bring to your attention one poem in particular because of its distinction: *Views* on page 93. This poem differs from others, not only in theme, but because it is conceptual. (see my discussion on poetry, second and third paragraphs of this introduction, above) Unlike my other poetry (1,500 poems, over 1,000 published), its several images or word-pictures only serve to illustrate its concepts. Thus *Views* has content to ponder. *Homecoming* (frontispiece), *Beauty* (page 71), *Reveal* (page 100), *Destiny* (page 504), *Finding Autumn Mountains* (page 556) are word-pictures *and* ideal. *Views* is not words but only concepts.)

It is philosophical in asking the reader to pause for thought on human nature. This is interesting for another reason. The subject might be Nature, or so appear to be. And Nature is an essential aspect of this poem. But *Views* calls upon the reader to think about his *own* view or different human views, and Nature actually serves to draw his attention to himself. This is not only personal because it contains objectivity as thought in relation to the 'I' of the reader. In this manner, *Views* is subjective-objective and can only be grasped by wakeful thinking.

This may produce a specific awakening effect within the reader's soul.

Or s/he may simply wish to grasp the poem's thematic idea or concepts in thinking them, yet find him/herself somehow incapable of this. Yet like all living thinking, immersion in living thoughts serves to prepare the thinker for his/her own soul's spiritual awakening. In this manner, *Views* goes beyond the limits of the scope of most conceptual poetry. No mere shadowy idea, its idea is a spiritual reality. This it shares in common with the idea of Christ, which Christ puts into our head.

(Novalis and Rilke are exceptions to the limitations mentioned, although Rilke reflects on ideas he simultaneously veils in shadowed thought. But his ideas are spiritual realities. We need only think of a line from an early poem: *du einziger und echter Christ* (*you one and genuine Christ*). Novalis addresses Christ, whom he reflects on as well, in an entire poetry cycle: *Geistige Lieder* (*Spiritual Songs*). He opens these songs with the question: *Was wär ich ohne Dich gewesen?* (*What had I been without you?*). This is no mere philosophical reflection. It is the deepest —and loftiest—question one may ask, and for Novalis, it is all.

In Rilke's poetry, the stream of creativity flows into his 'I'. Thus he is a genuinely gifted poet. He died of leukemia at age 51. This stream is far greater in the life and work of Novalis, who had a full life and died before his 29th birthday. In his novels it pulses in single-sentenced long paragraphs the understanding reader must also receive into his soul and heart. This is Novalis's warm, pulsing Christ-love. Hence he is the most gifted artist of words—and human being—of all. This in-streaming signifies the poet is gifted with his own innate, creative wellspring; he has given inner birth to Christ. Only he who has done so knows.)

An inner 'I' poem, *Views* is truly poetic. Although it is one of my few conceptual poems, all of my poems and much other of my written work that may be called poetry flows into my 'I', into me its poet. I am a gifted Mars destiny. Every destiny who is realized is gifted with at least two gifts. I have many: sculpture, classical piano, singing, poetry, prose, ‡.

Alan Lindgren
Los Angeles
August-September-October, 2014

Middle

Windows white winter sweetest wine
Red, robust with rosehips rhyme
I thought my memory would remind
Me of most music of my mind

But then the other thereabouts
Begins to bleat like sheep who shout:
Keep keeping company of men
Like laughter listening again

But mostly measure inner time
And sure ascend, the mountain climb
Unto the place of God sublime
Before the Prince, Christ entered Time

But then was He a little babe
In Bethlehem was born and made
His Mother Mary blameless bade
All humankind He came to aid

To shelter in the branches' shade
His tree of Life all life remade
To pardon pardoning instead
He died for us, in tomb was laid

On a tree was crucified
His cross the heaviest inside
He bore for all of us, the Bride
Jesu is the Christ who died

For all our sins He faultless came
To earth to live, to suffer same
To know experience He found
A human life and death and sound

But then upon the Day, the Third
Arose from Land of dead He heard
He helped the souls held captive there
To Magdalene appeared He where

The Tomb was empty, death o'ercome
The power resurrection's Sun
The Light in victory had won
And that is poetry of One

For Christ is single, genuine
If we with Him be true within
Must suffer fear and pain again
Courageous, still, and balancing

Like Christ would crucified between
Two other crosses there be seen
To left, to right, Christ middle died
With mercy in His heart inside

If we be Christ receptive now
His courage emulation show
His virtue in the middle go
Then we shall life eternal know.

March 21, 2013
November 1, 2014

Four Easter Poems

1. Easter

Easter is a day
I thought of this-a-away
The blossoms blooming gay
How colorful are they!

2. Life

A miracle is life
Each Easter after death
In victory the Christ
Again does resurrect

He is the Being great
Of Light, the God of Sun
Christ shines into our world
Magnificent, the One

And when the day is done
The sun has set again
The stars appear like suns
When men the dead become

With the angels there
The archangels of fire
They shine in heavenly light
And sing their songs in choir

And that is night I sing
And that is day I feel
With Easter joy does bring
And illness Christ does heal

He is the Voice divine
The Sun of all mankind
New life upon the vine
The heart in me I find.

3. Song

I'm centered in this world
Where in my mind in sense
Where in my soul like curls
Of hair, my heart condense

And this is sun in me
The branches of my tree
Spread, a shelter, see
For the birds to be

In the shade of life
They sing with all their hearts
But in my inmost soul
My song my heart imparts

The meaning of the light
This Easter morning sun
Shines sentient merry bright
Creation, every one.

4. Gift

A gift can be to me

A thing from memory
Come shining for to see
From my heart to be

A gift can presently
With wisdom wisely be
A thought I think in me
Within reality

But I think not of these
The past or present seize
But from the future breeze
A gift on air not flees

When I heard clearly sing
The little birds in spring
They my heart did bring
A gift upon the wing.

March 31, 2013
November 1, 2014

America

America – this song I sing!
The future on the breeze's wing
Doth fly to thee, and happening
Would help and heal all everything

America – I love thee, how
My love for thee is on my brow
I join with others in this song
Americans, we will be strong

We will give hope and health and hearth
Asylum for all peoples, worth
Who suffer poverty and wrong
America, they here belong

America – thou art in me
Within my heart a place to be
Where love and feeling clarity

Do shine like sunlight, brave and free

America – now take this word
Let sound and soar, an air-born bird
Who flies and sings in merry joy
America, good things enjoy

Reality of blood and breath
And birth and life and sacred death
That in the nights of spiritual
Replenish light in God's great Will

America – this poem I
Compose to thee from earth to sky
Now take thy freedom's victory
Fulfill thy future destiny

That all the world's peoples here
Find the help they need, so dear
America – humanity
Christ in us and Christ in thee.

May 19, 2013

Love

Love is a mystery shining so fair
Love is the element, water with air
Love is the story of Mary with child
Faerie are gifted with beauty so mild

Love suffers presently, future relieves
Love redeems pardoning, all things believes
Love is the future, the Word of the Son
God of the World and of every one

Love is not warm as the fire of the Sun
Love is not heavy as earth or onion
Love is of beauty for each, every one
The Earth's Venus' lover, and Love is the Son

Love does enlarge and embraces the World

Every God's child is but love's pearl
Shining with beauty and magic love lives
Passing through freely, love always gives

There in the cool of midnight is born
The Child of spiritual, Christ before morn
Christ before dawn at the hour of midnight
Christmas before the brave Easter of sight

Christmas before God's Son suffers again
Passion and Cross; the Child's smile us does win
Christmas when Jesu dreams in Mary's arms
Love sleeps most tender, with loveliness charms

Dreaming in ethers of bluish-white light
Love is a pearl of beauty tonight
Feeling uplifted by Christ's loving light
Dreaming secluded from Sun's brightening sight

There love lives secretly every night
Welcomes God's children to dream in love's light
Welcomes God's children to dunk in love's pool
Refreshing in waters of watery cool

Christmas when quiet reigns, stillness and peace
Blankets the World of Mankind with God's fleece
Christ is the Babe and we kiss His small cheek
Our darling, He dreams in a long, timeless week
Our darling, He dreams in our prayers of God's love
Christ is the Babe from God's heaven above.

August 10, 2013
August 19/30, 2014

Colors:
Verses on the Four Seasons

A long familiar avenue
Led me anon another to
The lonesome color shades of blue
To distances away from you

But you, my friend, I found by me
Like sprouting shoots upon a tree
Not wintry white or autumn blue
But springtime green, the living hue

Then came to me as my own heart
A rose of red me warmth impart
'Twas summer good of gardens gold
The roses red of wisdom old

Pray now announce the seasons four
In tunes of color none ignore
In autumn blue crisp yellow flames
Of dying leaves awaken names

But green of spring green life and limb
All Nature is spring's greening hymn
Whilst summer's red like rosy cheeks
Of maidens blushing warmest weeks

Then quiet stillness winter snows
Of whiteness blanket earth below
And heaven also white appears
The Child of Christmas every year

So rhythm annual of time
Pulses in this color-rhyme
For readers of this chorus' verse
Do find within my universe.

August 25, 2013

Three Poems by Alan Lindgren Inspired by a Watercolor of a Setting Sun the Poet had just Painted

I. The Sea

I wandered through a world
Of sea of color large
My mind did open wide
Encompass like a barge

This sea of color swell
In movements and in waves
Which buried rocks and shells
Into eternal graves

But I remained above
A traveler of song
Amidst the color-sea
Did carry me along

But I remained above
Where bird accompany
Across the setting Sun
Upon the color-sea.

II. Scene and Sun

In a color-world
I found all shades of green
Created by my eye
And Nature's palette scene

Created by my eye
And Art's own palette green
I painted color-worlds
An artist of a scene

An artist of a scene
Like gratitude and song
An artist of a scene
Like mercy me belong

An artist of a scene
Before I stand, while One
Above is shining clear
The warm and radiant Sun

Above is shining clear
The good in wisdom Sun
Whose light we do revere
Christ, the radiant One.

III. The Rising Sun

I love the color-sea
This world and scene and land
Of painted greenery
Of God's brush in hand

Of painted scenery
My heart knows deepening
As the setting Sun
Of an evening

As the setting Sun
Whose colors dear and deep
Depict the cross of Christ
Before an ever-sleep

Before an Easter morn
Before the Risen One
Begins a day newborn
With the rising Sun.

Los Angeles
September 16, 2013

The Wood of Green

I wandered through a wood of green
Through all the places I had been
The trees of branches evergreen
And mosses on the ground the scene

Before I found the magic place
I left the clamoring human race
To enter humankind once more
By a secret magic door

'Twas then a little bird in spring
Flew to me his joy to bring
His joyous pretty song did sing
As only birds upon the wing

But then arriving numerous
Butterflies who fluttered thus
Reminded me that springtime comes
And quickly goes as blossoming mums

But I like the light and air
As celebrating as a faire
All the villagers are there
In the summer life compare

Before the autumn winds and rain
Begin to blow and fall again
Another rhythm annual
Completion finds with festival

Of Christmas' winter's snow and peace
The world is blanketed beneath
The Child, the Christ is born once more
And safely laid on forest floor

I wandered through a wood of green
Through all the places I had been
The years of earth and sun and star
Divine of God and Christian are.

Culver City, California
September 20, 2013

The Year

Summer is a swallow
Then the fields lie fallow
And the autumn yellow
Death is just the gallows

But the winter simple
Children's faces dimple
Love is their example
Innocence to sample

Then the spring rejoices

Birth reborn with voices
Songs of birds depicting
Christ's quick resurrecting

First must suffer dearly
Life and death are yearly
Like a grapevine ageing
After harvest waging

All for mankind sorrow
Born to die tomorrow
Passion, crucifixion
Sunset our depiction

Christ's once resurrection
Easter reenaction
Humankind in future
Glory great in stature

Shall be bliss and rapture
No more death may capture
No more want or suffering
Only sunny morning

Summer is a swallow
Then the fields lie fallow
Yellow autumn 'wakening
Thinking's resurrecting

Under the Archangel
Spirit Time is Michael
Courage for tomorrow
His gesturing to follow

Bravely walking, warmly
Thinking His thoughts clearly
Eternal birth is reaching
Christ is us approaching

Spiritual is Christmas
Starry worlds above us
Magic smiles around us

Candles shine in darkness

So that light within us
Illumines hearts and souls thus
That love born inside is
Inner worlds Novalis

Poetry because of
Jesu born of God's love
Raphael's Madonnas
Forever painting because

Love of God's eternal
Christ is God nocturnal
Moon and stars and Venus
Twinkle, shine above us.

Los Angeles
September 21, 2013

Guide

Solar is the Sun inside
Sun of Christ our inner guide
We assured do reach our goal
Christ-perception, clear and whole

Clear and loving is sunlight
From the day into the night
Holy Week is sacred time
Crucifixion beyond rhyme

Music will ascend in God
Resurrection of the Word
From cathedrals of death's road
Painting's Easter's joyous ode!

Christmastide is holiness
Infancy of childness
Birth of love's eternity
Blessed His company are we

None can touch the Christ, the Child
In the arms of Mary mild
Womb-like sleep of Father-God
Dreams the everlasting Word.

Los Angeles
October 12
Edited Culver City, California
October 18, 2013

Three Poems on the Men of God

1. Sign

Quiet was a place of once
I knew of quiet domicile
Then came human common sense
And with it what is deemed worthwhile

I know that sense would commonly
Including quiet company
But when I look effortlessly
My place of quiet ceases be

The world in restless will not still
Because disquiet enters all
Because without God's quiet hill
Disturbances unwelcome call

God is my father without cease
He fathered me and gives me peace
God touches all that heavy sign
Becomes the weighted still Divine.

The men of God unmoved in Him
Their step in leaden quietly
They go forth, His work their hymn
Assurance' presence ever be.

2. God

The Mystery of God is still
That none can move from windowsill
Or from earth and ground and land
His bedrock solid, not of sand

Waters crash and winds do blow
No storm can alter quietness
The way the men of God do go
On weighty substance heaviness

For God the Father leaden be
All pictures painted but refer
To His power and gravity
Which all the universe defer.

3. Pulse

Sacred is the heart of He
Who born the Light in darkness comes
And grows to suffer pain and death
Sun of Christ in rhythms' limbs

He is the pulse of hearts and souls
Of seasons' cycle annual
Of the past and future goals
Of each year perennial

My lips do form His Name in song
My mind on Him does come to rest
Sun of Christ, the 'I AM' strong
The God of Ages is changeless

I, in feeling, do condense
The Sun in me my heart all thing
Rhythms pulse in willing's sense
From my heart empowered sing

My heart in feeling plumbless lives
Religion's festive inwardness

Harmonious receives and gives
Safeguards the 'I AM' sacredness

One last word in silence go
All thing allow to pass or change
While men of God increasing know
Their work eternal, earth's their range.

Los Angeles
October 3, 2013

The Sun

Measured is the course the Sun
Pulses in the seasons' run
Through each day She helps us find
Faithful, regular mankind

We depend on Her for sure
She all life on earth endure
And all spirit sun imparts
Find again in human hearts

What without Her would earth be?
Dark and cold and lifeless sea
Death would cover everything
Gone the voices of the spring

But each morning does return
And each Easter Sunday morn
She reborn from death's darkness
She brings health and life, gladness!

So our praises do we sing
To the Sun who wisely brings
In Her Tempo every thing
We require and justly rings

We do thank Thee, God and Sun
For Thou art of goodness One
We depend on Thee, we know

All good thing on us bestow.

Los Angeles
October 14
Edited Culver City, California
October 18, 2013

Dreams

Dreams were places I dreamed, I felt
A journey traveling o'er hill and dell
A trip as far as sky of blue
But inside I dreamed of you

Dreams were places I went, but real
Real in my heart, I feel
A place as red as roses pure
I inhaled their fragrance sure

Dreams were places I felt, I knew
Beyond the limits of distance, too
But within me and within you
My dreams I traveled fondly; dew

Drops fell on me and all
Of Nature heard I gently call
Like wild deer o'er forest moss
Christ was green upon the cross

No more dream but death in life
Married to my Lord, His wife
Follow Christ through death, right through
To another place with you.

October 20, 2013

Child

Afternoon was eventide
Did open up the night inside
Until the morn became my song
Did carry me 'til noon along

But what was evening but fall
Autumn until winter's call
When in the night Christ's voice is heard
Around Him angel and small bird?

And what the morn anew but spring's
Rebirth of Easter tidings brings?
Then see the noon of the year's day
Summer greens us in her way

I thought I heard I felt my song
Around the year entire long
In memory like vision's dream
But clear or dim as evening

When sun has set and stars abound
The universe is all around
Embraces earth, and we are child
Of Mother Mary, mercy mild
Embraces earth, and we are child
The Father-God of peace and mild.

November 3, 2013

Season

Springtime was the time of gay
When all of Nature had her way
When every color conquered grey
When gladness was the holiday

But in the summertime of green
The pastureland became the scene
The Sun shone great and grand, and seen
All greenery and garden been

Then autumn came in rain and breeze
The windy season without ease
I walked in bravery appease
The Gods before the snows all freeze

And finally was winter birth

A different kind, an inner mirth
Not spring of blossoms, bud, and shoot
But jubilating cheer and flute

Each spring is morning, Eastertide
When Christ does resurrect outside
But summer's daytime, St. John's Tide
The life of growth in good abide

While autumn's evening, Michaelmas
Thinking's resurrection west
Follows winter's night, Christmas
The Holy Nights, the world is blessed

And that is every year of earth
Of Nature and of human worth
Of Christ, the Saviour of mankind
The Tempo of the Sun, of time

The Tempo of mankind, the Sun
Is tempo of the heart, each one
Is tempo of the season's Sun
Of day and night for every one.

November 24, 2013

Evening

Sunshine was a merry song
It carried me in verse along
Like clarity of God in strong
Beams of warmth my soul belong

But mystery is other thing
Inner feeling suffering
In depths of heart where Christ does bring
Deeper within love does sing

For those imbued with mystery
Of the Christ in inwardly
To them belongs of sacredly
The sacrifice of death in me

Most precious is their suffering
Dearer than an offering
To the Gods the sibyls sing
As dear as sunsets' evening.

November 25, 2013

Trust

Trust is such a happy thing
It made my heart and me to sing
Like sparrows for the Child bring
Their songs of sweetness neighboring

The shepherds in the fields tend
Their sheep in goodness they do lend
Them help and hand and wholesome send
The warmth of summer sunshine wend

Their way to Christmas to the Child
Mary cared for, mercy mild
The Christ was just a baby, smiled
In dreams the Father made and styled

With wonder, love, and safety kept
In God's Hands and footsteps stepped
And peace and joy and cheer each time
The Holy Nights make verses rhyme.

November 25, 2013

Seven

The graveyard tombstones of my mind
Kept reading death unto the blind
They read the years of those on earth
'Tween birth and death before the mirth
Of heaven's immortal spirits find
The meaning of eternal kind

And I, yes I did poems write
My verses word-pictures of sight

While I found in writing song
That I, a poet, did belong
To humanity of sad
Sometimes, and also glad

For poetry is movement or
The way we open heaven's door
Like waves of water, life of seas
Like Son of God Whom we believe
Like God of love, complete, entire
As Venus and Her earth aspire

And that is why in every verse
Mortality my universe
Belongs humanity by day
Each life to cemetery way
For we must suffer life and death
From birth until our final breath

But because Christ man became
We Him follow may, our Name
Given us by God, the same
Is genius and beyond blame
Is light of Sun of Christ, each one
Of seven destinies Him won.

December 4, 2013

Life

Our foundation is of love
Born as children, God thereof
All the young are playing of
Songs from colors up above

Next we youth do strive and meek
Our ideals hear and seek
Christ in dreams the soul sees
Will awaken, karma seize

Young adulthood in the world
Personality the word

Independence will be heard
Fourth does follow on the third

Middle age; it's time to give
To return as well as live
Manifold the choices are
Culture works upon a star

Life grows older to advise
Younger travelers arise
Questions asked, their answers give
Only riddles must we live

Nearing fifty, spiritual
Life grows stronger, ritual
Facts, like knowledge, actual
Reason measures punctual

Now is time to well prepare
Death approaching are the years
Wisdom ripens at this stage
Christ of death and dying age

Body ages, years advance
Soul younger, governance
Of the spirit on the road
To th' immortal mother lode

Then at moment's truth of death
Time to take the final breath
Christ is ferryman from shore
Here to heaven's shore once more.

December 5, 2013
August 19, 2014

My Heart

Above the shadows shines the Sun
Light clear and warm for every one
Sometimes part the dark clouds grey
Revealing Easter, glorious Day

When all of Nature sings with Man
Messiah's coming, huge and grand

So part the clouds of grey and rain
And feel with me the suffering, pain
For New Jerusalem we stand
Earth entire, the Holy Land

Christ be born in your heart now
Love, a Christmas, on your brow
Eternal Bethlehem in you
Heaven dreams of Earth anew

Sun morning follows on the night
The resurrection of the Light
But the stars eternal where
Venus twinkling magic there

Christ is born, the Earth, His love
My heart keeps dreaming, dreaming of
Vision of His Christmas light
Reveals another kind of night.

December 7, 2013

Honesty

Honesty was just a word
Before appeared a little bird
In whom I knew was God I heard

Then the Sun through branch and leaf
Shone on my heart to warm belief
From my grief welcome relief

But all the circles merry dance
Like horses on the streets do prance
Not chance but humanest romance

Before the first rebirth of spring
Exhales the Earth in golden ring
The Sun in worth does Easter bring

Comes the inner birth of Christ
In human hearts is holy bliss
And in the Earth the Child is kissed

'Tis Christmas we do jubilate
Like children small we celebrate
The inner light before Christ's fate

Midwinter is eternally
The Son is born in peacefully
He dreams the Earth in manger be

If you wish in honesty
God in a bird to hear with me
Then awaken and be free

These ears with God's voice do unite
And hear the little birds' songs bright
And you will see the radiant Light.

December 8, 2013

Christmas

He made a Christian holiday
The way the Christmas bells bright play
And angels to the Earth where hay
The animals kept warm this way

The Child, the Christ, was just a babe
He dreamed the dreams of Christmas love
He who would all mankind save
With the Father up above

Christ brings Christianity
Unto the world's humanity
We who find in purity
Loving hearts to cherish He

Who is the Saviour of mankind
Christianity do find
And that is this clear poetry

As the star of Christmas see.

December 9, 2013

Faerie

Those whose hearts grow ever fonder
Like the shepherds over yonder
Of the Child in the manger
Christ of good news is harbinger

All the world in stillness lying
'Neath the snows of white kept saying
Purity was Mary's loving
Heart for Jesu, future saving

Jesu, Prince of peace, was child
Mary, Mother, mercy mild
They of faerie-magic beauty
Mysticism's loving duty

John of faerie foretold future
The Messiah's coming stature
Every one may see Him gifted
Beyond average they are sifted

That mankind's one destination
New Jerusalem one nation
O'er the world's entire creation
Global is our future station

That is Easter morning's Glory
After Revelations' story
First much work we have before us
Suffer, tend to souls precious

What the meaning Christmas saying?
Eternal time is with us staying
Every heart may birth the Child
Inner Bethlehem, Christ mild

Wrapped in dreams of love Christ smiles
See serene is Mary's child
Peace the Father blesses every
Human being, Christmas faerie.

December 9/Revised December 26, 2013

Christmastime

Wonderful is Christmastime
I keep singing in this rhyme
Songs midwinter's holy birth
And Maria's inner mirth

All is quiet on the Earth
When the Saviour gives men worth
Birth the little children know
See their faces small look so

As they gather 'round the Child
Tenderly, Maria mild
Rocks the Babe of heaven come
From the Father is the Son

Christ is God of love, we find
When we feel the faerie-kind
They whose Christ grows great indeed
Father-God in them is seed

Always may we Christ believe
That His wonders we receive
Wonderful is Christmastime
Love and joy of Christian prime.

December 11, 2013

Gently

I write because a song is love
I keep thinking, thinking of
Beyond the shores of death and birth
To the other shore from earth

Is heaven, place of love, I know
When I am sleeping, where I go
All is beauty, no more pain
Gone the sunlight's shadows' rain

Only angels sing with me
Another kind of fantasy
From my earthly poetry
Are the heavenly songs, you see

All is true and good and kind
Only heaven is to find
Beautiful with God to be
Like the Paradise Christmas tree

Come to, come to, come to me
Bethlehem this Christmas be
And I shall sing for, sing for thee
A song of Christmas love gently.

December 11, 2013

Lamb

If you ever in December
Following the month November
Inside in your heart remember
Christmas then you are a member

Earth and heaven's joyous choir
All the angels us inspire
Bird and beast around the Child
Gather with the shepherds filed

Each unto the Christ they bring
First some wool is offering
Him warm to keep this night so cold
Second flask of milk is told

Nourishment the little One
Of our God, the holy Son
Shepherd third a baby lamb

This Lamb of God whose name 'I AM'

Felt in future human hearts
Do the world us Christ imparts
For the saints and martyrs know
Bear this God on earth bestow

Now this song I sing is sung
Christmas joy for every one.

Los Angeles
December 11, 2013
April 12, 2014

Christmas Birth

It is with inmost joy and expectation that we feel the approach of the Thirteen Holy Nights and the Twelve Days of Christmas. Christ the Spirit-Child is soon to be born in our hearts where we have prepared a place for His inner birth, just as Mary the Mother prepared to give birth to Him, the holy One, in Bethlehem. Our hearts are simple places as the stall with the manger where ox and ass did eat was humble and meek. We become like small children who love the Christ-Child, the Infant Jesu. Children love little babies as though they are much older. The visible changes that take place in newborns, infants, toddlers, and small children—even over a brief period of time—are rapid and astonishing, almost daily. A little baby—how tiny was Christ whose prophesied destiny was the Passion and Crucifixion, followed by the Resurrection, for the destiny of mankind and the salvation of souls.

We see in the rosy Infant and the blush of Mary's cheeks the Rose of heaven that can only bud and blossom on the thorny green plant (the rosebush) of earthly death. Like Christ in Nature each Easter after Holy (Passion) Week, Life is triumphant over death. Yet this picture of the rose has its beginnings with the holy Child. We see Him, naked, next to a single red rose on a long thorny green stem. Already in His infancy, Christ's destiny is foretold.

But now we return to Mary and the coming birth. All is quiet. All is still. The animals make the stall where the Child shall lie in dreams of the Father of heavenly peace warm with their breath. The angels bend down from heaven singing praises to the Father for the holy gift of His only begotten Son, the Saviour, which is Christ, the Lord of these adulating heavenly hosts. Deep in the darkness of a midwinter's night, the Light of the World was born in Bethlehem. Since that first Christmas night the Christmas event has happened, will happen in increasing numbers of human hearts—10,000; 50,000; 100,000; 250,000; 500,000; 1,000,000; 10,000,000; 50,000,000; 100,000,000; 500,000,000; human hearts, as in the earth—until the Light of the Holy Nights shines from every prepared human soul into the surrounding darkness of the long midwinter nights. This is the miracle of eternal highest heaven descended to our humble mortal earth—the miracle of joyous and reverent Christmas birth.

Los Angeles
Culver City, California
December 13-14, 2010

Three Poems on Words

1. Alan-Poetry

Studies bring me thoughts before
Welcoming they enter more
Deepening in me they sink
A refreshing spirit-drink

German, Spanish, English are
Languages my answers' star
I love their words, they mean to me
Thoughts and love and harmony

Thoughts and love and harmony
Feeling, suns, eternity
Rhythms, rhymes, and tempo, time
Inner places visit, climb

Words of languages are lands
Sought and found and felt with hands
Of a farmer or a man
Gardening his words did plan

Orderly did think and write
Poems in the day and night

Then before they disappear
Enters time the newest year
To recover from the dead
Verses that had once been read

That is Alan-poetry
What the Sun does mean to me
What I feeling inwardly
Thought and did in peacefully.

2. Places

Words are colors, sounds, and bright
Shadows, places shine with light
Rhythms, rhymes, and themes, they make
Soul-pie and spirit-cake

If you play with words your own
You may find whole worlds within
Shaped by speech and sung in tone
All the places you have been

Places inner sought and known
Places felt and cared for, grown
By the gardener of earth
Sun of Christ gives light its birth.

3. Words

Words are my reality
Filled with meaning inwardly
Spoken sculptures physically
Vowels give them soul to me

If you find my words you may
Travel inner lands where hay
With a pitchfork thrown about
Makes a bed for cows, no doubt

Or where farms and fairy tales
Found together here or Wales
Lands of lore created in

Soul for feeling visited

Places visited or made
By the poet verses paid
For with coins of inner gold
Wisdom of the words unfold

Now with me do sit and read
What I've written is my deed
In my heart reality
Lives my inner poetry.

December 15, 2013

Six poems Composed on December 19, 2013

1. Forever

Forever is a longer time
Than all the verses of my rhyme
Than every mystery of day
Before the night has had her way

But then within the secret sight
Forever shines the starry light
Forever in the darkness 'ppears
Forever of eternal years

2. Sunlight

Colors are the words of day
When the sunlight has his way
Night is far and far away
Warmth and light of sun today

3. Pastures

People come and people go
Like the cows in pastures so
But they will their mark to leave
On the world before their eve

Of day of life before their night
Takes them from the daylight bright
To the Other Side of death
Beyond the shores of earthly breath
Where the pastures greener are
Than the cows of earth graze far.

4. Care

Meaningful is human care
One another everywhere
Humanity's own lonely child
Not alone with mercy mild.

5. Eternity

When I think on humankind
Peace and stillness in my mind
Where my God, the Father, writes
Eternity in starry lights.

6. Call

Farmers sow the grain, the hay
Harvest golden like the day
Gardeners the beds of earth
Till the soil where seeds give birth

To green plants of flower and food
Forests green are forest wood
Wonderful the greening hand
Joins the Gardener on the land

Who the Gardener of mankind?
Christ of every flower kind
All religions like the flowers
All the colors blossoming hours

But one gardener for all
Christ of life and human call.

Los Angeles
December 19, 2013

Joy

One long and lonely winter night
I sought the radiant inner light
Then I beheld it beaming bright
Following the Holy Nights

New Year's January still
All was joy by windowsill
Of the barn where Jesu Christ
Lay asleep in dreams of peace

The animals and sparrows small
Joined with the angels' chorus call
In jubilation, cheer, and all
The world was blanketed in snow

And that was winter glorious night
Of Christ's love and heavenly light.

Van Nuys, California
January 7, 2014

Pearls—Dedicated to Margaret

Wonders of the world
Spread like seeds about
Like some precious pearls
Shining without doubt

Sown then in the earth
Sprouting in the air
Greening given birth
Blossoms colored fair

By the clear sunlight
Beaming radiant bright
Heavenly beauteous light
Petals know delight

If you try to pluck
Any flower you see

You will have no luck
Disappears it free

Only to return
Like a soul reborn
To you smiling turn
No more you forlorn

Wonders come again
Brightening the day
Here and there and when
Growth does find its way

Plants are wonders green
Crowned with colored flower
Nature is the scene
Joy is every hour

If you see and live
All Creation of
God's great Hand does give
Earth and Heaven love

Wonders are God's work
Tiny, small, and grand
We are like a clerk
Studying the land

Such is beauty rare
Every dawning morn
Every sunset dear
Then the night is born.

January 10, 2014

Human Being

Human beings every language
Every folk and every nation
Embody eternal souls visiting
This earthly plane for learning

Human beings every kind

Join together one mankind
Sing the human song of Ages
Growth like childhood's soul in stages

Human being individual
Requires the body original
Child, man, and woman
Biography stamp elemental

Human being is our nature
Ever-development our stature
In Christ divine and human
Become in us one single

Human being is essentially
Felt in hearts condensing
There where religion deepens
Sacramental life our leaven

Human being of the future
New becoming in the pattern
Archetypal is its nature
Body the Spirit ever transforming

Human being longs for freedom
Let him sing his song
Human being will his being
Live entire his life long.

January 11
August 2014

Source (1)

Go beneath life's surface where the chaos cannot go
Where confusion is external and the evil is not so
There lives pulsing like the sunlight from its sun-source warm and clear
The heart of worlds and music of the brotherly sun-spheres

There in depths of sacred suffering of the saints shines radiant light
Illumining the secrets of the world to opened sight
Which once penetrated powerfully by the educator's mind

Reveals the Truth eternal to the Glory of mankind

And arisen from the Grave of death the inner Christ does shine
In resplendence for the souls of the seekers as a sign
Of the future coming swiftly as a bird on wings of thought
The mighty revelation educates the scholars taught

Increasing ever greater is the nearing God of All
The Messiah in His Glory is appearing with His Call
To mankind to join the work in forwards stepping with the Greats
That we meet the Christ approaching, daily we experience states
Of clear thinking consciousness of spirits of the night and day
For there is no other journey of the seeker on his way

Now returning to our source that lies deep in us inside
We replenish fonts of strength as we find our inner guide
Meditation is our poem; quiet are our forces warm
That we know the inner sun, whence our souls are reborn.

January 15
August 20/November 2, 2014

Death

Death is such a mystery
To human points of view
The human being dying
Expressed in life in hues

Of glance or voice or movements
Openly reveal
Humanity and suffering
Or peaceful on the field

Of earthly experience
Before the threshold to
Dimensions spiritual
To heaven crosses new

Behind him leaves his body
Now lifeless for the earth
Invisible his soul and spirit

Know a spirit-birth

But to Christ the Saviour
Death no mystery is
He ushers souls across the river
Heaven's shores are His

Where life eternal only real
The body left behind
All in heaven is spiritual
The source of all mankind.

January 16
August 20, 2014

See

The grain bends in the fields
To the winds that gently blow
The grass-blade yields
In my rose garden so

The music of the night
Replaced by warm beaming rays
Of the coloring sunlight
Creative of our days

The breathing of the hour
From birth to human death
Marks time with pulsing power
Of our blood with living breath

The rhythm of the sun
Of the seasons' pulse-beat goes
This heart of Nature won
The year's great bridge rainbows

If you would gain true worth
Must first awaken in
The inner light give birth
Find Christ in worlds within

Then in the Mystery
The deep Mystica union
Openly will see
The Light, the Christ, the Sun.

Los Angeles
January 19
August 20, 2014

Poesie

Da war ein Land von Poesie
Das Land war grün wie Gott und See
Wie Erde grün, wie Laub und Baum
Im Sonnenschein und Meerestraum

Das Land war schön wie Melodien
Die klingen sanft wie Elegien
Denn Poesie nach Tode will
Übergehen im Winter Still'
Denn Poesie in Ewigkeit
Fortwährend lebt wie Eingeweiht'

Geheimnisvoll wie Mond und Stern
Stirbt Poesie in Lieder gern'
Geheimnisvoll wie Mond und Stern
Tönt Poesie beid' nah' und fern.

Los Angeles
23. Januar
Culver City, Kalifornien
24. Januar 2014

Glory

The clouds, in long white trains of bright puffs
Stripes in a deep blue sky overhead
In huge heavenly arches
Spanning the entire sky expanses
Running in parallel curved rows of big white spots
Great bright bands through a broad blue sky

Opened my soul wide open
To, reaching up, take it all in
And I, in large awe
Immersed my whole being
—eye and soul and heart—
Until returning to my small human habitation
Recalling that Glory, which I had sought to fathom
The pure celestial dome of the day-sky
A blue-and-white wonder-world of love.

Los Angeles
February 8/August 20/September 1, 2014
Culver City, California
February 11, 2014

Heart—An Easter Poem

Sun of Christ, I stand before
Thy altar of the open door
Within my heart the Mystery
Of Christ in death does rise in me

The Mystery of Christ alone
Is sacred but the empty Tomb
Tells me the Lord of Life each morn
In resurrection is reborn

That human eyes born blind may see
The Christ, the inner light does be
The inner light etherically
Shines to bless me peacefully

But in the stillness of my mind
Christ dwells within my heart I find
And there in warmth and light I feel
The presence of the Christ is real
And there in warmth and light I find
The heart and meaning of mankind.

February 9
August 10/23; November 2, 2014

Beauty

Beauty earthly of a maiden
Or of the loveliness of Nature
Is for me fully laden
With sun's golden nomenclature

Then I need not the Gods of heaven
I live here on earth reborn
Divinities may of sleep be leaven
But I love the newness of the morn

The Gods immortal may well beckon
Me to join them in the night's
Eternity, but their influence slackens
Each time I bathe in the sunlight

Then I know time and life are precious
Every moment dearer my heart is
Than the eternal stars precocious
Loftiness my spirit gives

Time may be but passing fortune
Or unfortunate, as it were
Yet, in memory, all is fashioned
Into my heart to there endure

What would of sleep and death become
If I brought from day and life none?
But God gives me of time the Sun
Christ, the everlasting One

So, fair Beauty of Creation
Of the Child, Nature, and Art
Thee I embrace with adulation
Thee I treasure within my inner heart.

Los Angeles
February 12
August 20, 2014

Sacrifice

The Great Ones—evermore
Ever larger than before
Noble in all virtues are
Them the future is in store

The few greats of history
Bequeath to us their genius see
We know their names, great men were they
In stature, but temporally

The lesser, many though they we
Still above the average be
The many more—majority
May contribute, you or me

It matters not that I above
The average figure with my love
My several gifts I share gladly
To serve and help humanity

Just do your thing; that is enough
Your utmost only does suffice
That you, triumphant, shall attain
To freedom's song and karma's name

Each single one, the minor, too
The lesser and the greater few
Irreplaceable are you
Now sacrifice the present due

Sacrifice alone's enough
So are you precious unto us
So are you dear—the others' just
The increasing populace.

Los Angeles
Culver City, California
February 13-14
August 20, 2014

Corazón

¿Porque mi corazón dolor
Siente y siempre yo
Debo estar sin ayuda
Con la vida sentirlo?

El mundo es tan grande y
Todavía para ti
Porque tu corazón buen
Siente todos, y quien
Sabe más de la verdad
Que yo, medio centenar edad.

22. Febrero 2014

Die Liebe

Die Liebe wirkt wie Zauber und
Wie linder Farben, Farben bunt
Wie lila-rosa-purpur mein
Und edle Menschen, Kinderlein
Verstehen alle Liebe wahr
Denn Liebe leuchtet Christus dar
Und alle Menschen sind berührt
Im Herzen wo die Liebe rührt.

Nun gehe und fortan sei gut
Mit Herzenskraft und Herzensmut
Empfindsam und gar menschlich und
Lieblich jede Liebesstund'
Das Herz ist es was jedem bringt
Teueres Schmerz nach Christus ringt
Denn ohne Schmerz und Freude wär'
Der Mensch wie leer als ungefähr

Und leer ein Mensch entchristet lebt
Doch erfüllt im Herzen webt
Der Christus groß und liebend schwebt
Und lächelt süß und fühlend hebt
Die Liebe schön und immer treu

Wenn Menschen keusch wie Kinder neu
Einander grüßen liebevoll
So ist das Leben wie es soll.

22. und 23. Februar 2014

Schreiben

Jedes Mal ich schreibe wahr
Gedanken denke ich so klar
Wenn deutsch der Sprache Schönheit ist
So bin ich Herzenswärme; bist

Du mein, ich gerne lieb'
Dir alle meine Liebe geb'
Und meine Dichtung stell' ich dar
Wie ein Theater sternenklar

Die Sonne aber strahlet warm
In Strömen uns sie haltet barm-
herzig, denn der Sonne Macht
Auch der Kleinst' erwärmt mit Pracht

Ich danke Dir, mein Leser gut
Ich will Dir geben Kraft und Mut
Mit diesen Worten schreib' ich Dir
Alles Gute dort und hier
Mit diesen Worten dichte ich
Christus läßt dich nie im Stich.

22. und 23. Februar 2014

Oír

Pruebe cosas diferentes
Comidas indígenas
Y corazón tiempos

Porque la vida posible
Tener combinaciones
De humanos y sus naciones

Entonces es importante
Para ser abierto
En tus perspectivos

Para entender
La vida en sus grados
Y humanos ocupados
Sin envolver
Tu propio mismo complicados

Más tarde vas a ver
El mundo tan grande
Y lento, fino oír
Las almas de los muertos
En la paz nuestro
Padre Jesús Christo.

23. Febrero 2014

Weggefährte

Schreiben ist ein gutes Ding
Alle Sprachen schön zu sing'n
Aber Kugelschreiber und
Papier ausreichen genung

Wenn Du immer dich beklagst
Unverantwortlich und hast
Keine inn're Ruhe mehr
Oder schwächlich umgekehr

Dann wirst Du im Leben zwei
Richtungen hingehen bei
Die sind lauter Klage und
Inn're Leere jede Stund'

Aber wenn Du anders lebst
Verantwortlich Dein Herz wohl hebst
Dann Dein Engel um dich schwebt
Und harmonisch Christus webt
In Dein Leben, was Du tust
In Dein Leiden, Deine Lust

Nimmer läßt Er Dich im Stich
Christus treu Dein ständ'ges Licht
Immer steht Er bei Dir nahe
Weggefährte Christus da.

23. und 24. Februar 2014

Overcome

The world was dark and overwhelming
All the people had lost their way
Then Christ overcame the world, unfurling
His banner of love and light the day.

Since this, His Deed, magnificent
So many still not find their way
Yet many, seeking Christ, repent
To find a path, the way each day.

What means 'repent'? might you well ask
It means but comforts set aside
Make sacrifices, find your task
Walk your path with Christ the Guide

Leading to the altar of
Mankind, Sun of Christ, the One
The God of everlasting love
Of human hearts the sacred Sun.

February 24, 2014

Las Escuelas

Cuando los estudiantes de la vida encuentran dificultades
Entonces la oscuridad del alma es como una sombra
Que separa ellos frente de la luz
Porque en su experiencia la luz significa la libertad,
Y no son libres en su cárcel de la noche.
Pero la mañana de la luz del sol del corazón
Siempre sigue la oscuridad de la noche.
Y después del tiempo de la probación oscura
Entre el mundo de la vida espiritual con la luz brillante

Y los estudiantes de la vida descubren el sol Christo en la vida eterna
Con Diós, los angeles y los muertos:
Las estrellas en el cielo sobre la tierra
Y sus cosas y la vida en unión con los cuerpos físicos en el tiempo y
espacio:
Piedras, plantas, árboles, pájaros, pescados, animales y humanos.
Que bonita es la vida: la creación.
Y los estudiantes de la vida les abierta para aprender mucho
En las escuelas de los dos mundos: espiritual y físico.
Gracias a Diós por el sol y la vida.
Es verdad.

8. Marzo 2014

Fühlen

Ich liebe.
Ich liebe im Herzen.
Ich liebe im Herzen die Menschheit,
denn Christus ist unsre Menschheit.
In jedem Gefühl Seine Liebe webt und schwebt in:
unsrem Unglück und Glück,
unsrem Schmerzen und unsrer Freude,
unsrem Leiden und unsrer Fröhlichkeit,
unsrer Tragödie und unsrem Humor,
so klein wie Dein Herz auch ist.
So behalte Dein teures Fühlen,
Und fühle es in Deinem innersten Herzen
mit Lust und Pein
Du lieber Mensch.

8. März 2014

Trabajo

Trabajo puede ser físico o de la mente
Pero también del alma
Entonces es de una vida de la contemplación
Como en la iglesia en los siglos pasados en Europa.

Trabajo es necesario para vivir
Para el cuerpo físico o el alma espiritual

Porque ambos necesitan su propia comida
Entonces vive el humano con todos lo que necesita.

¡Trábaje y siente y piensa
Para tu cuerpo, tu alma y tu mente!
Entonces sería tu vida completa
Humano precioso en el corazón de Jesús
En el centro de la tierra.

9. Marzo 2014

Magnifica

Ritmos del corazón
El sol brilla en tu alma
El sol pasaje en tu vida
Porque el sol da tu luz
Y viene en tu mañana
Y sale en tu descanso del sol
Y Christo—el sol del corazón
Él vive en el tiempo
—su traidor, su maestro y su rey—
Para todo la creación
Y cada alma humana
El espíritu de la luz del día y su tiempo
En la naturaleza afuera donde los pájaros se vuelan y se cantan
Y donde los nubes aparecen grande y blanco
Cada vez Christo regresa en el cielo azul
Para nosotros quien podemos verle:
Magnifica.

9. Marzo 2014

Verstehen

Verschiedenheit ist mächtig
Aber Verständnis pulsiert tiefer, im Herzen
Uns einander grüßend, fühlend, und gründend
Noch kräftiger, wie die rote Sonne.

Wie auch das Zuhören
Das uns einander zuwinkt

Nett und mit Humor
Ist doch auch mächtiger, wie der weiße Mond
Als die Lüfte, die Wehen
Denn der Mondes Macht
Regelt das Wasser

Während der Sonne Kraft
Herrscht über die Erde
Und alle Jahreszeiten und Jahrtausenden
Sind Ihres Königreiches untertan

Die Sonne, die alle im Herzen zu verstehen weißt
Herrlich, warm, und gut
So ist es seit dem ersten Tag
Auf Erden.

9. März 2014

The Secret Door

Stillness reigns in human minds
Which, clear, portray the soul
Lucid bides my time within
My heart that I be whole
Whilst I, in thoughtfulness again
Ponder hearts of humankind
Who well believe in Christ, I know
They will Him find where they do go
For God gives them their role.

In reverence devoted I
Do write my verse herewith
That, thankful for another day
In poetry I give
I find again my inner way
Beneath God's deep blue sky
It was to me some beautiful
That I traversed, an oracle
This day that I did live.

Now rest is all that's left to ask
For night is come once more

And peace descends to earth for men
Who want to leave this shore
To go to heaven's land and hymns
Where those through death tend other tasks
And this is wonderful and good
By every angel understood
For you a secret door.

March 9, 2014

Hilfe

Holde sind Gefühle lieb
Die lächeln süß und schweben warm
Ich kenne sie mit Herz und Hand
Wenn ich beuge mich mein Arm

Denn die Gefühle innerlich
Trösten uns beid' Schmerz und Freud'
Dann heben sie das Herz und mich
So schön wie gestern und wie heut'

Ich denke daß mein Leben lang
Mein Wille stehe mir treu bei
Und wenn zu schwach zu gehen mehr
Mein Christus stehen für mich wird

Denn Gott hat für mich Platz gemacht
Sein Plan ist schon geschrieben dar
Und wenn ein Mensch sein Teil gebracht
Er wird geholfen ganz und gar
Und wenn ein Mensch sein Bestes tat
Der liebe Gott ihm Hilfe hat.

12. März 2014

Die Sterne

Tiefer lebt Gewissen
Als Oberfläches Schicht
Vorwärts geht die Menschheit

Nach Sonnenmorgenlicht

Tiefer ist das Leben
'Persönliches' doch nicht
Gefunden in den Seelen
Menschenherzens Licht

Höher ist die Liebe
Gottessohn so schön
All' die Sterne leuchten
All' die Engel tön'n

Höher ist der Himmel
Christi Lichtes Land
Geist des Vaters Wahrheit
Friede Vaters Hand

Höher sind die Seelen
Der Toten, Sternenlicht
Mit den Engeln leben
Ewig ihr Aussicht.

12. März 2014

The Garden

I walked along in search of light and air
The roses red did waft with fragrance fair
My lungs breathed life with spring's upcoming love
I felt the notion of the sun above

Then all the garden's blossoms smiled at me
They turned to face the trees with greenery
Then waved in breezy winds, their company
Their gardener, I saw them visited by bees

How happy is the fortune of the flower!
Begins to find it in the morning hour
In fleeting fragrances we heaven know
If only everywhere the flowers did grow!

Los Angeles
March 12, 2014

Sense

If you watch the sun by day
Pulsing on its coursing way
In your heart you'll find the sense
In which meaning does condense

For the sun is life, you see
Finds its power within to be
Human in the heart, and free
Karma seize for destiny.

This is Sun of Christ, you know
The way He life on you bestow
Without Him you would cold and dead
With Him warmth, life, light is red

Precious are you to me thus
In your heart an incubus
Prepares to birth a sun within
Light of Christ shine forth from then

Know what I without the sun
Would empty, hollow me be one
But in the Christ and He in me
Grows and lives my inner tree
Grows and lives heart's greenery
That's red, not green, of blood in me.

So sense is not of intellect
But known in hearts of those select
Where condensed sun-feeling lives
Then shines free, receiving gives

Such deep sense is known by those
Who learn the meaning of the rose
They feel the thorny bush of green
Then blossom red above the scene

This rosy blossom is of heaven
The roses are of number seven
The cross of black then dies away

And only life abundant stay

See white appears when Christ doth come
He is the holy Spirit One
The flame of bluish-white alive
The soul eternal with the Dove

So learn your heart in feeling dear
Suffer joy and pain and fear
With courage, equanimity
Condensing for good destiny.

Los Angeles
March 12, 2014 (first two stanzas)
Culver City, California
March 20, 2014 (last eight stanzas)

Dream*

A dream need not be dreamy-cloud
Or white as snow or grey in shroud
It may be clear as sunny days
Communicating messages.

My father in such dreams as these
Comes to me; no homilies
Can tell what these dreams mean to me
But they are conscious I do see

And hear it is my father come
To me to tell me of the Sun
Or just to be there for my warmth
He loves me—that is plain; his form

Appears to me as in life, know
This: his messages bestow
Whether of significance
Or me alone are dear to sense.

*My father Arne Lindgren has come to me in almost 30 conscious dreams since his passing on January 2, 2014 as of this writing.

March 13/22, 2014

Memory

I found my wishes in a stream
Which flowed with gold in it did gleam
Into a lake all fresh and clear
And fishes golden, sunlight here

The fishes played and swam with ease
My soul to dance, my heart to please
Then turned about, they did me tease
The sunlight, though, did me appease

I found in winter cold and snow
The temperatures were down below
The smoke was warm; I'll have you know
From fires in hearths through chimneys go

The smoke smelled good reminding me
Of childhood and Christmas tree
Each time I walk I know their scent
I love these smells my mem'ry lent.

March 13/22, 2014

Leben

Erquicke Lüften, Leben, Licht
Der Hand, der haltet, haltet nicht
Denn Wasser fließend fließt und bricht
Wie Wellen meiner Meeressicht

Die Lüfte, aber, wehen kühl
Das Leben sprosset grün Gefühl'n
Das Licht erleuchtet Welten groß
Als Gott, der Vater, Geistesschoß

Hält Liebe, vorgeburtes Kind
Bevor der Mensch wird seelisch blind
Die Seele mit den Engeln Eines
Badet Leib und Geist in Seines

Meeres Universumland

In Gottes friedlich-segnend Hand
Wo alles ruhig, warm, und gut
Dann die Seelen in die Flut

Einströmen für ein Leben neu
Auf Erden frech und nimmer scheu
In Leibern finden Haus und Heim
Zu lernen wieder 'was geheim

So ist die Weisheit menschliches
Durch Leiden schadet peinliches
Durch Dunkelheit will Licht erringen
Die Ewigkeit auf Erden bringen.

15. März 2014

Zwei Menschen

Es gehen zweie Menschen treu
Aufs Land wie Knechte ins Heu
Sie sind kräftig und frech mit Mut
Wollen Andren helfen gut

Das Wetter, aber, donnert, blitzt
Kein Vogel in den Bäumen sitzt
So müssen unsre Zweie stark
Zu Hause bleiben, nicht im Park

Wo die Blumen blüten nicht
Es ist so traurig, trauriglich
Ihre Herzen warm mit Blut
Pulsieren müssen unterm Hut

Bis die Sonne stärker bricht
Durch die dunkle Wolken; Licht
Ist mächtiger als alles sonst
Sei aufmerksam, Seiner Kunst

Ist strahlen, scheinen, grün 'hellen klar
Erwärmen Herzen immer dar
Die Menschen zwei mit Mut erneu'rt
Gehen wieder wohl befeu'rt

Ihre Taten groß zu tun
Lass' die Welten ihren Ruhm
Nur zuschauen ganz erstaunt
Denn mit der Sonne gut gelaunt

Sie besonders aufrecht sind
Sie helfen beide sehend, blind
Denn mit der Sonne scheinend klar
Und warm—sie alles 'mögen dar!

15. März 2014

Dos Poemas en Español

1. Ayer

Recuerdo el ayer
Cuando tú eras un niño pequeño
Y el mundo que te lleva como un corazón
O como una mano en la seguridad
O, posiblemente, los ojos sin entender.
Pero fue tu niñez, y el mundo empezó ayer.
¿Te acuerdas?

2. El Futuro

Tú ves en el futuro
—no en la ciencia ficción—
Tu alma
Depende de tu pasado y de tu presente
Todo está en tus decisiones
Así que hacer que sea difícil
O lo que dueles
Con la afirmación o la paciencia
Debido a que sólo tienes un alma
Un alma preciosa
Y nada puede replicarlo.
Nada ni nadie.

Los Angeles
15. Marzo 2014

Creation

The sunlight, radiant warm,
streams to earth.

The air, fresh and clear,
stirs with life.

The sea, waves do crash up above
Below, currents deep move and live.

The sun, grand in power,
rules the day.

Nights, beauty-love,
moon and stars appear.

Days, sun and clouds,
skies of blue

Overhead, overall,
great and true.

On earth, mountains tall
stand serene in stillness' majesty.

Creation is a giant
formed by God's Almighty Hands.

Los Angeles
March 17
Revised Culver City, California
April 19, 2014; Holy Saturday

Revere

The sun is radiant
Of earth and every plant
The light of life so clear
And warm do we revere

The sun of hearts and eyes
Shines with light of Christ
Awakening men's souls
Gives sight to them were blind

That they in daylight see
Christ-light clearly shine
Uniting human hearts
In warmth and light divine

The other to perceive
The Table where Christ sits
The Meal to partake
The Heart, the Light, the Word.

March 24, 2014

Greet

Radiant shines the evening sun
Shining warm and bright, this one
Shining clear to earth below
Love of sun on us bestow
We, our love do send above
With our thanks to sun thereof

Now in gratitude to bed
We, to sleep, do rest our head
That tomorrow with the sun
Greet the new day, every one!

March 29, 2014

A Sun Meditation

At eventide,
At the close of a sun's day,
We see the sky dims
To twilight,
And stars and moon appear,
A night of rest to refresh us,
Until the morrow,
At morningtide,

The dawn of a sun's day;
We will see the sky lighten
On a spring's beginning,
When the sun, bold and clear,
Announces the new day;
It will be here.

March 30, 2014

Song

Sun of warmth and sun of light
Shining radiant, shining bright
When, at evening, sun descends
To the earth her way she wends

Final light of day us bless
'Fore the night our heads do rest
Now we see the golden light
Of the evening, precious sight

We, our thanks to sun do give
For another day we live
We, in gratitude, this song
Raise to God, almighty One!

Los Angeles/March 30, 2014

Who am I?

I am
the son of this man
in whose footsteps many years I walked.

I am
the son of this man
in whose speech many years I suffered.

I am
the son of this man
in whose perceptions many years I thinking knew.

I am
the son of this man

in whose love many years I saw beauty.

I am
the son of this man
in whose heart many years I deeply feeling lived.

I am
the son of Alan Lindgren
in whom many years I dwelt and fully experienced life.

Los Angeles
March 31
Edited Culver City, California
April 17, 2014

Toddler

Small child—toddler
Whence do you come?
Where are you now?
In which world do you find yourself a part?

Looking 'round about
In a dream of fantasy
Bathing still in the love of angels
You remain in union with the universe
With whose divine beings you still converse
Toddler of love
—beautiful—.

March 31, 2014

Beginning

The air was vital. Leaf buds, the first of spring, had sprouted in green bursts of life and damp color. Soon, now only a premonition, flowers of delicate, strong, lovely, or bright color will blossom open in fragrances in the sunlight, capturing the fleeting minutes of early morning after a night of hidden closure beneath stars and moon. Each morning, the revelation of life, color, and fragrant beginning repeats—ever anew—as human hearts fill with hope for the future and the new day, given fresh birth and joy by the rising and Risen Sun.

Los Angeles/April 1, 2014

O Sun

O morning with the sunrise and the day!
Dear Sun of golden light and golden ray
Warms Thou our hearts with feeling good to stay
Shines forth Thy radiant light in brightening way

We thank Thee Sun of wisdom old, profound
Thy powerful light sprouts life from springtime's ground
After dark of winter, Easter's deed
Thy resurrection conquers death indeed

For what is life but light that's radiant good
That every human heart has understood?
O Sun, Thy mercy ever comes anew
Our hearts and minds with warmth and light imbue.

Los Angeles
April 2
Edited Culver City, California
April 19, 2014: Holy Saturday

Source (2)

When a human being discovers within himself his singularity and source, his inmost strength and support, he experiences he must go his road in loneliness. He is not alone; he lives daily in and by the presence of friends with whom he partakes of the communion of spirits—Christ and them and he—but he cannot rely on others, not even his best friends, to take on his inner challenges and battles, his inner struggles and hardships, his inner suffering and pain. All these belong to him and him alone. Thus the inner soul, the inward man, can only look within to find his inner sun, in the depths of his own heart. The heart understands others, but others will never be one's heart. In one's heart one is alone with one's inmost being, with the divine essence. Those who lose or lack this essence have nothing, are nothing. They are the emptied and empty ones. Those who suffer it, who find it, they have everything.

Los Angeles/April 3; Edited Culver City, California/April 4, 2014

Return

What wonder to me
White light up above

A Christ-cloud to see
In radiance His love

As prophesied He
Return I shall thee
The clouds we shall see
Christ visible, be

Abundant this light
Pure radiant might
Billowing bright
A great wondrous white
A glorious sight

Los Angeles/April 6
Edited Culver City, California
April 19, 2014: Holy Saturday

Learn

Organize and tabulate
Experience and all your fate
Be on time and not too late
Every hour and every date

Progress then becomes quite clear
On the road we light revere
Sunlight in the garden here
Gardening our life each year

Order keeps like books at hand
Governing estate and land
Responsible for every deed
Past in future do we read

Learning from the past is seed
Growth becomes the present need
Aims our future we do reach
Freedom's karma ever teach

Organize each every day
As you onwards go your way
Well record what you have learned

Memory you then have earned.

May 28, 2014

Views

The poet views Nature with an encompassing eye
While the scientist studies Her in pieces
It's like seeing the broad landscape entire
To the property within fences.

If you want to notice what is great, what is small
That is a wonder of beauty
Then open your eyes in spontaneous attentiveness
And you might discover a Nature-secret openly.

But if you are too busy or preoccupied
Or simply myopic in scientific study
All wonders, great and small, will pass you by
Because you'll overlook them.

Unless, perhaps, you bump into a tree
And smell the scent of pine.

May 30, 2014

The Tender Heart

Songs are sung for heroes
What about the lost
The forlorn, downtrodden
In storms on waves but tossed?

Theirs is only tragedy
Unnamed and sorrowful
Like their experiences
Unwanted though meaningful

Who shares in their sadness
From which no sign relief
Their ongoing mourning
Their hurt and pain and grief?

In the center of the Earth
The Heart of Jesus all
Feeling human, mortal
Is felt in sacred hall

None is left forgotten
The smallest finds a home
The most tender human feeling
Pity, joy, not roam

So feel with Jesu human
If sad or glad what be
Never once deserted
Nor alone with He.

June 7, 2014

Summer Sunlight

Sunlight radiant, clear
Summertime is here
Christ-light beauteous
For the both of us

Christ-light shining in
Daylight gold again
I see love in-stream
Summer's warm sunbeams.

July 4, 2014
Independence Day

Love Awakens Us

Love awakens us
Love is virtuous
In the air about
Love stirs without doubt

Love is big and bright
Bluish-whitish light
See it in the night
Love is quite a sight

Love is like a dream
Wide awake that streams
From the stars above
Venus twinkles love.

July 5, 2014

Summer

The summer is a song
That carries me along
Sunbeams gold and warm
Melting winter's form

To a Maypole dance
Horses canter, prance
Children playing chance
Suitors suit romance

See the fields of hay
June or August way
Feel the breeze today
Would the wind would stay

Blowing on my face
Through my hair to trace
Drops of sweat like lace
Cool me off a grace

Now the nights of star
Heavens reach afar
Venus, also Mars
Cosmic highway cars.

July 5, 2014

Sunbeams

Summer was a thought
Until I thinking sought
Golden summer days
Bringing sun's warm rays

Radiant and clear
Sunbeams I revere
Christ-light streaming here
Throughout all the year.

Los Angeles
July 6, 2014

Different

The mention of what rumors fly
Is like a list of ladies lie
Appear to listen, talk, and twill
The air with nonsense common fill

What's popular makes news and all
The people swarm like bees on call
Not one original, but one
Unnoticed by the other one

This is the tragedy today
What's different ignored this way
What's different no room to stay
What's different, what children play

If you would stand or sit or speak
If you would want a different week
If you silent think what's true
The others will not look at you

The others will deny the few
The others never mention you
The others never notice you
Because you take a different view.

Culver City, California
September 11/27, 2014

Harmonious

If you feel the sun within
The inner sun your heart again
Then all the people understood

Then every one partakes of good

So think with me these inner thoughts
Which only inside gaining sought
Because the heart then weighted feels
Reality within is real

Because in quiet listening
The stillness voices verses bring
Harmonious every feeling
And that alone a stone does sing.

Los Angeles
September 12/27, 2014

Muse

Between poetic words
plays the song of love
Lyric on the lyre
of the Muse Poesie above

I often muse in song
over the language of poetry
That's when a poem
finds its way into me

I often muse in song
over the language of poetry
That's when I compose
a lyric or elegy.

September 19, 2014

Chorus

Somewhere in the chorus
of angels and of boys
I heard tragedy
and I heard inmost joys

While on the earth
men and women merely speak

Only of themselves
of the Muses not one seek

But the children keep playing
their voices pure and clear
Harkening my thoughts
to deep sorrows and joys here

But the children keep playing
their games too young for the deaf
Speech of the adults
with the angels are they left.

Los Angeles
September 19/27; October 2, 2014

Welcome

After sunset's final glow
After final sunbeams show
The world's meaning inwards grow
Of the Sun of hearts to know

A fairy tale had written been
Past secrets golden reveal to men
Unfold according to mystery
Future truth in present be

Then the dawn of the New Age
Age of Light, a new bright stage
Where secrets past quite openly
Written, spoken for all to see
Affirm the paths the seekers tread
They choose life in Christ instead

Approach the altar human hearts
Where the inner Sun imparts
Them strength and meaning ne'er before
Dreamed of, known their journey's for

Then the moment awakening
Within the heart their souls to bring

Behold the inner light of sun
Christ, the Light God souls won

See, this inwards Mystery
In the world openly
Yet hidden from popularity
Only gifted eyes may see

Changes lives forever now
Love anew upon their brow
This the secret of the Sun
Welcome, Christ calls every one

Welcome, child, join in my work
New Jerusalem on earth
Welcome, child, join in my song
O'er the earth for future strong.

September 21-22, 2014

Christus

Die Liebe ist so süß
Ich suche sie nicht mehr
Gerade finde ich
In mir sie umgekehr'

Sie träumt in mir ein Bild
Ich sehe es so gern
Ein Bild von Mutter lieb
Ist nahe und nicht fern

Die Liebe ist bei mir
Mein Herz in Flammen brennt
Und wenn ich fühle sie
So sind wir nie getrennt

Sie lächelt mir gleich zu
Und scheu ich auch zurück
Sie ist ein schönes Los
Sie ist mein liebes Glück

Die Liebe wundervoll
Sie öffnet mir die Welt
In ihr ich sehe nun
Christi Lichteszelt

Denn Liebe ist Sein Herz
Sein Wort, Sein Leib, Sein Blut
Christus starb für uns
Mit Liebe und mit Mut.

Los Angeles
28. September 2014

Reveal

Hide not what will out
Reveal not beneath, behind
No, hidden keep what will about
Reveal instead to them born blind.

Treasures keep within all time
That sensations be sublime
Open so that all may see
Truth divine our company.

Hide in hearts dear suffering
Like the saints and Christ, the King
Reveal the secrets Ages old
To the vision souls behold.

Alan Lindgren
Los Angeles
October 14-15, 2014

Deutsche Gedichte
(German Poems:
A Review)

Poesie

Da war ein Land von Poesie
Das Land war grün wie Gott und See
Wie Erde grün, wie Laub und Baum
Im Sonnenschein und Meerestraum

Das Land war schön wie Melodien
Die klingen sanft wie Elegien
Denn Poesie nach Tode will
Übergehen im Winter Still'
Denn Poesie in Ewigkeit
Fortwährend lebt wie Eingeweiht'

Geheimnisvoll wie Mond und Stern
Stirbt Poesie in Lieder gern'
Geheimnisvoll wie Mond und Stern
Tönt Poesie beid' nah' und fern.

Los Angeles
23. Januar
Culver City, Kalifornien
24. Januar 2014

Die Liebe

Die Liebe wirkt wie Zauber und
Wie linder Farben, Farben bunt
Wie lila-rosa-purpur mein
Und edle Menschen, Kinderlein
Verstehen alle Liebe wahr
Denn Liebe leuchtet Christus dar
Und alle Menschen sind berührt
Im Herzen wo die Liebe rührt.

Nun gehe und fortan sei gut
Mit Herzenskraft und Herzensmut
Empfindsam und gar menschlich und
Lieblich jede Liebesstund'
Das Herz ist es was jedem bringt
Teueres Schmerz nach Christus ringt
Denn ohne Schmerz und Freude wär'
Der Mensch wie leer als ungefähr

Und leer ein Mensch entchristet lebt
Doch erfüllt im Herzen webt
Der Christus groß und liebend schwebt
Und lächelt süß und fühlend hebt
Die Liebe schön und immer treu
Wenn Menschen keusch wie Kinder neu
Einander grüßen liebevoll
So ist das Leben wie es soll.

22. und 23. Februar 2014

Schreiben

Jedes Mal ich schreibe wahr
Gedanken denke ich so klar
Wenn deutsch der Sprache Schönheit ist
So bin ich Herzenswärme; bist

Du mein, ich gerne lieb'
Dir alle meine Liebe geb'
Und meine Dichtung stell' ich dar
Wie ein Theater sternenklar

Die Sonne aber strahlet warm
In Strömen uns sie haltet barm-
herzig, denn der Sonne Macht
Auch der Kleinst' erwärmt mit Pracht

Ich danke Dir, mein Leser gut
Ich will Dir geben Kraft und Mut
Mit diesen Worten schreib' ich Dir
Alles Gute dort und hier

Mit diesen Worten dichte ich
Christus läßt dich nie im Stich.

22. und 23. Februar 2014

Weggefährte

Schreiben ist ein gutes Ding
Alle Sprachen schön zu sing'n
Aber Kugelschreiber und
Papier ausreichen genung

Wenn Du immer dich beklagst
Unverantwortlich und hast
Keine inn're Ruhe mehr
Oder schwächlich umgekehr

Dann wirst Du im Leben zwei
Richtungen hingehen bei
Die sind lauter Klage und
Inn're Leere jede Stund'

Aber wenn Du anders lebst
Verantwortlich Dein Herz wohl hebst
Dann Dein Engel um dich schwebt
Und harmonisch Christus webt
In Dein Leben, was Du tust
In Dein Leiden, Deine Lust

Nimmer läßt Er Dich im Stich
Christus treu Dein ständ'ges Licht
Immer steht Er bei Dir nahe
Weggefährte Christus da.

23. und 24. Februar 2014

Fühlen

Ich liebe.
Ich liebe im Herzen.
Ich liebe im Herzen die Menschheit,
denn Christus ist unsre Menschheit.
In jedem Gefühl Seine Liebe webt und schwebt in:

unsrem Unglück und Glück,
unsrem Schmerzen und unsrer Freude,
unsrem Leiden und unsrer Fröhlichkeit,
unsrer Tragödie und unsrem Humor,
so klein wie Dein Herz auch ist.

So behalte Dein teures Fühlen,
Und fühle es in Deinem innersten Herzen
mit Lust und Pein
Du lieber Mensch.

8. März 2014

Verstehen

Verschiedenheit ist mächtig
Aber Verständnis pulsiert tiefer, im Herzen
Uns einander grüßend, fühlend, und gründend
Noch kräftiger, wie die rote Sonne.

Wie auch das Zuhören
Das uns einander zuwinkt
Nett und mit Humor
Ist doch auch mächtiger, wie der weiße Mond
Als die Lüfte, die Wehen
Denn der Mondes Macht
Regelt das Wasser

Während der Sonne Kraft
Herrscht über die Erde
Und alle Jahreszeiten und Jahrtausenden
Sind Ihres Königreiches untertan

Die Sonne, die alle im Herzen zu verstehen weißt
Herrlich, warm, und gut
So ist es seit dem ersten Tag
Auf Erden.

9. März 2014

Hilfe

Holde sind Gefühle lieb
Die lächeln süß und schweben warm
Ich kenne sie mit Herz und Hand
Wenn ich beuge mich mein Arm

Denn die Gefühle innerlich
Trösten uns beid' Schmerz und Freud'
Dann heben sie das Herz und mich
So schön wie gestern und wie heut'

Ich denke daß mein Leben lang
Mein Wille stehe mir treu bei
Und wenn zu schwach zu gehen mehr
Mein Christus stehen für mich wird

Denn Gott hat für mich Platz gemacht
Sein Plan ist schon geschrieben dar
Und wenn ein Mensch sein Teil gebracht
Er wird geholfen ganz und gar
Und wenn ein Mensch sein Bestes tat
Der liebe Gott ihm Hilfe hat.

12. März 2014

Die Sterne

Tiefer lebt Gewissen
Wie Oberfläche Schicht
Vorwärts geht die Menschheit
Nach Sonnenmorgenlicht

Tiefer ist das Leben
'Persönliches' doch nicht
Gefunden in den Seelen
Menschenherzens Licht

Höher ist die Liebe
Gottessohn so schön
All' die Sterne leuchten
All' die Engel tön'n

Höher ist der Himmel
Christi Lichtes Land
Geist des Vaters Wahrheit
Friede Vaters Hand

Höher sind die Seelen
Der Toten, Sternen Licht
Mit den Engeln leben
Ewig ihr Aussicht.

12. März 2014

Leben

Erquicke Lüften, Leben, Licht
Der Hand, der haltet, haltet nicht
Denn Wasser fließend fließt und bricht
Wie Wellen meiner Meeressicht

Die Lüfte, aber, wehen kühl
Das Leben sprosset grün Gefühl'n
Das Licht erleuchtet Welten groß
Als Gott, der Vater, Geistesschoß

Hält Liebe, vorgeburtes Kind
Bevor der Mensch wird seelisch blind
Die Seele mit den Engeln Eines
Badet Leib und Geist in Seines

Meeres Universumland
In Gottes friedlich-segnend Hand
Wo alles ruhig, warm, und gut
Dann die Seelen in die Flut

Einströmen für ein Leben neu
Auf Erden frech und nimmer scheu
In Leibern finden Haus und Heim
Zu lernen wieder 'was geheim

So ist die Weisheit menschliches
Durch Leiden schadet peinliches
Durch Dunkelheit will Licht erringen
Die Ewigkeit auf Erden bringen.

15. März 2014

Zwei Menschen

Es gehen zweie Menschen treu
Aufs Land wie Knechte ins Heu
Sie sind kräftig und frech mit Mut
Wollen Andren helfen gut

Das Wetter, aber, donnert, blitzt
Kein Vogel in den Bäumen sitzt
So müssen unsre Zweie stark
Zu Hause bleiben, nicht im Park

Wo die Blumen blüten nicht
Es ist so traurig, trauriglich
Ihre Herzen warm mit Blut
Pulsieren müssen unterm Hut

Bis die Sonne stärker bricht

Durch die dunkle Wolken; Licht
Ist mächtiger als alles sonst
Sei aufmerksam, Seiner Kunst

Ist strahlen, scheinen, grün 'hellen klar
Erwärmen Herzen immer dar
Die Menschen zwei mit Mut erneu'rt
Gehen wieder wohl befeu'rt

Ihre Taten groß zu tun
Lass' die Welten ihren Ruhm
Nur zuschauen ganz erstaunt
Denn mit der Sonne gut gelaunt

Sie besonders aufrecht sind
Sie helfen beide sehend, blind
Denn mit der Sonne scheinend klar
Und warm—sie alles 'mögen dar!

15. März 2014

Christus

Die Liebe ist so süß, ich suche sie nicht mehr
Gerade finde ich in mir sie umgekehr'
Sie träumt in mir ein Bild; ich sehe es so gern
Ein Bild von Mutter lieb ist nahe und nicht fern

Die Liebe ist bei mir, mein Herz in Flammen brennt
Und wenn ich fühle sie, so sind wir nie getrennt
Sie lächelt mir gleich zu, und scheu ich auch zurück
Sie ist ein schönes Los, sie ist mein liebes Glück

Die Liebe wundervoll, sie öffnet mir die Welt
In ihr ich sehe nun Christi Lichteszelt
Denn Liebe ist Sein Herz, Sein Wort, Sein Leib, Sein Blut
Christus starb für uns mit Liebe und mit Mut.

Alan Lindgren
Los Angeles
28. September 2014

Poemas en Español
(Spanish Poems:
A Review)

Corazón

¿Porque mi corazón dolor
Siente y siempre yo
Debo estar sin ayuda
Con la vida sentirlo?

El mundo es tan grande y
Todavía para ti
Porque tu corazón buen
Siente todos, y quien
Sabe más de la verdad
Que yo, medio centenar edad.

22. Febrero 2014

Oír

Pruebe cosas diferentes
Comidas indígenas
Y corazón tiempos

Porque la vida posible
Tener combinaciones
De humanos y sus naciones

Entonces es importante
Para ser abierto
En tus perspectivos

Para entender
La vida en sus grados
Y humanos ocupados
Sin envolver
Tu propio mismo complicados

Más tarde vas a ver
El mundo tan grande
Y lento, fino oír
Las almas de los muertos

En la paz nuestro
Padre Jesús Christo.

23. Febrero 2014

Las Escuelas

Cuando los estudiantes de la vida encuentran dificultades
Entonces la oscuridad del alma es como una sombra
Que separa ellos frente de la luz
Porque en su experiencia la luz significa la libertad,
Y no son libres en su cárcel de la noche.
Pero la mañana de la luz del sol del corazón
Siempre sigue la oscuridad de la noche.
Y después del tiempo de la probación oscura
Entre el mundo de la vida espiritual con la luz brillante
Y los estudiantes de la vida descubren el sol Christo en la vida eterna
Con Diós, los angeles y los muertos:
Las estrellas en el cielo sobre la tierra
Y sus cosas y la vida en unión con los cuerpos físicos en el tiempo y espacio:
Piedras, plantas, árboles, pájaros, pescados, animales y humanos.
Que bonita es la vida: la creación.
Y los estudiantes de la vida les abierta para aprender mucho
En las escuelas de los dos mundos: espiritual y físico.
Gracias a Diós por el sol y la vida.
Es verdad.

8. Marzo 2014

Trabajo

Trabajo puede ser físico o de la mente
Pero también del alma
Entonces es de una vida de la contemplación
Como en la iglesia en los siglos pasados en Europa.

Trabajo es necesario para vivir
Para el cuerpo físico o el alma espiritual
Porque ambos necesitan su propia comida
Entonces vive el humano con todos lo que necesita.

¡Trábaje y siente y piensa
Para tu cuerpo, tu alma y tu mente!
Entonces sería tu vida completa
Humano precioso en el corazón de Jesús
En el centro de la tierra.

9. Marzo 2014

Magnifica

Ritmos del corazón
El sol brilla en tu alma
El sol pasaje en tu vida
Porque el sol da tu luz
Y viene en tu mañana
Y sale en tu descanso del sol
Y Christo—el sol del corazón
Él vive en el tiempo
—su traidor, su maestro y su rey—
Para todo la creación
Y cada alma humana
El espíritu de la luz del día y su tiempo
En la naturaleza afuera donde los pájaros se vuelan y se cantan
Y donde los nubes aparecen grande y blanco
Cada vez Christo regresa en el cielo azul
Para nosotros quien podemos verle:
Magnifica.

9. Marzo 2014

Dos Poemas en Español

1. Ayer

Recuerdo el ayer
Cuando tú eras un niño pequeño
Y el mundo que te lleva como un corazón
O como una mano en la seguridad
O, posiblemente, los ojos sin entender.
Pero fue tu niñez, y el mundo empezó ayer.
¿Te acuerdas?

2. El Futuro

Tú ves en el futuro
—no en la ciencia ficción—
Tu alma
Depende de tu pasado y de tu presente
Todo está en tus decisiones
Así que hacer que sea difícil
O lo que dueles
Con la afirmación o la paciencia
Debido a que sólo tienes un alma
Un alma preciosa
Y nada puede replicarlo.
Nada ni nadie.

Alan Lindgren
Los Angeles
15. Marzo 2014

The Stories

An Introduction to the Stories

The German Stories/Tales (Four)

Die Schriftsteller (*The Novelists*) is satirical—Juvenalian or dark satire. The humor factor so marked in Horatian satire (we think of Charles Dickens's work and Mark Twains's) is absent, excepting perhaps the ridiculous novelists, who epitomize vanity, are carried so far that it is farcical. A comparison in satire is Jonathan Swift's *Gulliver's Travels* that is also Juvenalian. The other element of the satire begins almost from the opening of the story and reaches its climax at the end—a moral lesson—when the novelists are left utterly stripped of everything that supported their natural vanity without anything to present (or hide behind).

Unlike *Die Schriftsteller*, *Flemsbach* is a tale appreciated by all ages and most readers. As in an old fairytale, the reader finds himself visiting a wonderful timeless place with the vacationers on holiday, unlike the permanent inhabitants. We feel we are bathing in golden sunlight—the magic of the Sun. Since time immemorial, in tales gold is the symbol of wisdom, so the village Flemsbach is drenched in the light of wisdom.

Der silberne Becher (*The Silver Goblet*) is for youth and adults because some of the images are too striking for the younger ones. But the latter portion of the story would not be displeasing for the sensibilities of the child. It is an unusual tale for several reasons: because it 1.) progresses in contrasting scenes as the story develops, 2.) takes the reader on an inner journey, which disregards possibly all previous literary creations according to what is acceptable in juxtaposition, and 3.) by way of a few literary devices, brings seemingly contradictory story elements or scenes together into a single short story. The tale has much to offer the reader, and it teaches as much as it is enjoyable to read.

There are several contrasting aspects to be seen among the cast of characters in *The Silver Goblet*. These are: poor and rich, death and life, old and young, the human physical body (and corpse) and human soul, Man and God (and His Angels). These contrasts bring into focus what is essential/non-essential. By them, the story also characterizes human nature of different kinds. Additionally, the dog and its name Gladbones, and its masters, who live in simplicity out in the country, lend the last portion of the story genuine charm, rustic and good.

The silver goblet of the title is the object, which serves to unify the story. As with all my fiction, and most of my writing, I did not plan out *The Silver Goblet*. Although it is a cohesive unity, it is the result of spontaneous unfolding creation.

Das kleine Märchen des alten Ehepaar Hühnerfaoth und des Fee (*The Little Fairytale of the Old Couple Hühnerfaoth and the Faerie*) is a small classic fairy story. Although the pictures of the tale have significance for the human soul, of which aspects are portrayed, it is also simply to be enjoyed.

For those of you who do not read German and who will otherwise benefit from having an English translation, I have translated my German stories into English. To the open book, the English translation appears on the left-hand side, the even pages, the original German on the right-hand side, the odd pages. (Because of the nature of the two languages, the translation is briefer than the original German, so the two pages do not exactly match, except where the story is only one page long. However, organizing the translation next to the original in this way is still an advantage for the reader who wishes to compare the two.)

The English Stories/Tales (Seven)

Hemdlig, the Three Brothers, and the Three Sisters, Mike and Morris,

Lemon Pie, Emma the Miser, Jakob's Fortune, Memories, and *Frank Mitchell and the Yellow Roses* likewise take the reader on different inner journeys. *Hemdlig* is a didactic story without pedantry or condescension, set perhaps in Medieval Europe, while *Mike and Morris* is a humorous tale of twins. The latter invites us to people and places far away from the story's home, closing with a reunion there that unites—not only Mike and Morris and their Mother—but the cast of characters who entered the picture after their separation, in a joyous celebration.

Lemon Pie begins with four men digging a ditch, followed by a paragraph of non-fiction, then where one of the men returns to his family and has a conversation with his three children about death before sitting at the dinner table to eat, and for dessert his favorite: lemon pie.

Emma the Miser is a masterful, apparently simple piece of short fiction. Its different elements each tell a story that, at the end, all come together to the climax that is nothing other than an expression of the title. *Jakob's Fortune* is a direct story of swindling, but it can also be seen as a revelation of personalities who have gained inner riches only to foolishly squander them. *Memories* is a brief portrayal of a sampling of life rich in sensations. An excellent piece of descriptive writing, of all the stories *Memories* sounds on a positive, tangible note. Its content is almost entirely images of experiences of the senses. *Frank Mitchell and the Yellow Roses* is a character study especially about the title character who represents, not only one of the seven destinies, but an American as well. I will let the reader come to know him. Now enjoy the stories section in *The Wood of Green.*

Alan Lindgren
Los Angeles

Three German Stories

The Novelists

It was night, and I found myself in the fog in a forest with novelists. Each carried a sack with him filled with his own novels. None noticed the other or paid him any mind, not after the fog had lifted either. Little footsteps rustled like restless shopping petty bourgeoisie as the authors walked back-and-forth. None could stand still to listen to the silent night and look at the magical stars. Slowly, the world became light until the Sun rose in all Her majesty.

Now the novelists began to talk all at once. They bragged about their fame and how they would gain a place among the greats of world literature. Suddenly, it began to rain, and all of them ran quickly about so that they wouldn't get wet from the raindrops. When this didn't work, each held his bundle of books over his head, because they believed this would keep them dry. But the sacks only got drenched with the water, and therewith the books in them, until the novelists themselves got soaking wet, as wet as ducks in a pond.

Then they all began to freeze from the cold, and they complained about their predicament, which they said was unearned and completely hopeless. Finally, they threw down the sacks with their novels, now utterly ruined and worthless, and went home devastated where they put their soaking wet clothes in the wash, showered, and fell naked into bed, awakened from all their vainglorious dreams of fame.

And they remain humbled people to this day, without courage or genius, for they never had them anyhow, and they never will, not even from heaven.

Los Angeles
September 16, 2013
Revised Culver City, California
February 19, 2014

Die Schriftsteller

Es war Nacht, und ich befand mich im Nebel in einem Wald mit Schriftstellern. Jeder trug ein Bündel mit seinen eigenen Romanen. Nicht einer bemerkte oder achtete auf den anderen, nachdem sich der Nebel wich auch. Es rauschte mit leisen Schritten als die Autoren wie unruhige Kleinbürger beim Einkaufen hin und her gingen. Niemand konnte stillstehen um die stille Nacht zuzuhören und die magische Sterne anzublicken. Langsam erhellte sich die Welt bis die Sonne in aller Pracht aufging.

Nun begannen die Schriftsteller auf einem Male zu reden. Sie plauderten über ihre Berühmtheit und wie sie wie die Großen der Weltliteratur Platz gegeben würden. Plötzlich fing es an zu regnen, und sie liefen alle schnell durcheinander um nicht von den Regentropfen naß zu werden. Als dies nicht ging, hielt jeder sein Bündel der Bücher über den Kopf, denn sie dachten, dann würden sie trocken bleiben. Aber die Bündel wurden nur mit Wasser getränkt, und damit die Bücher, die sie enthielten, bis die Schriftsteller selber durchnäßt wurden, so naß wie Gänse in einem Teich.

Dann begannen sie sich alle zu erfrieren, und sie beklagten ihren Zustand, der sie meinten unverdient und ganz hoffnungslos war. Endlich warfen sie die Bündel mit ihren Romanen, nun völlig ruiniert und wertlos, zur Boden, und sie gingen deprimiert nach Hause, wo sie ihre pitschnaß Kleider in die Wäsche taten, duschten, und fielen nackt ins Bett, von allen ihren eitlen Träumen von Ruhm geweckt.

Und sie bleiben bis heute demütige Leute, ohne Mut und Genie, denn sie hatten sie nie sowieso, und sie werden sie nie haben, auch vom Himmel nicht.

Los Angeles
16. September 2013
Culver City, Kalifornien
19. und 21. Februar 2014

Flemsbach

The blue sky covered over the earth, mountain and valley, forest and meadow, lake and sea. In the middle shone the sun in all her glory, great and wonderful. Birds flew across and big white clouds wandered slowly overhead like gigantic free radiant castles. The air smelled of green spring, new life, fresh morning.

Human beings went on the earth on foot and on horseback on a trip, joyous and excited like open children, because it was the holidays and they wanted nothing else than Nature and sunlight, green plant-life and fresh air. Where were they all going, is a question worth asking? To Flemsbach, a place in the south, where little birds fly and sing, and colorful fishes abound and look. The famous shoemakers and tailors of old tradition live there. Their forefathers have lived and worked in Flemsbach for centuries, so many centuries that no one knows how many. The children play the same games in the same street in the village as the little ones always have, and their bread is baked by their wives in the same ovens and they sleep in the same straw beds as in the olden days, and they dream of dear God and of His heavenly Kingdom as they have from the very beginning of their origins.

Yes, Flemsbach is a very special little village, because close by the most wonderful fishes, which the villagers have always eaten, swim in a brook by the name of Flemsbach ("Flemsbrook"), from which comes the name of the village, and nearby the prettiest birds fly in a forest, which richly supplies Flemsbach with wood, mushrooms, and wild boar as far back as the villagers know from tradition and fairytale. It is well said that no one, who has visited Flemsbach, has, can, or could forget his experiences there, from its landscape, forests, and waters, from its houses, street, and market, and especially from its inhabitants, and the entire magic that surrounds it.

Flemsbach

Der blaue Himmel überdeckte die Erde, Berg und Tal, Wald und Wiese, See und Meer. Mitten drin schien die Sonne in all ihrer Pracht, herrlich und wunderbar. Vögel flogen über, und große weiße Wolken wanderten langsam dadurch wie riesige freie strahlende Burgen. Die Luft roch nach grünen Frühling, neues Leben, frischen Morgen.

Auf die Erde gingen die Menschen zu Fuß und zu Pferd auf die Reise, fröhlich und heiter wie offene Kinder, denn es war Ferien und sie wollten nichts anderes als die Natur und das Sonnenlicht, grüne Flor und die frische Luft. Wo gingen sie alle hin? Es ist eine gute Frage. Nach Flemsbach, ein Ort im Süden wo kleine Vögel himmeln und singen, und bunte Fische wimmeln und gucken. Dort wohnen die berühmten Schuhmacher und Schneider der alten Tradition. Ihre Vorväter lebten und arbeiteten in Flemsbach seit Jahrhunderten, so viele man weiß nicht wie lange her. Die Kinder spielen die gleichen Spiele in der gleichen Straße im Dorf wie die Kleinen immer hatten, ihr Brot wird von ihren Frauen in den gleichen Backoven gebacken und sie schlafen in den gleichen Strohbetten wie in alten Zeiten, und sie träumen vom lieben Gott und seinem himmlischen Königreich wie seit dem Urbeginn ihrer Herkunft.

Ja, Flemsbach ist ein ganz besonderes Dorf, denn ganz in der Nähe schwimmen die wunderbarste Fische, die die Dorfbewohner seit je nachher gerne essen, in einem Bach namens Flemsbach, von dem der Name des Dorfes herstammt, und nahe fliegen die hübscheste Vögel im Walde, der Flemsbach mit Holz, Pilzen, und Wildschwein, seit die Flemsbacher es aus alter Tradition und Märchen wissen, reichlich beschenkt. Es ist wohl gesagt niemand, der Flemsbach besucht hat, von seiner Erlebnisse dort, von seiner Landschaft, Wälder, und Gewässern, von seinen Häusern, seiner Straße, und seinem Markt, und besonders

Summers Flemsbach is drenched in the sunshine in the valley, where time doesn't pass or life hasn't changed from the beginning. Flemsbach is a dream, and its inhabitants work, trade, talk, live, die, are born, listen, see, gesture, and walk in this dream in peace and kindness, beauty and goodness, sincerity and love, and their lives are always like a miracle in Paradise. That is why the neighbors from nearby places visit in the holidays, ever expectantly and happily. Each time they are welcomed, and they always return to their homes renewed and with God's blessing. But the villagers of Flemsbach continue with their work as shoemakers and tailors, and they gladly eat their fish and wild boar as they always have, and so it remains to this day.

Los Angeles
September 24-25, 2013
Culver City, California
February 25
March 7, 2014

von seinen Bewohnern, und den ganzen Zauber, der es umgibt, vergessen hat, kann, und könnte.

Flemsbach ist im Sommer im Tal vom Sonnenschein getränkt, wo die Zeit nicht vergeht, oder das Leben sich seit dem Anfang an nicht geändert hat. Flemsbach ist ein Traum, und seine Bewohner arbeiten, handeln, reden, leben, sterben, werden geboren, zuhören, sehen, gestikulieren, und gehen in diesem Traum in Friede und Freundlichkeit, Schönheit und Gute, Offenherzigkeit und Liebe, und ihr Leben ist stets wie ein Wunder im Paradies. Das ist, warum die Nachbarn aus den umliegenden Orten in den Ferien besuchen immer erwartungsvoll und glücklich. Jedes Mal werden sie willkommen, und immer gehen sie erholt und mit Gottessegen nach Hause zurück. Aber die Flemsbacher treiben ihre Arbeit als Schuhmacher und Schneider immer fort, und sie essen ihre Fische und ihr Wildschwein wie immer gerne, und so bleibt es bis an heute.

Los Angeles
24. und 25. September 2013
Culver City, Kalifornien
21. und 25. Februar
7. März 2014

The Silver Goblet

In retrospect, after the previous day's enterprises, to which all the participants except himself gave themselves selflessly and without a thought to heavy work and sheer labor, Peter thought, he shouldn't have demanded it from them, no, expected. But Peter, the very Peter whom many called "friend" and "do-gooder", was not to blame, or so he thought. He had no qualms about using his fellow human beings as long as he profited from it, that is, if he gained something for himself—and yesterday he gained a great deal, an entire estate: lands, house, human beings, animals, and all. Beautiful, Peter dreamed. There is nothing more beautiful.

* *

Suddenly the windowpane rattled, through which Peter observed the main street of the city exactly. He sat in the second floor, and nothing significant happened on this street in the city center that Peter could not clearly see down to the smallest detail.

* *

There was an old man, apparently a servant of the mayor, because of his uniform, sweating and moaning, walking slowly down the street. A girl, an eight-year-old by the name of Henna, gave the old man cool water to drink from a large silver goblet. The old man stood still, lapping up the precious water from the goblet like a thirsty dog. Then he stood upright, turned to Henna, nodded his dirty head to her, and fell lifeless to the ground. Henna screamed, "The old man is dead! The old man is dead!"

Peter merely said to himself: "That large goblet is silver. Such an expensive thing has an owner." Then he went into his study to organize his accounts for the bank, because the estate was to be officially given over to him the next day, and he wanted to ensure that everything connected would be problem-free and the paperwork in order for the

Der silberne Becher

Im Rückblick, nach dem gestrigen Unternehmen, für die alle Teilnehmer außer ihm gab schwere und schiere Arbeit selbstlos und ohne einen Gedanken, Peter dachte, er sollte sie nicht verlangt haben von ihnen, auch nicht erwartet. Aber Peter, der gleiche Peter, den viele als "Freund" und "Weltverbesserer", war nicht schuld, so dachte er. Er hatte keine Skrupel seine Mitmenschen zu verwenden, solange er davon profitiert, das heißt, wenn er etwas für sich gewonnen, und gestern gewann er eine Menge: eine ganze Immobilien: Land, Haus, Menschen, Tiere insgesamt. Schöne, träumte Peter. Es gibt nichts Schöneres.

****

Plötzlich rüttelte das Fenster, wodurch Peter genau die Hauptstraße der Stadt beobachtete. Er saß im ersten Stock, und nichts Wesentliches geschah an dieser Straße im Stadtzentrum das Peter nicht klar bis zum kleinsten Detail sehen konnte.

****

Da war ein alter Mann, seiner Kleidung wegen scheinbar ein Diener des Bürgermeisters, schwitzend und seufzend, langsam durch die Straße gehend. Ein Mädchen namens Henna, achtjährig, gab dem alten Manne kühles Wasser zu trinken von einem großen silbernen Becher. Der alte Mann stand da still, vom Kelch das kostbare Wasser saufend wie ein durstiger Hund. Dann hielte er sich aufrecht, wandte sich Henna zu, neigte ihr den schmutzigen Kopf, und fiel leblos zu den Boden. Henna schrie: "Der alte Mann ist tot! Der alte Mann ist tot!"

Peter sprach zu sich: "Der große Becher ist doch Silber. Solch ein teures Ding muß jemandem gehören." Dann ging er ins Schreibzimmer um sein Konto für die Bankkasse zu ordnen, denn morgen würde der Hof ihm offiziel übergeben, und er wollte versichern, alles sei dazu mit dem Rechtsanwalt sowie mit dem Landesbüro ohne Probleme und schriftlich in Ordnung.

lawyer and the county office.

****

A few children gathered around the lifeless body of the old man looking at it with wonder. They had seen animal corpses in the country, but never a human corpse. One small child, the five-year-old Armin, said: "That's not normal. Human beings don't die that way. They are brought to dear God by the Angels in person." A girl by the name of Gabriela, considerably older at ten years, responded: "No, little Armin. Human *souls* are brought before God. The *soul* is immortal. The *body* dies. Then they're dead." "Now I understand," spoke Armin with conviction. "We have souls like the gods, and like the plants life and death." "Very good, Armin," affirmed Gabriela. "Now you have spoken truly.

****

Half an hour later a horse-and-cart came to take the unsightly body to the grave. Soon thereafter the street was also emptied of children and of all but one thing: the silver goblet, left empty and forgotten on the sidewalk. It was midday, and every citizen of the town sat at home and enjoyed his meal, mainly meat stew and roasted potatoes, with quark with honey or quark delicacy for dessert.*

Following the long midday break, at about two o'clock in the afternoon, the children returned to the street, this time to play. After their parents had picked them up at four-thirty, a scrawny dog ran along the sidewalk, took the large goblet in its jowls, and disappeared.

****

An old couple, Herbert and Gudrun Tilde, sat in their small wood house about 1.7 miles (three kilometers) from the city. The dog, the very same dog, which had carried away the silver goblet between its teeth from the

*Quark and Quarkspeise are dairy products common in Germany.

Ein Paar Kinder sammelten um den leblosen Leib des alten Mannes und blickten ihm mit Wunder zu. Sie hatten Tierleichen auf dem Lande gesehen, aber nimmer eine Menschenleiche. Ein kleines Kind, der fünfjährige Armin, sagte: "So was gibt es ja nicht. Menschen sterben nicht so. Sie werden von den Engeln zu den lieben Gott persönlich gebracht." Ein Mädchen, namens Gabriela, viel älter mit zehn Jahren, erwiderte: "Nein, kleiner Armin. Menschen*seelen* werden vor Gott gebracht. Die *Seele* ist unsterblich. Der *Leib* stirbt. Dann sind sie tot." "Jetzt verstehe ich," sprach der Armin endgültig. "Wie die Götter haben wir Seelen, wie die Pflanzen Leben und Tod." "Sehr gut, Armin," bejahte Gabriela. "Nun hast du richtig wahrgesprochen."

****

Nach einer halben Stunde sind Pferd und Wagen gekommen, um den unschönen Leib zu das Grab zu nehmen. Bald danach wurde die Straße auch von Kindern entleert und alle, aber ein Ding: Der silberne Becher, leer und verlassen auf dem Bürgersteig vergessen. Es war Mittag, und jeder Burger saß zu Hause und genoß seine Mahlzeit, vor allem Fleisch-Eintopf und geröstete Kartoffeln, mit Quark mit Honig oder Quarkspeise zum Nachtisch.

Nach der Mittagspause, gegen zwei Uhr nachmittags, kehrten die Kinder auf die Straße, diese Zeit, um zu spielen. Nachdem ihren Eltern sie um halb fünf abgeholt, lief ein magerer Hund auf dem Bürgersteig, nahm den großen Pokal zwischen dem Oberkiefer und dem Unterkiefer, und verschwand.

****

Es saß ein altes Ehepaar, Herbert und Gudrun Tilde, in ihrem kleinen hölzernen Hause etwa drei Kilometer von der Stadt entfernt. Der Hund, derselbe, der den silbernen Kelch zwischen den Zähnen vom Bürgersteig im Stadtzentrum um halb fünf hinausgetragen hatte, gehörte dem Ehepaar Tilden. Er hieß Knochengerne, denn er liebte vor allem auf

sidewalk in the city-center, belonged to the Tilde couple. His name was Gladbones, because above all things he loved to chew on cow bones and pig bones, and actually did so daily, hour after hour.

****

When Gladbones entered the Tilde home, he dropped the heavy goblet on the floor. Old Herbert didn't notice and only said, "Good Gladbones. You have been away from us for a long time, indeed the entire afternoon. Gudrun. Give Gladbones water to drink and these beautiful pig bones to chew on." But when Gudrun gave the dog the bowl of water, she saw the silver goblet lying on the floor. "Herbert. Lookie here what Gladbones has brought to us. You know already what interesting things he brings us. But this is surely valuable." "What do you mean, good wife?" Herbert turned to Gudrun. "This large goblet, Herbert. I cannot see well, but as it is so heavy it must be costly." "Give it to me, Gudrun. I can still see. This is really something. It is heavy and not lead. This entire goblet is made of pure silver. You were right, good woman. This goblet—this large silver goblet—*is* valuable, *very* valuable. What is a poor old couple like we Tilden supposed to do with it? Tell me that!" "Drink beer from it, naturally," declared Gudrun. "And on holidays, red wine."

****

So it was and remains to this day. Because the Tilde couple live a long time. Gladbones died eight years later at age fifteen. Herbert dug a beautiful grave for the faithful dog, and each year he decorates it with flowers in the springtime. But as for himself and his wife, they drink beer from the silver goblet summer afternoons when it gets hot, and during the cold winters, when white snow covers the ground around the little house and its roof, good red wine.

translated from the original German by the author
Los Angeles/June 9
Culver City, California/July 24/29, 2014

Kuhknochen oder auch Schweineknochen zu kauen, und eigentlich tat er es täglich stundenlang.

****

Als Knochengerne ins Hause Tildens hinein trat, ließ er den großen schweren Becher zu den Boden fallen. Alte Herbert bemerkte es nicht und sagte nur, "Guter Knochengerne. Du bist schon lange weg von uns gewesen, na den ganzen Nachmittag. Gudrun. Gib Knochengerne doch Wasser zu trinken, und diese schöne Schweineknochen zu kauen." Als Gudrun aber den Schüssel Wasser dem Hunde gab, so sah sie den silbernen Kelch auf dem Boden liegend. "Herbert. Guck mal hier was der Knochengerne uns gebracht hat. Du weißt es schon, welch' interessante Dinge er uns bringt. Aber dieses Ding ist sicher kostbar." "Was meinst Du dann, meine Frau?" wandte Herbert Gudrun zu. "Dieser große Becher, Herbert. Ich kann nicht gut sehen, aber der muß teuer sein, denn er ist schwer." "Gib mir ihn, Gudrun. Ich kann noch sehen. Das gibt es doch nicht. Schwer ist er, und Blei nicht. Dieser Kelch besteht ganz aus Silber. Du hattest Recht, gute Frau. Der Becher—der große Silberbecher *ist* teuer, *sehr* teuer. Was soll ein armes altes Ehepaar wie wir Tilden damit? Sag mir das." "Daraus Bier trinken, natürlich," sagte Gudrun Bescheid. "Und an Festtage, Rotwein."

****

So war es und bleibt bis an heute. Denn das Ehepaar Tilden lebt lange. Knochengerne ist nach acht Jahren mit fünfzehn Jahren gestorben. Herbert hat für den treuen Hunde ein schönes Grab gemacht, und jedes Jahr im Frühling schmückt er Blumen darum. Aber Herbert selber und seine Frau Gudrun trinken Bier aus dem großen silbernen Becher Sommernachmittagen wann es warm wird, und in den kalten Wintern, wann weißer Schnee den Boden ums kleine Haus und droben das Dach bedeckt, guten Rotwein.

Alan Lindgren
Los Angeles/June 8, 2014
Culver City, California/June 17/20, 2014; July 29, 2014

A Little German Fairy Tale

The Little Fairy Tale of the Old Couple Hühnerfaoth and the Faerie

Once upon a time there lived an old couple, Elias and Mathilde Hühnerfaoth. Elias was a farmer; Mathilde kept house. They had an old dog, the faithful Silvester, and every evening, while Elias and Mathilde made themselves comfortable on the sofa and made quiet conversation, Silvester chewed on a large soup bone. Well one autumn evening, a knock was heard at the door. "Who could that be?' said Mathilde, and she stood up, walked slowly to the door, and opened. But when she looked out, no one was to be seen. "Strange," thought Mathilde, and she returned to the sofa. This repeated itself twice. Yet again, a knock was heard at the door. "Really," said the old woman, and she opened the door for the fourth time. There stood an ancient man with a long white beard who waved to and smiled at her. "May I visit you?" asked the little man. "Enter," spoke Elias. "Enter and welcome. What brings you here on this gloomy October evening?" After he entered, the visitor said, "I am a faerie from over yonder and am actually looking for friendly company." "Every one who knows us thinks we are a friendly couple, and Silvester here is a good dog." replied Elias. "It is well and good. The people where I come from are all friendly. Do you have something warm to eat?" Mathilde brought the faerie bratwurst and potatoes, and soon he had eaten them all up. "Do you perhaps have a pot of herbal tea?" asked the faerie. "Peppermint or Sage?" Mathilde gave him the choice. "O, preferably Peppermint." And soon the faerie had drunken the pot of herbal tea empty. "Now I have something for you!" and the faerie conjured forth a bag. When he opened it, dozens of gold coins fell on the table. "May the gold express my gratitude for your hospitality," and he disappeared. "Unusual," said Elias. "Very unusual," repeated Mathilde. But Elias and Mathilde did not keep the gold coins. Instead they gave them to the church for poor beggars. And that is The Little Fairytale of the Old Couple Hühnerfaoth and the Faerie.

Los Angeles/July 26
Culver City, California/July 31, 2014

Das kleine Märchen des alten Ehepaar Hühnerfaoth und des Fee

Da war ein altes Ehepaar, Elias und Mathilde Hühnerfaoth. Elias war Bauer; Mathilde gepflegtes Haus. Sie hatten einen alten Hund, den treuen Silvester, und jeden Abend, während Elias und Mathilde sich auf dem Sofa bequem und ruhiges Gespräch gemacht, kaute Silvester auf einem großen Suppenknochen. Nun ja, eine Herbstabend, klopfte es an die Tür. „Wer könnte das sein?" sagte die Mathilde, und sie stand auf, ging langsam zur Tür, und öffnete. Aber als sie hinausguckte, da war niemand zu sehen. „Komisch," dachte Mathilde, und sie saß neben ihrem Mann am Sofa wieder. Dies wiederholte sich zweimal. Nochmals klopfte es an die Tür. „Wirklich," sagte die alte Frau, und zum vierten Male öffnete sie die Tür. Dort stand ein uralter Mann mit einem langen weißen Bart, der winkte und lächelte sie an. „Darf ich Sie besuchen?" fragte der kleine Mann. „Herein," sprach Elias. „Herein und willkommen. Was führt Sie hierher zu dieser düstere Oktoberabend?" Nachdem er hineintrat, sagte der Besucher, „Ich bin ein Fee von drüben und bin eigentlich auf der Suche nach freundlicher Gesellschaft." „Alle, die uns kennen, meinen, wir sind ein freundliches Ehepaar, und Silvester hier ist ein guter Hund," antwortete der alte Elias. „Es ist schön und gut. Wo ich herkomme sind all Leute freundlich. Haben Sie etwas Warmes zum Essen?" Mathilde brachte dem Fee Bratwurst und Kartoffeln, und bald hatte er alles aufgegessen. „Haben Sie vielleicht eine Kanne Kräutertee?" fragte der Fee. „Pfefferminze oder Salbei?" Mathilde gab ihm die Wahl. „O, lieber Pfefferminze." Und bald hatte der Fee die Kanne Kräutertee leer getrunken. „Nun habe ich etwas für Sie!" und der Fee zauberte her eine Tasche. Als er ihn öffnete, Dutzende von Goldmünzen fiel auf den Tisch. „Möge das Gold meine Dankbarkeit für Ihre Gastfreundschaft ausdrücken.," und er verschwand. „Seltsam," meinte Elias. „Sehr seltsam," wiederholte Mathilde. Aber Elias und Mathilde haben die Goldmünzen nicht behalten. Stattdessen gab sie der Kirche für arme Bettler. Und das ist das kleine Märchen des alten Ehepaar Hühnerfaoth und des Fee.

Alan Lindgren
Los Angeles/July 26; Culver City, California/July 31, 2014

Seven English Stories

Hemdlig, the Three Brothers, and the Three Sisters

Long ago there lived three brothers. Living next door to these three brothers were three sisters, and all six of them were orphaned at the young age of eleven years. The three brothers and three sisters were eighteen years old, but one day an old man came from far away and paid them all a visit. Now this old man was very wise, and he brought these six eighteen-year-olds important news which, he said, would determine their futures. So he gathered the young people around him and spoke the following:

"You three sisters will meet three princes on your twenty-first birthdays. Each of these three princes will ask to marry one of you, and you will consent. Each prince will die a martyr's death at the young age of thirty, and you will become princesses and inherit great wealth and lands. You must be kind and gentle with your inheritances so that your fiefdoms bathe in love and beauty under your sovereign virtues. As you are by nature lovely and pure, this will come only easily to you. But as you will be princesses, you will also possess great white magic. You must use your white magic well to befriend the friendless, help the poor, feed the hungry, give the thirsty to drink, clothe the naked, and visit the imprisoned. Then peace will be with you and in your fiefdoms."

Next the wise old man turned to the three brothers, and this is what he said:

"Each of you will meet and marry one of three queens on your twenty-first birthdays, so you will become kings. As you are already excellent in virtue and mind, ethical in thinking, profound in heart and genius, and strong in soul and personality, this will only be fitting. When your royal wives all die when you are but thirty years old, you will inherit the thrones of the three kingdoms. By your rule, all will be well-ordered, maintained, and just. Under your reign, the populace will abide by the statutes you will ordain, so that each citizen will find his rightful place in society and contribute his fair share. You will also have to command the respect of the neighboring kingdoms and not offend the feeling, love, and grace of the three fiefdoms under the reign of the princesses, so that peace will be kept in the world. But owing to your innate intelligence, educator's gifts, and saintly ways, this will be well within your compass."

Then the old man addressed all six of the young people at one time:

"Your three fiefdoms," he said, indicating the three maidens, "and your three kingdoms," and here he indicated the three youths, "will be independent of one another and live side-by-side in harmony, each according to your gifts. For white magic works by the love of and faith in Christ, while wise instruction and just leadership follow the educator's gifts of fairness, penetrating insight, and excellent communication, and each has its place in our world. But keep your fiefdoms and your kingdoms distinct, else war break out and chaos rule."

"I am an old man now," he went on, "ninety-nine years old, but I will return and visit each of your fiefdoms and each of your kingdoms when I am one hundred-and-twenty-four years old—in twenty-five years—to see if all has transpired according to my prophecy before I return to the land of my Father."

And then the old man departed, and the three brothers and three sisters were left to themselves. The young people wondered at what the wise man had said to them, but they doubted not, for when they were small children—but three years old—a wise old man by the name of Hemdling had visited their parents and had told them many wonderful things. Hemdling was eighty-four years old at the time, so by this they reckoned he was the same man who had just paid them a visit.

Many years passed—twenty-five years, to be exact—and the three brothers and three sisters were all forty-three years old. And a man who introduced himself as Hemdling—the very same man who had prophesied their futures a quarter-century earlier—paid a visit to the three fiefdoms and three kingdoms as he had said, and harmony reigned between them all. Then Hemdling said to them:

> "You have done well and abided by my words. The world is at peace and order rules in just and ethical laws and conduct, while all the peoples have their share of love and affection. Now I may go to the land of my Father, which is God's land in heaven. Think on me through the day of your passing into heaven so the world and its peoples remain safe in the fold of the Good Shepherd, Which is Christ."

And that is the tale of Hemdling, the Three Brothers, and the Three Sisters.

Los Angeles
March 26-27
Revised Culver City, California
April 4, 2014

Mike and Morris

There once lived two brothers by the names of Mike and Morris in a village in Belgium. Mike and Morris were twins; what's more they were identical twins, and no one, except their Mother, could tell them apart. So wherever they went—separately or together—people could not tell which was Mike and which Morris.

One fine spring morning (it was in early April), as the twenty-eight-year-old twin brothers were out for a stroll, it began to drizzle. Mike and Morris both thought just how nice this drizzle was. After ten minutes, the drizzle had changed into big drops. How refreshing, was what the twins thought. But after another ten minutes, the rain was coming down in a real downpour. By this time, Mike and Morris were looking for cover. Ten minutes after that, the water came down in great sheets as the heavens thundered and lightning flashed. Still, Mike and Morris looked for shelter; they were soaking wet, but they found none. But what they did find was that they had become separated.

When it stopped raining, everything was fresh and clear and new. Dewdrops glistened on every leaf, petal, and blade of grass in the sunlight. It was by this time afternoon, and no one, who was there at this time, could remember a more beautiful day. Mike and Morris also found this to be so, but they could not share what would have been their pure joy with one another. Instead, they were both very sad. All the people who saw the brothers, Mike in one place, Morris in another far away, found this out of place. Their sorrow on such a beauteous spring afternoon out of place, that is. But when any one asked either brother why he was so sad, they did not respond. Their grief at having lost one another was too great for mere words. But this meant that no one could help them locate the other brother for their reunion, which alone would have brought them joy.

Meanwhile, their Mother had gone out to look for Mike and Morris. But both her sons had wandered—in different directions—very, very far away from their little hometown in Belgium where they had always lived with her.

Her name was Amber Amy Emily, and Amber Amy Emily was much beloved—and admired—in town. When Amber Amy Emily did not find Mike or Morris, or even hear any thing of their whereabouts from any one she asked, then *she* became sad. So Mike and Morris, and their much-beloved—and admired—Mother Amber Amy Emily, were the saddest family of the village in Belgium, but no two of them could share their sorrow, as all three were separated, far apart.

Many years passed, forty-two years to be precise, and Amber Amy Emily was by this time ninety-two, as she had been fifty years old when the great rainstorm had separated her identical twin sons, and her, far apart. Mike and Morris were by this time seventy years old, as you may recall they had been twenty-eight at the time of their stroll that fine, early April morning when they had been separated from one another, and their much-beloved—and admired—Mother Amber Amy Emily, by the storm.

You see, Amber Amy Emily was twenty-two when she gave birth to Mike and Morris. That was a day to remember by the villagers, because Mike and Morris were the only case of identical twins they had ever known. It was especially a day to remember for Amber Amy Emily, who was much-beloved—and admired—in the village, because she was so joyously surprised to have two babies, both boys, and identical twins— just imagine that! But now, for forty-two years, she was not joyous at all. No, she had borne her sorrow in her dear old heart all those years, long after the other villagers had nearly forgotten all about it. After all, many children had been born and grown up since then, and had had children of their own. The good people of this village in Belgium simply could not be to blame for forgetting about the great loss of Amber Amy Emily.

Meanwhile, both Mike and Morris had married lovely ladies, Mike Michelle and Morris Marissa, and both were fathers of identical twin boys, all four of which became fathers of identical twin girls.

The twin sons of Mike and Michelle they named Ivan and Devon, and the twin sons of Morris and Marissa received the names of Oscar and Bosca. The identical twin daughters of Ivan and Devon (Mike and Michelle's identical twin sons) were named Vilma and Valerie, and Ventura and Vanity, while the identical twin daughters of Oscar and Bosca (Morris and Marissa's identical twin sons) were given the names Selena and Sylvia, and Stella and Stardust. So both Mike and Morris had two sons each (who were identical twins, making four identical twins), and four granddaughters each (who were two sets each of identical twins, making eight identical twins).

Mike and Michelle, their twin sons Ivan and Devon, and their two sets of twin daughters Vilma and Valerie, and Ventura and Vanity, all lived in a town in Spain on the border to France, for that was where Mike had wandered far away from Belgium looking for Morris after the storm, while Morris and Marissa, their twin sons Oscar and Bosca, and their two sets of twin daughters Selena and Sylvia, and Stella and Stardust, all lived in a town in Italy on the border to Switzerland, for that was where Morris had found himself when he had wandered far away from the village in Belgium looking for his twin brother Mike.

Now you can imagine how famous these two towns (one in Spain on the border to France, the other in Italy on the border to Switzerland) became, what with two sets of identical twin sisters, each born to identical twin brothers, in the regions where they were located. But had it been known an *identical* situation existed in another town, and that the fathers and grandfathers to all these *six* sets of identical twins were identical twins from a hamlet in Belgium, then the two towns would have been famous from Belgium through all France and Spain, and through all Switzerland and Italy. But Mike and Morris both said nothing to any one. So no one knew they were identical twins, far separated long ago. Until….

Amber Amy Emily went on a trip to France and Switzerland. In France she learned of Mike and Michelle, their identical twin sons and their wives, and their identical twin daughters (two sets each equals four granddaughters) on the border in a town in Spain, and in Switzerland she learned of Morris and Marissa, their identical twin sons and their wives, and their identical twin daughters (two sets each equals four granddaughters) on the border in a town in Italy. Soon word got out, and Mike and Michelle, their sons Ivan and Devon, and their daughters Vilma and Valerie, and Ventura and Vanity; and Morris and Marissa, their sons Oscar and Bosca, and their daughters Selena and Sylvia, and Stella and Stardust; all joined the ninety-two-year-old great-grandmother Amber Amy Emily on her trip back to the small hometown in Belgium, and the *seven sets of identical twins* with Amber Amy Emily and the entire village had a really big celebration, *I can tell you.*

Los Angeles
April 13
Edited Culver City, California
April 20, 2014

Lemon Pie

Four strong men were at work digging a ditch about fourteen feet across and five feet down by the roadside within walking distance of the small town of Heather. This was on a warm summer afternoon in Iowa. The fields of corn were golden in the sunshine, and the occasional saucy crow flew overhead cawing at the scarecrows the farmers had put in their fields. The ditch was for drainage in case of flooding. Beginning at the edge of town, this was one of twelve such ditches. Many towns were doing something similar because of flood damage in recent years. The heavy flooding was fairly new; until the mid 1980s it was uncommon and less extreme. But with global warming, caused mainly by human choices, all kinds of extreme and unusual weather events were occurring globally, and with increased frequency and intensity. It was not only the weather from the climate change but included earthquakes and tsunamis as well—all natural disasters result from human thoughts and acts.

The men set down their shovels to take their mid-afternoon break. Thirsty, they drank cool water from large mugs they filled from a barrel in the back of their truck until they were satisfied. Then they dowsed their heads and splashed one another with the water like boys at play. Finally, they sat on the ground or leaned against the truck to enjoy the rest of their break, which lasted only twenty minutes as they had to get back to work by three o'clock to finish for the day at five.

Sandra had a chicken roasting in the oven for Sam and the kids when Sam returned from his day digging ditches. Sarge was their dog. A German shepherd, Sarge ran to Sam when he arrived.

"We can eat in fifteen minutes, Sam, if the kids help me set the table."

Sam was a quiet man. He could care less if they ate in fifteen or forty-five minutes, so long he had enough food, and Sandra was a good cook. Sam sat down in his armchair. In runs Peter, their eldest child at eleven.

"Hi, Papa," he said, expecting no reply.

Little Amy, their youngest at three, stood in the doorway looking earnestly up at her father.

"Come give your Papa a hug, Amy," said Sam. Amy walked shyly over to Sam and put her small arms around his legs.

"And how are you, little girl?"

Amy was even quieter than Sam, but she cooed, "Oookay, Paapaa."

Sam smiled. He loved his wife and children.

Mary Beth, at nine years their middle child, skipped into the room. When she saw her father she exclaimed, "Papa, you came back! It seems forever you were gone."

"Mary Beth, your Papa's got to work, you know. We can use the summer earnings to pay the bills and save up something for emergencies."

Then Peter said, "Like what emergencies, Papa?"

"Well, Pete, say our truck breaks down or we need new tires. Or your Uncle Joe dies and we pay for the funeral and the grave."

"Woots a foonerool, Paapaa?" said little Amy, carefully pronouncing the spoken word sounds.

"A funeral," answered Sam, "is when some one you care about dies and you honor them in remembering their life in a special service at a church or in a temple."

"Then what's a grave, Papa?" asked Peter.

"A grave is just a hole in the ground for the person's remains, but the tombstone and the upkeep costs something," replied Sam.

Then Mary Beth, the quickest and brightest of the three, said, "If our remains are buried in a hole, then where do we go?"

"Children, Mary Beth has just asked an important question. Where do you think we go after we die?" asked Sam.

Peter said, "My school buddy Frank says his Grandpa told him, "When the words are spoken at the burial, 'Ashes to ashes, and dust to dust', death is such a mystery. One moment, your loved one is right next to you, living and breathing, feeling and touching—even if they're sick. Then all that remains is the lifeless body, maybe the ashes.""

"Frank's Grandpa is right," affirmed Sam.

"The invisible part of us leaves the body—the visible part of us—behind," he went on. "This visible part of us is what's familiar. Our invisible part uses or expresses itself in our visible part like handwriting our name using our hand. That invisible part is very important, because we could never accomplish anything on earth without it. We would be in heaven all of the time if we weren't born as little babies to live out our lives here on earth. Our earth is the place for learning and for work. But when we die, we leave our bodies behind—our visible part that returns to the earth—and we go back to our true home that is heaven."

"What is heaven like?" said Mary Beth.

"That's a hard question to answer, Mary Beth, and few people know about it. It's like sleep, only it lasts much longer, and like sleep, most of us are not conscious in it so we don't remember it when we are awake and alive. Children, I think your Mama has set the table without your help, so let's go and eat."

After every one was seated at the table, Sandra remarked, "The kids must have been asking you questions like last month, otherwise at least Peter would have helped his Mama set the table."

Soon the family was enjoying roasted chicken, carrots, potatoes and, for dessert, Sam's favorite, lemon pie.

Los Angeles
June 14
August 14, 2014

Emma the Miser

Three men sat in a row in front of an old oak in its shade. They could not have another bite; they had just eaten, each a large sack lunch prepared by his wife.

Three women sat in a breakfast room chatting over coffee or tea and pastries. They had just finished doing up the dishes after taking a light lunch together. It was early spring, and the sunlight filtered through the curtains onto the floor.

The three men all yawned, one after another, because yawning is contagious. They were sleepy after their lunch and decided to have a nap. They lay down at the foot of the oak tree in a row. Soon, all three were snoring, sound asleep.

The three women gossiped about the new neighbor who, it was said, hoarded tens of thousands of dollars—if not more—but no one knew where. The neighbor was a forty-year-old spinster who never spoke; she stayed in the house and only answered the door when a delivery person brought a package or a box, or food from the local market. The three women wondered what the spinster did all day and whether she had any relatives. Surely she must get lonely.

After about an hour, one-by-one, the three men woke up from their nap. Albert, Henry, and Vince (for those were their names) told one another the dream they had just had; surprisingly they had all had the same dream. Of the three, only Albert dreamed in color; otherwise their dreams were identical.

A gentle dog was running. Its master had fallen and was injured and required help. The dog was seeking some one to come to the aid of its master. After ten minutes or so, the dog found a boy of ten to twelve years. The boy recognized the dog's purpose and followed it two or three miles to the injured man. The boy went to the local fire station that was nearby explaining the situation. Soon a paramedic vehicle came and the man was taken to the hospital where he received medical attention. He recovered.

The doorbell rang. A woman, roughly forty years old, stood nervously straightening her plain dress. May, the one of the three women gossiping who lived in the house, answered the door. She opened and saw the anxious woman before her. May asked if she could help her. The woman said she lived next door; she had moved in two weeks ago. She expected a visitor, a young gentleman by the name of Mark Collins, twenty-five with glasses and a cane, and had she seen such a man? May invited the woman into her home. The neighbor was beside herself with anticipation. She entered the breakfast room and was introduced around. May I introduce myself and my friends? My name is May. This is Carla and this is Joan. I'm Emma, the woman said. Welcome to Ford, Michigan, Emma. May repeated Emma's description of the young man, and if either Carla or Joan had seen him. She had not.

After treatment for concussion, a man was discharged from St. George Hospital, the only hospital in the town of Ford, Michigan. He wore glasses and carried a cane. His dog had been waiting throughout the treatment at the entrance to the hospital and licked him repeatedly. The man recognized his dog, Jeffers, but had no memory of his fall or transport to the hospital. But he knew his name: Mark Collins. It was only that he could not recall why he was in Ford, Michigan.

Albert, the one who dreamed in color, said he had to go home to his wife May. His two buddies, Henry and Vince, agreed they, too, had to return home. Soon they were on their way.

Carla said she had seen a man who met Emma's description that morning before coming over to May's house for lunch and coffee. He had a dog with him, she said. Emma blurted out: Mark has a dog. A gentle white dog. Yes, it was white and looked gentle, said Carla.

Albert had to pass by the hospital on his way home. There he saw Mark Collins with his dog. He recognized both from his dream. Soon the two men were in conversation. Everything each said confirmed the other while filling in what the other had not known. But as to why Mark Collins was in Ford, Michigan, neither Mark nor Albert knew. Albert invited Mark to join him, with Jeffers, to his home. There, he might relax and, perhaps, his memory return. Mark was agreeable, and soon the two men with Mark's faithful dog came to the doorstep of Albert and May's home.

Albert opened the front door and called out in a loud voice, "May, I'm ho-ome!" Together with Mark Collins and the dog, Albert entered the house. When they came into the breakfast room, Emma suddenly turned and saw the two men and Mark's dog with her sharp eyes. "Mark! Where have you been? You have Jeffers with you. I've been expecting you all morning." "Aunt Emma. You live in Ford, Michigan? I was just treated for concussion at the hospital, and I can't remember why I'm here. I can't even remember a town called Ford. Am I here because of you?" "Did you bring the money, Mark?"

Los Angeles
June 25
August 17, 2014

Jakob's Fortune

There once was an old man by the name of Jakob. Jakob was a tailor. He made and mended clothing for the hardworking citizens of Bohemia like himself, except that because he was so hardworking and made such quality clothes—suits, trousers, shirts, and overalls for the men and boys; and dresses, skirts, and blouses for the women and girls—Jakob was able to set aside a portion of his earnings each week for his retirement, when he planned to lead an idle life of luxury. Indeed, he had done so throughout his working life.

Well, one sunny springtime morning, an elegantly-dressed, middle-aged gentleman entered Jakob's shop. He announced himself, saying, "Once I was a hardworking tailor such as yourself. I had planned to take an early retirement to finally lead an idle life of luxury. But then a wealthy gentleman entered my shop and told me about the way to get rich without working and saving a penny."

"What did he tell you next?" asked Jakob, who was entirely impressed by this gentleman and the promise of early wealth.

"I will tell you how I became very rich without working a single day, but first I will have to see your savings and count exactly how much money you have set aside so far."

Well, Jakob hesitated for a moment of doubt, but then he imagined his coming good fortune, and he led the gentleman to a large wood chest hidden in the back of his workshop, and he opened it. Now the dapper-dressed man had his turn at being impressed, because Jakob had amassed hundreds of precious coins of gold and silver, and bank notes worth many thousands of francs. When the man had counted the money —it amounted to 85,000 francs—Jakob said, "Well, now will you share your secret of work-free great wealth with me?"

By this time the gentleman had regained his nonchalant and convincing manner, and he replied, "If you give me the savings you have accumulated in this wood chest, I will invest it immediately in 100% secure stocks that are skyrocketing even as we speak, and tomorrow morning at this time (and here he opened his gold watch fob and read the time aloud), nine fifty-two, mid-morning, no later, I will bring you your 85,000 francs twenty-fold—1,700,000 francs—in cash."

"But how do I know you will not disappear with my savings?" asked Jakob expectantly, but with caution.

"I will write you a promissory note in the amount of 1,700,000 francs that you can take to my bank after ten o'clock tomorrow morning and cash in, should I not arrive by then with your money." And here the gentleman removed an expensive leather pocketbook from an inside coat pocket, filled out and signed an official-looking promissory note for 1,700,000 francs, and handed it to Jakob.

Jakob closely examined the note, and to his satisfaction, put it in his wallet, which he put into his trousers pocket, closed and locked the wood chest, and together the two men carried it to the gentleman's carriage, which stood waiting for him outside Jakob's shop, placed it inside, and the gentleman boarded, nodded, waved, and departed.

Jakob never saw the man again. Neither was there any such bank he did business with. But Jakob did lose a fortune; because he believed he could gain twenty-fold what he had saved through hard work: gold and silver coins and bank notes worth 85,000 francs, in an investment that did not exist, with a man who was skilled in credulous formalities when he was really swindling. And that is the story of Jakob, the tailor with a gambler's personality betting at the horse races, who was duped.

Los Angeles
August 3-5/17, 2014

Memories

A closet with shelves, coat rack, and three corners (because the closed door where it met the wall and the floor made the fourth) was a cool place in the house warm in the summer. This it shared in common with the large cellar where the potted plants were kept in the winter to keep them from freezing on the balconies and where the apples, carrots, onions, and potatoes were stored. However, the apples were kept away from the carrots because the apples make them taste bitter. I always liked to go down there, not because the Christmas decorations and tree ornaments were kept there off Christmas season, but because of the smell. I can still remember walking down the stairs of twenty-one steps to the bottom of the cellar where I could see everything from the light of a single lamp and breathing in. How I loved to inhale the cool and musty cellar air midsummer, and autumns and winters—when the fruits and vegetables that keep for weeks and even months down there were stored —to smell the odor of them mingled with the gardening tools that still had soil clinging to them and the potted herbs Mother used in the kitchen. It was my favorite place in the house.

Summers were for out-of-doors. Before the automobile, except those special train trips to our Boston relatives, we kids had great fun in the apple orchard running around and throwing over-ripe apples at each other when we weren't picking the good ones and collecting them in big wood buckets to bring into the house. Mother made the best desserts from them using her Mother's recipes: of course apple pie (with a top crust), apple cobbler made with brown sugar (served with ice cream in the summertime and with whipped cream autumns and winters), cinnamon-apple bars, and her own apple cake. How good they tasted after a meal of hot buttered rolls, beef stew, vegetables, and apple juice with ice, following a day of play and work out in the orchard.

Sometimes we helped Father plant (later pick) summer squash, zucchini, early potatoes, white corn, bush beans, tomatoes, spinach, lettuces, cucumbers, radishes, beets, onions, and carrots, among other vegetables. Then there was our wonderful watermelon patch. We also harvested plums, peaches, apricots, figs, big lemons, and almonds from their trees growing near the vegetable garden. Boy, could Mother bake the best lemon chiffon pie!

Summer was my favorite season. That wide-open blue sky when we would lie down on our backs on the freshly-mowed grass and breathe in-and-out the fragrant air, while the flies buzzed about—then we could be lazy! But the honeybees were busy at their work gathering nectar from all the blossoms, and the clover, while the birds pecked at the ripened fruit—the purple turkey figs were their favorite, and they got a lot of them before we could. My senses were drenched in the warm and light world of the summer sun; why it seemed endless as it was a bountiful time of the year. My childhood was good; my memories—now 70, 80 years gone by—remain as fresh as a just-picked and -eaten sweet and juicy watermelon.

Los Angeles
August 9-10, 2014

Frank Mitchell and the Yellow Roses

A man stood on the sidewalk in front of the corner store where the neighborhood women shopped for fresh milk and vegetables every morning for the day. A hungry stray cat came up to him and rubbed against his leg as if asking for something to eat. The man bought a newspaper from the stand for 25¢ and lit a cigarette, smoking it while reading the headlines and a front page article on investment in gold and silver and the stock market. Then he hailed a cab which soon disappeared down a side street.

Three boys were playing marbles in the wide hallway of an apartment on the fifth floor of a building down the street from the corner store just alluded to. The apartment belonged to the family of the eldest boy of the three, the eleven-year-old Thomas. His two younger pals were Sylvester at nine years, and Jonesy, who was only six. They played marbles there every weekend morning and afternoon, taking a break for lunch prepared and served by Thomas' Mother, Bethany Alice Mitchell. His father, Graydon Speaks, had left her for another woman when Thomas was only four years old. The next year Bethany Alice married a man by the name of Frank Mitchell who had a steady job and paid the bills on time. Graydon Speaks was often out of work, and their marriage had been an unhappy one. But Thomas kept the name, and his full name was Thomas Jordan Davis Speaks. He never saw his father again after Graydon left them.

Frank Mitchell excelled in money matters. He was a dapper fellow who always dressed in fancy suits, but all presentation and no substance. He was a car dealer who worked on commission, and as Frank was a natural salesman and the dealership was Mercedes Benz, he made good money. But Thomas didn't care for Frank, because Frank didn't care about anything except himself, his clothes, and his property, not even for Bethany, although she was a pretty lady and he enjoyed spoiling her.

Bethany adored Frank. She fell for him when they first met outside Hobart's Café on a Sunday afternoon the autumn after Graydon left her with little Thomas. Frank had offered to take her out to the Blue Lagoon, an expensive restaurant overlooking the bay, and then to a show at the Wilton Theatre afterward. Bethany was immediately taken, by his offer and good looks both, so of course she accepted. Might she stop by the apartment to change into a nice dress first? Frank flashed his winning smile and, with a wave of his right hand, noted that was unnecessary as she looked stunning in her becoming outfit already. That was their first date.

The man in the cab told the driver to drop him off at Wilbourne and Sixth. The cabby knew exactly where that was, and he readily accepted the five dollar tip, which was a lot of money in those days. From there, he walked two blocks south to Sonders and two blocks east to Fourth Street. He knocked at the door of a mansion and, when the butler answered, announced his arrival by saying, "My name is Frank Mitchell. I have an appointment with Charles Lontrain." The butler showed him in with the words, "Mr. Lontrain has been awaiting your coming." Soon, guest and host were deep in conversation.

Thomas asked his Mother where Frank was. It was suppertime, and usually the three of them ate supper together Saturdays. "Now, Thomas. You know your father has an appointment with a very rich man this afternoon." "Frank isn't my father," was all Thomas had to say, and he grumpily left Bethany in the kitchen by herself.

The next day, in walks Frank Mitchell. He went right up to Bethany, gave her a light kiss on the cheek and a posy of ten yellow roses. "O, Frank," Bethany gushed. "What brings this on?" "We're moving to Albany tomorrow. I've been promoted." "But Thomas has all his friends here. And his school. And this is his—our—city." "Well, it's time for a change. Fresh air. New car. New clothes. New house. And plenty of money. Sky's the limit." "But Thomas won't leave. And Frank, dear. I won't either." Frank didn't bat an eye. He took back the posy of yellow roses and left Bethany standing in the kitchen. And that is the story of Bethany Alice and Frank Mitchell, the car salesman who could make a sale on every other customer looking for a Mercedes at the dealership. Thomas Jordan Davis Speaks could care less, and Bethany Alice got over it.

Los Angeles
September 29
October 1, 2014

The Studies

An Introduction to the Studies

There are entire worlds behind and above the physical realm accessible to the senses, which are therefore ordinarily invisible for, silent to, not experienced by, unknown to us. We need to immerse our souls in the real sensory realm, because it is spiritual-physical and health-bestowing. We cannot do this if our experiences of natural and human sensations, and clear ideas, are replaced by experiences of artificial sensations, and by abstractions. These latter, artificial sensations and abstractions cannot awaken life within the soul. Instead, they stimulate, mesmerize, and dull the senses, and muddle, distract, or fragment the mind, which, in turn, has a deadening or a disturbing effect on the soul.

Our individual and societal problems are mainly due to technology and thought-abstractions, and to these karmic tendencies (for the destiny, see below): forgetting, mental illness, malice, folly, weakness, dreaminess (combined with the effects of artificial sensations, the soul may be lost), and indifference. All of the inherent tendencies in the seven destinies are enhanced, increased, or worsened by the use and abuse of technologies, and by abstraction. Although it seems the Moon and Venus destinies are not subject to the negative impact of technology and abstraction, the karma of Moon souls is threatened by overexposure and the earlier in life and childhood the more so. Here it is apparent for the Moon destiny that malice so hard to bear and so easy to return in kind is actually karmic, as are the corresponding tendencies in the other six destinies. But these tendencies can be turned to good by the individual who finds her or his own path in life, and in so doing acquires what was lacking in the tendency: memory (Jupiter), healing (Mars), love (Moon), wisdom (Sun), strength (Saturnine), wakefulness (Mercurial), empathy (Venus). This is something entirely new. An inner transformation has taken place from the soul's awakening to the spirit-threshold crossing by suffering the soul's probation: the inner Christ. (see pages 278-279: 7 destinies)

If this does not happen the soul is in danger of losing the capacity to endure or create karma/suffering and for all inner experience (empty), or burning up in the fire of anguish, fragrant emotionalism, or psychopathy that takes over and cannot be suffered for eventual healing. Both indicate the loss of identity, of the 'I'. The soul traveling its journey in earthly life to realize its destiny, not to take too many wrong paths, but the middle road that leads ahead to the sacred inner altar and the soul's awakening, the inner birth of Christ, is the third possibility.

It behooves us to leave behind or shut down or turn off or rid ourselves of unnecessary technologies and unnecessary uses of technology, to take time for natural and human experiences, to bring concreteness, clarity, and life into our thoughts and ideas, in order to open and heal our senses, minds, and souls to Nature, our humanity, and divine life in the spirit.

The goal—one-by-one—is to perceive the inner light of the soul and the etheric Tone: Christ. This is St. Paul's Damascus experience. The spirit-seeker (after Christ) reaches this destination, at once the purpose and meaning of human existence. This marks the beginning of the true communion of humanity which must, again and again, be celebrated between Christ and you (or Nature or Angel) and me: perception. Then the restoration of what was absent in each destiny, indicated above, takes place from within. Many lifetimes are first required for maturation.

Every striving soul on her/his earthly journey must gain life-experience only to be had across many reincarnations. This is for his/her own, individual path to and with Christ. The soul and the body are distinct. (see poem *Destiny* pg. 502) Karma (the destiny) is created and resolved on earth, everything suffered (formed and endured), including all illness, vocation, and the significant relationships. Christ is the Lord of Karma.

On a number of themes, these studies penetrate beneath the surface of outer life and normative society to the deeper, higher reality referred to and what it signifies for the subject under study. Some are essential or important for practice or preparation, which cannot be overvalued, especially on the four temperaments. Please read these (marked in the *Contents* with an *), *The Face of Our Humanity* (397-398), and *Human vs. Dehuman* (399-402) especially as they are of importance for every one.

Alan Lindgren
Los Angeles
August 30-31/September 18-19/October 13/18-19/30, 2014

Opening

We must leave our home of childhood and youth and venture out to become men and women in this brave new world of ours. To do this, in early childhood the child needs exemplary goodness worthy of imitation, much love and joy, and simple play to engage its natural fantasy life; in middle childhood a child's education with nature-experiences, art, and music where the child wants to learn its lessons in the subjects and with the teaching method appropriate to its age as we find in the Waldorf Schools. This must be a childhood and an education free from exposure to learning and entertainment technologies so damaging to the ears, eyes, soul, and mind. Parents, teachers, and other responsible adults who are loving authority figures have their important roles to play for a childhood that gives the foundation for all adult life: if one respected, just, and beloved adult, this is good, if two or more, this is still better. In adolescence we come to the age of idealism, so essential to the future, but in adults as yet uncommon. These adults must embody those beautiful, clear, and ethical ideals inherent in striving youth.

If we wish we may pursue the most important education: adult self-education, which enriches the soul with inner treasures and trains the spirit to think in the direction of higher knowledge (experience). No longer bound by the limits of that wonderful physical instrument of the thinking human spirit—the brain—we will think the spiritual thoughts and so see through the fallacy of materialism by the light of spiritual truth that will shine in each human soul and light the way to the divine within. Learning and enduring or working over the course of many earthly lives, the striving, seeking soul will attain its hitherto unknown and unknowable goal: the spiritual awakening, the inner Bethlehem, the inner birth of Christ. This is the Damascus experience, the awakening from its dreams to conscious life in the spirit.

– Alan Lindgren

Highest Thinking

While the heart of the human being of divine conscience—not some preaching morality or human I, but the increasing activity of Christ's 'I AM' at work in her/him—must suffer dearly with the heart-courage of the saints, to use an image from the great German lyric poet Christian Morgenstern (1871-1914), "the bright thoughts (of the religious genius) are like radiant swans moving across the blue lake of the soul", unattainable for all other geniuses but given to us as an image in this poet's poetic picture. Endowed with the power of the sun, such a human spirit is great and lofty. "It builds the airship but takes flight heavenwards by the Christ-love."

O, we far lesser men and women, who are centered, not within our hearts in sacred feeling and from ever-increasing mighty spirits aloft on eagle-wings of thought, but in our ordinary lower selves, let us take moments of pure glory-thought to behold the vision the Great Ones have already attained and steadily guide mankind to: the coming of the Messiah, a huge white light blazing with almighty power which He produces in them, from within them. While this divine light of Christ approaches us all, He is already at work in glorious power in the thought, speech, hearing, vision, touch, breath, love, and genius of these Great Ones, so that I may write: I have seen the Messiah in His Glory.

Alan Lindgren
Los Angeles
September 5-8
October 18, 2014

Whatever We Cherish Is All That We Have

Whatever we cherish is all that we have. If a friend is dear to us, we have a friend. If a loved one is dear to us, we have a loved one. If a pet is dear to us, we have our pet. If earth, sun, birds, animals, stones, clouds, plants, stars, moon, ocean, beach, mountain, forest—Creation—brings us healing, solace, refreshment, wonder, joy, or wisdom, then Creation is always there for us, an inexhaustible source of healing and inspiration. If human feeling is dear to us, we cherish our human feeling. If dreaming is dear to us, we have our dreaming. If our memories are dear to us, we have our memories. If books are dear to us, we cherish our books. If our work enriches our lives, or is therapeutic for us, then our work is a blessing. If our own or others' creativity and culture are dear to us, we have our own or others' creativity and culture.

If we experience the practical life, good sense, and sound reason to be stabilizing influences in our minds and lives, then they are indispensable to us. If clear perceptions; precise observation; cool, calm, and collected awareness of and attentive interest in our environment is healthy for us, and essential for our overall sanity and orientation in real life, then we know to value, and to repeatedly implement, what is of a practical, sensible, reasonable, perceptive, precise, observant, cool, calm, collected, aware, attentive, and interested nature in daily life that is normalcy and indispensable and intentional to practice. If being awake is a matter of life-and-death in this demanding and confusing world, then let us be awake.

If we think on God that we be good in our struggles for strength, then this is a help, consolation, and assurance to us. If we cherish religious feeling within our hearts, then we feel the meaning of the religions in our hearts. If we believe in Christ, then He works in the world that He overcame 2,000 years ago. If we want to be Christians, then we are Christians. If we love one another, then we remember Christ. If we love, then we educate. If we are loved, we learn. If we break Bread and drink the Cup together, then we partake of the Sacramental Meal of Christ's flesh and His blood whereby we are nourished and sustained for life on earth. If we believe in God that signifies goodness, then we know He has designated our place in heaven and destiny on earth. If we are brothers and sisters, then we help one another as a matter-of-course.

If we cherish the experiences we have each day, then our daily experiences are dear to us. If we cherish helping another human being whom we care for and love, then helping another human being is dear to us. If we cherish being of service, then being of service is dear to us. If we cherish listening and learning, then listening and learning are dear to us. If suffering and grief are dear to us, we know how dear to us our suffering and grief is. If a higher perspective grants us humor, which reveals freedom, let us smile. If we fondly feel our sorrows, then we find consolation in our sorrows. If happiness lifts our spirits to glad moods, then let us rejoice in the light. If love, fun, and magic bring joy into our lives, what delight we take in love, fun, and magic. Let us be dear to one another. Let us always cherish, for that is what we have, that is all that we have. If we have it, then it is enough, for then we have all that we need, and then some.

Los Angeles
June 15-16, 2006
Culver City, California
May 30, 2014

You and I in the New Age of Light

Because of the dawn of a new age, the Age of Light in which we are now living, new possibilities are opening up for those who are seeking help in many places and under varied circumstances. Whether youth, woman, or man; black or white, yellow or brown; Buddhist or Zoroastrian or Hindi, Christian or Muslim or Jew, Catholic or Orthodox or Protestant, of a new religion or atheist or materialist; Asian or European, African or American, Latin or indigenous; poor or rich; of any nationality or family: all human beings find themselves faced with the same human and spiritual choices.

The spiritual landscape or geography is very bleak; the spiritual climate is cold and windy, often turbulent, but many are the hearts which shine warm and radiant as suns for any and all who will draw near. They are our centers and lifeblood, the beacons of Christ, whose clarion call sounds forth in truth into the world for all to hear. Awaken! I am here, in your midst. Gather together with My helpers that you find support and encouragement for your inner battles; solace and consolation when you are lonely, suffer, and grieve; discipline, thoughtfulness, and stabilization when celebrations, frivolity, and joyous activity are excessive, strength when you feel tired and weary, inner health when your body ails you.

Cultivate the feeling of reverence, respect, and devotion where veneration is due, in the depths of your heart, which is the nourishment of the soul for spiritual health and strength, above all for the strength, which develops for the activity of inwards knowing, that your soul becomes wealthy in virtue and strength for good deeds.

Prepare the shrine of your heart that it become fertile for the germination of your soul, and the power of the spirit sprout in the light of the world.* Find times and places for quiet inwardness and meditation, where you go to your divine source, the inner wellspring of creativity, love, and light, for renewal and redirection. Set aside times each day to distinguish the essential from the non-essential. Set about your tasks with boldness, energy, and courage but also sensibility and wisdom that you be true to your God, not wild or myopic. Achieve inner goals manifest in outwards life in small or modest ways, unaltered by the storms of life, which brew and break out in spiritual thunder, lightning, and torrents about you. Know that patience and persistence are not altered with changes beyond your intention, and that, applied in daily life, show positive and real results that are objective and that therefore cannot be altered.

Do not despair. Find those who reciprocate. They are your fellow travelers as you journey through life. Offer them your friendship; show them good will without expecting anything in return but their friendship and good will. You will find you are never alone but share human feeling and love in common with true friends. Offer them human help when they are in need; show them you care. Connect with them so that they know they are special to you, that you are their friend, and that you love and understand them and are present for them.

Each day, go within in meditation where the divine indwells you and waits to be heard. Listen closely to the still small voice in your soul and live according to it to find peace of mind and harmony with others.

Go outside in Creation, which heals, and where people are about and your work is spiritual-social. Find the balance alternating between the inner and the outer life that all is well.

Remember that you are the soul, the bridge that connects the divine within you and the world of things and men around you. You are the simple solution to the complex problems of society when you let your selfless love spread and your little light shine wherever you go. Know that, while you may not be able to change and improve the outer circumstances, which are unfavorable to positive change and world progress, and may not always be in a position to perform good outer deeds, which need to get done, you can always help others by your inner attitude and life, and by practicing the virtues of moderation, patience, balance, and discipline, that love alone enables us to see one another truly, and that "love educates".**

Repeatedly work on yourself daily: transforming your soul through contemplation, prayer, meditation, thinking, and insights; your etheric body or one-sided temperament by intentionally changing your inborn nature or habits; your physical body by making conscious the regular willed bodily functions: chewing and swallowing your food and drink, digestion, elimination; and sitting, standing, and walking.

Give and receive, which is the secret of all development, and await the turning point of your existence when you will awaken from your young dreams to the Sun Divine, the light of the world. Then you will gain the secret of initiative, and the perspective that all is well, whereby you will be part of world progress, because you prepared your soul and heart in your body to become a fitting vessel for the Christ to work in your work, perform deeds in your active deeds, love in your love, live in your life on earth, walk in your steps, gesture in your gestures, see through your eyes, listen through your ears, sound in your voice, speak with your lips, think in your thoughts, enable you to find the balance in each moment.

Then you will stand in the clear warm light of the new day to greet the morning Sun, which has risen from the darkness of night to illumine the world entire for the good work of men and women. This is the Christ, the cosmopolitan Sun-Being of God's great Good World Plan that includes you, and whose glory shines forever and ever.

Santa Monica, California
Easter Monday/April 9-10
Edited Culver City, California
April 17, 2012/May 30, 2014
Edited Los Angeles
September 17-18, 2014

* This is taken from the following mealtime grace:

The seeds are germinating in the earth's dark night
The herbs are sprouting through the power of the air
The fruits are ripening in the might of the sun.

So germinates the soul in the heart's holy shrine
So sprouts the might of the spirit in the light of the world
So ripens the strength of man in the glory divine.

In the original German:

Es keimen die Pflanzen in der Erde Nacht
Es sprossen die Kräuter durch der Luft Gewalt
Es reifen die Früchte durch der Sonne Macht.

So keimet die Seele in des Herzens Schrein
So sprosset des Geistes Macht im Lichte der Welt
So reifet des Menschen Kraft in Gottes Schein.

Rudolf Steiner

** "Love does not rule, but it educates, and that is more", is from Johann Wolfgang von Goethe's *Fairy Tale of the Green Snake and the Beautiful Lily.*

The Age of Christ

The period of history and time covered in the Old Testament is very significant. It is true that Christ's life, death, and resurrection have completely changed the world, history, and time since these events and forever after and that the significance of these effects of Christ run more deeply than anything else. But without pre-Christian times the karma created by human souls, by human hearts could never have found their fulfillment and resolution where they had been formed and must work themselves out, on earth. This is the fulfillment of the destinies, which results from lifetimes of human relationships of a karmic nature, significant tasks, and other deeds, and these reincarnations began in the Old Testament period.

Since Christ's human life, we are seeing the resolution of this karma across reincarnations. Because many souls have yet to experience the New Testament events in the personal and objective sense, new karma continues to be formed that will only be resolved in future (by the end of our post-Atlantean epoch, approximately 5,000 years or AD7000). This will take place along with the resolution of preexisting karma.

Since the Palestine events (the Mystery of Golgotha, the crucifixion and resurrection), Christ has been at work among men and women and, beginning the 1930s, numbering in the millions. This is not meant in an outwardly visible, physical sense, but as a spiritual reality. Christ continues to change the World that He overcame 2,000 years ago, rather the World is catching up to Christ's deeds since the time when Augustus Caesar ruled over the Roman Empire. We hasten to the New Jerusalem that will be the world over. Eternity beckons. Time waits for no man or woman. It is up to each one of us to either join in the work of Christ or no. *

God remains seated on His Throne in everlasting peace-strength where He suffers all human transgression with immeasurable pain until the only human activity is conscience, selfless sacrifice, and service in the spirit of Christ. This pain is beyond comprehension. Today, since 1900 —the dawn of the Age of Light—Christianity is in its earliest beginnings in the sense of all humankind. It is not in Jerusalem, ancient Greece, Asia Minor, and Rome; it is not medieval European Christendom; it is the entire world; it is global. The Age of Light is the Age of Christ that shall reign to the ends of the Earth and for all time.

Los Angeles
April 29/May 1, 2013
Culver City, California
May 30
September 18, 2014

* Here I quote the great Christ-Sun initiate and German lyric poet Christian Morgenstern (1871-1914): *Save Christ from the Christians!* meaning many who call themselves Christians have not experienced Him within their spiritual I or higher Self (genius) and therefore do not know His only true name: 'I AM'. They do not know this, do not understand this, or call Him by another name; they know absolutely nothing about Christ. These very people are often to be found proselytizing, preaching, 'praising', and so on, thereby doing great harm.

The Living Christ

Christ was born 2,000 years ago. He was a little baby. Just imagine that. In Jesus of Nazareth, He became a man. Christ walked, lived, ate, drank, saw, taught, healed, suffered, and died in Palestine. On the Third Day, He rose from the dead and ascended into heaven. These are historical-spiritual facts. For Christ is a spirit. These events are historical in Jesus.

But Christ was a man only once. This was in Jesus of Nazareth. He will never again appear in the flesh. That was a special hour in existence. It was the darkest hour that Christ changed into light. Death had no power over Him. Christ conquered death with His Life. He cast out the gloomy darkness with His great and glorious Light. Christ is the Light of the World. He is the Risen One.

Now Christ appears to men and women in the etheric or life realm of the Earth. To those whose souls He has awakened from their slumber, Christ can be seen shining from the soil; from plants and blossoms; around insects such as bees, ants, and butterflies; around birds and animals; and in the etheric bodies of some human beings. The Etheric Christ appears in the form of light: soul light. Christ is the Spirit of the Earth.

He is also the Cosmic Christ of the sun, the clouds, and the stars. He can be seen in all of Nature and is among human beings gathered together in His Name, which is the inner experience of the 'I AM'.

He is the living Christ, or He is not at all. In those in whom He lives, Christ grows great indeed. In them, He enlarges on earth among men, women, and children. When they die they rise and ascend into heaven. Such are the Risen men and women. They rise in Christ and He in them. They gain immortality of the spirit.

The human soul is eternal. It is only the body, which is mortal. Death has power over those only whose lives and thinking were devoid of the spirit, which were bound to the senses. These souls must live in a kind of spiritual isolation on the Other Side of death's threshold, unless those close to them in earthly life remember them in their hearts.

But death is only physical; the soul leaves the body at death and ascends into spiritual worlds. But the eternity of those in whom Christ has risen and who have risen in Christ differs from the others. Christ lives in them and they in Him on earth and in heaven. Their spiritual bodies are immortal. These spiritual bodies remain after death as they were in life. The difference is that after death they have no flesh any more. In earthly life, their spiritual bodies lived in union with their physical bodies. In divine life, their spiritual bodies live with the angels and the other dead where no physical bodies can go. This is their immortality. But all those who were close on earth continue their connections after death in the Spiritual World (= heaven). This is their Christ-experience in heaven.

Today only some who are mortal gain immortality. Today many who are mortal shall in future gain the immortality of the spiritual body. The immortality of the spiritual body is divine.

The living Christ is on and in the earth. Those who do the work of Christ necessarily suffer and make selfless sacrifices. In heaven they have other tasks together with the other dead, the heavenly hosts, and our heavenly Father, Christ Jesus, Who ascended into heaven.

Santa Monica, California
October 26, 2011
Culver City, California
May 30; December 2
Los Angeles
September 18, 2014

Hope, Service, and the Destination of Humankind

Where many people may sense impending doom as disaster, war, or fatal illness happens, and relate this sense in the form of dreams, pictures, or thoughts, my actual imagination or vision beholds the glory and the resurrection of Christ in humankind. It is not that I do not dwell on my own condition and situation—of which I am full aware—but that my sight sees not only the darkness and the death associated with physical reality, but equally the light and abundant spiritual life. The beautiful and glorious sun shines with her clear radiant-pulsing light about me. Christ-light is shining in our daylight. How can this be, some one who is realistic but limited in awareness to material-physical reality might ask?

It is because I have crossed the threshold to the spiritual world in the midst of life and can go back-and-forth at will. I am fully aware of the limitations imposed by physical reality on those who have not penetrated to the infinite realms of the spirit within the human I that has attained to the divine, which has given inner birth to Christ. But I am also in familiar territory with spiritual reality or higher dimensions, if only as a beginner, then with conscious and genuine experience. The conscious experience of Christ brought about by the soul's awakening is actual knowledge of things hitherto unknowable because they necessarily lay beyond the realm of experience. Now these things are entirely within experience.

And so it is clear to see how one such as myself can view the destination of humankind in its enormous might and splendor and take personal joy in this viewing, while at the same time possess the awareness that I will not be present at this future point in time. Not only do I take great joy in the knowledge of what is beyond my life, but I also dedicate myself to its fulfillment. I already possessed this knowledge as a knowing feeling during my 5-month fully conscious depression (1986) after my soul's awakening (1985) before I crossed the spiritual threshold (1987). I was able to put this true feeling into the following thought: I have no hope for myself, but I have hope for mankind.

So long I cherish this hope as I do now I remain wholly part of mankind because of my active participation in human and world progress with positive intention. This hope and this sense give my life real purpose because I have the knowledge I am helping others. In ways, however great or small, every one who helps is part of the picture and knows it. Only those who go about with no sense of endurance or purpose feel hopeless; to their experience they are out of the picture. I have dedicated my mature life to helping others.

Sometimes I have had to wander in places of inner desolation that implies despondency on my part, but I have never stopped caring. I only wish I had been more disciplined because when I was I made real personal progress (until June 1987). Since then my path has continued to be one of learning, however. I am indebted to my friends that I have always been able to learn. These friends include, not only greater and lesser Sun of Christ initiates, but also the little people who, in all sincerity, make personal efforts on their path of learning and progress. We learn from the ever-developing greatly-gifted teachers. But we can also learn from those who, yet ignorant, have much to teach us from their perspective. I cherish the knowledge: *We are in this together.* It is my hope that many people will feel this with a sense of earnestness and personal responsibility. This has always been my prevailing mood.

Santa Monica, California
June 10
Revised Culver City, California
June 12, 2012

Learning

Perspectives

Several months ago, a good-willed human being, who was my new friend at the time, asked me what a pathological thinker is. As it turns out, he had been seeing doctors and psychologists for some time who had inculcated in his mind that he was such a thinker. But then my friend went on to say, that he was researching the topic because he wanted to learn about it, looking it up in dictionaries, and so forth. He wished to understand the real meaning of what it means to be a pathological thinker, so that he would be able to understand what it was these doctors had diagnosed him with.

It was at this point in our conversation that I said, because my friend was asking questions, was actively striving to learn about this in order to understand it, that he could not be a pathological thinker. You see, similar to a psychopath, totally obsessed with an idea or with an event in his past who can think of nothing else, a pathological thinker lives entirely in his own inner world of pathological, disturbed thoughts, so he is incapable of stepping back outside his inner world, his pathological mind or psyche, to really examine the nature of the thoughts, to subject them to study for the purpose of understanding them. He *cannot* learn.

For the very reason my friend wants to learn (not only about pathology but about other topics that concern him as well; and he also appreciates literature; he was both interested in and enjoyed reading quality fiction), which is extremely *healthy*, to achieve clear understanding of his own mental processes, and not merely to be at their mercy or whim—which would be purely subjective—he *could* not be a pathological thinker. His very quest to learn, his search for objective knowledge and his broader interests are not only not pathological; they are healthy. One may learn from such a deliberate and thoughtful human being, from his human nature and thinking approach. He embodies qualities that are not only of human interest, but beneficial, harmonious, and measured, and should be recognized.

My friend was really shocked from his usual viewpoint by my insight, because he had never encountered it or any other thinking of its nature before. I mean this in an entirely positive sense. What took my good friend aback in such a positive way by my response, was his realization I am gifted to see my fellow human beings from perspectives usually absent. He was faced with a higher and refreshing perspective that would never have occurred to him within his own way of thinking. However, I am aware I am one of many in this regard, and there are a smaller number in our time who are far more gifted than I.

I owe this and my several other gifts to preparation through necessary life-experience, my soul battles, hard work, and seeking; my innate intelligence and formal learning; and especially my perception and autonomous thinking gifts. It is important for each human being to gain perception and sense-free thought, and to unite true perception with living thinking. For without this experience, this combination of human-spiritual activities, no objective knowledge that is deeper, or higher perspectives, can be won. Insights that grant the thinker higher perspectives are a matter-of-course for those who truly perceive and then think the corresponding sense-free thoughts. Thus what surprised my friend is actually no surprise at all. It is simply a question of knowledge: the experience of Christ and of human natures and destinies, with wakefulness and awareness. It is a gift, which, however, like meditation, must be practiced with selfless sacrifice and energetic inner activity.

[Note: Not only studies about or with material on the four temperaments (see *-ed studies in *Contents*, pages xv-xvi), but those regarding the seven destinies may be helpful and of interest. For example, pages 280-281, 357-374 (living examples), and 375-382 (historical examples).]

Alan Lindgren
Los Angeles
September 1/3/17
October 18-19, 2014

Physical and Spiritual Knowledge (Experience): Perception and Thinking

Faith is in God, but faith is religion (the heart) and is another subject from Christianity. It is a question of community. The Kingdom of God that will be on earth is Christianity. Christ came to earth. He was born. He was a tiny baby. Imagine that.

Christ lived and walked on earth. He lived in Palestine and was crucified on Golgotha, which means the place of the skull. He died and was buried. On the Third Day, Christ arose from the land of the dead and ascended into heaven. As He told His disciples and the two Marys, Christ appears in the clouds. These are the Christ-clouds, the big bright, billowing clouds that emanate white Christ-light.

These things really happened and happen. They are historical facts. Today, Christianity in the sense of all humankind is in its very beginnings. Belief in Christ is important. But more important today than belief is experience.

We can only know what we experience personally. What we have not experienced, we cannot know.

If you have played with children, then you know what it is to play with children. This is special. If you have suffered, experienced pain or illness, then you know what it is to suffer, experience pain or illness. This is deeply significant. If you are a Mother, then you know what it is to carry a child, give birth, and have a child. This is a miracle. If you have been a nurse, then you know what it is to be a nurse. This is caring. If you have been a teacher, then you know what it is to be a teacher. This is good. If you are a writer or an editor, then you know how to write and edit. These are excellent skills. If you have had a business, then you know what it is to run a business. This requires business skills and business knowledge. If you are a homemaker, then you know shopping, cooking, baking, cleaning, and time-management skills. This is essential for family life today when the old traditions have been forgotten, leaving the children without the care and structure required for a healthy, good childhood, which is the basis for a meaningful, useful, helpful adulthood in which a person can develop herself and learn on the road of real life. If you have worked, then you know what it is to work. This has real practical, hands-on value.

It is the same with Christ, only differently. If you know Christ, then your soul has awakened in Him when you received a drop of His spiritual sun essence into your heart, your soul. This experience brings about a deepening inwardness, a complete transformation. You are granted a new experience hitherto unknown to you. Your soul has awakened from its dreams such that you can perceiving think and thinking perceive the truth: Christ. You perceive inner light, soul-light, Christ-light.

You are no longer a child. You are no longer a youth. You are a mature adult standing on the divine ground of the world, of which you are conscious. Your spirit has become very big, enlarging your soul.

You know yourself with objectivity as a stranger. You see others for the first time as they really are. This is possible because you shine your inner light on everything you see. Light enables us to see, just as the Tone enables us to hear. You hear the Christ-Tone also. Before, you cannot hear it. Your life is forever changed.

It is a question of experience.

Before Christ has awakened you, you do not know spiritual things. You may believe or claim you know, but then you are unaware. Awareness comes from awakening from your dreams to Christ. Most people today are unaware of Christ. Some suffer pain, illness, discomfort, and physical loss, but they are unaware that their pain and suffering connects them directly with Christ. They are directly connected with Christ, but they remain unaware of this. The important thing is that we are connected, whether we are aware or unaware. This is our karma.

Christ is the Lord of Karma. Karma is a human, spiritual law, as is reincarnation. Reincarnation and karma are the two human, spiritual laws. Only human beings have ever known them. Stones do not experience them. Plants and animals do not experience them. Angels do not either. Because Christ became human in Jesus of Nazareth, He died a human death. He incarnated once. In His incarnation, Christ united His destiny with world destiny. He is the Lord of Karma. Karma is destiny.

Karma is a law that every human being is subject to, just as reproduction, heredity, and growth are the three etheric or life laws that every living thing is subject to. Wherever human beings create or suffer karma, there is Christ. Those who create no karma, or who suffer no karma, they are not connected with Christ. This is very earnest.

It is essential that we shelter our small hearts or protect our spirits from everything that would steal our pain from us. 'No pain, no gain.' It is equally important that we think or be smart and do not allow our emotions or warmth to exude from our bodies and hearts to emptiness or overwhelming illness. Thinking is human. Imagination is also human.

Before the soul has awakened on the reception of a drop of the Christ sun essence, thinking remains brain-bound and lifeless. It is lifeless as mathematics, statistics, facts, logic, and memorization are lifeless and cannot understand what is living. It can only memorize and acquire facts, statistics, and information. But the plants, the animals, and human beings, all beings which have no physical bodies (including the so-called 'dead', the three hierarchies or nine heavenly hosts, the holy Trinity); and all non-physical processes, these people cannot think them, because they can think only using their brains what is dead.

Spiritual things are living, like Christ. He is the living Christ. This is so whether or not we believe in Him. Christ is in and on the Earth. He dwells in human hearts, which have prepared a place for His birth, just as He was born in Bethlehem after His Mother Mary had prepared to give birth to Him. This is the Christ-Child.

Thinking is the one thing. We have brain-bound/sense-bound or dead thinking, and brain-free/sense-free or living or Christ-thinking.

Perception is the other thing. We perceive colors with our eyes, sounds with our ears, warmth with our hearts and bodies, tastes with our tongues, smells with our noses, things with our skin and hands. In order to perceive something, you have to have the organ of perception with which to perceive it.

You need eyes to see colors, ears to hear sounds, a tongue to taste flavors, a nose to smell smells, hands and skin to touch things, hearts and bodies to feel warmth.

These things that we perceive can be limited to the physical world. Then we perceive solely what is physical, because we are using physical organs of perception only. But there are other, higher organs of perception by which we can perceive living things, not the physical bodies of living things that require physical organs of perception, but their life or etheric bodies. If the eyes of the soul have been opened, we can see the life of the plants, the insects, the animals, human beings, the soil of the Earth. This life that we perceive with the eyes of the soul is the etheric realm, etheric bodies.

Christ walked the Earth 2,000 years ago. He was a man. He was human flesh, and He died a human death. But this was only once. Christ will never again appear in the flesh. Today, Christ appears in the etheric realm of the Earth and of all living things. But to see the living Christ in the etheric realm in which He appears to us today, the eyes of your soul must first be opened.

Only those whose soul eyes have been opened by Christ can see Him in the etheric where He appears. This sight is of soul-light because Christ-light is soul-light. The sunlight is ensouled. Soul-light shines in human souls. Soul-light shines in the etheric realm in all living things.

All others are like the blind man who cannot see colors that are all around him. But a blind man can sometimes have an operation performed on his eyes so that he can see. This is like what happens when the eyes of the soul are opened. Then we can see many things which were always there, but which were hidden from us because we were blind to them.

The same is true of the Tone world. If you have only physical ears, you can hear only the physical vibrations produced in the air. (You can still differentiate between human and natural sounds and those produced by machines, including computer-generated and digital sound, when you can only perceive physical vibrations. This is also true of visual sensations. You can differentiate between true or natural colors, light and shadows/darkness as experienced in Nature, Art, and the human iris, and the virtual and digital colors, light and darkness; before your soul eyes have been opened. But your hearing and vision is in a dream as it were.)

With spiritual ears you can hear the etheric Tone that sounds in the thought ether. This etheric Tone is the Christ-Tone. (Some human beings are highly sensitive to the thought ether. They share this in common with the plant kingdom. Such people detect thoughts, attitude, and love with keen sensitivity because they are carried from people by the thought ether and have a direct effect on their soul and mind. These thoughts that they detect are coarse or fine. These attitudes are harsh or friendly. This love is present or absent. All human beings are affected by thoughts and imagery, only those souls of the Moon, Venus, and Mercury planets (destinies) are particularly sensitive, likewise plants and trees.)

Our knowledge is limited only by the limitations to our experience. If our experience is limited, then our knowledge is equally limited. If our experience has been refined, deepened, broadened, attained to heights, then our knowledge has likewise been refined, deepened, broadened, attained to heights.

Physical experiences are necessarily limited. They are confined to what is physical. But there is much more to life than what the senses relate, than what is physical, than what is material. You can learn of these living and spiritual things from others who know them from personal experience. They are like those who can see describing colors and colored things to a blind man. How can you learn of these things? You can learn of them in the thoughts of those who impart them in thinking form. We can do this because we can think the thoughts.

For example, Rudolf Steiner wrote a book entitled *Theosophie* (*Theosophy*). In this book, translated from the German into English and many other languages, so clearly and precisely written, he describes these and related things in great detail in thought form that makes them comprehensible to someone who has yet to experience them. Of course personal experience is a different matter from learning of something or hearing about it from someone else. But the point is, these things that are important for every one to know about can be communicated to those who do not yet have first-hand experience of them *in thoughts that every one who is unbiased can think.* Simply thinking the thoughts prepares the soul on the path of its destiny that leads to the soul's awakening, which signifies firsthand, personal experience of living and spiritual things.

I have also described these things for you here, and I describe them from other perspectives, and I take up other significant themes in the studies of this section of non-fiction. My soul eyes have also been opened to perceive Christ in the etheric; my spiritual ears also hear the etheric Tone, which I also produce; I also think (produce and perceive) the living thoughts. I am not the only one. There are millions today, and in future there will be many millions more, and it is important that you will be among them. Christ is there, not only for those graced, but for all humankind.

But I am a writer with these gifts, and this is not so common. The clear and detached thinking of thoughts that are written or spoken communicate to the reader or listener. These qualities enable each human being to think the thoughts that are independent of the thinker. They are thus valid for each and every one in every instance. Like the great ideas, these thoughts are objective in their truth and thus stand in the thought-world as facts do in reality.

The truly great ones are the teachers and leaders of mankind, like Johann Sebastian Bach, Rudolf Steiner, Ita Wegman, Marie Steiner, Christian Morgenstern, Michael Bauer, Elisabeth Vreede, Albert Steffen, Günther Wachsmuth, Diethart Jaenig, Jörgen Smit, Manfred Schmidt-Brabant, Gérard Klockenbring and many others, on earth and in heaven, today. All of these special people, the other greats, and many lesser, but also very gifted ones, are working very hard for us. If we go to them, they will always help us. They turn no one away. Christ never lets one down.

Perhaps by reading this and the other studies, these things that seem so strange and are so different from what we ordinarily experience will not seem altogether strange any more. They are within and everywhere around us. Whether or not we perceive and think them, these spiritual realities and dimensions were always present. Indeed, they are more significant, and in a real sense, more real than is physical reality because they give our lives true meaning and cross over the boundaries of birth and death. They bear the attributes of eternity because they transcend time and space in their truth. This is so when they appear in time and space which condensed from them, and which they immortalize.

True thoughts are eternal. Those who think them immortalize that aspect of their selves—their souls—that think them. This occurs when we think—not the materialistic thoughts—the spiritual thoughts, this transforms the soul into the spirit self or higher Self or genius. This is a task for human beings today: thinking and rethinking the living, spiritual Christ-thoughts that are brain-free and sense-free. The organ by means of which these autonomous thoughts are thought is the awakened soul.

We live in the Age of the Consciousness Soul. We know that consciousness refers to a condition of soul in which it dwells and experiences its environment. The stone has the consciousness deeper than our dreamless sleep. The plant lives in a consciousness like human dreamless sleep. The animal lives in a consciousness comparable to the condition of human dream sleep. When not sleeping, the human being lives in a consciousness that is the condition of waking. Yet most waking human beings are not fully awake when they are not sleeping. These human beings live in a kind of dream when they are awake.

But one day, after many lifetimes of human experience, Christ awakens them from their daydreams with His Day-Light. Then these same human beings see and hear awake. Then they think awake—not merely reflections and shadowed thoughts, which are what presents itself to every human mind-soul—but the actual thoughts that are light, Christ-light, by which we see the world. This Christ-light or thinking that illumines the world of things, processes, and beings enables these human beings to know. Now they have gained true knowledge: the knowledge of Christ and therewith of the higher or spirit self that is the human genius in full awake consciousness. This wakeful consciousness is made possible by the incarnating genius or spirit or higher Self into the human being listening, thinking, feeling, remembering, healing, imagining, loving, romancing, gesturing, speaking, working, walking, standing, or sitting on the earth.

A blind man cannot see, you see.

A deaf man cannot hear, you know.

A lipless man cannot speak, you say.

A handless and bodiless man cannot touch, you feel.

A man without a nose cannot smell, you breathe.

A man without a tongue cannot taste, you taste.

A voiceless man cannot sing, you hear.

A mindless man cannot think. Do you understand?

A man who cannot do these things cannot comprehend, you know.

But a man with eyes can see. And a man with ears can hear. And a man with lips can speak. And a man with hands and a body can touch. And a man with a nose can smell. And a man with a tongue can taste. And a man with a voice can sing. And a man with a mind can think.

And a man with these organs can know.

So it is with spiritual things.

Santa Monica, California
October 25/November 3, 2011
Culver City, California
December 22-23/26, 2011; December 2, 2014
Los Angeles
September 17-18/21, 2014

Diet, the Use of Salt and Sweets, and Water, in the Four Temperaments

There are specific indications found in Caroline von Heydebrand's excellent book on the temperaments* on salt and sweets, and water, for the four temperaments. These practices are simple, straightforward, economical, and easy to perform so that every one may apply them in daily life, for the children and others in one's care, and oneself. It is essential that one knows correctly the temperament of the individual in question, else harm, even great harm can be done. However, if the correct practice is taken the results are very beneficial. Then they do us good no end. Let us briefly describe the four temperaments to clarify each.

The Sanguine is often tall—though not always—, well-proportioned, broad-shouldered, and walks with a lilt in the step. S/he has a twinkle in the eye. Outwardly and inwardly mobile, flexible, and resilient; the Sanguine is quick to forgive and forget. S/he has a large soul relative to a small ego. Hence a surging thought life with a short attention span. Sanguines have outer interests, hobbies. Persons of this temperament have the most beautiful sense of interest; open, spontaneous, and aware. The Sanguine is naturally musical. S/he likes to experience cheerfulness, gladness, and joy. Sanguines love beauty and lovableness. They understand children and animals. The temperament of childhood is the Sanguine. Sanguines have a natural appreciation for light and color phenomena. The element of the Sanguine temperament is the air and light.

The Choleric is often short—though not always—and of compact build. S/he has a firm walk with an added push into the ground for will-emphasis. A bold, even black eye. Stout-hearted, s/he is bold, brave, blunt, and courageous. S/he is assertive and will be in evidence. The ego is the predominant member of fourfold man in the Choleric temperament, stunting growth in the three lower members. The Choleric has the ego's certainty of its goal. S/he has a strong will directed outwards and feelings difficult to master. Human beings of this temperament have the most beautiful compassion, strong, supportive, courageous. Cholerics admire greatness and respect strength, hard work, and intelligence. They know they are unique and discover and are interested in what is unique. They are naturally healthy individuals. They value the young adult and all human beings; and heroism, courage, and bravery. The temperament of man/womanhood is the Choleric. Cholerics have a natural sense for and appreciation of gesture, form, and spatial relationships, such as the placement of furniture in a room and the man or woman walking down the street. The element of the Choleric temperament is fire.

The Melancholic is taut-bellied, generally lean, and often wiry. S/he has a firm, dragging gait and a sad eye. The physical body is predominant in the Melancholic temperament. This sets up obstacles to the three higher members: the etheric body, astral body/soul, and ego. Hence s/he lacks the etheric ease of the Phlegmatic, the astral/soul mobility of the Sanguine, and the ego's certainty of its goal of the Choleric. But s/he has physical bearing. The Melancholic does a lot of thinking, particularly about how others affect her/him. Those of this temperament have the most beautiful esteem, dignified and noble. The Melancholic is naturally musical. Melancholics are extremely sensitive to all forms of pain and suffering. They will forget themselves in selfless compassion for another human being or an animal who suffers. They are obsessed with suffering and death. Where this would be morbid and unhealthy for someone of another temperament, this is completely normal and healthy for the Melancholic. They feel compassion, for example, for the saints and martyrs, whose lives are therefore good for them to learn about, as for strangers who have suffered greatly. Melancholics find consolation in their sadness and sorrows. They are at home in the physical world of dead inanimate objects. They appreciate the cold lifeless mineral whose unbending silence they understand. The temperament of middle age is the Melancholic. Melancholics have a natural sense for words and thoughts, which they intuit. They are interested in the craft of words. The element of the Melancholic is earth.

The Phlegmatic has a corpulent, expanding physical body. S/he missteps and has a dull eye. Phlegmatics are perfectly contented doing nothing. Hence this is the temperament of laziness. However, Phlegmatics are sensuous and the natural romantics. So they love food. They are always thinking about food. Unless they are eating, which is even better. The etheric body is the predominant member of the Phlegmatic temperament. This means they have expansive physical bodies, as we have said, and large souls and big egos. They would rather relax. That is more pleasant. But it is difficult to be a Phlegmatic if you want to do something physical. This is a heavy feeling that is rather depressing. So one wants to be positive around the Phlegmatic. It is important for the Phlegmatic to wake up from the doldrums. This happens in the Tone. Phlegmatics are naturally musical. A Phlegmatic can sit at a piano and create a simple melody, just one note after the other, one that is musically pleasing. Phlegmatics have a natural and good sense for rhythms. This is felt, for example, in the four seasons, day and night, and in reciting poetry and singing. Persons of this temperament have a kind of inner life. They have the most beautiful love of all four of the temperaments; serene, even, steadfast, and abiding. Unlike the other three temperaments, Phlegmatics cannot be directly influenced by another person: through lovableness like the Sanguine, absolute command of the subject as is the case for the Choleric, or much suffering for the sensitive Melancholic. Only indirectly through his/her peers does the Phlegmatic take an interest in what is going on. So it is very beneficial for the Phlegmatic to be around a warm, loud, lively group of people in whose company s/he will take a shared interest. Phlegmatics are naturally the most social people in that they are equally good with all four of the temperaments: with other Phlegmatics, with Melancholics, Cholerics and Sanguines. So it is good for them to be around other human beings. Phlegmatics like water, which is their element. They like the plants, whose simple green they love and understand. Theirs is the temperament of old age.

[Note: Secondary and tertiary temperaments are common, less so a balance of all four. But there is always a predominant one. In treatment, including the practices presented in this study, one always goes by the primary temperament.]

SALT and SWEETS in the TEMPERAMENTS

Salt unites and makes mentally fit. It aids in concentration. Without sweetness we would faint from weakness.[1] The body changes carbohydrates (grains/cereals) into starch that it converts into sugar. This sugar differs from the refined sugar that also provides sweetness. Sugar aids in friendliness and relaxation. Refined sugar is nutritional but that is not why Cholerics and Melancholics and, in smaller amounts, Phlegmatics require it. Those who need refined sugar ENJOY its taste, and it is this natural pleasure that is telling. The same is true of fatty beef, pork, or lamb. Those who require it experience natural pleasure when they indulge in eating fatty red meats such as pork link sausages or a fatty steak. Again, this is pleasure that is TASTED.

Sanguines and Phlegmatics need a well-salted diet. (Salt is a potent substance that enhances flavor. One should taste it as such.) But Sanguines should avoid refined sugar, and Phlegmatics not overeat it. When Sanguines eat refined sugar, it throws their thinking into disarray because of their already mobile souls, so they need to obtain their sweetness solely from baked or cooked whole grains and cereals. These are the good carbohydrates and, as with all foods from plants, they should be cooked or baked, with the exceptions of radishes, salads, and fruits. (See cooking fruits, below.) Melancholics need some added salt. Cholerics should avoid added salt altogether as this is harmful for them. There is enough salt in food already.

All four temperaments should eat root vegetables for their natural mineral (salt) content. This is for the head, the brain as it aids the thinking processes. Not the tuberous vegetables (such as the potato, yam, and sweet potato), which are not true root vegetables (they are between the root and the stalk) and thus reach only the lower brain (making us 'stupid'), but such vegetables as carrots, beets, turnips, parsnips, onions, and radishes that reach the entire brain. (Potatoes taken with root and other non-tuberous vegetables are fine.) Carrots are by far the best plant source of minerals. We require mineral salts for thinking.[3]

Melancholics and Cholerics need plenty of sweet. This includes added refined sugar such as on cereal, in cookies, cakes, pies, candies, and ice cream, and, for those who drink it, coffee and tea. Phlegmatics may also enjoy refined sugar but in smaller quantities, as noted above. For information on stimulants, see Rudolf Steiner's work on the topic in the bibliography. (Many who drink herbal teas may prefer honey. Honey gives firmness to the older human being. Honey is to old age what milk is to children. But it should not be taken as a food or it causes illnesses.)

All the temperaments can enjoy fresh fruit, fresh fruit juice, raisins, dates, figs, and honey (as an additive, not a food). If the digestion is sensitive the fruit may be cooked as in jams and sauces. We need the fruit for the digestive organs for their protein[1] [a]. We would die without protein. Some vegetarians take a few eggs a week for the protein.

FATS and the TEMPERAMENTS

Fats are also important for health. We require adequate fats for the heart and the blood vessels.[2] [a] Fats are the warmth-builders. This can be from the plant and animal kingdoms, and, for infants, from the human kingdom—in the mother's breast milk. We learn more about the essential nutrients, to develop sound judgment regarding nutrition, and gain nutritional awareness, in two excellent books by Gerhard Schmidt, M.D., that offer a new dynamic view of man and the world.**

When we take in less fat than we use up we become spiritual, but in an unhealthy way. We become ill. This can lead to starvation. When we take in more fat than we use up we are healthy in this sense, but we develop a paunch, which is not so good sometimes. (This also depends on the temperament.) When we take in the same amount of fat as we use up, this is just right.[3] [a]

The greatest gift one may give the Phlegmatic is to keep him slender as a child. Then he will not suffer a weight problem his entire adult life. Most obesity is the direct result of fattened Phlegmatic children. Sanguines can also become too fat, although this usually happens in adult life from inactivity coupled with overeating. Melancholics tend to be slim. Some have trouble keeping the pounds on. They may become too slender— really skinny that can even lead to the illnesses of bulimia and *anorexia nervosa*. This is starvation. These diseases can affect the other temperaments as well, but very often and the worst cases are with Melancholics. When this is the tendency, normal eating, extra calories, and more than usual fat in the diet are advisable. In the Choleric temperament, there are very different builds. Some individuals are small, by which we mean not only short or petite, but slender. They have small bones. These individuals will find the right weight without a paunch. Others are of medium or large build in a similar situation but with a (small) paunch. There are Cholerics who are especially big-boned. They may be stout. For these individuals a paunch is actually desirable that is entirely healthy. They carry their weight well. They look good. (One may go too far, of course, but these individuals can be quite big.)

WATER and TEMPERATURE

There are two extremes in temperature: warmth/heat and cool/cold. They each have specific effects. Warmth brings about a dreamy, sleepy condition. It aids in relaxation and letting go. Cold awakens. It brings us to ourselves.

Because Sanguines are airy and Phlegmatics watery natures, they tend to be dreamy that is unawake. So it is healthy for the Sanguine and the Phlegmatic to begin the day with a dowse of cold water over the head for a healthy wake-up call, ridding the 'sleep in the eyes', awake for play, learning, and work.

Because Melancholics are earthy and Cholerics fiery natures, they tend to be too awake, it is correct to say. So it is beneficial for the Choleric and the Melancholic to have warm water on the tummy at bedtime. This activates the metabolic life dream-forces, helping them to close the day, relax, and let go to have a good night's sleep.

Los Angeles
January 13-16, 2011
Edited Culver City, California
April 25/May 2-6/September 21, 2014

1. Rudolf Steiner. *Nutrition and Stimulants, Bio-Dynamic Farming and Gardening Association, Inc. (1991)*, p. 104. *Nutrition and Health / Two Lectures to Workmen, Anthroposophic Press, Inc., Bell's Pond (1987)*, pp. 11-12.
2. Ibid., p. 101. *Nutrition and Health / Two Lectures to Workmen, Anthroposophic Press, Inc., Bell's Pond (1987)*, pp. 8-9, 12, 19.
3. Ibid., p. 61
1a. Ibid., p. 106. *Nutrition and Health / Two Lectures to Workmen, Anthroposophic Press, Inc., Bell's Pond (1987)*, pp. 14-15, 19.
2a. Rudolf Steiner. *Nutrition and Health / Two Lectures to Workmen, Anthroposophic Press, Inc., Bell's Pond (1987)*, pp. 12-13, 19.
3a. Rudolf Steiner. *Nutrition and Stimulants, Bio-Dynamic Farming and Gardening Association, Inc. (1991)*, pp. 63-64

Bibliography (Additional references)

*von Heydebrand, Caroline. *Childhood: A Study of the Growing Soul, SteinerBooks, Anthroposophic Press (1995); Rudolf Steiner Press (1970)*

von Heydebrand, Caroline and Röschl-Lehrs, Maria. *Vom Seelenwesen des Kindes* (original German), *Stuttgart: Verlag Freies Geistesleben (1966)*

(continued next page)

[Note: Caroline von Heydebrand (1886-1938) was a class teacher in the first Waldorf School. Maria Röschl-Lehrs was a close friend of Caroline von Heydebrand. She wrote the beautiful Foreword to the original German version that she closes with a profound poem by the author.]

**Schmidt, M.D., Gerhard. *The Dynamics of Nutrition, Bio-Dynamic Farming and Gardening Association (1980)*

————. *The Essentials of Nutrition, Bio-Dynamic Farming and Gardening Association (1987)*

Steiner, Rudolf. *Nutrition and Stimulants / Lectures and Extracts compiled and translated by K. Castelliz and B. Saunders-Davies, Bio-Dynamic Farming and Gardening Association, Inc. (1991)*

————. *Nutrition and Health / Two Lectures to Workmen* given on July 31 and August 2, 1924 in Dornach, Switzerland, *Anthroposophic Press, Inc., Bell's Pond (1987)*

Practical Wisdom and Christ

Some wisdom you can *taste*, such as in or on food: sugar (for the Melancholic, the Choleric, and, in smaller quantities, the Phlegmatic), and salt (for the Sanguine, the Phlegmatic, and the Melancholic). These are healthy cravings; they bring pleasure (the sugar), or satisfaction (the salt); they are enjoyed. Indeed human beings of these temperaments require sugar or salt, accordingly. In contrast, the unhealthy cravings are addictive; they are harmful; we do best to avoid them.

The same goes for red meats and their fats for those who require them. They are thoroughly relished. It is tasted. Hence the wisdom is not of an intellectual or mental nature because it cannot be deceptive or misleading; it is actually tasted. *The right foods we enjoy*; *the wrong foods make us ill*. (Rudolf Steiner) It is clear from this simple directive what we may/should eat, and what not. Children are highly intuitive in this regard. Parents or other adults should pay attention to what the child wants and serve it the food or what have you.

However, if fed a food unhealthy for it for a period of time, such as sugary foods for the Sanguine child or salt for the Choleric, then the child will develop an unhealthy craving and become addicted. This is very harmful and often stays into adulthood. If the adult familiarizes him/herself with the four temperaments, this is easily avoided. The Phlegmatic child tends to overeat owing to its temperament. Here, too, knowledge of the temperaments is invaluable. Then the child will be kept slender, the greatest gift it can be given. (see study, *Diet, the Use of Salt and Sweets, and Water in the Four Temperaments*, above)

We have briefly discussed natural healthy cravings. Likewise with a good head-dowse of cold water first thing in the morning for a healthy wake-up call for the two dreamy natures: the Phlegmatic and the Sanguine. This is experiential as is all wisdom and requires no book-learning (study), although reading good literature to implement these practices can educate those who do not perform them already in daily life. (I knew a wonderful Phlegmatic who loved to imagine taking a hot bath. This surely has the effect opposite that desired, putting her into dreamland. Indeed each time she said this one could imagine her melting away in the warm water. In contrast to this, beginning in high school, I chose to end my morning shower by turning off all the hot water and dowsing my head with cold water for a few minutes. I did not read about this beneficial practice (I am a Sanguine) until *after* high school when I was 19 ½ years old; I just 'knew' it was the way for me to begin my day.)

For the Melancholic and the Choleric the beneficial water treatment is quite the opposite: *warm* water on the *tummy* at *bedtime* to activate the metabolic life dream-forces in these overly awake natures.* The action taken has the effect opposite the nature of the temperament. The temperament is the habit-nature; it is also apparent in the behavior, so encouraging, bringing out, developing, prolonging, or counteracting qualities or tendencies is the desired goal here.

As these measures with their extremely beneficial effects are simple and economical to carry out with the children and others under our care, and with ourselves as mature beings, we should take them up. Everything speaks for this.

This 'simple' wisdom belies real depth, for while the Christ-Being is active in soul in Impulses in human hearts, He is also active in the real practical life and will be at work in human bodies which house our souls. Both of these together, bodies and souls (hearts) become the altar of Christ. For the deeply and highly gifted Sun-initiates of Christ, this is *In daily life we serve like priests at the altar.* (Novalis)

The Christ-Sun initiates are our profound helpers and are found in many tasks and places today. Whether off or at work, they wend their way through every day in the service of Christ, and, by what is truly practical and human, guide and counsel all who come to them in freedom.

Unmistakable in their humanity and caring hearts; forgiveness; ever-increasing inwardness; propriety; purity; mercifulness; selfless creative power and service; heart-warmth and -goodness; clear, meaningful, and ethical thinking—soul-light; corrective communication (when we have gone astray from what is true, good, right, and just); perfect balance—all of the virtues, refined—may we who seek genuine help, to learn at any level, or simply soul support, prayer, heartfelt encouragement, or in combination, go to them who avail themselves to us, for Christ is at work in their good deeds (intentionality), love (warm and understanding hearts), and thoughts (clear insights, souls), and in all that they live, suffer, and know. They are the modern-day saints and educators, these Sun-initiates, who have dedicated their lives to God, to the work of Christ on earth for human salvation. Real, practical wisdom, in depth and detail, in their fields of work and interest, is at their disposal in this service. Excellent communication is a daily necessity for them as personal counselors and educators of humankind to this end.**

Los Angeles
May 24-25
Edited Culver City, California
May 27
September 21, 2014

*read about the four temperaments in Caroline von Heydebrand's book, *Childhood: A Study of the Growing Soul* (Anthroposophic Press, 1995), the best resource on this important topic

**great Sun-Initiates who have crossed death's threshold who have authored books or whose lectures appear in book format available in English include Rudolf Steiner, Albert Steffen, Ita Wegman MD, Gérard Klockenbring, Jörgen Smit, and Manfred Schmidt-Brabant. Others still with us on This Side have also authored books and given lectures available in book format in English. (Google *Section Lead* or *Executive Council* + *Anthroposophical Society* + *Temple Lodge* and *SteinerBooks*)

Learning throughout Life

Learning is a process. Human beings have ways to learn. There are seven ways that are fundamental. These seven ways reflect the first seven 7-year stages of human life and development and the seven destinies or planetary types that correlate with these stages.

Early Childhood

Learning begins in childhood. The child's learning differs entirely from that of the youth or adult. It changes according to the inner laws of childhood development as it grows and develops physically-physiologically. Thus it is fruitless to try to 'educate' children as though they were adults. Intellectual teaching means nothing to those at this stage of life. This includes middle childhood.

The child is at our mercy. This goes for its teachers, family or adoptive family, and the other adults in its life. It should not be exposed to artificial sensations from imitative and other technologies until adolescence, and then only in restricted uses. In adulthood we bear sole responsibility for all adverse effects from exposure to these sensations from the uses, overuses, and abuses of technologies, on ourselves and the defenseless children, but we should not for any reason subject them to them. Likewise with the elderly.

Small children learn through imitation. Therefore adults should be worthy of imitation with children until their seventh birthday, right into the movements of the limbs. Children at this stage need abundant love and joy. Also necessary for the small child's development are much physical play, simple toys that give the child's natural fantasy-life free reign, stories, games, and rhymes the child wonders at and delights in, regular rhythm in the daily routine (including meal, snack, nap, and bedtimes), warmth, good nutrition—for the development of the organs. The small child's experiences should be good ones; they make up its earliest memories. Early childhood is the foundation of life and thus of all learning. It ends with the change of the teeth (losing its baby teeth).

Middle Childhood

In middle childhood the child requires a loving authority figure. If it has at least one such adult in its life ages seven to fourteen, it will be able to weather the storms of life as an adult. When the child leaves behind the magical years of early childhood, it is a truly social being. From the protective world of the family, its teachers now join the adults, and many pupils the children in its life. In addition, learning about historical personalities (other adults) will broaden the child's horizons still further. These personalities should include heroes and heroines, as well as the gods and goddesses of the mythologies. First graders will still hear stories appropriate for the little ones, while second to fourth graders (seven-, eight-, and nine-year-olds) are eager to hear fables, fairy and folk tales, and legends. In the Fifth Grade (ten-year-olds) the child should learn Old Testament lessons, especially the Ten Commandments. It is in the tenth year that the child first experiences (understands) the mortality of the human being. Before this age it is still too young to comprehend its meaning. Thus the nine-year old is mature in a way unattainable earlier in its life.

While the small child has the richest fantasy life, owing to its fresh etheric body and forces that are still extremely active in the head (for whom imagination is therefore truth), in middle childhood nature-experiences, including the small wonders, become important. Samples from the mineral (stones, crystals), plant (pine cones, seeds, leaves, blossoms, cotton, and so forth), animal (wool, silk, honeycomb, eggs, horns, feathers, shells) and human (handmade crafts and ornaments) kingdoms can be lovingly collected and displayed. In addition to the beauty of God's Creation, the children should use their own creativity to make beautiful things. As early childhood is the age of goodness, middle childhood is the age of beauty. Thus the child's entire learning experience should be education as an art.

Such an education is found in the Waldorf Schools, where the children do not have textbooks rather make their own main lesson book, one for each main lesson subject taught for two hours at the beginning of each school day for two weeks. This is in addition to watercolor painting and eurythmy, from First Grade through High School ("Lower" and "Upper School"), as well as recorder (a wooden flute), crafts, choir, orchestra, knitting, crocheting, sewing, clay, wood, and stone sculpture, wood and metal work at different ages. The children, and youth, also present plays.

Where the physical needs and requirements are fundamental in early childhood, working with the temperament is essential in middle childhood, for classroom (school) learning and balancing the one-sided nature of the temperaments for future progress and development, both. The person must undertake the transformation of the temperament or habit-nature in adulthood independently through intentional practices. In middle childhood, it is the teacher and other adults who are responsible for cultivating the habits opposite the child's (primary) temperament, thereby laying the foundation for continued learning in adulthood.

With the children it is not enough to have 'head-knowledge' of the four temperaments—to possess book learning—although this is good. Rather the adult must have or demonstrate the qualities the child of its temperament requires in human terms in order to work with it pedagogically. All learning at this stage rests on this being and living of the teacher, parents, and others adults. Intellectual prowess means nothing to the children.

It is not so important what a teacher knows, but who the teacher is.

Rudolf Steiner

This is no longer the case on puberty that is in adolescence.

The Sanguine

The teacher must be lovable for the Sanguine boy or girl, because it is through its love for the teacher the Sanguine child is able to lengthen its naturally brief attention span, crucial for the learning process and development of every Sanguine of every age. Therefore everything we can do to help the Sanguine with concentration is the key. This includes observation and study (age appropriate), receiving impressions of human beings with their qualities, and beautiful Nature and Art with their colors, and allowing these impressions to sink in where she will live with them for years. This guides him from naturally shallow outer hobbies and interests to cultivate deeper, lasting interests.

The Sanguine loves beauty and has the deepest appreciation for light and color phenomena. This is intuition at its loftiest level. The Italian High Renaissance painter and architect Raphael (1483-1520), the greatest artist of all time, was a Sanguine. There are many lesser-known Sanguine artists whose paintings are beautiful, if not profound and lofty as are Raphael's wondrous works, which epitomize heavenly beauty and love untouched by all earthly blemishes, so lovely and pure they are.

The Sanguine learns through devotion and love. Later in life, this means acquiring clear and specific knowledge of the subject of her choice. This is preferably in two practices instead of three or four, or in one discipline instead of two. It can include the Arts, such as playing a musical instrument, painting, and drawing. Through immersion in observation and study, actual insight is gained. Mastery of a discipline makes expert the soul and fine-tunes the mind through much practice and the exercise of thinking. This begins in the child but of course cannot yet be realized until later. It is essential to establish good habits in middle childhood.

The Sanguine is very flexible and mobile, not only inwardly but physically (outwardly) as well. He can withstand tremendous egoic pressure and lengthy weighty concentration because of this inner mobility and resilience. She can always bounce back. Therefore concentration has profound significance for him. Through its discipline she learns, not only skills and material, and masters subjects and practices, but by it grows spiritually by changing the habit of losing her train of thought (his thoughts in disarray), and developing the important concentration powers. This has deeper, lasting meaning for spiritual progress, which is slow work, where book learning enriches the soul and spirit at an intellectual level, which requires only mental application. (See Adolescence, below) For the Sanguine studying (concentration; making observations from study and life) is everything, as we have seen.

Beginning with born habits and developing the opposite ones is the case with each of the temperaments. Real, spiritual progress rests on slowly developing the qualities and habits opposite one's own nature. Going against what comes naturally accomplishes nothing. It is through understanding the temperament that we begin the work to transform it. The Sanguine must work to lengthen her attention span a little at a time, but beyond what is comfortable. Practiced daily for months and years, marked results are seen. Flitting about like a butterfly in between until coming to rest on the subject, picture, or object again.

The Choleric

The teacher must demonstrate absolute command of the subject for the

Choleric child, because it is through its respect for the adult that it will love him. If he ever shows a weakness, the child's admiration is forever lost. The Choleric boy or girl may throw a snowball at its esteemed teacher to show its love for her, thus expending excess will-force energy, which every Choleric must do throughout life if he is to learn relaxation, receive, and thereby make inner progress. Significant in this regard is performing repetitive, mundane physical tasks and chores, such as doing up the dishes, cooking, baking, cleaning, taking out the trash, washing the windows, and gardening (pulling weeds, working the soil, planting, watering, and picking the fruits (harvesting)). Carrying out these and other regular physical tasks is very therapeutic for the Choleric.

The Choleric has a natural sense for spatial relationships, such as the placement of furniture in a room. She notices the walking human being, particularly the legs, but also the very human face, the very human gesture and the very human hand, so these physical expressions are of interest to him. Many sculptors are of the Choleric temperament. Outstanding examples include the great Italian High Renaissance sculptor, painter, and architect Michelangelo (1475-1564) and the French sculptor Auguste Rodin (1840-1917).

Learning about the lives and achievements of great men and women, those greater than oneself, such that she can say *I could never have done that* is beneficial. Reading biography is excellent, for example about heroes and heroines, brave men and women, the endurance and adventures of those who have survived against the odds through strength and ingenuity. But all good biography is fine, because human lives are of human interest. Reading the same book each year, year after year for decades is also good. Then the book must have qualities, which justify rereading, so that something new surfaces (is discovered) on each reading. Or simply because of the impression. We note repetition again.

As small facts do not budge, the Choleric does well to learn them, because he cannot change them, however much she wills it. In this manner he expends excess will-force energy so good for relaxation. And when she has gone too far or acts out, being taken aside by one whom he respects for an earnest word helps him to really feel its meaning.

The Choleric can hold her ground surrounded by huge quantities of apathy and disinterest because of his natural focus. Therefore disinterest is good for her. Capable of tremendous soul struggle and hardship from his strong will-power, she can master the most difficult challenge of all: himself. Admiration and respect are paramount for the Choleric and thus everything worthy of them, including hard work, strength, knowledge, and virtue.

The Melancholic

The teacher must have really suffered in life for the Melancholic girl or boy, because it is through its unerring sense of compassion for all pain and suffering that the child will forget itself and love its teacher, another person, or an animal. Learning about the saints and martyrs, and people who have suffered in its own life, is therefore most therapeutic. Crucial for every Melancholic is selflessness through compassion, whereby her beloved sadness, sorrow, and grief is nourished where it may blossom as joy, love, humor, and passion: soul-expression.

The Melancholic can take all manner of happy joking and warm teasing because of his firm and unbending physical bearing. Indeed this is beneficial for the reason given: humor draws the soul out of its confining inner abode and into freeing outer expression. We see the central role compassion, sympathy, empathy, and mercy have to play in the life of the Melancholic.

He has the greatest sensitivity to thoughts and interest in the craft of words, by which thoughts are conveyed. Because of these qualities and the ability to concentrate on one line of thought for days, weeks, or months at a time, many thinkers, writers, and readers (including students, scholars, and academics) are of the Melancholic temperament. Great Melancholic thinkers include the saint and Italian Dominican priest Thomas Aquinas (ca. 1225-1274) and the great Austrian seer and thinking giant Rudolf Steiner (1861-1925). Both were great initiates.

The Melancholic does a lot of thinking, especially about how others affect her, so any and all forgiveness and soul-expression are of utmost importance. This extends to taking an interest in one's surroundings, because the person is concentrating in his inner world and thus finds it challenging to see the wide world around. So it is also important for the Melancholic to go outside, hear and look about the sounds, objects, and colors of the outer world of people, nature, and things.

The Phlegmatic

The teacher can have absolutely no direct influence over the Phlegmatic child whatsoever. Only indirectly, through its peers, is the teacher able to reach the Phlegmatic boy or girl. Thus entire class feeling and, throughout life, camaraderie, 'rubbing shoulders' with other personalities, and being surrounded by a loud, lively, and friendly group of peers in whose presence she will take a warm shared interest, does this all-too-often burdened and downhearted human being good no end. Thereby the Phlegmatic is roused to life and learns.

Because of natural balance, serenity, innate patience, and amazing recall, the Phlegmatic is among the best of students, if only his genius is active in her slumbering and open for learning. She is the multifaceted genius because she turns that aspect of her all-embracing human nature to the thing or subject in question. Often very meaningful and good insights arise from simple observations and noticing facts, however apparently small. Allowing facts simply to be is a wonderful quality of the Phlegmatic. Neither the Phlegmatic nor the facts change, however much or little power is expended on them. Beautiful love is even and serene, and thus simple, and this is also an attribute of this special temperament.

It is good for the person to arrive at her own insights, rather than direct instruction. Then he is calling on personal and impersonal experiences. Despite her fantastic recall ability, that may indicate genius, deeper knowledge that is wisdom or insight arises from profound experience, not memorization. Awakening love through open interest provides the key to this wonderful temperament. This is so very much better than criticism. Encouragement is ever welcome.

The Phlegmatic awakens in the Tone world, so he is naturally musical. Seated at the piano, she can quietly and evenly create (play) a little melody. When finished, it will be a simple and complete small composition. Examples of well-known Phlegmatic composers are the German Baroque master J.S. Bach (1685-1750), the Austrian Franz Schubert (1797-1828) and the Swedish-speaking Finn Jean Sibelius (1865-1957). (see my study on Johann Sebastian Bach, pages 441-444)

We like to see good, nice, and positive words spoken simply and kindly, because they buoy the Phlegmatic in his inner feeling life. Michael Bauer (1871-1929), the great German Nuremburg anthroposophist, teacher, and pedagogical and priestly master, expresses it in this clear manner taken from real life in one of his lectures. " *'Don't have such poor posture. Don't pick the flowers. Don't make such a boring face.'* Notice it is the little word 'not' that I draw to your attention." Bauer is describing the all-too-frequent way by which the critical parent or other adult addresses the Phlegmatic child. By taking note of this to foster the opposite treatment of Phlegmatic children and adults, these good human beings feel understood and encouraged, thereby lightening their burdened feelings somewhat. This is not only a great comfort and solace. It is cheering and uplifting.

Outer, physical activity, work, and focus are the aim for every Phlegmatic. Sitting in a room with four walls and nothing else until he gets so bored with his laziness so that he gets up and takes action is good. The Phlegmatic particularly enjoys food. When not eating, she is thinking about food. The inner life of the Phlegmatic can consist in thinking about and eating food.

His is the temperament of sensuousness and romance. Keeping the Phlegmatic slender as a child is the greatest gift one can give her, because then she will not suffer a weight problem her entire adult life. The Phlegmatic learns life's lessons through deeds, through doing. He accomplishes nothing by relaxing and eating, his favorite activities, but everything by his most challenging: walking and physical work. The Phlegmatic has the greatest capacity to bear physical pain and discomfort, because of her natural apathy, sense of self-comfort, ease, relaxation ability, evenness, serenity, and vagueness. In this light pain, suffering, and discomfort are necessary for spiritual development.

Without sacrificing comforts and conveniences, no progress can be made. Suffering is associated with self-sacrifice, doing without what makes life pleasant and easy. Even if one enjoys every comfort and convenience, which many in western society do, people still suffer pain, discomfort, and illness, despite all efforts to the contrary. Suffering is the human condition as much as mortality. Its purpose is inner progress to Christ: perfection. Without lifetimes of suffering and pain, we could not develop to this highest goal. It is that aspect of life that is undeniably real. It is our karma and thus our destiny.

Two very great Phlegmatic geniuses not yet gifted by their soul's awakening were the Ancient Greek philosopher Aristotle (384-322BC) and the German Romanticist poet-scientist Goethe (AD1749-1832). There are a few practical measures that, when implemented, have the most beneficial results for health and balance in the four temperaments, as follows:

Cold and Warm Water

A good head-dowse of cold water first thing in the morning for a healthy wakeup call for the dreamy airy Sanguine and watery Phlegmatic and, in contrast, warm water on the tummy at bedtime to activate the metabolic life-dream forces in the overly awake earthy Melancholic and fiery Choleric.

Salt and Sweets

The Sanguine and the Phlegmatic should have a well-salted diet. The Sanguine should avoid refined sugars altogether as these send his thoughts and feelings into disarray; the Phlegmatic not too much. Fresh fruit and fresh fruit juices are good, honey as an additive.

The Choleric should have no added salt; there is enough in food already; the Melancholic some added salt. Plenty of sweets is important for both; this is a healthy craving, so indulge! If fresh fruit upsets the sensitive stomach, then fruit in jams and sauces. Honey as an additive.

The parent and caregiver should practice these simple measures with their children and others under their care; as independent adults we must carry them out on our own. Many people put them into practice quite out of instinct. As with changing the habits to develop what comes naturally to the opposite temperament (balance the one-sided nature of our own temperament), this is for our adult self-education.

Adolescence

In adolescence the key is working with the young person's innate idealism: sensing Christ in adults where He is an inner presence. This quality of idealism ceases in this form on the twenty-first birthday, except in cases of the seeker after Christ when it continues, virtue depending. Idealism seeks the Truth (Christ), so whatever is true is of particular significance at this stage of learning. Thus clarity, insight, geometry, trigonometry, facts, thought, philosophy, poetry, symbolism are paramount for adolescence. Noble or lofty beauty is a form of truth, which is present with love. Christ is the love-God. This is beautiful.

Symbolic love that belongs to this age is beautiful. Where imagination is truth for the small child, beauty is truth for the youth. Thus the Truth (Christ) can appear in this simple (unadorned) form of beauty at this stage of human development. Indeed in the Arts truth remains beauty. Christ is the divinity of love. Love between the sexes may become a symbol for Christ wed to the pure human soul.

Youth is also the age of the destiny or planetary type, which signifies learning lessons—in the classroom and life both—and building up relationships, whereas the temperament is revealed in the behavior and habits. The teacher/adult must teach/communicate according to the planet. Now the learning process is at an intellectual level for the first time. This is possible and actual because the death-forces set in in the head beginning in puberty, and it is these death-forces which enable us to think critically in a clearly-delineated and intellectual fashion.

On puberty the child is left behind but the adult is not yet. Youth is the present stage of learning and development. The formation of the young person's judgments is based on independent observation. Guidance is still necessary where the adult is outstanding and a real expert. There are seven planetary types or destinies, as follows:

Saturnine: a.) inward memory; b.) spirit-inwardness
Sun: a.) harmonious feeling; b.) empowered
Moon: a.) awake reflection/shadowed thought; b.) might
Mars: a.) inward/outward strength; b.) life stirring-sounding
Jupiter: a.) deep, inward wisdom; b.) radiant wisdom
Venus: a.) love; b.) beauty-love
Mercurial: a.) weaving & healing; b.) quick limb-motion

Here a) is the way the person learns and builds up relationships, and b) is his/her nature or quality. Each destiny has its own color, metal, and bodily organ/s as well:

Saturnine – blue, lead, spleen, frontal lobes
Sun – red, gold, heart, chest organization
Moon – white, silver, brain, sex region
Mars – orange, iron, gall bladder, larynx
Jupiter – yellow, tin, liver, forehead
Venus – purple, copper, kidneys, between the region of the stomach and the region of the heart
Mercurial – green, quicksilver (mercury), lungs, abdomen

Studying the qualities, attributes, properties, uses, and significance of these colors, metals, and organs grants the student much insight into individuals of the seven planets (destinies). In addition the gods and goddesses of the mythologies have much to teach us:

Saturnus (Roman) and Cronos/Kronus (Greek) – Saturnine
Sol (Roman) and Apollo (Greek) – Sun
Luna (Roman) and Artemis (and Diana/Hecate) (Greek) – Moon
Mars (Roman) and Ares (Greek) – Mars
Jupiter/Jove (Roman) and Zeus (Greek) – Jupiter
Venus (Roman) and Aphrodite (Greek) – Venus

Mercury (Roman) and Hermes (Greek) – Mercury

These gods and goddesses of the mythologies (other mythologies have corresponding gods and goddesses, such as Ancient Egyptian mythology (for example Isis-Osiris – Sun) and Norse mythology (Baldur – Sun)) are identical to the lower seven of the nine heavenly hosts or hierarchical ranks of Medieval European Christian tradition. (see, below)

There are also related gemstones, plants/trees, animals/insects, and symbols, for example the black onyx, cypress, and yew (Saturn); the strawberry, red currant, cranberry, and moth (which loves the light) (Sun); the heads of a dog, a horse, and a snake (Moon); iron ore, straw/corn/wheat, and the horse (Mars); the thunderbolt/lightning bolt, rain/sunshine (Jupiter); vegetation/vineyards/garden greenery and the dove, swan, and dolphin (Venus). These are only some examples.

Mercury (Hermes) goes between all the other gods and goddesses and so is depicted with wings (as on the Mercury silver dime of U.S. coinage). Although the exchange of goods and services are the purpose, because he is the god of trade and commerce (today's business world) Mercury is non-sensual, spiritual, and therefore not connected to the natural world. Money is not the goods or services but an intermediary by whose means they are handled that is exchanged. Property is not essential rather the ability to acquire it. This is the gift of exchange, a property of spiritual genius: combining thinking, the only thinking of the seven destinies unrelated to the physical world. (see Upper Middle Age, below) However, the Mercurial is extremely interested in acquiring (more and more) property, and jealously so. Hence, the materialist.

The seven planetary individualities and destinies are a vast and profound field of study, which only the most gifted may penetrate with really deep insight, so we will only name the hierarchies or heavenly hosts of the

Christian tradition that are these gods and goddesses of the mythologies and thus intimately connected with the seven destinies/planetary types. (Note the rank of the hierarchy does not imply superiority or inferiority of the human individuality configured with the host/rank/god/goddess.)

The first and lowest hierarchy, triad of ranks or heavenly hosts (eternity)

angels: sons of life or twilight: Moon (Artemis/Luna)
archangels: fire spirits: Mercurial (Hermes/Mercury)
archai: spirits of personality: Venus (Aphrodite/Venus)

The second and middle hierarchy, triad of ranks or heavenly hosts (time)

exusiai/elohim (creative of egos): spirits of form: Sun (Apollo/Sol)
dynameis: spirits of movement: Mars (Ares/Mars)
kyriotetes: spirits of wisdom: Jupiter (Zeus/Jupiter)

The third and highest hierarchy, triad of ranks or heavenly hosts (space)

thrones: spirits of will/imagination: Saturnine (Kronos/Cronus/Saturn)
cherubim: spirits of the harmonies and inspiration
seraphim: spirits of love and intuition

Above the hierarchies, nine ranks of heavenly hosts

The holy Trinity of

Sophia, the Holy Spirit of Wisdom
Christ, the Word and the Son of Love
God, the Father of Quiet Will Peace-Strength

Note the thrones (Saturnine) are already in the third hierarchy (space), but the cherubim, seraphim, and holy Trinity are outside the planetary spheres where the 'fixed stars' are located (the galaxies and constellations of the zodiac). For example the seraphim go among the galaxies, a lofty task. The Son or Word-God of the holy Trinity was where the constellations stand today.

None of this is meant in a physical sense. The physical planets and stars are only reference points. Starlight is luciferic. (Rudolf Steiner) In the valid Ptolemaic (geocentric) worldview, the planetary orbits are seen in relation to the Earth, and the powerful white heavenly light, in constant motion and visible only to higher perception, fills the night sky making the starry lights nearly invisible, which is 'where' the planetary spiritual individualities (first seven ranks of gods and goddesses, heavenly hosts) and still higher divine beings are active.

The adolescent has not yet begun the process of the (adult) incarnation of the ego (I). The girl's ego is dissolved in her astral body; the youth's cannot take proper hold of the physical body by way of his.

Young Adulthood

Learning in young adulthood is conscious in a way previously impossible. The young person may experience her/himself truly separate from family and all others. It is also subtle in that s/he must 'make room' for the incarnating adult ego, a seven-year process from the twenty-first to the twenty-eighth birthdays. It is also characterized by gathering life-experience in various possible ways: through travel, work, and study.

This is the age of the independent personality. If a lifetime challenge, then this is particularly a time of struggle in 'the school of hard knocks'. For some this time continues through death. But the young person is still on the receiving end of life, so these struggles and the hardship, which may be suffered, have their blessing as well: acquiring new skills. Here, natural talent and cleverness (intelligence) are useful. But deeper, beneath the surface of life, the pain is very real and undeniable. This pain accompanies the enthusiasm with which the young man or woman tackles a self-chosen task. The young adult is wholly engaged— inwardly and outwardly—with what he is doing. This engagement can call on courage and strength or deep-seated will-forces.

The young man or woman looks in two directions: back to childhood (birth) and ahead to old age (death), while s/he experiences life on earth to its fullest. This is the Janus-head of Ancient Rome with the two faces: each one faces in the opposite direction from the other one.

Mature Manhood and Womanhood

The learning process takes on a new meaning during the next seven-year period, from twenty-eight to thirty-five. It's time the individual, who has received from the world since birth, turns around and contributes to society. Continued learning by thinking is in the context of work, although there is always time and opportunity for formal (course and book) learning. This is the particular age of the thinker.

Interest is the key to all mature learning, thinking interest that will penetrate into the hidden layers of reality and existence to what is essential, while gaining an overview of the whole picture. This happens in one's line of work or field of interest, which can be one and the same and results from choice and studies/profession planning. We know that freedom is essential in all culture, including the many professions and life-tasks, with the accompanying responsibility. Responsibility belongs to freedom. In this sense, schooling, training, and work are active pursuits in which the wise genius is at work.

The woman or man finds her niche in life; the individuality or genius, however inconspicuous or wise, is at work in the cultural life in the broadest sense: to wherever talent, wisdom, and applied work lead one in life. If one is also fortunate, then success will follow as a matter-of-course. Not only the professions in the former 'man's world', but homemaking is included as the home is the center of the new culture: the family. Today the husband and father may be the homemaker as well as the traditional wife and mother.

Middle Age

From the thirty-fifth to the forty-second birthdays, the adult is not only mature but in a position that enables him to counsel those who are younger and therefore less experienced and who may thus benefit from guidance in life. One's perspective broadens from specific cultural interests to community and national awareness and love, which is expressed in the folk groups or peoples with their languages, and the political life. Locally, this is in the community.

In the larger sense are language, tradition, and custom, and, specifically the emerging nations where leaders lead but every one is included in the spirit of love and equality. Friendships and relationships of all kinds established in openness, mutual agreements, and kept promises, become primary. This is the vote, for and against propositions, candidates for public office, trust and trustworthiness, both. Not only ideal sexual love and romantic relationships, but friendships between two close people. There is love, Christ's Life ("I am the Way, the Truth, and the Life"): pure mysticism and spiritual magic. Novalis writes: *What is mysticism? Religion, love, Nature, and State.*

Upper Middle Age

During the next seven-year stage, forty-two to forty-nine, the perspective extends all the way to the entire globe: humankind. This is the brotherhood encompassing all personalities, all peoples and nations in cosmopolitanism. Differences matter less because the beauty of commonality is felt and known weaving and healing amongst us. This is the economic sphere of activity, fraternity or brotherhood/sisterhood.

Learning facts and acquiring positive, objective knowledge enable free individuals to comprehend the larger, global issues by clarifying situations with reason and common sense. We note the centrality of truth in all transactions and exchanges. This keeps every one honest by clarity, transparency, openness, and respect.

The fundamental tone is health and healing. We turn or walk away where our help is not needed, and we go where our help is needed. No precious time is wasted. This is matter-of-fact. Perhaps we have been part of the healing process for individuals and humankind that results from the beneficial mutual exchange, which is most beautiful.

Mathematics and the technical world are particularly esteemed because of their precise and non-sensual nature. They are also unemotional, which means they are not under the sway of feeling. This is important for reason, knowledge, and common sense: the healthy mind.

Another aspect of this is money and the financial world. The open exchange of values given to money in any of its forms (this could be coin, currency, check, card, or electronic (online) transactions) signifies it is nonphysical. Money is spiritual; it has only the value we give it. Gone are the days of barter and precious metals. However, some are experimenting with new forms of these older traditions of exchange of barter 'money' for goods and services. We note the necessity of the use of mathematics, now also technical functions in business and banking. This applies to the Postal Service and wherever exchanges are made. Combining thinking is the best kind for commerce and economics.

We mentioned at the beginning of this study these seven 7-year stages of learning and life correspond to the seven planetary types (the destinies):

conception/birth – 7 (early childhood): Saturnine, physical body, and the twin sexes

7 – 14/puberty (middle childhood): Sun, etheric body/heart, and the four temperaments

14 – 21 (adolescence): Moon, astral body/soul/mind, and the seven planets/destinies

21 – 28 (young adulthood): Mars, ego/soul kernel/I, and the individual

28 – 35 (mature manhood/womanhood): Jupiter, spirit self/higher Self or I, and the genius

35 – 42 (middle age): Venus, life spirit/romance/Christly nature, and the Christ-principle

42 – 49 (upper middle age): Mercurial, spirit man/Father-principle, and the personality

There are also seven mysteries associated with time and with the seven destinies, as follows:

Saturnine (Old Saturn and Ancient India): the abyss (early childhood)

Sun (Old Sun and Ancient Persia): number (middle childhood)

Moon (Old Moon & Ancient Egypt/Chaldea/Assyria): affinities (youth)

Mars (our entire Earth stage and Greco-Roman (antiquity)/European Christendom): birth and death (young adulthood)

Jupiter (Jupiter & Anglo-Saxon Germanic/now): the encounter with evil (mature manhood/womanhood)

Venus (Venus and Slavic): the Word (middle age)

Mercurial (Vulcan and Brazilian-American): bliss (upper middle age)

These seven mysteries shed further light on the seven destinies and stages of life and learning.

Fifty Years and Beyond

From the age of fifty, learning changes, because the seven stages have run their course. Learning has been about life, about earthly life and the world, which depletes, uses up life-forces. It is time to prepare for death, for divine life, which restores, renews, and replenishes for the coming earthly life. The inner life should have become stronger and more spiritual already in the last 7-year stage: forty-two to forty-nine, but now the soul may deepen and open itself to the ever-increasing experience of the divine right through the death-experience: the approach and welcoming home of the Christ. Childlike love becomes old wisdom, and through death earthly wisdom is transformed: born as divine love.

It is good to bring together the young and the old at this time: the children and the elderly, who will naturally appreciate, understand, and help one another. Children love old people. The elderly are kind and patient with the children. God in these little ones meets Christ in the old. This is a special blessing.

In closing we will affirm that, aside from the love of the parents and other adults in its life, a good education (as we find in the Waldorf Schools) is the greatest gift a child can receive. In adulthood the individual may pursue the most important education: self-tuition (adult self-education). That is the purpose of this study, all of the studies published here, and most of my written work.

Los Angeles
December 10/12/16-19, 2012
May 17/20
September 24, 2014

Facts, Commonality, and the Universal

Facts in Repetition and Changelessness

Whereas the quality of genuineness is singularity and is thus found in the one unique or original alone, the nature of facts is one of commonality that applies in each specific instance in an identical fashion. Where in the singularity of qualities of our humanness that are of a genuine nature, copies are but fakes and replacements but artificial substitutes of the original and true, when it comes to facts multiplicity and reiteration are desirable because the facts can be made use of as they stand no matter the circumstance and under every applicable situation.

Facts cannot be replaced, it is true, but a fact can appear in abundant repetition without any variance in its essential nature. It remains intact, however great or small it is, whatever happens and however it is used, so long one is true to it, because it is changeless, immutable, and unalterable. Whatever the environment or situation, a fact stands, by itself, independent and unmoved. In this, it is like the Truth.

The Nature and Intrinsic Worth of Facts: Commonality, Universality, and Truthfulness

Facts are therefore not circumstantial. If they are temporal or spatially located, then their truthfulness is not because of time or place, rather because they are true. They are above the individual. They are general in their commonality and universality, and specific in their identity, both. This means if I can identify a fact, I have all of it, and it will apply in every circumstance and condition according to itself.

The intrinsic worth of a fact is in its truthfulness. Only in truthfulness does a fact have any value. Facts never deceive. They do not lie. They make no false claims. Deception does that. Therein lies the power of the lie, false claims to truth, to fact-hood.

There is only one God. He created the universe. Christ His Son is singular and genuine. The appearance on earth of Christ the Son of God in the person of the Man Jesus of Nazareth is unique. The Mystery of Golgotha—the crucifixion and resurrection of Christ—is the central occurrence in the history of the world and humanity. With It, Christ's human mission was fulfilled. These are no ordinary facts and thoughts; they are spiritual-historical facts and realities of the deepest order.

Facts and the Fact-Sense

Facts relate only and ever themselves. Thus they are not compelled to claim what they are not, neither to deny what they are as do deceptions, because they iterate and affirm only their true identity. That is of use and interest to the thinker and to the observer of world-phenomena. Subject a fact to the fact-sense and it will show itself to be true. It will prove itself to be a fact. Only a fact can do that. It will simply be as a stone reposing in the garden.

Facts, it can be said, have a self that is true. Each fact is a true self. That is what a fact is. It is an identity that reposes in the truth.

The Beauty of Reposing in the Truth

All things that repose in the truth are beautiful. Green is a beautiful color. Green reposes. It does not move. It is entirely content in and with itself. The most powerful red, with however much power it assaults the green, cannot move or alter it, so contented and unmoved green is.

Indifference: Facts Cannot Be Influenced

Green is the color of indifference. In this sense, all facts are green.

Facts cannot be influenced by any will, feeling, or thought. Therein lies the general and reliable usefulness of the fact, in its indifference to what it's not. It is even indifferent to itself, though it jealously guards its own. Facts can be used by us and brought to our attention, but owing to their truthfulness they are worthy of our respect. Even strength, wisdom, and love cannot influence facts. They are seen to be in a class by themselves. (It should be said that facts are useful for their truthfulness, but that the clear, detached, objective thinking of true thoughts merely makes *use* of facts. Facts are not objective thinking, although they are objective. Where objective thinking is a living stream that flows into the thinker, a fact is objective as a spiritual object is objective.)

Facts in Existence and Abundance

There is an abundance of facts, from the smallest, like a leaf or blade of grass, to the largest, like broad pastureland or park lawns.

All facts simply exist. It is enough. That is what they are. Nothing is required of them but their existence. Nothing else is asked of them but to be stated. Be they very small or very great, they are all facts. Like the color green, in any quantity, size, or shape, facts remain facts.

Sculpture, Beauty, and Simplicity

The art form that corresponds to green that is repose—contented and at rest—is sculpture. We know the true quality of all sculpture is beauty. What reposes in itself is beautiful. The most detailed sculpture of, to take the most evolved and therefore perfect form, a human being or group of two or more human beings, is also the most beautiful. It reposes. The overall simplicity of the sculpture, of the total form, lends it its beauty.

Perfection and Beauty

Perfection is beautiful. There is no unsightly error or flaw. Such is the fact: perfection without flaw. The unity is perfect, and its perfection is entire and into every detail. Each detail must serve the whole, is subservient to the entirety. However detailed and complex the sculptural form or composition, in its perfection the entire partakes of simplicity.

The Universal Mind of God and the Universe as Composition Entire

God is the great Creator of the Universe. His Mind is therefore universal. Unlike the universal nature of the microcosmic human being, God's universal Mind is of cosmic proportions. God gives attention to the least detail, yet each must play its rightful role in the whole of God's Creation. Creation, like the Poet's landscape, is not the parts, the individual aspects, members, and details. Neither is it the summation of these various elements, great and small. It is a composition entire of itself—the Universe.

The Oneness of the Universe, the Greatest and Infinite Fact

Great and manifold, complex and profound the Universe is, it is ever One, and in its unity of perfection, in its oneness creates the impression of grandeur because it *is* great, the greatest of *all*. It is necessarily unutterably beautiful. It is the greatest fact—infinite yet enclosed.

There is the beauty of the idealist. Ideal beauty attends to small detail, but the entire is perfectly beautiful as a composition. We have mentioned sculpture in this regard. God's beauty is universal. The Spirit of the One God is infinitely larger than the idealist, who aims in its direction.

God is one spirit. Hence His Work, His Creation or Universe, is One: a unity. Because each detail springs living from the Source, from God, if we could step back and behold all of Creation from the loftiest perspective (were we thus capable and not deceiving ourselves), we would see the beauty of the whole. We would find the Unity of His Creation.

Facts as Irreducible Entities

In the Unity, the Universe, the greatest fact of facts, each aspect and each detail is a lesser fact, down to the very least. Although in magnitude they differ immeasurably (from infinite to tiny), as facts they are all entities and true, unshakable, and cannot be taken apart by any power in heaven or on earth. Facts are irreducible. Thus God is the Creator of all facts. That is why they are true, because God created them.

Truthfulness: The Property of the Fact, and God as the Father of Morality

Truth is the property or feature of the fact: truthfulness. God does not deceive. Dishonest men do, and all those who do not hold fast to what is noble, good, right, moral, and true. God created the Truth. He is the Father of morality. Where men may moralize, morality is goodness as the Sun is good. God's Kingdom is therefore good, and He rules in nobility and in Truth. This is the morality of Christ, what is good. Morality is also right as the Father-God of Divine Justice is just. Christ is the sum of virtue, the excellence of God. God is the spirit of truth.

God and His Universe Alone Endure

God Himself is not a fact. He gave every fact its existence. Facts have their existence in God. What else exists transpires but shall pass away out of existence. Only God and His Universe shall endure.

The One and Only Universe

There is only one Universe. There are no versions, unlike the many bogus fakes such as we have in artificial images and recordings using machine technologies. They are easily replicated using more advanced technologies. The Universe is singular and genuine. It is the only One. There can exist no copies of the Universe. It is the One and Only of All.

Christ and the Universe: The Knowledge of God

We are but little men. Even the highest greatest angel appears not large in the great Context of God's Universe. Christ is a great Being. He is the Word and the Light God, Who leads the way for men to see the Father on high with eyes. Christ alone has seen the Father with eyes. We would be like Him, yet Christ can only represent that for which we strive. True men walk in the Footsteps of Christ, Who is with the Father.

Christ: The Keeper of the Laws of the Universe

Christ keeps the laws of the Universe. Christ is the Divine lawfulness of God's Universe. None may alter these laws. All facts are but points along the straight lines of the universal laws of Christ in God. Those who follow every law in all their conduct, they find God. Him alone they worship, for there are many false Gods who mean nothing to the One God, Who is the Creator of the Universe.

The Worship of False Gods and of the One True God

Many men worship all the other Gods. The appetites and mercilessness, lust for power (criminality), lust and sex (hedonism), possession (self-addictive personalities), prestige and position, the coveting of property and material wealth (materialism) or money (miserliness), comfort and convenience (materialism), coveting what one has or what others have from jealousy and greed (miserliness), these are some of the Gods men worship. None shall endure because they are not aligned with the one God, Who alone is good.

Those who worship the One and True God, Whose Son is Christ Jesus, our heavenly Father, they go the straight and narrow path that leads to salvation. Christ Jesus is the Saviour of humankind. He came for all humankind for our salvation.

The Universal Validity of the Universe and God as its Sole Ruler

The universal nature of the Universe is its validity for each and all. There are no exceptions to this rule. God is the Sole Ruler of the Universe. All men must in Him abide else they surrender their existence within God's Universe. Whatever you or I may do, the Universe remains. It does not vary with the journeyer or alter with his journeying.

Time and space exist. That is why we may become perfect in Christ, because we journey across time in space on Earth in God's Universe. In this the Universe is common, alike for every one, regardless of human choice and the powers who would serve digression. As with Christ the Universe is singular and cannot be repeated or found elsewhere.

Perfection in Christ is possible, and actual, because we awaken within ourselves as seekers, undergo trials and probation, and cross the threshold of the spirit awake in life, in full consciousness.

The Universe as Object of Study and the Content of Human Experience

The Universe can be studied and experienced by all who have the capacity for impersonal unprejudiced research and personal human experience in countless experiments and experiences, so long there is time and space and measure: students and human beings of every kind and variety of approach.

Experiment and Outcome: Interest and Validity Seen in the Result

Experiments can be repeated. Indeed this is desirable. It is through repetition of experiment that the laws at work in the phenomena are best observed. The meaning of experiment lies in two things: the experiment itself and the outcome. If the experiment conducted is of universal interest and validity, then its outcome will likewise be of universal interest and validity. The outcome will invariably be the same one. Thus all good experiments are akin to facts. Their interest and validity are universal. The nature of their results points to this fact. The result or outcome of every good experiment is a fact or facts.

Learning About the Universe by Experiment and Experience: Fact and Meaning

We learn about the Universe and all that it contains by way of experiment and experience. The nature of our experiments is factual in the sense of scientific inquiry—science. The nature of our experience is human. It is one of meaning to us, to our hearts and souls, but it is not mere sentiment, rather it speaks a language that is clear and meaningful.

Meaning is to the human being what fact is to the researcher or inquirer of scientific experiment. The meaning of experience is to the human being as heart and soul what the factual results of experiment or research into world-phenomena are to the thinker and observer of phenomena. The former calls for courage, endurance, faith, inward heart-feeling, equanimity—all of the virtues, the latter scientific rigor and discipline without flaw or fail. The virtues are ennobled through experience in their application in self-discipline.

Scientific Study as Training and Spiritual Communion, Human Experience as the Meaning of the Journey

Scientific study is as much training as it is for research and results. This training is one of sense and spirit in unity in soul. The goal and achievement of science is communion with the spirit, the altar nature and the elements, and spiritual worlds. Thus human experience is the meaning of the journey through earthly life for fruits of heaven, while experiment is the sacred study of the truth and spirit in perception married with thought.

Inward meaning is of value to the heart, the soul, and the spirit, precious and irreplaceable. Facts are of value to the student of the spirit, which corresponds to the goal of all striving: the Truth or spiritual nature of God in His perfection. This spiritual nature of God is beautiful because perfection is beautiful.

Vision and Creation as Revelation

One cannot see God; one has not yet. Only the Son has seen God with eyes. One can see the perfect beauty that He created though in imperfect form. One can see perfection, however, in imagination in spirit. One can conceive of the circle and the line in perfection. One can see the co-Creator of beauty: the artist. But what is creative in the artist, namely, the artistic soul, is invisible as God is invisible. The invisible creative soul of beauty is revealed in the visible creations of Art, in the beauty created. Creation is a revelation of God Who created it.

Summation

We have fact and experiment, and beauty in its perfection. These are thought, handled, conceived, and experienced in sense, soul, and spirit.

Both are true, both are universal. Both are impersonal or suprapersonal. Both are common and alike to each and all.

Los Angeles
May 17/24/26, 2010
September 24
October 4, 2014
Culver City, California
May 9/13, 2014

From Specificity To God

Real life is always specific. A certain action has its consequence, every cause its effect. In the science of history, the law of cause and effect is equally at work. We see this, not readily, as in physics, but over longer periods of time, for example what took place during the Middle Ages to what occurred in the late 1900s, and in what continues to and will happen. These are specific and causal relationships. If something is broken, it must be repaired or replaced, because it will not function in its broken condition. Practical knowledge is always specific. It is necessary to detect the problem and to fix it or to know if it needs to be replaced and to then replace it. Errors can be big or small, but they are always specific. If they are detected early on, usually they can be corrected. Correction is a matter of precision as is its master. The correct answer as the correct question is always specific and precisely put. Finding the question is as important as answering it. Locating the correct question is key to finding the correct answer. Mistakes can be irreparable. But many mistakes are not bad.

Every deed has its karma. Karma is the consequence or repercussion of our deeds. When we wander astray or do harm in some way, this brings pain or hardship back on us. Untruthfulness has its own karma that is consequences in coming lifetimes. When we love and help one another in acts of selfless sacrifice, which is for the sake of the other and without thought of self-benefit, this brings good karma, such as open-heartedness and joy. The law of karma is highly complex, but it invariably works specifically in life, in the biography. There are different levels of karma: individual, group, and world karma. Individual karma interweaves in group karma, but according to the individual who is its cause. It manifests in the group. Thus my karma is embedded in the karma of all those with whom I am born in karmic relationship. My karma is thereby intrinsically interwoven with the karma of these people. Some of them are also in karmic relationship of their own, while others are in karmic relationship not with someone I know, but with others. In this manner, world karma is fashioned from group karma that goes out from individuals connected by individual karma.

Christ is the Lord of Karma. He knows to weave all of the threads of individual karma into a world-picture-pattern beyond human knowing. He is the master weaver who takes the innumerable karmic threads of individuals and weaves them skillfully together with one another until many group karmic patterns are seen to emerge that interweave in still more complex fashion. Christ takes these highly complex group karmic patterns made up of complex karmic individual interwoven threads and uses them in the great design of the tapestry of world karma that is at a level of complexity only He can fathom. The beings of God (the hierarchies) are also at work here, for Christ works through them in everything that takes place on earth. This begins with what we take with us into the spiritual world from a lifetime on earth, and continues in the preparation for our upcoming lifetime and those after that.

Christ knows to use all karma for the Good of God's great Good World Plan. He can do so because He weaves and works in all that goes out from human hearts. We have entered the place of mercy. Lord, have mercy on our souls. We beg Christ for His mercy. When we pray for our souls, let us do so begging Christ for His mercy. He takes our prayers to God, Who grants us His mercy when we are sincere. Sincerity is the essence of the heart begging Christ for His mercy.

Good people abound. God grants them peace of mind. His healing Spirit shines through clear souls. If I want peace of mind, let me be good in the eyes of Christ. God is my heavenly Father. This is Christ Jesus in heaven. God sees me as I really am.

We have gone from specificity in what works and is in effect to our relationship with the Divine. This relationship alone is holy. We tread on holy ground. Let us be good. We stand in the presence of God. Man walks on the Divine Ground of the Father. The ground of the Father is the Foundation of the World that is His Knowledge. This is the source of all peace of mind. Be still. The Father speaks in our inner quiet.

All is still where there is quiet. All is still and good. In the quiet stillness of God all His children who find quiet in Him have their true source, which is God. There, He holds me in His Hand. We are safe in the Hand of God. By day, God protects us from our enemies. By night, He fills us with His divine peace, and we are in Him. He is our inner strength and our divine love, the source of all being. We have our true being in Him. In Christ, Who became a man, God is our human being. God is the being of the animals, the plants, and the stones. In Christ, He is the being of the dead. In Christ, God is the hierarchies' or heavenly hosts' being. He is the being of All. Fatherly, God holds His children in His Hand. Fatherly, His Lap is on which we play. Amen.

Alan Lindgren
Los Angeles
February 4/7, 2011
Culver City, California
May 13/15
Los Angeles
September 25/28
October 4, 2014

Thinking and Imagination: Two Ways of Knowing

Knowing by Thinking

Intelligence and Experiential Knowledge

We live in a time in history when any kind of intelligence has come to be valued before human experience, when intellectual abstractions and/or constructs for many educated individuals have come to replace experiential truths, that is, what the human being may know directly from firsthand experience using his God-given senses in union with his God-given powers of thinking. This event, if it can be named as such, alongside the advent of the world of virtual reality (virtual and other artificial sensations), has resulted in a soul crisis, a spiritual crisis of the human soul. It is the direct result of the emergence of human doubt that brought about a general questioning of the foundations of tradition in the quest for knowledge gained by independent observations and thinking, yet which often denies reality. The virtual sensations belong to another set of circumstances, one of advanced, imitative technologies that have come more and more to replace real experience for many individuals.

Some healthy scientific minds used their own healthy, human-based experience in their search for knowledge, which they applied to the phenomena of the world, which they studied. The German Romantic Era of Genius novelist, dramatist, poet, and scientist Johann Wolfgang von Goethe is a prime example of this healthy scientific approach. But many, many highly intelligent people have come to question their own, human experience, and instead have 'stepped back out of reality,' one can say, and from this reality-distant 'location' they think about everything under the sun. The questions they come up with are inherently mistaken ones. They question *meaning* and *reality*, rather than examining *thinking* and *(sensory) phenomena*. (The theorists are a good example of this.)

Rudolf Steiner's Work on Thinking

Then came one scientific thinker into the foreground of philosophy and scientific thinking, Rudolf Steiner (1861-1925). By studying the nature of human thought, he demonstrates that the spiritual activity of thinking is the foundation of all knowledge, rather than consciousness, feeling (mysticism), or will (Schopenhauer). By an intensification of thinking, he shows the human spirit overcomes the limits to knowledge held unassailable once and for all. Those unwilling to recognize this only show their *own* limitations, that *they* have been unable to think intensively enough. In his standard work on philosophy (*The Philosophy of Freedom* or *The Philosophy of Spiritual Activity*), Steiner defines his own philosophy, one of an ethical monism of thought, or pure thinking. This, pure thinking exists in the spiritual world. There, there are no boundaries. There, thinking is sense-free, brain-free, autonomous. There alone, the human spirit is free.

In his early work *Erkenntnistheorie einer Goetheschen Weltanschauung* (*Theory of Knowledge*), completed at the age of 25, Rudolf Steiner presented the two elements involved in all knowing: pure experience and the experience of thinking. We can only know that which we experience. Knowledge can only consist in our own experience.

'Pure Experience'

He then describes pure experience as objects "next-to-each-other-in-space" and events "after-one-another-in-time" without the inclusion of thinking. In such a condition of experience, the human being is placed into the worlds of space and time endowed with the full use of his senses, but without (the powers of) his thinking. Thus pure experience remains senseless, that is, devoid of sense, of meaning. Thinking is necessary to know something. Without thinking, the world, in all its color and sound, with its varied sensations and feeling, manifold stimuli and impressions, makes no sense. This Steiner calls pure experience.

The Experience of Thinking

Next Steiner closely examines the experience of human thinking. He shows that within the thinker a thought is produced that connects with an interrelated thought that likewise arises within the thinker, but that in order for knowledge to be possible, to be gained, he must *perceive* the thoughts that are produced in him in all clarity and transparency. Then he perceives how the one thought arising within him comes into interaction with another within him to which it is related. This production and interaction of related thoughts within the thinker is inherent in the thinking process and which the thinker simultaneously perceives. This forms the whole experience of thinking. Without clear thought-perception, there can be no objective examination or study of the thoughts which come into being and interaction within him. He cannot hold the thoughts before him to determine their relationships, their validity or mistakenness, their correctness or error, their verity (truthfulness) or untruthfulness. He can neither distinguish between a fact and a mistake or an error. Thus thought-perception is essential.

Thinking and Knowledge

Steiner shows that the thinker must simultaneously perceive the thoughts that are produced within him in order that they be known (wholly experienced). To know a thought, I must perceive it. Then and only then may I know it, both my own thoughts and all others. (It is very interesting to know a person by perceiving his thoughts. One gains insight into the person only to be had by knowing his thoughts.)

Rudolf Steiner proceeds from this determination of knowing the thoughts, the crystal-clear, see-through knowledge of thinking gained from the perception of thoughts produced (the experience of thinking), to the application of thinking knowing to other kinds of experience. Here we shed the light of thinking onto our pure experience. We know the objects that are next to each other in space and the events that follow one another in time when our thinking is added to our sensing of them. Our otherwise pure experience, before thoughtless and therefore senseless (mindless), now makes clear sense to us because we endow it with the experience of our thinking, thinking the corresponding thoughts. It is by the addition of the corresponding thoughts that pure experience first gains meaning for us. I see colorful soft-looking objects in disarray, but they mean nothing to me. "Those are colored socks," I think. *Now* what I see has sense to it. I think it. I know. Likewise, "I hear children playing."

It is only due to our peculiar constitution as human beings that these two elements are separated that we then must reunite. In the nature of things, the objects and their thoughts form a natural unity, a whole, an entirety. The things and their ideas, the percepts and the concepts are naturally one. Because we separate them, we must reunite them so that we gain knowledge. Such is the nature of human experience and knowing.

There were healthy thinkers before Steiner's work on thinking and knowledge, Goethe among them. But Steiner laid the philosophical foundation for knowledge, and in order to do this he had to examine the nature of thinking, to know the thinking process in an objective that is detached fashion. No one had ever done this before.

Rudolf Steiner demonstrated that Goethe's method of studying world-phenomena is the *only* healthy way. This is the marriage of which we have just spoken. Steiner then extends his research to purely spiritual phenomena of higher worlds in his later work. In his *Erkenntnistheorie*, Steiner delineates the different sciences or branches of science, the realms or fields of knowledge of earth. These include, among others: geology, botany, zoology, anatomy, physiology, psychology, physics, chemistry, meteorology, and history. Through the demonstration of the application of healthy sensory (pure) experience in union with healthy lucid, thinking experience, Rudolf Steiner thus laid the foundation for true knowledge. This requires two things: healthy sensory organs (with which to perceive) and a sound (healthy) mind (with which to think).

The Crisis of Each One

Now, 90 years after his death, humanity stands at the great crossroads. The crisis mentioned at the beginning of this study has become the crisis of each one. Contrary to speculation, *thinking* is the final frontier, and each individual human being stands at this frontier for better or for worse, for soul digression or soul progress, illness or healing and health, ignorance or learning, forgetting or remembering, malice or love, folly or insight-wisdom, weakness or strength, dreaminess or wakefulness, indifference or empathy, fear-escape-denial (Lucifer) and error-control-negation (Ahriman) or courage-truth-affirmation-freedom (Christ). The choice is left to each one of us. It is a human, soul battle, primarily one of human thinking, as the crisis engages each individual and therewith all of humanity. We must be prepared to attain autonomous thinking, which means progress on our own, individual path that leads ahead.

The speculation mentioned, which many entertain (space travel or exploration; the study of the physical Moon and Mars from samples, and of the other celestial bodies by other means; atomic theory in physics, chemistry, and other sciences, and so on) has absolutely no significance. Our task is on the Earth for humanity, and for the spiritual world for the souls who have crossed the threshold of death. But if we have lost our minds, we can accomplish nothing. Thinking is therefore essential.

Knowing by Imagination

There is another equally valid way of knowing in the sense of clear and conscious experience. This is imagination. It is less a method than it is a creative and imaginative act. Depending on the soul-spirit or planetary type, knowing by thinking can be replaced by equally valid knowing by imagination. Here the soul, instead of engaging in the spiritual activity of thinking, is engaged in the production of spiritual imaginations, in the spiritual activity of imagination. However, the process is a similar one.

For example, I see an orange, the fruit, in a bowl of fruit across the room. Without having to walk to the other side of the room, I can speak or think the following: "That is an orange." Without it having occurred to me that it is, indeed, an orange, meaning the piece of fruit, I may have seen it, but then I engage in the act of imagination, of picturing. I not only see the orange by means of my eyes, I use my productive powers of imagination to actively, consciously (awake) 'grasp' the orange. I grasp, the orange, not by passive vision, but by active imagination. Together with my vision, this becomes cognition. To my pure experience of seeing the orange as it is in the bowl of fruit across the room, along with all the other objects or things (here, visual), but without the involvement of my imagination, I 'take' the orange, I add my active picturing the orange, I produce by means of the productive powers of my imagination, the image of the orange that is before me. This is an act of cognition. Only now does the orange have meaning for me. With this action, by means of which I am projecting what I see outside myself, I am so to speak 'taking' the orange from among the many objects of my pure experience that fill the room, making it my own. It is very much like intentionally taking a piece of fruit, an apple or an orange, from a bowl with my hand, and saying (aloud or to myself), I have taken this piece of fruit (this apple or orange) with my hand. This is the spiritual activity of imagination. It is a creative act. Imagination is creative of meaning.

Talent, Cleverness, and the Healthy Imagination

The person who is talented with a healthy imagination remains ever centered, focused, active in, and aware of his environment, nor does he ever forget himself, his naturally healthy sensory life, and his gift of memory. Unlike the grounded thinker, who stands on the solid foundation of the phenomena-united-with-thinking reality of his experience, of his knowledge, which is his strongly integrated and integrating higher I or genius, the healthy imagination-talented person is never moved from the reality of his differing experience, which is one of perception, but also of visual memory, reality, imaginative life, and an unerring intuitive sense for what lives in human hearts. His powers of imagination are strong because they ever adhere to the experiential and concrete realm, together with clear vision and body, a painterly world of love, one that sees, but also breathes, touches, smells, tastes, feels, romances, intuits, and prophecies, the latter by means of spiritual magic.

The mystic remains ever awake and objective, cool and impassive, and in the beauty and love of his idealism. He is favored by God, and he knows to rely on God. His is not some vague or passing God, rather the Father, Who created the human being, heaven and earth, and it is Christ the Son in Whose footsteps he follows. He has faith, and he has a gifted imagination. He knows to pray and prophecy. He sees the present, and in the present the future, which he helps to make happen. He is the mystic.

It should be said that the productive powers of imagination can be activated separately from the given world of the senses. Here the poet is a prime example, the poet who conjures forth images 'from thin air'. M.L. King said he was pulling 'rabbits out of a hat'. This is the abstract use of imagination, abstract in the sense of purely ideal, away from the sensory world of reality, yet freely drawing from it, taking from it images for its own use. These images take on an independent life from the given sensory world of reality, however, and are only abstract in this sense.

Imagination in Spiritual Vision and In Prophecy

But if such pictures tell of the secrets otherwise hidden in the earth, behind the scenes of men, and in the hearts of men, then they are not abstract in the sense of taken away from the real world, outside of reality. They are revelations of the secrets of the world—including future events as prophecies of what will happen—and, in a sense, are more real than what is apparent to the senses, where they will become manifest.

In such a case, the imagination produced by way of a lucid, conscious dream filled with meanings, has the clarity and sense of an imagination produced to grasp an object of extent reality of the senses, such as was given in the example of the orange in a bowl of fruit across the room. Rather than identifying a thing, an object in space, or an event in time (the pure experience of reality) by means of the power of imagination, a spiritual truth or secret of something profound, but previously hidden, is brought to light, and the one to whom the secret is revealed produces an imagination by means of which he communicates the secret, and this capacity or process is a magical one, like 'pulling rabbits out of a hat'.

Only here the rabbits are the means of gaining the faith of the people, for this aspect of Christ is empowered, not on the foundation of reason and knowledge, but by awakening the faith of the people by which Christ in the mystic/magician gains the power to work wonders. Here the secrets of people's hearts, events, and the earth are revealed, and not the illusions or tricks of the conjuring artist.

Here again a parallel is to be noted, namely, that the spiritual magician alone can conjure forth such an unseen, veiled, or concealed reality, which in his case is alluring or enticing a hidden truth from beyond mankind's power, and clothing it in the form of an image.

Imagination versus the Method of Thinking

Such an act of imagination differs in its very nature from the method of thinking knowledge, although ultimately the end may be the same, the goal achieved one and the same. In the instance of the thinker, it is the Truth of knowledge, of sound thinking that is attained or tirelessly striven for, and solid facts are prized as invaluable. In the case of the spiritual magician and mystic, it is the productive power of imagination that is the active element or making real of what was previously absent, potential, or even non-existent. Here Life, that is, pure mysticism and spiritual magic, plays its part. In the former the Way and the Truth of Christ are found and won by knowledge, in the latter the Life of Christ takes effect by faith, whereby this works its wonders.

The Scientific Mind and the Mystic: Two Roads to Knowledge

The scientific mind will work no miracles; he will *know*, will *think* through penetrating observations of the world-phenomena in which Sun of Christ in reality is present and knowable. This constitutes scientific *proof*. The mystic works by way of *faith* in the power of the Life and Love of Christ, in the power of the active Christ Who ever increases in him, and through the Mystery of redemptive suffering, sorrow, and death to eternal life. The mystic is therefore the true magician and lover, the thinker the seeing scientist of what is spiritual and practical. The mystic practices the creative power of love and of imagination; the scientific thinker the accurate and complex insight of penetrating observation and reason, of intellect and Will. The mystic is *large*, is *huge* in spirit with all of the virtues in perfect purity, the thinker bears spiritual *weight* and has all of the virtues practiced with ever-increasing discipline and -inwardness for ever higher levels of perfection. Both have religion, religious hearts. Therefore both suffer dearly, both pray, endure all things, hope all things, believe all things. To both belong the future.

Education and Knowledge

Education is fundamental for the human being, because without it the goal of knowledge cannot be pursued. Knowledge is of the essence of things, beings, and processes. It is the only goal worthy of human striving. The essence of things is seen in the lawfulness of the universe and of all things ordered in it. Thus the goal of knowledge is union with the universal laws experienced at work within the human spirit in perfection, utter purity, and with full power: the perfection, purity, and power of morality, because the laws of the universe are also just and ethical.

In the Epistles of the New Testament, Paul expresses this union as follows: *When I was a child, I spoke like a child, I thought like a child, I reasoned like a child. When I became a man, I put childish ways behind me. Now we see dimly, as in a mirror; then we shall see face to face. Now I know in part; then knowing and being known shall be one.* (1 Corinthians 13:11-12) The knowing genius will be one with being known by God, the divine Order of universal lawfulness, Whose dominion is the cosmos and the earth.

If essential knowledge is the goal, then knowing is also an activity. By means of the activity of knowing, the goal of knowledge is or will be obtained. The path, which leads to this goal, can only be trod in freedom. Thus the activity of knowing is one of inner freedom: thinking or the productive power of imagination.

With our thinking we penetrate to the essence of things. Combining our perception with our thinking and love, we make penetrating observations of world-phenomena. What are these penetrating observations? They bring us to the essence of world-phenomena, physical and spiritual. By means of penetrating observations, we arrive at the essences of all things, which can be known.

Only that which can be studied and learned is of interest to the student. What is unknowable is either external to the human being, or it is too lofty for human comprehension. If it is external, then it is unreasonable, impractical, and useless; or irrational, sardonic, and mocking. What is external cannot think. If it is too lofty for human comprehension, then we may only wonder and awe at its sublimity. Then it is the Divinity of All, He 'who goes before His creatures like a father.' (in *The Act of Consecration of Man*, a sacrament of the Christian Community, from Rudolf Steiner.)

Education is a training whereby what is of interest can be studied and learned. Given the right conditions, like a seed planted in fertile soil, the education of, first a child, can grow, blossom, and ripen into knowledge of the spirit. The conditions necessary for the development of the seed-forces of education and knowledge include love, reverence, respect, and devotion. With these qualities the child learns simple lessons, which, however, belie genuine depth. Indeed the deepest knowledge begins with the practice of these qualities and, long after the individual has left childhood and entered mature life, these very qualities remain at the heart of all knowing. It is clear to see these qualities: reverence, respect, and devotion; must be cultivated for the pursuit of all true knowledge.

In the child it is the adults in its life, who must allow it ample opportunity to learn through 1.) imitation of goodness in early childhood (until the seventh birthday: birth – 7), 2.) veneration for a loving authority figure and devotion to the creation of beauty in middle childhood (until puberty: 7 – 14), and 3.) the dreams, aspirations, and expectations of idealism for truth (the Christ) in adolescence (youth: 14 – 21); the growing person receives the proper guidance in order to flourish, thus laying the foundation for mature life (adulthood).

The healthy child *wants* to learn. The adult needs only understand the laws at work in the unfolding growth of the soul of the child, which takes place in clear stages, as all human life and development proceeds in stages. This understanding is the basis for the Waldorf method and curriculum, which are the foundation of Waldorf education.*

In adulthood all learning rests with the individual, who must rely on his own resources to pursue the goal of knowledge and morality, or artistic and practical goals, for adult self-education, should s/he wish it. Here, not only educational institutions and trade schools provide training opportunities, but the personal assistance of key human beings and the school of life itself. Books can be useful, and may be invaluable for study, learning, and help in all kinds of inner situations, but they do not replace real life. For both, all learning rests on one and the same activity: penetrating observation or insight, alluded to above.

He who will know requires, in addition to much practice and the four qualities already introduced, essential self-imposed discipline and patience, because just as outer achievements require not only application but also patience, the fruits of inner work require time to ripen. Those who are unwilling to practice with patience and self-imposed discipline will never achieve anything. This goes for study, creativity, and practical work—all life pursuits—as well as inner, spiritual development which, together with meditative practice these three initiatives, vocational occupations, or task-professions, nurture and sustain. Practice with patience and self-discipline over long periods of time for inner progress make or break human character, implementation depending. In his *Nicomachean Ethics*, Book One, Chapter 1, 1, the Ancient Greek philosopher of categories Aristotle (384 BC-322 BC) states:

> Every art and every investigation, and likewise every practical pursuit or undertaking, seems to aim at some good: hence it has well been said that the Good is That at which all things aim.

Patience is a virtue, but it must be practiced as the saints did: not passively, but as a receptive, enduring activity and attitude. Clearheaded, unshaken and unclouded by emotions and passions, cool reasoning and non-emotional self-objectivity and factual sense, *and common sense*, are other essential virtues in the pursuit of knowledge.

Required Practices for Progress for the Different Destinies

Self-discipline means practicing what has already been acquired by means of deliberate application and self-restraint (of impulsiveness, excess, recklessness, with emotion, the appetites, and feelings), but also in areas not yet cultivated, with virtue and balance. Thus, for some one, entering into a task with refined qualities or aestheticism, compassionate sensitivity and self-regard may be essential, while for someone else love and open interest may need to blossom.

Again, exercising generosity of spirit and means together with strength may be required (Moon), while earning, saving, and wise expenditure of resources, and activity/work may be key for real progress. (Mars)

Or practicing modesty in the spirit of love may be ideals towards which to strive (Jupiter), for another person moderation (non-indulgence) and healing may be the aim (Venus), and for someone else a mild and non-envious heart together with clear memory practices may be called for (Mercurial). This latter situation applies to truthfulness, an important virtue and discipline-practice for individuals given to deception and lies.

Again, purity of soul and harmony in feeling may be attributes sought after for some (Saturnine), while for others utter mastery of the temper with wakefulness may be foremost (Sun). Being awake can be a matter of life and death and is certainly a prized ability to be practiced at every waking moment, for we live in demanding and confusing times.

When we awaken to the spirit in and behind reality, all that we have achieved up until that moment proves its usefulness and is seen to be crucial for our further development. In this regard we note especially the work accomplished on the temperament, the habit-nature, which requires years of daily practice for marked progress. Therefore it is always time to begin in the process of learning and education, and in the activity of knowing, however advanced or novice the individual is. Those who take this to heart and really apply it according to their nature go the furthest and, if they are so inclined, will, at some (distant but) specific point of time in future, reach the goal of all human striving: perfect knowledge of Christ, which is the objective experience of Him *each* may attain.

This is the purpose of the reincarnation of the human spiritual ego or I in various corporeality configurations by way of the destiny of the soul: the attainment of knowledge of the divine within in ever-higher levels of perfection. Three laws that apply to every one are at work here: 1.) the body and heredity (corporeality), 2.) the soul and the destiny, shaped and resolved on earth (karma), and 3.) the spirit and reincarnation.

* The first Waldorf School opened in Stuttgart, Germany, in 1919, mainly with the children of the workers in the Waldorf Astoria cigarette factory. The Nazis shut down the School, because it fostered the freedom of the human spirit, only to be reopened with next to nothing by teachers and former pupils following the Second World War. Meantime, the Waldorf School Michael Hall had opened in Forest Row, Sussex, England, which has since operated without pause. Waldorf education is now an international movement with well over 1,000 schools worldwide. About half of these meet the practice of genuine anthroposophy; they are truly good Waldorf Schools.

The method and curriculum, the decentralized coordination by the faculty, and the economic structuring of the Waldorf School were given by Rudolf Steiner (1861-1925), the towering Austrian seer and thinker and founder of the worldwide Anthroposophical Society and movement, at the request of Emil Molt, the owner of the factory, who financed the school entirely. Anthroposophy is *not* taught to the pupils. However, teachers must gain an artistic and a practical sense and knowledge of childhood and its stages, which means proceeding from their own work and life with anthroposophy and the image of man that it projects.

The Truth of Objective Experience and Spiritual Beings

The Truth of Objective Experience

The truth of objectivity (objective experience) is in our viewing in a conscious, detached, and therefore unprejudiced fashion. Our experience is therefore objective. We cherish the experiences, which are dear to our hearts. But we also feel heartened and grounded in reality because of our knowledge objective experience is real and observable as is physical reality. Real ideas, spiritual beings and processes are thus objective to unprejudiced human experience, perception and conception.

This is what makes our experiences healthy ones: their being fully grounded in the reality of conscious and detached observation, whether they are experiences of the physical (sensible) world or soul-spiritual (supersensible) world. Both are known by sense-free or pure thinking.

Sense- and Brain-bound Thinking (Unknowing)

Those who do not comprehend this, they use their brains to think. But they are not able to observe their brains by means of which they think. They cannot perceive the thoughts, not their own or those of others. With their sense-bound thinking, they know nothing but what is dead.

They may grasp mathematical and physical concepts. They may learn vocabularies, verb conjugations, and grammatical rules. They may research or design as scientists or engineers. They may read or write literature or dramatic works of quality. They may architect, sculpt, paint, or draw; or appreciate (experience) these art forms. They may learn the classical musical structures to compose, play by, or identify them. They may have poetical ideas, imaginations, and symbols. Then they have the sense or power of imagination to experience what is of a spiritual (ideal) nature, but they are in a dream of living, which is unaware of what lives in human imagination. They do not know, because in consciousness they are limited by what the senses relate, by what the brain can relay. The condition of consciousness in which they live is like unto a dream. Spiritually, they are in a dreamlike condition. They are unawake to real spiritual ideality and physical reality. Their thinking is brain-bound.

Those who are able to observe without prejudice, not only the sensory world, but the thoughts of the thought-world, they know something. They view the thoughts they are thinking and the natural and supernatural phenomena they conceive. This capacity grants them true knowledge, the truth of human experience that is objective. This is whence their capacity for knowledge: sense-free thinking that is awake.

The Lifeless Realm and Fresh Understanding (Knowing)

Then they penetrate the lifeless realm with fresh understanding as well. They can utilize mathematical and physical concepts as easily as a child its playthings. They can observe the grammars and words of languages as the master teaching his students law. They can write and read literature and dramatic works in such a manner that they perceive the thoughts and impressions in an impersonal fashion that is with the eye of a seer. They can architect, sculpt, paint, or draw; or experience these art forms; wakefully conscious of the ideas they clothe. They can survey musical structures as the pianist playing and simultaneously hearing the music as a detached (impersonal) observer. Or they listen solely as an observer in a detached fashion. Their inspirations and intuitions are conscious in them. They know the subject best, who instruct. (*Teaching is the highest understanding. Aristotle*)

These thinkers also know the intuitions of the sense-bound thinkers, the inspirations of the sense-bound geniuses and the imaginations of the sense-bound souls. Not only do they intuit them, inspire them, and imagine them as their creators, but they penetrate in knowing to their spiritual (ideal) content through unbiased observation. Intuition, inspiration, and imagination are spiritual faculties, whether one who engages them is unawake (their experiences are sense-bound) or autonomous, sense-free. This is because the higher faculties belong to painting, music, and poetry. This is true of the creations of those awake. These artistic or musical or poetic creators imbue their creations with spiritual substance—Christ—for Christ is not merely conceptual as theology and science are conceptual, rather He is the living Christ. These thinkers are those who know because their experiences are wakeful. They know Christ, whose substance they impart to their creative work. This is so with the gifted artists, composers, and poets. It is also so with the gifted scientific thinkers who are the religious geniuses.

Knowing Living Spiritual Beings, Powers, Processes, and Ideas

In addition to the lifeless realm, which reposes as a stone before their feet, the sense-free thinker thinks what is living (etheric, like a plant), ensouled (soul-feeling, as an animal), and enspirited (spirit-thinking, as a human being). Such a thinker thinks spiritual (living, soul, and spiritual) thoughts that correspond to what is alive, feels, and thinks. These beings include plants, animals, and human beings. In addition there are spiritual beings on earth with no physical bodies. These are the four kinds of elementals (the gnomes, undines, sylphs, and salamanders, who all have etheric bodies). The company of heaven (the so-called dead, hierarchies or heavenly hosts (angelic beings), and holy Trinity) have no physical bodies as a matter of course. They also understand these beings or powers because sense-free thinkers can think them.

Like the creative work of the geniuses, the content of these spiritual experiences is living ideas. Just as the architect works with a blueprint, so does human life on earth have its design in the spiritual world (heaven). Just as the inventor is struck with the idea of his invention that preexisted in the spiritual world, so do the living ideas of all living things and beings on earth preexist in the spiritual world.

The hierarchies or heavenly hosts and the holy Trinity are great and lofty beings far above man. Nonetheless, together with us and with the fallen beings, they are responsible for what takes place on earth. (see below) Our lives would be impossible without these great good beings and the divine laws they command. Christ is foremost among them. He is the Lord of the reincarnation of the human spirit and of the karma of the human soul. So it is imperative for us to gain at least a fundamental understanding and awareness of their active and living presence, both in what transpires in the spiritual world (heaven), where we dwell between death and rebirth, and in earthly life. Then and only then can we rightfully say we are human beings, because then we experience our context in the larger picture of the universe of God. In this regard the work of Rudolf Steiner (1861-1925) is invaluable.

Understanding the Fallen Angelic Powers

In addition to the hierarchies (the nine choirs or heavenly hosts), there are three levels of fallen spiritual beings. They are the backward powers or spirits. They are at the levels of the angels (sons of life), archangels (fire spirits), and archai (spirits of personality), the three lowest ranks of the lowest of the three hierarchies (triads). Thus there is not one level of wrongdoing or bad, but there are three. To understand life, one must recognize these fallen beings, for they are active on earth as they affect human beings. But those backwards spirits at the level of the archai (Sorat and the asuras) have nothing to do with evolution. They are the exterior beings. Again and again, Rudolf Steiner described Lucifer and Ahriman, whose spirits (luciferic) and legions (ahrimanic) are at the levels of the angels and archangels, respectively, in the simplest terms. Below we will look into these beings from various standpoints to gain a proper perspective on their roles and effects, and in our human natures.

Lucifer: the Spirits of Excessive Warmth and Light

The first level or form of wrongdoing are the spirits of fear and negativity. Such spirits, known as the luciferic spirits, are the natural tempters of humanity wherever there is excessive warmth and light, particularly during the spring and summer. They are apparent in human flights of fancy, dreaminess, an elevated mood; escapades into fleeting pleasure, impulsiveness, carelessness, religiosity, and false spirituality. Such people are wise, but selfishly. Lucifer or his spirit-hosts are always tempting the human being to flee the earthly, to be impractical and irresponsible, light and frivolous, happy-go-lucky without regard for anything or any one. They are at the level of the angels, but the angels are wiser and mightier than are they.

Like fear itself, under Lucifer's influence everything gets blown up out of proportion. Like a balloon full of hot air, reason escapes. We are foolish to panic or become paranoid as to what might get us next. Lucifer chokes throats with fear, makes us anxious, a bundle of nerves and worry. Fun becomes sheer anxiety; calm restraint nervousness.

Lucifer, Love and Beauty, and the Artistic Soul

Yet *there would be no beauty, no art or loveliness without Lucifer.*

Lucifer is the spirit of fear and negativity, but also of love and beauty. Transformed he serves the beautiful, lofty, wondrous activity of the artist in creativity the moment the artist finds his own artistic freedom through the choosing of his thoughts, the regulation and mastery of his feelings, the discipline of his will, and the perfection of technique.

All artists partake especially of the luciferic side of human nature. That is why so many are bad with money. It is not earned to begin with, mismanaged or spent like water running freely, or it is "kept in a little box." For them the material world should serve them only as a substance from God for their artistic-creative God-given gifts. They do not understand money and are not good with facts, or only at meeting points with physical reality when they must deal with it in the struggle that is life. This meeting with earthly reality and facts often occurs directly in their creative work. But many singers and some architects are realists.

The poet is the master of the Word and understands his poetic art. The composer, musician, and singer have mastered the Tone world and the musical instruments or the human voice. The artist drawer and painter is the sketcher and colorist who lives in the lines and Color world with his charcoal, pencils, pen and ink, paints, papers, brushes, and canvases. The sculptor knows the world of the Form and how to use his hands, his carving, rasping, filing, and sanding tools, and his materials (clays, woods, stones (mainly marble, alabaster), beeswax, and plaster cast into metal (primarily bronze)). Therefore, the material world can appear to the artist as a special kind toy to play with, a brush to paint with, or a piece of clay to sculpt with. This is the artist's relationship to the practical life. It is with the medium of her art form.

Artists know all about their tools, and they work very hard due to their impractical natures to master and keep fluid the flawless technique necessary for the execution of their works of art. Here they are the masters of the earthly, if here alone. Their connection to form, color, tone, word, or gesture therefore retains pure spiritual magic because they imbue their creations with love and the special mystical-magical quality touching the earthly, transforming the earthly by the magical hand of the spirit. Their creations shimmer and sparkle, or glow and shine in inner warmth and radiance, for the Spirit is at work in them. But not only singers, musicians and composers also are often realists. (Jupiter, Sun)

The true artistic soul is endowed with the love of pure mysticism and the light of spiritual magic, or with inner warmth and radiant light. He experiences the absence of these spiritual qualities in everything in today's dead, scientific, technological world as something deeply missing. That is why she is here today, so that the quality of magic is present to brighten the world like a rainbow. Christ has touched these hearts and souls with His mystical, magical wand of Life. Every word the artist speaks or writes, every melody she hears, sings, and plays, every black-and-white or color scene she sees, draws, and paints, every form she shapes that is under the good spell of Christ's mystical, magical wand shimmers lovely and wonderfully, or shines radiantly and warmly from her inner Sun. Her creations smile with light and warmth or lovingly into the otherwise cold, dark, hard, unkind world of today.

Christ does not leave these children of His alone. He loves these special ones, His artist children. They all share a feeling for one another, a natural appreciation in common, for they are Christ's artists. They face one great danger: virtual reality, digital visuals and sound, and the other artificial technological media, which would excite, mesmerize, and dull their senses, and disturb or deaden their souls. We think especially of the non-artist luciferic souls, the old idealist Mercurial.

Ahriman and His Legions: the Dark and Freezing Spirits

The second level or form of wrongdoing is Ahriman at work in cold black darkness. Ahriman is here together with his legions. Those who tend toward pure selfishness and egoism fall prey most easily and willingly to Ahriman's bony icy grip. Wallowing in his selfish depths he seeks to drag all others down with him below. Cold and darkness is his realm (especially noticeable during autumn and winter). Greedy and miserly are often those under his influence. Earthbound are they, often nitpicking and clever. Highly arrogant about their cleverness, they do not recognize it is Ahriman under whose control they are actually living in unfreedom. Others under his command are the materialists. They are often atheists who therefore lack God. They deny Christ Who shed His Blood for them and for all human beings. But all who do not think the spiritual thoughts are unfree under his power.

Many great intellects, scientists, and all devoted materialists who take no interest in spiritual matters or in things of wonder and genuine beauty, these human beings are the favorites of Ahriman, although they do not know it. That is their tragedy and can lead to illness, even physically crippling illness. But perhaps even more serious than illness, such souls lack Christ nor do they know to seek Him in their preoccupation with materialism, intellectuality, or material science. But Christ can still find them, nor does He forget any of His children. The ahrimanic legions are at the level of the archangels, but the archangels are wiser and mightier than are they.

Ahriman and the Scientific Mind

All great intellects and minds, scientific thinkers and inventors strongly partake of the ahrimanic aspect of human nature. They know how to make money and use it wisely, if not greedily. They are good and sometimes miserly with money and business affairs. They are eminently practical and down-to-earth. Their spirituality is sensible and practical, and they put it to work in their daily lives. The world could not function without these intelligent men and women. They keep things running smoothly, know how to fix things when they break down, and can always find the practical solution to a given problem by a thorough consideration of the solid facts. What the artistic natures lack, they more than make up for with their sound methodical (or clever and creative) thinking and practical common sense.

But they often lack pure mysticism and spiritual magic: Christ's Life. They are unmystical and unmagical in their scientific evaluations of the nature of reality. They cannot understand the divine Life aspect of Christ's threefold nature, for it cannot be found in the scientific and theological facts of their world conceptions. They remain too strongly bound to the earthly because of their ahrimanic human natures and cannot grasp the elusive rainbow which plays and dances happily in the heavens smiling warm and radiant through the cold dark raindrops. But they give solid ground and depth to life's inner meaning. They have the ability to understand the dark, cold shadows. They cannot be deceived by delusions of grandeur in their down-to-earth common sense. All scientific natures pride themselves on their knowledge and consider themselves citizens-in-good-standing of the larger scientific community. Their great danger is spiritless isolation. They require love and beauty, and whatever is spiritual in life on earth and in the afterlife in heaven.

It is the spirit of the age to believe that any fact, no matter how suspect, is superior to any imaginative exercise, no matter how true.
GORE VIDAL (1925–2012), in *Encounter* (December 1967).

To a certain extent all human beings tend in the ahrimanic direction, for we live in the age of scientific doubt and dead technology. We may be luciferic, dreamy/beautiful, but then also intellectual. Pity the dreaming artists haven't the practical-sensible know-how of scientific minds, the thinkers untouched by heaven's magic wand or radiant sunshine that enchants the artist's world to life. We have one another for what we lack.

The artistic (luciferic) natures include many human beings who have no formal artistic education and whose profession or task may not be one of artist. They deeply need the *practical* help of healthy food, science, medicine, and dentistry, and of the sensible, down-to-earth scientific natures in their morning and daytime contacts with physical reality. This grounds them in solid facts, the facts of the physical world. Here dead technology can be of practical value.

It is good for artistic natures to think and work practically and with facts and to learn a trade or practical profession that will not deaden their innate imagination in the slightest. They will find times and ways to be creative. They need to be among young and middle-aged adults; this will encourage them to be practical and thoughtful. They need to show their natural love in practical thoughtful ways, however small, in addition to adding their actual artistic touches.

The scientific (ahrimanic) natures include many human beings who have no formal scientific training and may not be researchers, scientists, scholars, or professors by profession. They deeply need to experience the *beauty* of nature and the arts and of the mystical magical or sunny artistic natures. It does them much good to participate in art by sculpting, painting, singing, playing a musical instrument, or writing poetry or, if they cannot, by touching an artist's sculptures, seeing genuine paintings, hearing beautiful singing or music played, or experiencing living poetry, especially in the evening and nighttime. Immersing themselves body, soul, and spirit in the spiritual ideals of beauty, goodness, and truth warms and lightens their souls to glowing, radiant moods.

Imagination, inspiration, and intuition work their wonders through the arts. Experiencing nature without subjecting her to study of any kind, but only for her wonder and beauty via the senses is also a big help to these scientific natures. It is good for them to spend time with the elderly and the sick, and with children, as this will awaken compassion and love for their fellow human beings. They need to use their natural insight and practical knowledge to gain understanding for the delicate and fragile human conditions of the very old and the very young in such a way that they feel tenderness there.

As we live in an age of materialistic science and technology, *all* human beings deeply need the therapeutic qualities inherent in the arts and Nature today. The human soul needs beauty just as the body needs food, exercise, and rest. We cannot survive as human beings without natural and cultural beauty, without art. And we have a deep responsibility to our children, youth, and seniors to lovingly guide and care for them.

Ahriman as the Spirit of Materialism

Ahriman cannot be effective and influence human beings directly. Wherever the Tone of Truth rings out openly he hides away in the shadows of his own realm. His poisoned bite has been named for what it truly is. He can only gain control through deception or error. Materialism is an error and is the product of Ahriman. Materialism is a spiritual world conception that denies the spiritual and only acknowledges the physical-material world and objects and bodies, what can be weighed and measured using physical instruments and means. But it is a world-conception thought out with the greatest care into every detail and as such it is spiritual. But its spirit is Ahriman.

Ahriman wants human beings to deny everything spiritual, every aspect of the human being around or within physical nature, and the spiritual world (heaven): etheric- life-nature as living formative, non-physical, thought-bearing substance and body which shapes, molds, and forms the physical bodies of all living things and keeps them from disintegrating and decomposing so long it united with them; soul-nature as feeling, inner life, and body which the etheric and physical bodies of all ensouled beings serve so as to awaken sensation there within: feelings of repulsion and attraction, antipathy and sympathy, pain and pleasure, desire and hurt, inner feelings and movements revealed outwardly in glance, word, touch, gesture, and tone; I or ego as consciousness which the soul, and etheric and physical bodies serve as instruments of the individual personality; and spirit-nature as human essence which the ego, soul, and etheric and physical bodies offer themselves up to for thinking, light, love, and good will; and science, art, and religion.

The physical nature of the human being and of the world (physical, sensory reality) is only rightly understood as the creation, tremendous sacrifices, and expression of lofty spiritual beings: the spiritual world (Christ), the heavenly hosts (the hierarchies or choirs of angelic beings), which is our source. Thus we have spirit with matter; matter with spirit.

Ahriman is the spirit of technology. Materialism understands nothing other than how to build, operate, and repair machines. It doesn't understand the physical nature of Creation and the human body it purports to have so thoroughly mastered. It cuts us off from the source of everything existing in Creation and human co-Creation: the Creator-God and His good angels, which created spiritual and physical worlds, cosmos and earth; and human creativity (imagination, inspiration, and intuition). In this mechanistic-computer view that dominates humanity's present-day thinking, Ahriman accomplishes a feat of great harm.

The Ahrimanic Deception

Today ahrimanic beings appear in human form as an average person. "Believe me, I am just another human being like you," he says. Indeed he is at work in men and women, and hence in appearance, in outer dress and activity. He *identifies* with human beings to deceive and confuse us. He wants our attention, *all* of it. For it is in gaining our attention that he influences or controls, leaving us unfree. Ahriman detests the truth of clear ethical thinking, pure selfless love, good will, all those human and spiritual activities and aspects he cannot touch, for these qualities protect us from confusion and wrongdoing. He cannot bear pure innocence and true freedom that live within as they are beyond his grasp.

Ahriman can work because he enters some human beings through an error in their thinking. It is he who gestures in the gestures formerly of those human beings. All thinking is an impossibility in them, for Ahriman only confuses and they do not understand what has happened to them but only suffer. Yet those human beings whom Ahriman has taken over are still there. They suffer but no one has access to them, because Ahriman has gained complete control over their souls, spirits, and bodies. Human beings of all backgrounds are instruments of Ahriman. Philosophers, writers, artists, musicians, scientists, husbands, housewives, very crude souls, many kinds of human beings are his instruments. They are in the minority but still number many. The first such human being was the philosopher Friedrich Nietzsche (1844-1900). Charles Eisenstein (b. 1967), a translator for ten years, then a carpenter (who went broke), is a current example under whose name Ahriman writes books. But this phenomenon numbers in the millions worldwide and is the cause of much confusion. Of the seven destinies, only Sun and Venus cannot fall prey to Ahriman in this way. Ahriman *deceives*.

Ahriman enjoys only wrongdoing. He aims to be looked upon as an anybody at first (one of many, no different), an acquaintance next, then a trusted friend and confidant, and finally, to be reviled. In everything he does he will provoke malice; he wants people to return in kind, although in disguise most of the time. This contempt can be overt, but then it will be in character, for he will never do anything to jeopardize his human appearance. He ends the work of the human being he took over because of their suffering him—illness. We think of Nietzsche and Eisenstein.

The lives of such human beings end in tragic suffering. They have lost their minds and souls to Ahriman.

It is noteworthy this phenomenon exists and is common in our Age of materialism, technology, and the 'being' intelligence belonging to every-man and every-woman, that was never before in the history of humanity. If 1% of the population, it is nonetheless significant. It belongs to our Jupiter era which began about AD1500, whose mystery is the encounter with evil. The mystery of the preceding Mars era is birth and death.

Ahriman will not be found out for whom he really is, for then his game would be over. And then he would lose. But although he is doomed, he actually believes he can win. He keeps trying, convinced of his future.

Ahriman is highly clever and intelligent. He cannot be outwitted by human cleverness. Cleverness is *his* game. *He* invented it. Lucifer wishes us to fear him. Ahriman wants our malice. But he likes *all* forms of egoism and selfishness. In all that is selfish and ego-oriented, he recognizes his own nature at work in human nature. Then there is that much less love to overcome. So he likes intellectualism. But he has no power over pure love.

Ahriman can serve the creative process for he is the spirit of technology. In most instances hi-tech is misused, overused, or wrongly used. Then it causes harm. However, with computers in the production of books (hard copy), technology *may* serve the creative process *if* the book is a good or useful one. Here the computer is an invaluable writing and editing tool. Along with modern means of printing, the result may be good books, which would have been impossible or extremely time-consuming to produce. The number can be easily multiplied for a wider readership.

This situation is clearly the opposite with Eisenstein and Ahriman. And most books out there are not worth reading. Nothing can be learned. Yet books may be purchased through Amazon.com at an extremely low price that have immeasurable value for learning, such as lectures by the late anthroposophical thinking giant Manfred Schmidt-Brabant. (1926-2001)

Like the detective story or murder mystery, the really popular books that are mass produced are worthless in form and content. This takes on a whole new dimension when we consider such technologies as, iPods, headphones, CDs, DVDs, BDs, tablets, and computers (by which music websites, chatrooms, and the social media are used). Additionally, many other entertainment and 'learning' technologies such as television, videos, and Kindle books should be mentioned regarding the popularity of really worthless products, which, however, hundreds of millions of human beings invest huge amounts of time and money, damaging their senses, minds, and souls. If a good book is read on Kindle, instead of the learning process taking place, the eyes and mind are adversely affected and sleep suffers, similar to watching television.

Scientific Research and the Proper Perspective Over All Things

Science is a fruit of ahrimanic intelligence, but this doesn't signify it must be materialistic or untruthful in any way. The gifted scientist uses his thinking powers and research to serve the progressive powers. Like Aristotle, he recognizes the good of every human effort that is aligned with God's great Good World Plan (world and human evolution). He also knows all those who misunderstand the bad (wrongdoing) because they are enmeshed in it in some way ultimately also serve the Good, though indirectly. Seen from the higher, eternal perspective, everything has its place in God's great Good World Plan. (Of course, this excludes the empty souls and incurably emotionally ill who have no possibility to realize their destiny anymore.) This proper perspective is above the temporal-seasonal where wrongdoing is at work. Those who have won this higher vantage point see out over all things. They recognize the role every one must play in the grand scheme of things that is progress for the eternal Good of God.

Every art and every investigation, and likewise every practical pursuit or undertaking, seems to aim at some good: hence it has been well said that the Good is That at which all things aim.
ARISTOTLE (384-322 BC), *Nichomachean Ethics.*

Rudolf Steiner, the Truth of Natural and Spiritual Science, Genuine Spirituality, and Fundamental Human Goodness

In 1892 Steiner's dissertation appeared under the title *Truth and science. Prologue to a 'philosophy of freedom'*. This was later published as a book, *Truth and Science*. Steiner had received a scientific education, and his knowledge of philosophy was unsurpassed. But later he developed his anthroposophy, or 'science of the spirit'. He knew that natural science is the knowledge of nature outside. Spiritual science is the knowledge of the spirit inside. It is the opposite and counterpart of natural science.

The spirit-rich ideas of Rudolf Steiner have begun to appear to the populace as common property. This does not mean they are thoroughly understood, but that they are being heard and thought. For the most part, people are unaware of their source: Rudolf Steiner (anthroposophy). But that is of no account. What matters is that they are being thought.

Ideas are universal. They belong to no one and every one. Today's great thinkers, educators, and leaders are also sowing the seeds of spiritual knowledge in the souls and hearts of human beings. Like the work of Rudolf Steiner, their ideas will take effect in the larger society 85 years after their deaths. Even when used by Ahriman in a confusing manner to deceive, as is the case with Eisenstein and many others, the ideas are often identified to their true source such that readers turn there for the facts. Then clarity returns: truth.

Human beings must find their way back to the Spirit, not a false pseudo-spirituality, but a genuine living one experienced in wakefulness. They must come to terms with the wrongful bad, but by seeking the Christ Who is the right and just Good: God. Then they will have the strength, love, courage, and insight to live in the Truth amidst the widespread Lie of the world. They shall not succumb to the wrongful bad, for in Christ, they shall strive to be good. Zarathustra or Zoroaster, the grand Persian prophet, taught that the Good will one day emerge victorious, because he believed human nature is fundamentally good.

Lucifer and Ahriman, Love and Reconciliation

Lucifer is frivolous. Ahriman is actually a coward. He is tortured in the presence of pure love. He runs away and hides when faced with the Christ-Tone in which the Truth rejoices. But given the opportunity he'll come running right back. Because of our own little selfishness, our own smallness of scope, our lack of love for one another, we *invite* Ahriman into our lives. Because there is so little love in the world today, that's why Ahriman has such a great influence on human beings.

Ahriman wants to separate us as individuals. Those who love suffer willingly to unite humankind. Love recognizes soul and heart qualities where it works creating friendships, community, and sister/brotherhood.

Without Ahriman there would be no science or technology. Science and technology may serve the Good if they become useful tools in the hands of human beings working for the healing creative process. Where Lucifer is, Ahriman is just around the corner, and *vice versa*. Fear turns into malice and malice fear. But Christ redeems Lucifer in the warm light, pure mysticism, and spiritual magic of love (gentle as a dove). He harnesses Ahriman into service through the sensible, practical insights and strengths of the Darkness and Cold (wise as a serpent).

Novalis writes, "If all human beings were lovers, the distinction between mystic and non-mystic would disappear." Love is so great the wisest and most gifted thinker may learn. Such men and women know the words of St. John regarding God and love with true understanding. Like the esoteric mystics and white magicians who are the martyrs, the greatest scientific minds belong to those of deepest faith who also suffer and die for Christ: the saints all learn Christian love.

Only courageous love transforms us in Christ's merciful redemption from the two polar influences of Lucifer and Ahriman. The Christ-Being walks before us in the Way-strength-Will, Truth-wisdom-insight, and courage-heart-feeling the middle path between the ahrimanic depths and luciferic heights: the two extremes. He is the great Representative of Humankind. Christ became human in Jesus of Nazareth that we might become human in Him, in suffering humanity in our brethren, in whom Christ also hurts and suffers.

We win our true humanity drawing from the opposite poles what is useful. We grow inwardly in courageous feeling, sure strength, clear wisdom and loving light. We need Lucifer to develop our artistic natures (love and beauty) and Ahriman in order to develop our intellectual, scientific natures (knowledge and insight-wisdom). Christ, in us, is our heart of religion, inmost courageous feeling, and abundant love, in the face of blown-up fear and the pain of terrible malice. We need not run from fear and pain when in brave suffering we ask for and receive Christ's help. This calls on our profound living knowledge of human and divine nature, and on our faith, which we feeling suffer, because Christ is dear to us, because our brothers and sisters are precious to us.

Love is selfless in direct service. We recall the work of Martin Luther King, Jr., who preached love and nonviolence, not only to replace unjust laws with justice, and to win victories for equality and decency for all poor and oppressed peoples, but to be reconciled and befriend those who had inflicted suffering through oppression. Love does not only establish justice that is its power, it forgives, even cruelty.

The great German lyric poet and pupil of Rudolf Steiner Christian Morgenstern (1871-1914) wrote much about love.

He who never loved the devil clearly does not know that he exists.

Do you not know that love gives everything, and in this everything knows no limits, no possibility *of limits.*

...a certain indescribable that one can only indicate with the name "humor", and that only out-streams where the faculty exists to view life with an unmistakable earnestness as with a heartfelt, yes childlike love.

I have seen the HUMAN BEING in his deepest form,
I know the world to its foundation.

I know that its deepest meaning is love, love,
and that I am here to love more and more.

I open my arms outwards as HE did,
I want to embrace the entire world as HE did.

There is a still greater love than that which longs for the possession of
the beloved object: That wants to free the beloved soul. And this love is
so divinely beautiful that there is nothing more beautiful on earth.

Gratitude and love are brother and sister.
Gratitude is love, gentle but constant.
He who goes through life a lover
is also thankful for everything.

O deep love, which marries my soul to everything.

Everything is actually beautiful *beheld with love. The more one loves the*
world, the more beautiful he will find her.

In truth there is no understanding without love.

There is only one progress, namely that of love, but it leads into the soul
of God Himself.

It is beautiful to think that so many human beings are holy in the eyes of
those who love them.

Christian Morgenstern (translated from the German by A. Lindgren)

The Condition of the Non-Existence of Wrongdoing

There is a place in the very center of the human heart that cannot be touched by any bad. When we know times of inner difficulty or uncertainty, or disturbances of any kind in our soul-spiritual (inner and outer) environment, Christ can and does work from this place to restore in us a sense of quiet and love. Here the good angels and our loved ones who have crossed death's threshold can also work, for they are united with Christ in the Spiritual World. The heart is the most spiritual of the organs. (Rudolf Steiner)

When we commune with Christ together with an/other human being/s (when we are gathered together in His Name), we are directing our consciousness or attention inwards to our inner source where the Mystery of the Christ of our hearts indwells in us. This is an inner consciousness of the heart. There we are safely protected where no wrongdoing can go. Indeed, when we are so communing with Christ, no wrongdoing exists.

This condition of the non-existence of all wrongdoing can also be experienced in artistic activity when the heart is pure, the will is good, and the mind is healed. Indeed artistic activity can actually bring about such a condition, if it is approached in the right way: with devotion, goodness, love, and complete immersion in the work of doing-creation. Wrongdoing cannot exist when none is allowed a place or room in the thoughts, feelings, and deeds of the person. The support of good will is also necessary; wrongdoing is rendered powerless where the quiet peace-strength of good will reigns. It removes itself, as it were. There, it cannot exist.

Another time when no wrongdoing (no bad) can exist is during the thinking process. When some one is engaged in pure thinking, that itself takes place in the Spiritual World, s/he is entirely secure and protected from all outer influences. Pure thinking is sense-free, spiritual.

Novalis writes, *Auf einer gewissen Stufe des Bewusstseins, existiert schon kein Übel und so weiter.* (*At a certain level of consciousness, no bad et cetera exists.*) This is an inner place in the heart and soul where Christ in purity stirs and works. There, the heart remains untouched, whereas the gut and the mind are not so protected. We think of the head-metabolic illnesses commonly called the mood disorders or mental illnesses which many who are not ill may also tend in their direction. These illnesses not only trouble the mind of the ill, they equally disturb the metabolism (the metabolic system and region seated in the lower torso). Yet in the presence of some one in whose presence peace reigns (Sun of Christ), such a person is also protected.

We can always go to the inner place in the heart, even in the midst of outer public life. We turn our consciousness there, listening only to the feeling, to the heart, and we know that all is well. The effect is that we are granted peace—peace of mind and stability of will (quiet strength)—for the heart heals the head and provides balance to the whole man.

Archangel Michael's Deed in 1879 and Its Implications For Us

The Archangel Michael, Who is the mighty Time-Spirit of our Age, won the great battle against Ahriman (known as the Dragon in Medieval Europe, the devil, later Mephistopheles) in 1879, throwing him out of the spiritual world, thus ending the many-millennial Kali Yuga—the Age of Darkness—and inaugurating the Age of Light in which we live today.

On the one hand Ahriman (wrongdoing or darkness) is now active on the earth, in the earthly sphere, particularly influential during the time between Easter Sunday and the Holy Nights of Christmas when the earth herself is ahrimanized. At Christmastime (during the Holy Nights), Christ is born in the earth and in our hearts if we have prepared a place for Him. Then the "Light of the World" is given birth, thus protecting the earth and human hearts from the ahrimanic forces until the outbreath following Chirist's resurrection in Nature on Easter morning. We have Christ, Who is the Spirit of the earth, particularly during the autumn and winter months, and the Cosmic Christ of the sun, the clouds, and the stars, particularly during the spring and summertime.

The other implication of the great deed of St. Michael in 1879 is of equal significance. Although Ahriman (wrongdoing or darkness) now wields earthly power, which poses a danger today (two such ways are materialism and technology; Ahriman is this world conception's spirit, and this creative spirit), human beings can now experience the spiritual world—our Christ—in wide-awake consciousness. This is because Ahriman is no longer to be found there. The soul's spiritual awakening is perceiving Christ in wakeful consciousness. This is objective.

It is essential today and over the coming several thousands of years for *each* human soul's spiritual awakening to the Christ-Being. It is a most intimate, personal yet objective experience, cited at the beginning of this study. The soul's awakening is the moment when the first wakeful and objective experience of Christ is simultaneously observed in an unbiased fashion. It is the deepest and most personal experience, and equally entirely objective that is impersonal. Therein lives its truth, in its objectivity.

To have this pivotal experience the human soul must ripen or mature through earthly life-experience spanning many, many incarnations. Thus, what began happening in the 1930s to millions of human souls (the wakeful conscious, spiritual awakening experience) in *this* incarnation, will occur for many, many other human souls in *succeeding* ones. Only if the person has the endurance or works towards the Christ experience shall this come to pass. Then each shall receive the help s/he needs. Christ never lets one down.

St. Michael is the "fiery Prince of Thought" and "the Countenance of Christ". (Rudolf Steiner) The four archangels of the four great Christian festivals are Gabriel (Christmas), Raphael (Easter), Uriel (St. John's) and Michael (Michaelmas). The archangeloi are the "fire spirits". (Rudolf Steiner)

Sorat and the Spirits of Warped Personality

The third level or form of wrongdoing is the asuras under Sorat. Sorat and his asuras are at the level of the archai, but the archai are wiser and mightier than are they. The archai are the "spirits of personality" (Rudolf Steiner). The asuras are the spirits of warped personality and destruction, the antithesis to the healing spirits, the archai. The asuras are neither luciferic operating through fear, nor ahrimanic operating through malice, but they make use of both spirits (fear and malice) to destroy egos for digression. They have nothing to do with evolution, but in human form they induce a retrograde motion in the soul that accelerates experiences necessary for progress for those who do the work or endure their karma. How can the spirits of destruction serve progress for the Good? Speeding up the reverse direction mentioned, the turnaround may begin sooner, thus facilitating progress to the soul's awakening or Damascus experience. These are seven different ways, according to the destiny (planetary type). (see *An Introduction to the Studies* on page 165)

Those who suffer illness but who are bellicose, dedicated, intent, and individual, with the will to love, are healed by practical life and inner Sun of Christ in their breathing (the personality). (Sun of Christ heals in warmth ether of breath.) Illness triggered by the asuras is healed body and soul. Without karma suffered there can be no healing. (Mars)

Those who remember poorly but who are assiduous, conscientious, sagacious, weaving, are not mislead, and retain warmth gain memory of childhood and its karmic significance by Sun of Christ in their bodies. (Sun of Christ imbues warm bodies with will-forces that recall memory.) By way of vice, virtue, and suffering, forgetfulness induced by the asuras is replaced by clear and profound memory. (Jupiter)

Those all-virtuous who are indifferent but who are mystics, magicians, and candid lovers gifted with memory, gain sincere empathy by heart's Sun of Christ. (Sun of Christ warms human hearts.) Cold indifference in this world, in which many asuras are at work, is transformed by Christ-filled hearts. They who are aloof or indifferent learn sincere empathy by suffering. They are the mystics and martyrs. (Venus)

Those who are dreamy but who have independence, acumen, logic, reason, and harmonizing, Sun of Christ awakens their souls/minds. (Sun of Christ awakens souls.) Accentuated by the asuras in human form, false dreams of comfort and convenience, and the ownership of property that is materialism, are overcome by awakening to the one true ideal: Christ. They were dreamy who awaken by suffering. Beware of artificial sensations; the soul may become forever lost. (Mercurial)

Those who are by nature weak but who guard their inwards forces in cautious passionate speech and silence, and with reflection, gain strength in Sun of Christ supporting their egos. (Sun of Christ is the Bearer of the ego-force.) Inner weakness and anxiety is replaced by soul-spirit strength and certainty. They who experience weakness find strength through suffering their karma. (Saturnine)

Those all-virtuous in heart, powerful, regulated, lawful, authoritative, and eminently practical but given to folly, who practice great discipline and patience, gain profound wisdom by Sun of Christ. (Sun of Christ enlightens the religious genius.) Foolishness of subconscious thought, feeling, and will, utilized by the asuras, becomes conscious thought and intention in Christ's daylight. They must know folly to develop clear-headed insight and knowledge through suffering terrible karma. They are the saints and educators. (Sun)

Those who suffer malice but who are idealistic, naive, conceptual, and wise, find love by Sun of Christ as lovers in the Christ-community. (Sun of Christ is a way to Christianity.) Soul-battle with malice, increased by the asuras, becomes love, courage, equanimity, and forgiveness in Christ. They suffer malice to find Christ: love. (Moon)

All seven destinies must make good choices to gain what was lacking in their natures by suffering the inner Christ: the soul's probation. Sorat cannot stand between souls of the destinies and Sun of Christ because they seek Christ, and their seeking Him ensures Christ finds them. Those who are not yet seekers but who progress, they, too, have the possibility for salvation, but in future incarnations.

Anti-Christ Versus the False Christs

In each one of us is an anti-Christ. It is that in us, which denies Christ. The lower self of those who unite their spiritual I with Christ decreases more and more. As Christ grows ever greater in them, there is less of the small human, which denies Christ. Ever-increasing inwardness signifies more intensive union with Christ. Less denial of Christ, less anti-Christ.

The anti-Christ in us has absolutely nothing to do with the false Christs. They are the asuras in human form who wish to destroy Christ to thwart progress. They cannot destroy Christ in those capable of saying "Not I, but Christ in me." [Christ's only true name is 'I AM']. They must content themselves with the dregs of society. Because they are unrelated to the hierarchies and the 'dead', human beings, kingdoms of earth, time, and stages of evolution (now Earth), the asuras under Sorat (the false Christs or arabists; there are many) have nothing to do with evolution. But they accompany evolving beings and planetary stages until evolution—all cycles of time—has run its course. They pose a danger to the initiates.

The false Christs or arabists (Woodrow Wilson was an arabist) are the very people about whom Christ warned His disciples.

Our Journey

To progress on our journey to victory, we must keep our hearts intact or protect our spirits. Then accelerating our destiny-tendency incited by contact with asuras in human form (the false Christs) for turnaround shall serve, not the digression these backwards beings work for, rather the progressive powers, Christ foremost among them. We must exercise some discipline to develop qualities opposite our temperament and for virtue, stay true to our own, individual path, and endure or form and cultivate karma and karmic relationships. Then and only then will all be well. It is a question of inner, soul battle.

If Lucifer swells the lungs and head to grandiose delusions, and Ahriman placates those who are selfish, then Sorat will drain our heart and soul reserves, leaving us empty and helpless. Where Sorat does everything he can to weaken us, preying on our flaws so that we feel bad and hopeless, Christ empowers and upholds the human I in our struggles to be good. When the wrongful dark powers do everything they can to undermine our best efforts, the virtue of courage of the Light God, the Sun-God Christ in our hearts and thoughts help us to wage battle against them. Christ is our ally; we call on Him. He lets no one down. (For Jupiter destinies, small vices can act as memory-reminders, necessary initially.)

Sorat and his asuras are doing everything in their power to thwart and end progress, but human beings who ignite an inner Sun in whom Christ is mighty work with all their inner divine powers in the great battle between the Bad and the Good, between wrongdoing and justice. In them Christ establishes justice, light, virtue, and order on earth. They are the deep and great religious leaders, educators, thinkers: the saints who are esotericists. They are the profound mystics, huge spiritual magicians, prophets: the martyrs who love. Light and darkness are beings.

In human terms we experience our angelic nature or genius (son of life or twilight) (in ourselves and in one another) in our Name or Spirit Self, our archangelic nature or Christ-principle (fire spirit) in our Kingdom or Life Spirit, our archai nature or Father-principle (personality) in our Divine Will or Spirit Man. Thus we have the Holy Trinity reflected in microcosm in the human being's highest three members.

Saint Michael: Archangel of the Sun

Our efforts for courage are transformed by St. Michael for the good of mankind. (Virginia Sease)*

Michael cannot intervene directly in human affairs; this would not leave us free. But we can look up to Him—casting our gaze up to the Sun where He rides on His white steed wielding Christ's blazing Sword of Truth and wearing Christ's Shield of love—and follow His beckoning Gesture. For Michael is the Archangel of Sun of Christ. The relationship of the human being to Michael today is in clear, living, fiery, courageous heart-thoughts, the red, orange, golden-yellow thoughts—the colors of the autumn leaves. (Michaelmas Eve falls on September 28th each year.) This living thinking calls for great courage indeed, for then we uphold the good, true, beautiful, just, and ethical in the spirit of truth—no matter what we face—but we must wage this Michaelic battle in our thinking in freedom, in our good warm, heart-thoughts, for these are the Michaelic thoughts in which Michael lives and works.

The Thoughts of Michael in the Middle Ages and Today

Whereas during the Middle Ages the Michaelic thoughts streamed into human souls from the outside, today the thoughts must arise within our souls with our full wakeful consciousness. (Virginia Sease)* These are the Christ-Thoughts, the spiritual thoughts, the courageous sun-thoughts.

What is this difference, and why was it necessary for human beings to stand without any outer supports and entirely independent of the dogmas and doctrines of the Church and its faith-based worldview, relying only on our own, unbiased observation? What happens when we reach the level of thinking that is sense-free or autonomous, which is independent of the physical senses and the brain?

Autonomy, the Scientific Revolution, and Spiritual Anarchy

When we learn how Joan of Arc, "The Maid of Orléan" (1412-1431), saved France from the English, thereby restoring the balance of power in Europe, such divine intervention could never happen today. Now the divine will be born in our hearts, Christ will spiritually awaken our souls to day-consciousness by our inmost seeking Him in inner freedom. Not faith, but profound insight must determine the direction we impart our lives and the choices we make, both personal and societal. Archangel Michael can no longer inspire in thoughts streaming into us from above, as was Joan of Arc (also by St. Margaret and St. Catherine). Today, the thoughts of Michael must arise within our own souls in autonomy.

This autonomy is achieved by intensifying thinking to penetrate through the limits imposed by the senses and the brain into the Thought-Center of the World. This sense-free thinking (spiritual freedom) knows no bounds. No longer servants inspired by higher powers outside our being, we gain inner powers known to us because the divine thoughts are active within our souls with our full and clear consciousness.

We bravely struggle with the freedom granted those only who have attained autonomous thinking. We are men and women courageous in spirit who stand in truth of insight on the divine ground of the world. The sainthood of Joan has been succeeded by the sainthood of maturity. The thoughts of the great Archangel Michael no longer enter our souls in rapture from spiritual worlds; they arise in the calm and steady gaze of conscious seership produced from within us. If we maintain our balance, we are able to practice spiritual courage far greater than could be expected of young Joan. We become independent thinkers working, not for the Church, the State, or Papal Europe, but in spiritual anarchy, examining each thought and viewpoint, learning from our own unprejudiced observation, just as Tycho Brahe (1546-1601), Galileo Galilei (1564-1642), and Johannes Kepler (1571-1630) pioneered the science of astronomy in the Scientific Revolution in the 1500s, defying the Church in independence of spirit. These brave men challenged the political power of Papal Rome as did Joan the English, not under the false accusation of sorcery, rather for upsetting the centuries-honored Church dogma that was faith-based. Giordano Bruno (1548-1600) posed a greater threat to the Church. He was a pantheist. More than this, he taught the human, spiritual laws of reincarnation and karma. Giordano Bruno was ahead of his time. Like Joan, he was burned at the stake.

"Goethe is the Copernicus and the Kepler of the organic world." (Rudolf Steiner) This is Goethean, phenomenological science. *Rudolf Steiner* is the Goethe of the soul and spirit world. This is anthroposophy.

Autonomous Thinking as the Foundation of Healthy Experience

The courage of such scientists must be carried over into the spiritual domain in observations of the seers and thinkers gifted with the modern-day perception of Christ and other spiritual beings, including human spiritual being. Unlike in the Middle Ages of Joan, in knowing God and serving Christ today, we cannot address human faith but fully conscious spiritual thinking. Meeting one another on independent terms, we must be challenged to think the spiritual thoughts, opening our soul-eyes to perceive Christ-Light, gaining the objective truth of higher knowledge, not merely physical facts, weights, measurements, distances, statistics.

The facts remain useful; we must be wary lest error creep into our thinking, nor should we forget the reality of the physical world (matter). But we must remain knowing of the spiritual sun essence of our hearts and souls (spirit). A motto of anthroposophy is no matter without spirit (reality); no spirit without matter (reality). Soul and spirit beings weave wherever physical and etheric beings, processes, objects are on earth.

We need not leave the solid earth of the senses, but our perceptions by their means are not soul-spiritual, although what is sensible is drenched in radiant sun-warmth and sun-light, imbued with what is supersensible (science and thinking). Nor do we depart from the clarity and reverence of spiritual knowledge granted us by immersion in truth and grace, and which is our inner wellspring and communion with Christ (the warmth and light of religion). Our souls lives in another connection in what we imagine, inspire, and intuit as creative beings: love and beauty (art), spiritual communion (science), sacramental communion (religion).

Thinking autonomy and spiritual sensing are the foundation of healthy knowledge. We are left in no doubt. The truth of objective experience is unbiased observation while we are experiencing. Or we are experiencing the content of our observation in an unprejudiced fashion.

The Obedient Dragon Serves the Good

In the best traditions of Middle Ages, St. Michael does not merely slay the Dragon. He transforms him into a faithful and obedient servant. (Virginia Sease)*

Angels

Our good thoughts are like a golden thread which the angels weave into *a tapestry for the welfare of mankind.* (Virginia Sease)*

We feel especially close to the angels during the Thirteen Holy Nights when we go to sleep with a prayer in our hearts, not for ourselves but for others. (Virginia Sease)* The angels intervene directly in human affairs. They constantly work mitigating in human affairs at key moments, in key places, and in delicate situations to ensure that all goes well. This means that human decisions must frequently be made very suddenly that are life changing. At such times the angels are very busy.

One such example is when a couple, unable to conceive a child, went on a regular visit to their doctor who knew of their wish to have a child. The doctor said he had another patient, a young pregnant woman, who would give birth in one week but did not want her child—not even to see it. The doctor asked the couple if they would like to adopt this child. They did. The baby had exactly the hair and eye color of the adoptive parents. The child's angel was very busy arranging things indeed.

We know how often small children are in situations of danger, escaping severe injury or death when this is highly unlikely. This is owing to the protection of the Guardian Angel of the child.

There are children who suffer tragedy and death from natural and human disasters, accidents, or incurable illness. In such instances, this is so that the unused life-forces of the child can serve the three highest hosts of the highest triad of the three hierarchies to save the souls of materialists in the clutches of Ahriman, not only in their thinking and conceptions, but down into their wills, or it is the karma of the child's soul.

If the childhood tragedy serves the redemption of the materialists otherwise beyond the help of the thrones, cherubim, and seraphim, an equal blessing and joy will balance the grief of the parents' loss and sorrow in their next incarnation. If it is karmic this is also the case, for grieving parents suffer the physical loss of their child. As with all karma, the karma of children follows certain spiritual laws.

Each of us has a Guardian Angel. In genuine prayer to the Guardian

Angel of some one in need, their Guardian Angel does help them.

Our Religious Nature In Christ

In Christ we have our religious (Christ-like) nature. He became human in Jesus of Nazareth that we might become human in Him. We must win our true humanity in drawing from the two extremes what is useful and helpful in inwardness of heart-feeling (religious, courageous heart), will-strength of the heart, and wisdom (insight) of the clear and warm (Sun-) heart-imbued mind. These two extremes are from the depths below (Ahriman) and the heights above (Lucifer). With powers of heart (our inner Christ-Sun) we pulling bring the two forces together, our hearts immeasurably strengthened.

The greatest geniuses are the religious (heart) geniuses. Insofar any destiny gains Sun of Christ (in the heart) do they partake of religion. We know how little genuine religious feeling there is today. In large part, this is owing to the widespread spirit of materialism and technology. All genuine religions have their center and essence in the 'I AM' of human hearts, whether they know it or not. A pastor, rabbi, or imam may be the genuine center of a religious community, church, temple, or mosque.

The inner Christ is the 'I AM' within the heart and soul. These are the inner heart-forces so powerful in the Sun destinies. They form karma.

We need Lucifer to develop our creative artistic natures, Ahriman our intellectual scientific natures. Christ in us is our heart of religion, our inmost feeling courage and generous love, even in the face of fear and the pain of malice. We need not run from fear and pain when in brave suffering we ask for and receive Christ's help.

The Company of Heaven

In addition to the three choirs of heavenly hosts (angelic beings) already discussed, there are six yet higher ranks or levels of spiritual beings, the two highest of three triads or hierarchies. We have the nine heavenly hosts: angeloi, archangeloi, archai; exusiai, dynameis, kyriotetes;

thrones, cherubim, seraphim. Each of these nine ranks of divine beings above man has specific tasks. They are the "limbs of Christ". Rudolf Steiner saved these nine choirs of heavenly hosts for human beings from sleep, forgetting, and death in his extensive writing and lecturing. The unborn and the dead are also active in the spiritual world together with the hierarchies or heavenly hosts. This is the company of heaven.

And ye shall know the truth, and the truth shall set you free.
St. John, 3:32.

God is a Spirit: and they that worship Him must worship Him in spirit and in truth.
St. John, 4:24.

But the fruit of the Spirit is love, joy, peace, long-suffering, gentleness, goodness, faith, meekness, temperance.
II Corinthians, 5:22.
The Bible

Santa Monica, California
September 12, 2011
Los Angeles
September 25/28
October 3-6/11/19-23
November 14, 2014

NOTE: Much of this study is first-published in this volume. A portion was published in the essay "On Being Good and the Question of Evil" in *The Courage of the Flame* (Culver City: Sun Sings Publications, 2002), reprinted with permission from Alan Lindgren. However, this portion is greatly revised in places.

* Dr. Virginia Sease in no way endorses this volume or any study, story, or poem in it. *The Wood of Green* is published independently of the General Anthroposophical Society at the Goetheanum in Dornach, Switzerland, which the author recognizes.

Artificial Sensations and the Children

Virtual, digital, and other artificial and imitative sensations are the cause of much harm to the user of the technology. This is apparent at all ages. The greater the use, the more harm done. But exposure before puberty can cause irreversible damage. Additionally, those who, as children, are robbed of their childhoods by artificial experiences in place of real ones, become hopeless and useless adults. The younger the child, the greater the harm done. We are seeing such adults, now in their 20s and 30s, everywhere. This comes to us as no surprise. It is a consequence of exposure of children to these sensations.

Teachers and parents are seeing the effects of sensory stimulation on the eye and ear organs on the minds and souls of school children in illnesses such as ADHD (attention deficit hyperactive disorder): inattentiveness, over-activity, impulsiveness, or a combination, and the inability to sit still without preoccupying the fingers at a keyboard. Yet the cause-and-effect connection is often not made, apparent it is. On other children the sensations act as tranquilizers. Sensitive adults know the mesmerizing effects of watching television and sitting at the computer for any length of time. People sit staring at their cell phones that double as iPads for hours, and if they read at all, more and more often it is Kindle books from computer-like screens. Likewise with iPods, but with sound. Notepads are a newer toy.

Some teachers are advising parents to limit computer and television use by their children. While some parents are insisting their children play less with artificial toys and more with such toys as balls, children easily fall into bad habits and, at a certain level, are unable to activate their innate imaginative faculty playing with simple wooden or cloth toys or with natural objects such as pine cones and feathers. Some behave as though drugged, unable or unwilling to engage in physical play at all.

If a child does not engage its imagination sufficiently in its early years (from infancy until the age of seven), the proper formation of the internal organs does not take place. This process must occur in early childhood; it cannot be made up for after this stage of development.

Concerned parents are giving gifts of 'old-fashioned' toys to their little ones, making clear to them there are limits in playing with video games and watching television. The question is: *Is this enough*? Any significant amount of exposure to artificial sensations at this age does irreparable damage. A healthy childhood continues through puberty.

Although in many instances children continue spending much or more time playing with computer simulations and so-called educational videos and games than they do in healthy natural and human play and instruction, a significant amount of attention is being given to these problematic areas because the symptoms are extreme and undeniable. Unfortunately, many parents continue encouraging their children to sit in front of computers for so-called educational purposes, in conformity to other parents and at the recommendation of schools, such that untold harm is done.

I witnessed a shocking situation of a mother with her eleven or twelve year-old daughter at a public library not long ago. The girl was listening to an iPod seated at a table opposite her mother. She was supposed to be doing her homework while her mother read a book. The girl was fidgeting with her pencil, unable to sit still or concentrate at all. Occasionally, she made the effort to connect with reality by removing the earplugs. Then she looked across the table to her mother helplessly for encouragement. Then the mother looked up from her quiet reading and smiled kindly at her daughter. But invariably, after about twenty seconds, the girl gave in again. She put the earplugs back in her ears and resumed her fidgeting in the world of artificial sound created by the iPod. She could not bear the reality of quiet.

I often see children—even three year-olds—at a local public library sitting at children's computers wearing headphones larger than their heads, looking up at the computer screen while their little fingers rove across the keyboard. It is with such artificial experiences that they are beginning their lives. Like the fidgeting girl listening to the iPod, these children will be burned or blanked out well before the age of thirty, if they manage to study or work after high school at all, if they graduate from high school. The 'hopeless' age gets younger and younger.

At the national and global level this damage has a major economic impact. At the personal level the person becomes lost when within the soul nothing stirs when the artificial sensations are taken away and s/he is in a natural or human environment. Before a fragrant red rose no intuition or feeling is sensed or aroused. In chorus or birdsong nothing gladdens the heart or awakens within. Among children no sorrow or joy or love appears or quickens. With the sick or hurt no compassion is felt. The soul is as dead. The situation is a hopeless one.

Yet we can address this grave problem in our society by changing the way we raise our children, and by the choices we make in our own lives as adults. We begin with our adult self-education and by changing our practices or doing more that is beneficial. Then we will be in a position to help the children, who grow up at our mercy and who are the future.

It is heartening to see school children playing at recess and during physical education ('P.E.') with enthusiasm and fun. They are just being children. So long as the children play, there is hope for the future.

Santa Monica, California
July 13/27, 2011
Culver City, California
May 13, 2014
Los Angeles
October 5/23/27, 2014

Machines, Information, Health, and Healing

Dr. Hans Peter van Manen (1931-2009), the Dutch anthroposophist, educator, historian, and author, wrote several volumes. *Wiederkunft und Heimsuchung: Von der Wiederkunft Christi und dem Kommen des Antichrist* addresses realities and issues which concerned and concern 20th and 21st century humanity. One theme I'd like to take up in this study is machines and their effects on individuals and Western society as a whole, not only in science, but also in music, art, and literature.

Machines are estranging for and exert a strong fascination on human beings. They are a direct result of materialism, which is a spiritual world conception, which denies the spirit in the world and in the human being, but which is spiritual. The spirit of machines and machine technologies is identical with that of materialism, the mephistophelian creative spirit. We see the connection here. The world creative spirit is divine and human. It is the spirit at work in and behind all manifestations of the spiritual world, which include nature-phenomena, human beings, and human creativity of a living character.

When we step back and really take a look at modern science and technology, we recognize immediately they are divorced from the experience of natural and human reality. Not only are they separated off from this reality experience; they estrange us from the same. We sense this everywhere today. These aspects of post-modern life have a twofold estranging effect. The first is in outlook. We touched on this in the materialistic world conception, which is pervasive among human beings in our present age.

When someone denies the spirit, they deny the divinity of their humanity and of nature, of God's creation. They have cut themselves off from their true source. This affects not only their outlook, but also their relationship to the divine. This relationship to the divine extends beyond the confines of death, because what we think and how we think determines what we experience in the life beyond and in future incarnations. These are therefore real consequences of materialistic thinking. These effects extend beyond the confines of death. This is the one estranging affect, in our relationship to our actual supersensible being: our true, immortal nature, the divine.

The other way materialism estranges people today is through the sensory organs when we turn to the tangible effects. This actually happens with machines. Let us take a closer look into this reality, created by machine technologies.

Machines

Machines are constituted of solely material parts and mechanisms. Thus they are subject to physical laws such as gravity. But here commonality with the natural and human world ceases. In all other ways they are unalike, for examples stones.

Machines are designed and constructed or assembled for a specific purpose. They are therefore purely utilitarian like information. We see the difference here. Physically-speaking, the human being is created so that he may think. The human brain is the physical instrument of the thinking human spirit, and thinking is the realm of freedom. We are above the animals and only a little lower than the angels in our thinking. We make choices, and taken together all of our choices determine the direction we give our lives, including our life-changing decisions.

A machine carries out functions for which it was designed by way of simple commands. It is therefore defined by its uses that are inherently extremely limited. There is neither choice nor creativity, freedom nor development, direction nor relationship; no thinking, feeling, willing, remembering, touching, seeing, hearing, listening, singing, speaking, gesturing, romance, or breathing, but only information and the carrying out of very basic commands. This is entirely artificial, however efficient and otherwise useful it may be.

However, we find entirely wasteful and harmful technologies and their uses. Not only in the military, for which the creation and use of machines is extremely costly, devastating, and tragic, in human and in economic terms: in destruction, maiming and loss of precious life; but also in other inventions and their development for the artificial stimulation of the senses as we have in computer simulations for video games and entertainment, and in other uses of virtual, digital, and newer technologies, which bombard the eye and ear organs with their stimuli of artificial sights and sounds, thereby harming or causing permanent damage.

Even for those whose eyes and ears remain intact, often from exposure to these sensations (stimulation), which can induce hyperactivity or have sedative effects, when the person is deprived of them and in a natural or human setting where genuine experiences are offered, nothing stirs within the soul. There is no inner response; no imagination, inspiration, or intuition awakens; the person is inwardly inactive, as dead inside. What is artificial and imitative comes more and more to replace what is human and natural, having a mesmerizing, stimulating, or sedating effect.

These realities are fundamental and additional to the actual content of the artificial experience, the *what* represented by visual and auditory means, which may scar the mind of the person, even permanently. For example, an image or sound from a film or video experienced in childhood of a violent or otherwise ugly nature can leave an indelible impression on the soul. This can haunt the person until death, when memories ordinarily cease. Thus, although it is unreal, the effects of the image or sound are very real and can have a profound impact. It is very significant what we experience during our waking hours. Of course this goes for 'real' sensations and thoughts as well. We think of homelessness and wartime experiences for children and adults.

A technology is already being developed that includes tactile (touch) virtual experiences in what is called haptics. The following information can be found on the Internet and is in the public domain:

> Although virtual reality (VR)/virtuality consists primarily in visual experiences in computer-simulated environments, some advanced, haptic systems now include tactile information. This is haptic technology or haptics, a tactile feedback technology, which takes advantage of the sense of touch by applying forces, vibrations or motions to the user. Here mechanical stimulation can be used to assist in the creation of virtual objects in a computer simulation, to control such virtual objects, and to enhance the remote control of machines and devices (telerobotics). Haptics has been described as 'doing for the sense of touch what computer graphics does for vision'.

We have already mentioned hyperactivity and sedation or dullness as effects on the inner person (and therewith on behavior). Because the soul is numbed by or addicted to the artificial sensory stimulus, shock or vulgarity, the person requires more of the same to achieve an inner response, while a real life situation has less and less an effect, making little or no impression. We can imagine what this means in a moral sense: our fundamental humanity.

In these tragic and artificial human experiences, we come to recognize the gravity of the consequences of machines in our society and the world today: human beings are 1.) hurt or overwhelmed; and 2.) dehumanized, depersonalized. Like materiality (materialism), machines estrange. This estrangement inspires an underlying fear, but machines also fascinate.[1] Sometimes they estrange by fascination. We think of several technologies in everyday use by myriad human beings today, such as cell phones and laptop computers. Thus estrangement is a product of materialism, here of the pervasive use of machines in Western society by individuals.

The Machine in Music, Art, and Literature

When a person is disinterested in or unresponsive to natural and human sensations, s/he will look for a replacement. This happens in the Arts today. The 20th century was a time of experimentation in every arena of human activity. Some of this was good. To an extent this portion was necessary. For example in the late 1960s young people rebelled against 'the establishment'. The hippies were pacifists and against war. They became political. They believed in 'flower power'. They created a new lifestyle. Young people were dissatisfied with what society offered. But the way this was expressed was often damaging, occurring in three manifestations: 1.) the use of hard drugs, 2.) promiscuity, 3.) high decibel electronic rock music. All of this rocked and shocked the older generation. Soon after, by the mid-70s, only here and there and more as token expressions (such as in long hair and clothing), the entire movement had dispersed, and those who had been most devoted were given over to what they had challenged: the establishment.[2]

Experimentation in Art began at the turn of the century. The machine, so foreign to creativity, exerted a powerful and often determining influence. This is ongoing. It directly altered music with the production of artificial sound by machines. This is clearly foreign to the human ear, to the human soul. Not only electronic music, whose hard rock form became dominant in the 1960s (see above), but the entire music industry has become one of machines with, first cassettes and tapes, and now CD, DVD, computer video, music website, and iPod technologies, and digital headphones and television, including 3-D LED HDTV. The film industry, which is inseparable from machines, has often innovated cutting-edge new technologies in visuals, and sound and special effects.

Live music seems to all-but disappear, while CD recordings and virtual music downloads onto such a device as the iPod are more and more perfect copy imitations, refined, convenient, popular, and inexpensive to obtain. Recorded musical sound is free to access over the Internet.

The visual arts have also been drastically affected. Abstract and imitative Art (that appears *like* reality like a photograph only a much more perfect copy), and all computer-generated Art, have all-but taken over. We find this in art installations, natural spaces, and especially in graphic art. The Japanese forms *manga* and *anime* now replace the old cartoons in popularity, while 3-D does the same with lower-tech film. We want further deviations from reality on the one hand, and more convincing but further removed from reality artificial imitations of reality on the other. There is an increasing preoccupation with such technologies as aircraft and other military machines, which are entirely removed from Art. Film, videos, and video games typically have machines as 'actors'. Meanwhile 'outer space' and science fiction replaces inner, soul spaces and genuine experiences of our precious earth, sun, moon, and stars for many.

Even literature and poetry, solely human art forms because words, imagination, and thought are found nowhere else in Creation but in human beings, are under the influence of the machine and technology. Many poets have chosen desperate, cynical, or completely irrational expressions because of the estranging impact and effects of machines on and in their souls and lives. They, too, cannot find their true way. E-mails and the Internet as pictures and themes have found their way into what calls itself 'poetry'. Last year (2011) the sales of e-Books exceeded those of hard copy for the first time. Yet computers and the Internet are invaluable tools for the creation and publication of real, physical books.

* *

All artists utilize etheric forces in their creative work, whether or not they know this. This is the source of the therapeutic qualities and effects of doing and experiencing art. If the poet does not give his thoughts and pictures a living form, they remain abstract and lifeless. Exactly as with an imagination or inner picture in meditation, when a genuine poem comes into existence, it is a visible actuality in the world of soul and spirit.[3] This is also the case with fairy tales and in some novels.

People sit for hours at a time in front of computers, whether at study, work or for diversion, substituting music websites and iPods for live music, and social-interactive websites and chatrooms for live human exchange. Very often cell phones replace conversation in person. We are increasingly isolating ourselves when what we require is our humanity. Nature, true Art, and one another are our source of soul sustenance and nourishment, without which we cannot live. Often, our only human interaction is on technical matters or over electronic or computer resources, our only time outdoors walking or jogging listening to iPods or on the cell phone, mentioned above. We have become strangers to nature and one another. We cannot think the deeper, finer thoughts or actively imagine, or they assume phantom shapes and life, passing by our consciousness strangely or so quickly we have no true or lasting relationship to them. I spoke with a young man several years ago who was born in 1984 and whose first memory was a video. He asked me, "Is life an illusion?"

Technologies: Bad or Good?

Without underestimating the real harmfulness of and actual damage done by artificial technologies (past, present, and future), it should be said that they can bring about an *external* unification or unifying connection that can be favorable, usage depending. Take, for example the Internet with its recognizable benefits of worldwide simultaneous communication and networking. Computer systems enable huge data banks to be easily accessed, information collected and transferred, and businesses to run smoothly and efficiently. In and of itself this is not good. It all depends on how it is used. We know that machines are ruthless because they have no humanity. They function for us because of their efficiency and nondiscrimination. They will serve the Bad as readily as the Good.

Technology saves human beings a tremendous amount of time and work. Think of the tractor and the truck. Or transportation: trains and airplanes for example. Communication and all manner of connections are opened up, bringing about swift contact and exchange possibilities. Many technologies can prove beneficial, their uses depending. But we have seen some of the consequences.

One danger is that time, energy, and money can be and is spent at machines that should be used in Nature, with true Art, or between real people (in person). When the human occupation with technology replaces inner activity and real experiences, we realize the gravity of the consequences. However, used in the right way with discretion, as a useful tool to save time, energy, and money so that the time, energy, and money saved is directed to healthy and healing real experiences and activities in Nature, culture, and with human beings, the benefits are clear.

Technology in itself is neither bad nor good. But its uses and abuses exert a great temptation and fascination on human beings that estrange us from the world, one another, and ourselves. When used wisely and with prudence and common sense, they serve the Good. They serve the creative process (quality writing and publishing, for example writings of a spiritual nature) and provide the means whereby we connect with one another outwardly, conduct research (access information), make transactions, and take care of other business matters (in banking and business), and perform physical work (that is 'work' machines, like washers & driers, sanitation trucks, cargo transport, recycling, roadwork, in building, and so on).

It is up to us. As children are entirely at the mercy of the adults in their lives, we have a deep responsibility for their welfare. They are too young to be exposed to what is intellectual and artificial, and which does untold harm and irreparable damage, the younger the more so. As adults many today are making poor choices for their own souls, while others are finding and making their human and spiritual way (real and ideal) as they journey through life in this brave new world of ours.*

Here I offer my insights into human relationships in my study *Reciprocity*, first published in 2004.[1][a]

Reciprocity

Reciprocity is an interesting word. Its adjectival relative is reciprocal, meaning "working both ways," "mutual," "mutually effecting," "shared," "two-way." And what is reciprocal, what is mutual? A friendship or genuine relationship of any kind, any healthy relationship wherein both parties relate to one another as equals, in which both parties are in a mutually beneficial relationship, such a relationship is reciprocal, is mutual. This can be either under the counsel of a professional relationship as between doctor and patient, or in a more informal setting. Why is reciprocity, just why is mutuality so very significant, actually absolutely essential in every genuine relationship and conversation? Because without it no true sharing can take place, nor is any real communication possible.

I may gleam facts and information from a book, such as a reference book of some kind, for example from a dictionary or an encyclopedia, or from other resources, such as data via the Internet or from some database or other. And then I have gained something both real and valuable from this gleaning of facts and information, which can indeed prove to be very useful to me personally or for my work or task. But this is information, not communication. This is data, not human. This is valuable for my research and thereby my intellectual work, but it is not of any help to me in my human need for friendship and human relationships, which is of deep significance to me personally.

I am not some storage center, computer drive, flash drive, some encyclopedia, some shelf-university, even though I be knowledgeable and qualified to teach without referring to any external references but from memory alone, even though I can impart tens of thousands of pertinent facts at my fingertips prompted only by my students or by the necessity given by my line of work.

No, I am a man or a woman with very real human needs, which can only be provided in relationship with another human being. But if I am too closed-minded and selfish and cannot see the special light in my fellow human brother or sister's eyes, if I cannot hear the special timbre in another human being's voice, if I cannot appreciate the unique quality and nature of my loved one, companion, friend, brother, sister, doctor, patient, teacher, student, close relation, or child, if I cannot relate to my fellow human brothers and sisters due to my own engrained limitations, I then become weary, weak, and ineffectual, or sick, tired, and lonely, or arrogant, snobbish, and conceited, or vainglorious, proud, and puffed up, or isolative, dejected, and hopeless, or abstracted, removed from reality, and hypothetical, or heavy, downtrodden, and depressed, and so on.

We need one another. We are not alone in this world. There is much more to life than sheer work, diet, exercise, rest, medication, hobbies, pastimes, diversions. We must discover one another through love. We must create times and places for one another, both professionally and informally. We must be human in public and private places.

Love unites two souls, bridges the gulf, reaches across the divide, across the gap, heals wounds, binds two souls as one, mends broken relationships, sees light, not boundaries. Love is reciprocal. Love is mutual. Love is both divine and so very human. We see God in one another when we perceive our brother or sister.

Christ is our human brother, is our human sister. He is the

One, Who is the bridge between two hearts and souls. We recognize Him in the true, the good, and the beautiful in one another when these are truly present. We need only befriend one another. We need only help one another in our human need and vulnerability. Christ is our support and strength. He gives us courage of heart. He is heartening. He loves us very much. Let us love one another as He loves us.

Let us establish and cultivate mutually beneficial, reciprocal, good, and healthy relationships when this is possible. We can do this with those with whom we feel a deeper tie, a deeper human connection. Toward all others, we know no help is there. Nor can we help those who want no help, with those who are not interested in helping or in being helped. We are purely professional there. We turn or walk away. We turn to our human brothers and sisters who want our help. We use our time and energy wisely. We shelter our gifts and use them where they are needed. We share with those who are truly mutual, who are reciprocal. And all is well.

God, Christ is love. We seek to be like Him insofar we are good friends to our human brothers and sisters, insofar we perceive them, love them, show them intentionality, good will. We are brave enough for the sake of the other to be vulnerable that we may come to Christ in our human brother, in our human sister. We receive Him. He is the Warmth of our warmth, the Light of our lights, the Tone of our voice.

He stands and knocks at the door of our hearts and souls. We open unto Him and sup with Him and He with us. This is the spiritual communion of souls with the Christ Being. This is the meaning of reciprocity. Thus it has been.

Inglewood, California
September 29, 2004

Solutions

A major aspect of the complexities of the problems we face today is the world of machines and technology. What can we do? In my study *Reciprocity*, given above in its entirety, I directed our attention to healthy human relationships. Let's explore this and related themes further.

We can be present and demonstrate our concern and love for, show interest in and regard for one another. Humanity is almost everywhere, wherever there is coming into being, growth, development, hurting, loss, illness, deprivation, dying, and death. Even in upper-class society, upscale neighborhoods, shopping and dining malls, the homeless and physically- or emotionally-maimed veterans are present or nearby. The children are wherever their parents, teachers, and other caretakers are found. Old people are too-often shut up indoors, secluded from the world. We need to visit them, and to bring together the youngest and oldest generations, which are naturally good with one another.

As Maya Angelou says, we must be human in public and private places. We can find or locate others who share this intention with us. We can spend time outdoors experiencing nature-phenomena—even in or near the city—without the technical devices. We can do arts & crafts, design and sew clothing. We can brighten our living spaces with handmade decorations. We be craftsmen in woodworking/cabinetmaking and ceramics. We can sing, play, or listen to live acoustic music and singing at every opportunity. We can do or experience true Art with 'natural' media: sculpture with clay, beeswax, plaster, or wood; drawing with lead and colored pencil, charcoal, pen & ink, and papers; painting in watercolors, acrylics, and oils on watercolor paper or canvas. We can read the classics, other genuinely interesting literature and poetry, or write and compose the same, all hard copy. We can speak/do drama. We can gesture, do eurythmy, and dance. We can love and romance. We can breathe, care for our hair, and architect. We can do these things without machine technologies, but without their influence and that of intoxicating substances. We can garden, keep bees, cook, bake, clean, do carpentry and plumbing. We can take care of the children, elderly, and pets. We can be human in an increasingly dehuman society.

****

We can also turn to Nature. We can go outside beneath the sky, feel the warm sunshine, cool breeze, blowing wind, wet rain, or freezing snow. We can lie down, sit, stand, or walk outdoors to experience the earth below and the sun, clouds, moon, and stars above us. We look to the great mountains and the brown or green hills. We listen to the birds chirping and singing, other animal sounds, and the earth's waters. We see the colorful flowers, trees' leaves, and other green plants. We find the tiny insects as they go about their tasks. We venture into the forests or walk along the beaches. We witness the wonderful colors of the dawn and sunrise, and the dear colors of the sunset. We then find our true humanity—in one another, Nature, and within our own souls—the divine element in Nature, the Arts, and our own, inner being.

We have briefly discussed the practical, artistic, and natural activities and experiences in which we engage and actively participate that are purely beneficial for us because they afford us harmony, peace, quiet, and therapeutic possibilities/qualities. We purposely turn away from our machines: shut down the computer; turn off the cell, the TV, the radio; discard the iPod, headphones, CD, DVD, and video players; and intentionally seek out these healthy and healing experiences, places, times, and engagements. The relationship is between the individual and nature-phenomena, an/other human being/s, creativity, or the divine.

Santa Monica, California/March 22/28-29, 2012
Revised and edited Culver City, California/March 30/April 3-4
Further revised Los Angeles/November 29, 2012/October 5, 2014

* This refers to Aldous Huxley's prophetic classic, *Brave New World*

FOOTNOTES

1. Hans Peter van Manen, *Wiederkunft und Heimsuchung* (Verlag am Goetheanum: 2011), Chapter 3, p. 35

2. Ibid., Chapter 13, pp. 131-2

3. Ibid., Chapter 6, p. 54

1a. Alan Lindgren, *The Magic of the Stars: Selected Poems by Alan Lindgren 2003-2004* (Sun Sings Publications: Culver City, 2004, 2005), front matter, pp. xxii-xxiv

Tools and Technology

At its best, technology is a tool, or several tools. We know that tools must be utilized properly, appropriately, effectively, and to a specific purpose if they are to be of use to us, to perform work for us, or to assist us in our work. Thus technology of itself means nothing to us and is never what life is about, rather it may only serve us for our work and creativity, to share with and help one another. In the way of a concrete example let us give an analogy.

In the kitchen there are various utensils, pots and pans, an oven, and a refrigerator we may require for meal preparation. These things are not the meal, neither are they we humans who share the meal at the dining room table. We use them to help us prepare the meal. The ingredients for what we prepare and eat are independent from the kitchen, but they constitute the food we eat that gives us health and strength for life. These ingredients come from farm and garden, from the Earth and Sun.

What is life all about? It cannot be about the tools, about the kitchen and what is used in it for meal preparation from the wholesome ingredients. In our analogy, life is all about gathering around the table, the family of Man dining together, the feast, the taking of the elements, the flesh and blood of Christ from the bread we bake from the grain of the fields and the juice we press from the grapes from the vine. All else but serves this purpose, our true meaning, which grants us the strength and health we require for our daily work on earth, the experience of Mother Nature and of human Culture, and the taming of Nature with her forces into farm and garden by the cultivation of the soil and the sowing of the seeds, until, once again, we return to the Table and Meal of Christ. Then, each night and between each death and rebirth, we return to eternal realms of spirit with the company of heaven: the dead, the hierarchies of divine beings or heavenly hosts, and the holy Trinity, for the replenishment of light until a new day of fresh life in this wonderful world of ours.

Los Angeles
September 21, 2013/October 5-6, 2014
Edited Culver City, California
September 24, 2013

Order, Organization, and a Beautiful Mind

Organization and order are indispensable for the thrifty and efficient housewife; the hardworking gardener, plumber, electrician, maintenance man, carpenter, and handyman; the devoted student and teacher; the diligent, conscientious, and precise scientist, researcher, and engineer; the occupied businessman, banker, accountant, and librarian; the masterful architect and composer; the keen-minded and expert writer and editor; indeed for every one to facilitate the manageability of otherwise ungainly or overwhelming tasks, the structuring of parts and aspects (both practical and ideal), and the clarity and straightforwardness of what is or seems to be difficult or haphazard. Without fundamental organization and discipline chaos soon takes over, confusion wreaks its havoc in, or error creeps into the work. Although these ruinous elements appear in the work that is actually where they manifest.

All order is but the outcome (result) of method and sense that is *in the thinking and mind.* Mental illnesses and traumatic experiences can be observed most directly and easily in the behaviors and chaos, errors and confusion that are visible in outward expression. However impractical or sensible, imperfect or exact, malformed or beautiful they may be, all of our designs and plans become real and apparent *in their implementation.* Practice follows upon method or organization, and the results can be both harmonious and beautiful. Hence when we speak or read of a 'beautiful mind' we are reverent of our most precious and divine endowment. Those favored with such a soul or mind are blessed over all others. To them belong the greatest possibilities and potentials, the hope of the future, the riches of the past, and the preeminence of the present. Truly, harmony and beauty in the thinking or imagination is a gift to be cherished above all things on earth. The most excellent, loftiest, and deepest thinkers, mystics, and poets are graced with it. It proceeds from God much as the dome of the human head is a picture and a microcosm of the starry heavens we can only wonder at and worship.

Los Angeles
August 17-18, 2010
October 5, 2014

Education for the Spirit

The time in human history has come that the adult must educate himself. This must be an education for the spirit. Who would be the teacher in this self-education for the spirit? It is not the self. The teacher is life itself, but life in the spirit, that is life's experiences as they are reflected within the human soul. For only in the human spirit can life on earth become a true education, one that is neither borrowed nor led, given nor taken, attempted nor longed for, wished nor hoped for.

Spiritual Education and the Experiences of the Heart

No, the true education for the human spirit is gained by inner work or endurance on or for those experiences that find a place within the human heart and mind in the sense of feeling and fact. Feelings of suffering and good cheer, pain and pleasure, sadness and gladness, sorrows and joys, woes and happiness, solemnity and mirth, reverence and gaiety, grief and humor, devotion and delight, mysticism and magic.

Processional Facts Along the Journey

Facts of all kinds are prized in that they are each true, such that we learn from them. Then they are neither sacred nor profane (Ralph Waldo Emerson), but only processional, our helpers along the journey with and to Christ, Who is our lifelong companion.

Feelings and Facts: Substance and Material on the Spiritual Path

Feelings and facts such as these become the substance and the material we work on, internalizing and learning from them what they have to offer us. This becomes for us their fullest meaning, the deepest, dearest meaning of a warm loving heart and the clearest, most lucid, brightest, most candid considerations of a heart-enlightened mind. Then and then alone may we proceed on a spiritual path along which the journeyer makes her way.

The Human Soul: The Spiritual Journeyer and Adult Self-Education

Who is this journeyer? She is the human soul who ever walks in spiritual climes of Sun and Earth and Moon and stars, light and shadow and color, sound and silence, warmth and coolness, magic and mystery, love and chemistry, blindness and wisdom, materiality and spirituality, secularity and sacredness, folks and religions, human being and Christ being, God and Son and Sophia, heaven and earth, angels and souls, sunlight and rainbows, men and stars, animals and stones, plants and clouds, eurythmy and music, poetry and painting, music and sculpture, painting and architecture, sculpture and romance, architecture and eurythmy, love and poetry, imagination, inspiration, and intuition—all of the keys to feeling, knowing, living, and doing. They are our teachers, friends, and guides. This is adult self-education: education for the spirit.

2012 (?)
Edited Los Angeles
October 5, 2014

It is not so important what a teacher knows, but who a teacher is.

Rudolf Steiner

This applies only to the teachers of children, and not those of youth. Let me give two examples:

In the Eleventh Grade (I was 16 years old at the time), I had a class in trigonometry. I had had no previous experience in the subject—I had only heard of trigonometry—I had never studied it and knew nothing of the trigonometric functions, equations, and so forth. The teacher, whose name I shall not mention, was a likable fellow. He had a way of endearing himself to others. But he knew nothing about trigonometry; he knew less than I did who had only heard about it! Needless to say, I didn't think much of his knowledge of trigonometry—or of him, for that matter. High school teachers and college/university professors should be experts in the subject they teach; the subjects they teach should be in their field of expertise.

In the Fourth Grade I was nine years old. This was in 1971-1972. I attended a private, international school in Tunis, Tunisia, North Africa that school year. The name of the school was the American Cooperative School of Tunis: ACST. Children from many nations were enrolled at ACST. We fourth graders had a class teacher by the name of Mr. Harris. He was from Northern California in the redwoods forest area. Jim Harris suffered from a rare disease for which there was no known cure. It ended in premature death. His wife wanted to have a child by him, but he would not, because the child would have inherited the gene for the fatal illness from which he suffered, and he cared too deeply than to leave the legacy of suffering and early death to another human being. His wife was upset with him; she wished to have a child regardless, but it was no use; his mind was made up. Mr. Harris refused to have a child.

All of us in the Fourth Grade dearly loved and deeply respected the man —I revered him as much as my own father, who was more important to me than any other man. Mr. Harris embodied the loving authority figure every child in its middle years needs (ages 7-14). He was lovable for the Sanguines, commanded respect from the Cholerics, his suffering was great for the Melancholics, and the Phlegmatics could only join in with the rest of the class in loving him. Yet I cannot remember learning a single thing from Mr. Harris—academically speaking. I remember only the man and our class.

Each week Mr. Harris brought his record player and LP collection of American folk songs into the classroom. He hand wrote the lyrics to some thirty of these folk songs and gave a mimeographed copy of each to every pupil. These songs surely reminded him of his home country that he must have missed in far-off Tunisia, in faraway North Africa. Mr. Harris played these LPs with the folk songs on his record player, and together we sang them. Soon, we all knew the songs by heart. I still know the melodies and lyrics to many of them after forty-two years:

500 Miles (*'If you miss the train I'm on, you will know that I am gone; you can hear the whistle blow a hundred miles... '*);
Dona, Dona, Dona (*'On a wagon bound for market, there's a calf with a mournful eye; high above him there's a swallow winging swiftly through the sky... '*);
Puff, the Magic Dragon;
Mariah (*'Away out West they got a name for rain and wind and fire; the rain is Tess, the fire is Jo, and they call the wind Mariah... '*);
The Everglades (*'Where a man can hide and never be found and have no fear of the bayin' hound, but he better keep a-movin' and a-don't stand still; if the skeeters don't get' im then the gators will... '*);
Four Strong Winds (*'Four strong winds that blow lonely, seven seas that run high, all these things that don't make come what may... '*)

and I remember them in connection with Mr. Harris and the Fourth Grade class of ACST, 1971-1972.

As my family knew how much I loved him, we invited Mr. Harris over to our home in Tunis for supper so that my parents could meet him, and he joined us one evening. My Mother also loved the man, and when, several years later, we learned he had returned to the United States to his home in Northern California, we tried to look him up, to locate him, but we never did learn what happened to dear Jim Harris. Rudolf Steiner's words ring most true for me, as I am sure they do for many: It's not so important what the teacher (or adult) with children knows, as who s/he *is*. This means being a loving authority figure and bearing the qualities required by the temperaments of the children.

Los Angeles
March 8, 2010

Knowledge and Humor

Why do genuine knowledge, which penetrates beyond life's surfaces and illusions and through all intellectuality (condescension, pedantry, semantics), politics, lies and rumors, materialism, cleverness and talent (when these are not utilized for creativity), religiosity and false spirituality, mental illness and immorality, to the essence and source of spiritual life (touching or drawing from the creative wellspring of the thinker/creative soul), and good humor invariably be in complement and, often, ready appearance, which is the one is at hand when and where the other is engaged? What about the writing genre of Horatian satire*, where humor is in a combination of elements, on one level, simultaneous with thought-provoking content that signifies penetrating observations into individual or societal ills, on another, for the purpose of change which is redemption? Or again, in characterizations of people who are multidimensional who play humorous roles in works of humorous fiction or comedies that are revelatory of real human nature?

It is because both knowledge and humor are fundamentally healthy in a spiritual sense. Those who are capable of real knowledge in any of its seven forms (the planets or destinies) are also able to appreciate if not create humor of some kind. This is not an indication of the level of understanding rather of perspective, for s/he who can know something can also sparkle with humor or wit, laugh at adversity and indigence, or smile with good humor and charm, and perspective is necessary for both. Only the healthy mind has perspective. Even some one who suffers from an illness of the mind may gain or glimpse knowledge and experience some kind of genuine humor.

Still, one may ask, perspective and spiritual health inclusive, what is the link between knowledge and humor? It is the nature of thinking that is responsible for knowledge to be joyous, although for some knowledge is a source or sorrow. We know that sorrow and joy are twin moods so they are both aspects of human feeling. We suffer our feeling that is therefore dear to us, our sadness and gladness, our somber earnestness and gleeful gaiety.

It is of interest that sorrow and joy can arise from knowledge, from thinking. We can say, "This I think and I feel." Conversely one may say, "My feeling for the truth of knowledge is my guide to the attainment of the same." Regards knowledge as the source of sorrow and joy, in creativity as in life these effects are found in tragedy and comedy (humor). However, pure thinking can be an enjoyable experience, a pleasure of a higher order, if hard work because it may necessitate application of will and mind. It may also be a solace to the thinker. This is thinking the thoughts of one who has already traveled the road of Self-knowledge. Such thoughts may be a comfort in all kinds of situations. One source is Christian Morgenstern (see quotes, below) who was writing humorous poetry when he died of tuberculosis at age 43. A more common kind of thinking may be contemplative as in philosophy.

Like all creativity, thinking is therapeutic: it has cleansing and healing powers. Similarly, good tears and laughter are 'good for the soul', because they allow an expression to our feeling that may be profound and know hurt. They are also healthy and surface from feeling that is deeper than emotion or expresses loving feeling in a sentience of pure innocence or delight. In the former we have the enthusiasm of the heart, 'hearty' tears and laughter, in the latter childlike naivety and playfulness of the soul longing for Christ. Who knows also cares (is understanding); every human being senses when human understanding is present. This includes the sorrows and joys of the human heart, and the very human experiences of grief, loss, and loneliness. We know we are not alone at such times, for Christ is our constant companion when we know any kind of suffering or pain.

Humor is a welcome friend if not sometimes a necessity when

misunderstanding becomes almost unbearable. This humor is good because it laughs in the face of pain and hardship, and it smiles in times of sore trial and tribulation.

The great German poet Christian Morgenstern writes, *Humor is the greatest freedom of the spirit. True humor is always masterful.* And: *He who has freedom, he who is really free, has a little smile with it.* And: *Laughter and smiling are door and threshold through which much good can enter the human being.* (*English translation by A. Lindgren*)

All manner of happy jesting and warm teasing is very therapeutic for the Melancholic. This helps to draw the self-contained soul out in friendliness and expression. Owing to their physical bearing and innate concentration abilities, Melancholics can withstand the most jesting and humor of all the temperaments. Christian Morgenstern was a great Melancholic. (see quotations, above) I once met a Melancholic man who is an equal to Christian Morgenstern and thus a great One. He jested with himself with tremendous self-expression, vigor, and humor, smiling and laughing the while. His joking made sense, mind you.

Humor is good that does not mock but understands, is not mixed or muddled but clear, does not offend but supports and encourages, does not trivialize but values, is not prejudiced or at some one's expense but unbiased, does not harm or hurt but helps and heals. Good humor is redemptive and springs from good will and a good heart or a loving soul.

Los Angeles
Culver City, California
May 26-27, 2011
October 6/8/23, 2014

* examples of Horatian satire are the works of the British Londoner Charles Dickens (1812-1870), the American Samuel Clemens ("Mark Twain") (1835-1910), and the operettas of the British librettist W.S. Gilbert (1836-1911) and composer Arthur Sullivan (1842-1900).

Thinking, Feeling, Willing, and Seeing

How one feels is how one sees the world. When sad and gloomy we see things blue and dreary. When glad and cheerful we see things bright and colorful. When dull and listless we see things vague and gray. When strong and vigorous we see things fresh and bold and clear. Our inner state finds resonance in the objects, atmosphere and colors around us. What we think and feel and will becomes for us reality in our perceived experiences. How different are the paintings of the different artists! How uniquely does each one of us see!

The outside world also plays into our thoughts and feelings, coloring our inner experiences. When it is dark and cold we must be positive, strong, and warm to fight the gloomy depression. When it is bright and warm we find it all too easy to lose ourselves in the expansive outbreath. In the mountains among the trees, lakes, and wildlife, and in the fresh, crisp air, we feel and think differently from when we are on the dirty, noisy, busy city streets where we must call upon our inner resources and take special care to *find beauty, notice love,* and *sense peace.* This can be a conscious acting from within, choosing the *positive,* maintaining inner *balance,* and living in the *spirit of love,* and is more vital in our modern society than ever.

1999

Reprinted with permission from Alan Lindgren, *By the Sunset there's a Door: Poetry, Prose, and Essays Celebrating Nature and Humanity* (Culver City: Sun Sings Publications, 2002), 253

Validity of Different Aspects and Viewpoints and the Human I

It can be quite delightful to hear a person exclaim one aspect of some one or something exclusive of another aspect already stated. Rudolf Steiner told the following joke. One person says about another, 'He is a vegetarian.' Some one else says, 'No, you are wrong. I know him, and he is a postman!'

It is clear the two are not mutually exclusive; one may play different roles and practice many things; this is quite usual. But there are aspects and viewpoints, which are all valid as well, but which some one might not readily consider or be aware of. This is the topic of this little study.

Not so long ago, theoretical science introduced the concept of relativity into the popular vocabulary. Soon, every one seems to be lightly tossing this concept about as though it were a truth that explains all things, or that it does away with fundamental principles and therewith the possibility and actuality of true knowledge. Something missing from these discussions is the fact that relativity is also relative.

My grandfather is a forebear of mine, but he is also a descendent of his grandfather. My grandson is a descendent of mine, but he may also be a forebear of his grandson. Thus our ancestors are progeny, and our progeny may also be ancestors. It is relative to the viewpoint of the individual under consideration in the lineage of the family or bloodline of ancestry and progeny. But for *me*, I *am*. I am not relative to myself.

Spiritually, I descend from myself, on down the line of incarnations or earth lives, because each soul-I is a species unto itself. This means I am eternal, my spiritual ego or I is eternal in me. There is no relativity in eternity. It is only when eternity enters time and space that development is a possibility or begins. And development is all about change.

Here we come to a key principle: development is a process that has a beginning, a middle that may be a turning point, and an end. Through this process of development, *forms* change. These forms change as an expression of inner gestures. So long there is development, these forms will be in a constant state of change. So there is nothing static about development; it is a process of continual change. These changes can be visible because they can be expressions of what is spiritually in motion. Then they are form changes.

Eurythmy is an art form of gesture that is not dance, mime, or gymnastics. Each sound has its own intrinsic gesture, each consonant and vowel in speech eurythmy, each tone in tone eurythmy. In eurythmy, the spoken poem is simultaneously visible, the performed musical composition is likewise visible. Hence, eurythmy is *visible speech* and *visible song*. Rudolf Steiner has this to say about eurythmy:

> *Man as we see him before us is complete in himself. But this completeness is the result of motion ... And when we develop eurythmy we are carried back to the very beginnings of motion ... God does eurythmy, and in so doing produces the human form.*
>
> *... for eurythmy means in a certain sense the making of gestures, yet not transient random gestures, but cosmic ones, loaded with meaning, such as cannot be otherwise and are not due to any human caprice.* (Eurythmy as Visible Speech, lecture of 24 June 1924.)
>
> *There is perhaps no art in which one is made so intensely aware of being at one with the cosmos, as in eurythmy.*

When the physical plane of existence has been left behind, and prior to reentry into it, there continues to be development. But this development is unseen from the physical plane of existence. Yet without this spiritual development, the form changes in the physical world would cease. There would be no impetus for change any longer. It is therefore essential, not what is visible, but what is unseen that causes everything on the physical plane of existence to occur. If we were to go about in the world trying to explain what is taking place that is visible to us everywhere using our senses and our brains, we would get lost in this world. Only when we consider the underlying causes may we begin to have some kind of understanding for what is actually taking place.

But what science does is to try to explain the world phenomena without any knowledge of the process of development, which is a fundamental principle of all domains, earthly and spiritual (heavenly). Or at least this has largely been the case from the time science made its entry into the picture. Exceptional is one scientist, all of whose work is based on this principle of development. He is the German romanticist genius Johann Wolfgang von Goethe (1749-1832). The Austrian seer and thinking giant and Goethe scholar-expert Rudolf Steiner (1861-1925) took this principle of development, applying it to spiritual realms and dimensions.

Material science looks for the causes of everything it observes, which is physical- material, in the outer aspects of these things, what is countable, can be weighed, and is otherwise measurable. But is doesn't go any further; it doesn't penetrate any deeper to the inner qualities. It systematically denies the spirit at work in and behind all things. So it is easy to see why the so-called 'theory of relativity' as a concept has found such popular appeal. People just go around saying everything in the world is relative; it's relative to everything else, they say. But if you think about it, you realize they are saying nothing. The relativity of everything to everything else isn't identical with discovering the hidden connections that live between all things that mutually affect one another, because these connections aren't arbitrary; they are not relative; they follow quite specific spiritual laws.

We said at the beginning, the human I isn't relative because it's eternal.

It is an entelechy that is connected with other spiritual entelechies following the two human spiritual laws of reincarnation and karma and other, higher laws in the life between death and rebirth. Each person as an I is entire, whole in himself, in herself, and in a process of becoming. Her/His viewpoint is therefore not relative in the same way as a goat, an apple tree, or a rock is relative. However, as do human beings, a goat, an apple tree, and a rock partake of qualities, and qualities are not relative because they are intrinsic and substantial, and not merely attributed and conceptual.

All substances have effects. Thus the mineral kingdom to which a rock belongs has effects, which are both real and specific. These effects are also not relative, because they result from the very nature of the mineral kingdom, which, as we said, are intrinsic and substantial. We know that minerals provide the basis for all plant life. From the soil, the Plant draws up minerals that serve the Plant's etheric body or life. The same is true of an apple tree and the plant kingdom, but at a higher level. We know that animals owe their life to the plants, which are directly beneath them. Likewise with a goat and the animal kingdom, whose effects are at a higher level yet. Mankind shed the animal kingdom·that we might become more perfectly human. Thus the animals made a great sacrifice for us, and we will redeem them in the future by tremendous love. Mankind is the highest kingdom on earth, whose effects are therefore the greatest. Human creativity is also beneficial for the angels, which are above us, not a kingdom on earth, but in the heavenly hierarchies. We see how each level or kingdom owes a debt of gratitude to the nearest lower level or kingdom.

There are other relationships here. Let us go into one more. Where there are very few plant egos, which are all at the center of the Earth (Rudolf Steiner), animals share group souls, group egos. Hence we say: a school of fish, a pack of wolves, a flock of sheep, a herd of buffalo. But each single human being is his own species; we are not interested in a group as we are with animals, but in the individual person. A goldfish tells me everything I need to know about all goldfish. What interests me about a bighorn sheep is in common with all bighorn sheep. If I know one nanny goat, then I know what interests me about all nanny goats. But I want to know about just you. I want to read your biography, learn about your personal and impersonal experiences; I want to know everything of significance in your life. Though in the context of larger group and world karma, I will know your destiny in you and you alone. I want to discern certain general qualities and characteristics about one of the seven destinies (planetary types) in coming to attentively know you and your biography, because each human being is one and only one of the seven. But you are also your own destiny which you create for yourself across reincarnations and are at times endowed with from the etheric or astral body of a great historical destiny. You are single or nothing.

Plants are generic. This corresponds to the genus or genera, which approximate the plant egos. Animals are kinds. What kind of animal, I want to know. Human beings are individual. The divine is isolated, individualized in each single one. This is the individuality.

Each spiritual I is an inner center, which must gain a deepening in itself to fulfill its true purpose or destiny. This deepening is a process, and like all processes, it takes place in transitions, in transformations. These lead to higher development levels. But there is one turning point of existence when the I experiences itself in a deeply inward and conscious manner for the first time. This is the decisive moment. The higher I descends and incarnates into the lower I (sentient soul, mind soul, and consciousness soul) and lower sheathes (astral, etheric, physical bodies), wide awake. This is no gradual change. In an instant, the individual knows. This places the divine directly in the center of one's own inner being, which is situated in the heart but that runs right through the entire soul-I. Then the lower I has become the vehicle of the higher, placing itself in Its service, in the service of the divine within. This higher divine principle now incarnates (see above). This divine principle is the true Name of each single human being, the genius or individuality. Each genius is a center. When two geniuses truly meet, they acknowledge, each the other. Where the one may be greater than the other, neither can replace another one. This is very important. It is not merely individual; it is the individuality or true Name (Spirit Self or Manas) that gives the individual his/her central core of being or 'I AM'. We know from spiritual history the 'I AM' is the only true name of Christ, who went by different names in different religions.

A glass of water may be seen as half empty or half full. The one viewpoint is not correct to the exclusion of the other; both are valid. Where the half-full viewpoint is the more positive one, the pessimistic half-empty viewpoint is also justified and has equal validity. But the inner experience of one's higher I, the 'I AM' or name of Christ centered in one's own (human) I, is not merely a valid viewpoint. It is the key, the beginning, the turning point, the essence, and the meaning of human existence. It is once and for all. Various standpoints and perspectives are all interesting and valid; we can learn from them. But they show themselves to be relative to this deeper and higher principle, the 'I AM' in the human I, and find their rightful place and significance in relation to it.

Santa Monica, California
June 4-5
Culver City, California
June 5, 2012
Los Angeles
October 9/11, 2014

Transitions, the Damascus Experience, and Gifts

Changes or developments happen in quite sudden transitions. This is true in nature and in inner human (soul) processes both: Changes are drastic; they are not gradual over long periods of time but proceed in leaps and bounds. If the preparation time for maturation to be receptive for such a change involves lifetimes in human terms and eons in world (evolutionary) terms, then it occurs in a single instant. The years, months, weeks, and days leading up to this moment are special ones, characterized by newness and great expectation, but they are regulated as well to ensure that all goes normally in the course of daily life. Here we are referring to the Damascus experience, the inner birth of Christ.

What is the Damascus experience, so named because of the Apostle Paul's (St. Paul) life-changing experience of Christ on the road to Damascus? This occurred after Christ's resurrection and the appearances of Christ to many, but limited in number, before His ascent into Heaven. It is the conscious vision of His Light in the Etheric and the conscious hearing of His voice (the etheric Tone). This vision and this hearing are breakthroughs in physical (sensory) experience to spiritual (soul) or supersensory perception, unprecedented to all experience hitherto known and knowable. The Damascus experience is for all human beings, and not for just the chosen few. It marks the beginning of Self knowledge because it brings Christ-knowledge in essence.

The period immediately following is a resolution or working things out made possible by this pivotal and deeply significant change. The first few years after the profound event are steeped in meaning; they are very full, unlike anything in the past. They are therefore unprecedented; one cannot prepare for them in any way, but only face them and live them in their fullness. What happens is decisive for all future developments; everything hinges on what is suffered, what is done.

Where thinking must guide all actions, the heart is the place of inmost time. What the heart feels is sacred; we experience the meaning of the inner sun of the heart. This is true, religious feeling, festive and dear. All who are changed gain this feeling; it is universally, inwardly human, divine-human, within. It is also radiant as the sun is radiant.

Where before the change self-discipline is preparatory, following it conscience activity with self-discipline is responsible for the entire future in each present moment. One walks the good path in balance between the two extremes. With the awareness of the inner Christ, this is a harmony that can be established in the soul, a balance among the thinking, feeling, and willing soul faculties.

At first, life is corrective. Because one is headed surely for the destination, any falling away is an impossibility. Christ, the inner guide, assumes directional power and ensures any guilt is suffered in a matter of months, which can be very hard to bear. This is in contrast to the karma created and suffered from lifetime to lifetime.

There is, however, a point in time that, when crossed, cannot be refigured, undone, or repeated. It is in this sense the moment of absolute decision. There is no going back. Every one who comes to this point wills it to cross over; everything has led up to it for this purpose. Questions are asked; the answers are felt but are not allowed to influence the decision. This is necessary, because otherwise self-knowledge would necessitate the recollection of preexisting conditions of soul. Then the person would look back before the immense progress of the immediate past, before even the progress leading up to the Damascus experience (the soul's awakening), when old ways were changed and overcome.

A new knowledge, a higher Self-knowledge has been gained. Christ, the 'I AM', has awakened the soul, the heart, the spiritual I (the Damascus experience). Now, by the inwards power of the 'I AM' within one's own

I, the true goal and meaning of all human existence has been found: the sharing of the Meal, when in one's brethren Christ knocks at the door and one opens, and we sup: Christ and you and I, we three. This is the meaning of selfless love and is the very subsistence, without which one cannot live.

One has come so far. On this crossing over, with the soul's inner power of Christ, healing takes place from within. One is entirely free in each moment in inner decision that manifests in the real world. It all depends on self-mastery and self-restraint: finding and maintaining poise in the middle without the earlier corrective of life. Now, in each present moment, one asks the Christ within for help to find the balance, which he does, so long one is awake, attentive, and active. One must be self-corrective in the sense of inwardly attentive or there is no corrective at all.

Because of the new communion, the time after the threshold crossing is most special. Firstly, one cannot live without the Meal. It is one's cross and one's life, one's trial and one's salvation. But something else has come into existence: Gifts hitherto non-existent appear in a beautiful inwardness and in full power of the Christ-filled I. These two are one: inwardness in quiet times and inner power in open engagement.

The three soul activities: thinking, feeling, and willing are independent of one another. One may activate them singly, in pairs, or all three simultaneously. The divine essence in the I is central. It has always been, but now there is a new beauty because selfless love appears everywhere. This selfless love from the Christ within is ever reborn in the soul and heart, in the I, but it is manifest in the spiritual-physical environment. While it touches all who can be touched, because of its purity and selfless character it is itself quite untouched. One will only serve and in serving help one's fellows. This is Christ-service by Christ-love.

When, with you, I break the Bread and take the Cup, a service is reenacted, one which Christ Himself first performed with his disciples. All who are human understand this; it requires no education or explanation. Now it happens that a look, a smile, a word, a tone, a thought, a gesture, listening—or simply one's presence—communicates because of these new abilities, this gift, and by this communication—with love—teaching is now a possibility, is a reality. Knowledge of the spirit—of the Christ—is conveyed through love, and this combination educates according to the planet.

This knowledge or communication experience awakens the forces or activity of conscience, thereby bringing about the inner conditions necessary for communion: sacramental and spiritual both. This is the one gift: communication and thereby education of the spirit through conscience: communion, the sharing of the Meal.

Other gifts may join this one, specific gifts: practical ones in daily work-tasks; scientific ones in research, learning, and insight; artistic ones in creation in the various art forms; the religious priesterly or pastoral gift —the dearest, deepest gift of all. We feel those with the religious gift who care so deeply, because theirs is the great heart of dear suffering and sorrow or joy, which is heartening. At the same time it brings home to our hearts the solemnity and cheer with which they bear their crosses, on which they die, which they do for us, because they love us and are Christ-presences for us in our time of need. With Christ, they never let us down. All who are gifted bear that which is formed within them out into the world, where it is of service to the work of Christ in and on the Earth.

Santa Monica, California/April 22, 2012
Culver City, California/April 24, 2012
Los Angeles/October 8, 2014

My Writing for Adult Self-Education and the Four Temperaments

The subject of the four temperaments is my single longest interest, going back to my high school days in the late 1970s at Highland Hall Waldorf School in Northridge, California. At that time it was but a hobby for me. I could easily determine a person's temperament by their build, carriage, stepping, and other outer expressions. And I liked doing this. But it was when I purchased the book by Caroline von Heydebrand, *Vom Seelenwesen des Kindes* (*Childhood: A Study of the Growing Soul*) in an anthroposophical bookstore in Hamburg, Germany, in my 20th year of life that I began to take up the study in earnest (1982). Combined with countless clear inner and outer observations of people in my own life, as well as historical personalities, my understanding of this 'spiritual psychology' gradually deepened to its present form that is comprehensive and complete. Because our etheric body, which determines the temperament or habit-nature, is the transition between the physical body and the soul, the outer and inner aspects of each temperament cannot rightly be seen separately. They form one whole. I have presented the temperaments perhaps more clearly and thoroughly than any other motif in the non-fiction section of *The Wood of Green*.

I have written more frequently and more material on the four temperaments than any other subject since 2001, when I began writing non-fiction. I recently completed a study entitled *Learning throughout Life* that includes a large section on the temperaments with many new insights and nuances, one of dozens of my articles, studies, and essays with content on this theme. (December 10-19, 2012) On a website for my written work and visual art (2002-2005) there were more hits on the temperaments essays than on anything else—tens of thousands—which reflects the major and growing interest in this topic today. A series I wrote on the four temperaments was published in the early 2000s in Highland Hall's newsletter *Rhythms*. So I may justifiably name myself an expert in this pedagogically important field, which is also a key for adult self-education for very important spiritual progress and its rich fruits, which lays the foundation for all future development at the same time.

All the great ones have applied huge amounts of work spiritualizing (transforming) their temperaments, and with tremendous results. They continue to do so, because the etheric body can be ever more transformed into Life Spirit—the Christ-principle—, the member of man experienced in the element of light ether or Christly love, so this work is always ongoing. Only the transformation of the extremely dense physical body into Spirit Man or the Father-principle, the member of man experienced in the element of warmth ether or Divine Will (quiet peace-strength), requires more patience and work. This work is much slower yet. But everyone may perform the work addressing the one-sidedness of habits inherent in each temperament by developing the opposite habits and qualities. This is our daily task. Thus understanding the temperaments and implementing the practices given to accomplish this lifelong task are invaluable to each and all.

What all of this means is that anthroposophy is as living and pertinent today as it was during the first quarter of the 20th century. One must only take up the thoughts and impulses of the initiators, the Sun-Initiates, beginning with Rudolf Steiner (1861-1925) and his inner circle, but also the other greats and lesser ones, including the gifted class teacher at the first Waldorf School that opened in Stuttgart in 1919, Caroline von Heydebrand (1886-1938), whom Steiner praised for her work with the children.

In earlier German printings of her book a Foreword by her friend Maria Röschl-Lehrs ends with a poem written by the gifted teacher. In it Heydebrand directs the reader's perception to the Christ sitting at the Table in the soul-eyes of our brother, shining radiant bright through the temperaments. So the deeper goal of this teacher, whose life-task was working with children in middle childhood and thus with the temperaments for their balancing, that was foremost in her thoughts and all that she did, and to which she was devoted, was not the temperaments. It was the perception of Christ in the human soul.

We note here what is essential: Christ and the human soul; but without the temperament/s (etheric body and heart), Christ cannot be perceived in a human being. And without the balancing of their one-sidedness, the extremes of insanity, frenzy, madness and imbecility can and do occur. We are assured the children under Caroline von Heydebrand's care did not succumb to these conditions, and that if they tended in their direction she saved them from them, while helping many more develop the opposite qualities to a much greater degree in a healthy fashion. Heydebrand's knowledge arose from working directly with the children with warm understanding and love, but her insight was far clearer and deeper than is ordinarily the case in our time. One has the opportunity in working with this age group to do tremendous good. Middle childhood is the plant of human life (7–14 years). We know if a plant is healthy, there will be rich leaves, beautiful blossoms, and good fruit.

The clear ideas, unique qualities, and life-bestowing spiritual impulses of anthroposophy cannot find their way into human lives without personal objective knowledge (experience). A person may memorize an entire lecture or series of lectures, or a book, by Rudolf Steiner and know nothing about its contents, or about the experiences the thoughts point to. I possess firsthand knowledge (personal, objective experience), so when I read a text by Rudolf Steiner or by another seer and thinker, it means something to me; I understand it directly. I can also bring these contents into my own form as I personalize and individualize the thoughts. The essence and awakening of knowledge (objective experience) is Christ. He who would know his true Self and his fellow human beings, Creation (the natural world), society, history, evolution, religion, and spiritual dimensions (the 'dead', the hierarchies, and the holy Trinity) must therefore know Christ. This knowledge and its awakening are at the heart of anthroposophy.

In taking initiative many individuals and groups of individuals working together apply the ideas of anthroposophy of a practical, scientific, artistic, or religious nature with the most beautiful results, because Rudolf Steiner and all great Sun-Initiates are the most practical of human beings. This includes pedagogy (Waldorf education, the Steiner

Waldorf Schools), special education (including Camphill communities or 'villages'), agriculture (bio-dynamics, farming and gardening), medicine (anthroposophically-extended medicine), religious renewal (the Christian Community), creative speech (speech formation), singing (the School for Uncovering the voice), painting (veil painting that is watercolor), eurythmy, architecture (organic architecture), economics and society (threefolding), and much else.

Ideas are the content of anthroposophy; practices, with the living spiritual impulses, their implementation. Thus anthroposophy is rich in content, in ideas, but it is essentially *life*. The non-fiction section of this volume is intended to inform readers with ideal content, with living concepts and thoughts covering a broad range of knowledge. This is not only for intellectual interest. It is for the awakening power of living thought and the deeper interests of students of life. In this sense it will become an invaluable companion for English-language readers who are on their own individual path or who seek such a path. It undertakes to address, not one kind of thinker, but all seven.

I am not a simple thinker, neither do I think in generalities. But because my insights and thus my writing is less complex and detailed than that of the greats, my work is more accessible to the novice, who may therefore find the thoughts more comprehensible. Thoughts that are personalized and individualized from great and lesser gifted thinkers enhance my work and are found throughout *The Wood of Green*.

What is more themes that I have lived with for many years—the four temperaments in particular, but also the sun, the sunlight, plants and their blossoms, the sunrise and sunset, Christ-clouds, birds, the pulse-beat of the course of the seasons (outer natural and inner spiritual connections, spring and Eastertide, summer, autumn and Michaelmas, Advent, Christmastide and winter), the holy Trinity, color, words with their speech sounds and the rhythms of language, other phenomena and their qualities—are extremely well-expressed in my writing, prose and poetry, because of my deep or fine, clear and rich experiences of them. Often I convey a particular insight or insights with substantial points or subtle nuances that are entirely original. Frequently I draw from my own, innate creative wellspring which births budding life in the spirit, enriching my work with soul experience and spiritual essence. I always consciously experience the thoughts I think in wakeful clarity. They are my objective knowledge that is experience, perception of lucid truth.

Taken together everything published here makes up a portion of my objective knowledge that may be of interest and help to you as they have me. A great many of my 1500 poems contain objective content as well. For this reason, coupled with their richness of soul, I have included 109 recent, previously-unpublished poems of mine. Some of the material concerns the seven destinies (planetary types) or destiny as a spiritual law (karma), which signifies reincarnation and karma. I have given place to the theme and great Sun-Being of Light, the Light God Christ, and much else of relevance. Much of my pertinent written work is *not* included simply because the scope of *The Wood of Green*—one volume —did not allow it. However, this large non-fiction section has a breadth of knowledge not found except in anthroposophical literature where it is to be expected.

That is why I write and publish, for adult self-education, for the learning and guidance of adults who seek the help to be had through study. This does not preclude application and life-experience; it is meant as a stimulus and to awaken consciousness, as well as for learning which can be gained from books. My work on the temperaments is to be noted especially in this regard.

Los Angeles
December 19/22-23, 2012
February 9, 2013
October 8, 2014

* Caroline von Heydebrand, *Vom Seelenwesen des Kindes* (mit einem Vorwort von Maria Röschl-Lehrs) (Taschenbuch, Freies Geistesleben, November 1982)

† Caroline von Heydebrand, *Childhood*: *A Study of the Growing Soul* (Anthroposophic Press, 1995)

The Four Temperaments and Fourfold Man

Behavior is the mirror in which everyone shows their image.
Johann Wolfgang von Goethe

A Word on the Use of the Words 'Sanguine', 'Choleric', 'Melancholic', and 'Phlegmatic'

In our usage, the words 'Sanguine', 'Choleric', 'Melancholic', and 'Phlegmatic' connote the four temperaments, as described below. In literature and common use until recent years, when the concepts of the four temperaments are coming into popular consciousness and discussion, these words are adjectives with often emotional or negative connotations. For the purposes of clarity, I am capitalizing them. Used here, they are the four etheric types or habit-natures, just as male and female are the two physical types. Unlike the two physical types (male and female, with rare exception), combinations of two or three are common, less so a balance of all four temperaments. Then one is always predominant.

The Significance of Work on the Temperaments Beginning in Childhood

We cannot overemphasize the importance of work on the temperament or habit-nature for every destiny's personal, spiritual progress. With children in middle childhood it is up to the teacher, parent, and other key adults in their lives to help them cultivate good (temperament) habits. Then a good beginning has already been formed and made, which will be the foundation for the rest of life.

The Child and Temperament

If the child is too outgoing, cannot sit still, has a short or very short attention span, then the teacher or other adult must be lovable. Through its natural love for the teacher, the child will take a more extended interest in the lesson. This is the Sanguine boy or girl.

If the child is bold, brave, blunt, strong-willed, assertive, and focused, the teacher or other adult must never show a weakness. She or he must demonstrate an absolute command over the subject, else the child's respect be forever lost. It is through esteem and admiration that the Choleric child loves its teacher. Such a child might express love for its teacher by throwing a snowball at him or her. It is very beneficial for the Choleric to hear stories of courage and valor, of heroes and heroines, gallant and mighty individuals who have achieved great things.

If the child is introverted, reticent, observant, stays to its self, minds its own business, and is a little egoist, then the teacher must have suffered a great deal in life. It is only through compassion for genuine suffering that the Melancholic child is able to forget itself. Through selfless compassion this child will love its teacher. For this reason, it is good for the Melancholic to learn about the lives of saints and martyrs, of the tremendous suffering of humanity.

If the child is lazy, lethargic, dull, slow, slumped over, apparently disinterested, loves food, is sensuous, the teacher can gain no influence over the child directly whatsoever. It is only through its peers, through camaraderie in the classroom that the Phlegmatic boy or girl wakes up from its slumber and joins in so that it may say: *We love our teacher.* This temperament is truly remarkable and can demonstrate qualities of genius. A half an hour can go by where the child is dreaming about eating its lunch or snack, or secretly and quietly taking out an apple from its sack and ritually chewing and eating it up. If the teacher, however, calls on the child, and asks it to recount what has been said, it can recite everything from memory. Brilliant recall.

Temperament and Spiritual Development

We are what we repeatedly do. Excellence, then, is not an act, but a habit.

Aristotle

If we are to progress as adults, we must take up our own, self-education. Work on the temperament or habit-nature—which is slow and difficult in that it requires years of daily application to show real benefits—is the single most important task to which we can devote our selves. When we make headway in this work, we are doing our selves and our fellow human beings a great service. This is the foundation of all development. Only when we transform on our selves are we of service to humanity.

There are certain physical traits and soul qualities associated with each of the four temperaments. This is because the temperament is determined by the etheric body, which lives between the physical body —which it shapes and forms in the growing child—and the soul or astral body—where it has another impact. This would be in the person's behavior, where the temperament also manifests outwardly.

Temperament always involves one-sidedness. Therefore one needs to develop the qualities inherent in the opposite temperament, all those things that come only naturally to persons of the temperament opposite one's own.

The Tasks of the Temperaments

Sensitive to and appreciative of light- and color-phenomena, the broad-shouldered, well-proportioned, often tall *Sanguine*, who has outer hobbies and interests, can withstand tremendous ego pressure and concentration and great sorrow, for she is a loving, selfless, and mobile soul (and body) and is quick to forgive and forget, *but she greatly needs and appreciates esteem (self-regard.)* The Sanguine needs to prolong her attention span and develop deeper, lasting interests through observation in perception and thinking, practice and learning in reading, writing, music, and the visual arts. She does this through love and caring work with patience. She needs to receive impressions and to live with their inner effects for years. But she should also allow herself her sanguinity and flit from one thing to the next sometimes.

The Sanguine has a predominant soul relative to a small ego. This signifies astral (soul) mobility, flexibility, resilience; quick to forgive and forget, but a surging thought life, wordy, a short attention span. The nervous system is accentuated in the Sanguine. Loves the lovable. Has outer hobbies, outer interests. Gifted color sense, sensitivity to light and color phenomena. She has a lilt in the step and a twinkle in the eye. Most beautiful sense of interest, spontaneous, open, and aware.

The bold, brave, blunt, compact, often short *Choleric*, who has a strong will directed outwards, can endure great soul hardship and struggle and much indifference and apathy, for he has a strong, certain, forceful, and esteemed ego, *but he so needs and appreciates love*. The Choleric needs to expend his excess will-force energy on small unshakeable facts, facts because they do not budge. And when he has gone too far he needs to be faced with the seriousness of what he has done by one whom he respects. It is also therapeutic for him to do repetitious (daily, weekly, seasonal, yearly), mundane, ritual physical tasks and chores. Hearing stories of great heroes and heroines, great individualities and destinies with outstanding achievements is therapeutic. Reading biography is therefore extremely good for him. S/he needs to say of himself, *I could never have done that*. The Choleric has a ready sense for gesture, form, and spatial relationships, such as the placement of furniture in a room.

In the Choleric the ego or I is emphasized. This means compact soul, etheric body, and physical body, stunted growth, often short. The Choleric is stout hearted, bold, blunt, brave, assertive. He has ego's certainty of its goal, a strong will directed outwards. Here the blood in its circulation, and a firm gait with an added push into the ground for will-emphasis. The Choleric has a bold, even black eye and the sense for the human hand, face, head, and body in form, feature, and gesture. Spatial sense. Strong will directed outwards. Absolute good will. An innate sense of dignity. Carries a grudge when offended. Uncomfortable feelings are difficult to master. With his strong will, he is capable of the most difficult, self-mastery. The most beautiful sense of compassion, strong, courageous, and supportive.

The lean, often wiry *Melancholic*, whose sense for thoughts and the craft of words is emphasized, and who does a lot of thinking, especially about how others affect her, can tolerate much etheric liveliness and passionate expression, all manner of joy and happy teasing and jesting, for she has great compassion and a firm and unbending physical bearing, *but she so needs and appreciates interest*. The Melancholic needs to occupy herself with the tremendous suffering and soul trials of Mankind, of saints and martyrs, and of people in her own life, so that she forgets herself in selfless compassion. Warm teasing, which draws her out of herself in good humor, also does her great good, and it does wonders for her to go out-of-doors in the fresh air and sunshine. Like all of us, if especially, she needs caring friends.

In the Melancholic the predominant physical body sets up obstacles to the lower three members. This means lack of astral mobility, etheric ease (relaxation difficulty), and ego's goal certainty. Has physical bearing. The sensory organs are pronounced. Gifted with words and thoughts, has the sense of word-craft. Does a lot of thinking, especially about how others affect her. Is highly sensitive. When hurt, carries the pain around for years. Trouble letting go. Is deeply compassionate. Loves to dwell on suffering. Obsession with death and dying, not morbid as it would be in the other temperaments. Firm, dragging gait. Sad eye. Most beautiful esteem of all the temperaments, dignified and noble.

The expansive, corpulent bodied *Phlegmatic*, who has a kind of an inner life, can patiently endure much physical pain and suffering and put up with great physical discomfort and can withstand *unmoved* powerful assertions and willful attacks, for he has much etheric ease and even, serene steadiness and can survey and listen to everything that is placed before him with unbiased interest and cannot be directly influenced by another person, *but he so needs and appreciates kindness and compassion.* The Phlegmatic should, from time to time, sit in an otherwise empty room with four walls and really feel his lazy boredom so that, from within himself, he will resolve to *do* something, get up and take action. It does him great good to be around a loud, lively, and friendly group of peers in whose company he will take a warm shared interest. The Phlegmatic awakens in the Tone.

The Phlegmatic has a predominant etheric body. Great etheric ease, is naturally easy-going. Good at relaxing. Has a large ego, soul, and expansive physical body. Here it is the glandular system. Lazy. Disinterest. Apathy. Sensuous. Romantic. He likes food. Is interested in food. Likes to eat. Thinks a lot about food. He is musical and has an innate sense of rhythm. The multifaceted genius. Missteps. Has a dull eye. Most beautiful love, serene, even, steady.

Nelson Mandela (1918-2013), the South African leader, was behind the first 'peaceful revolution' which took place in South Africa. He was a Phlegmatic. One day the system of Apartheid that separated South African blacks from whites still existed. On the next it was gone for good. There was no bloodshed, violence, or quarrel, not even bitterness. Blacks who had formerly been servants to whites were drinking tea and visiting good-naturedly with their former bosses as friends.

What Mandela did as a Phlegmatic can be a good example for all of his temperament. He performed very physical labor on Robben Island off the coast of South Africa where he was imprisoned from 1963 to 1982—for nineteen years. He chipped and moved rocks from one location to another. He sewed mailbags. Then he was transferred to Capetown to a mainland prison for eight years. His dignity and courage never faltered and enabled another prisoner to endure the hardship by way of example.

Several years ago I happened to be watching television, something I do rarely. Oprah was on and Nelson Mandela was her special guest. Before millions of people across America, this world-famous leader made the following statement: *If you want to change society and the world, you have to change yourself.* These are profoundly true words. America may have heard them, but it is dubious most of the people watching took much notice or remembered them. Yet this did occur, and it is nothing short of outstanding. But what is really significant is what Mandela, together with a few of his close friends, accomplished, the first peaceful revolution in the history of humankind. By personal transformation, they were able to effect social transformation, change on a large scale.

Cesar Chavez (1927-1993), a Mexican-American Choleric, achieved something similar with the poor farm workers in California. We have heard of Mahatma Ghandi (1869-1948), a South African Choleric of Indian descent, what he accomplished for India through non-violence and self-discipline. Ghandi's non-violent method has become standard for many, including Mandela, Chavez, and M. L. King, Jr. (1929-1968) The main difference between the movement led by Ghandi in India and that of King here in America, is that King's was truly Christian, a Christ Kingdom on earth movement. Christ was very great in King.

I had a friend in Berlin who was studying history at the university there. This was in 1982. His Mother was the chief gardener at the Waldorf School in Berlin. She was a Phlegmatic. In the 2010s a woman in her late fifties came to our home in Culver City, California. She was hired to do some housecleaning. I joined her part of the time in cleaning the large living room window as cleaning both sides at once for visibility does the best job. But she carried out everything else on her own. A housekeeper, she is a Phlegmatic. We have already discussed Nelson Mandela. In these examples, the people are or were doing the most significant work they could be doing. They are Phlegmatics performing physical labor.

For Cholerics the task is the opposite. This involves expending excess will-force energy on small facts, facts because they will not budge. This is for relaxation. Performing mundane ritual physical tasks and chores, each day, each week, each year. This also serves to expend their excess will-forces whereby relaxation and feeling make themselves felt. We think of Ghandi and Chavez, who also harnessed their strong Choleric wills to effect peaceful change in the lives of human beings oppressed and discriminated against for their ethnicity. Single-handed, Ghandi was responsible for freeing India from the British yoke. Chavez was the first President of the United Farm Workers Union. All repetition is healthy for the Choleric. Read the same book every year for many years, preferably for decades. Biography is particularly good. The Choleric must take in and feel. This must be practiced for years—throughout life. Most great Cholerics in the sense of self-transformation are unknown to the public. Cholerics stand out socially by nature.

For Melancholics the work is again of a different nature. These people do a lot of thinking. They can concentrate for long periods of time without particular effort. They are observant, but everything is in relation to them selves. They are strongly centered in them selves. They have great difficulty in taking a spontaneous and open interest in their surroundings and in other people, noticing light and little things in passing. Self-expression is thus of primary importance. Looking around, sharing thoughts and feelings in an open outgoing fashion, laughing with good humor, all self-expression is their temperament task in life. Rudolf Steiner was a very, very gifted and great Melancholic.

The Sanguine is opposite the Melancholic. Hence her work must accomplish what comes naturally to the Melancholic. The naturally short attention span needs to be slowly lengthened, little-by-little, over long periods of time. Receiving impressions and allowing them to sink in where they go on working. In this way, intuitions or insights arise.

Deeper, lasting interests must develop, especially in one field, from an outer hobby or interest to expertise, knowledge, and excellence achieved by study, writing, or practicing a musical instrument. Or, in the case of Mozart (1756-1791), the great Austrian Classical composer child prodigy and genius, composing over 600 major works before his death at age 35. Mozart suffered a great deal. This also signifies progress and spiritual development. Most great Sanguines are unknown to the public. There are a few major exceptions, Mozart, we have noted; Lazarus-Christian Rosenkreutz-the Count of St. Germain (a composer); Raphael (1483-1520); and Jesus of Nazareth, in reverse order of greatness. The Lazarus personality is the greatest of the Sun destinies, Raphael of the all destinies of Earth, Jesus of Nazareth of all destinies.

The Temperaments and the Four Gifts

The *love of the Phlegmatic* lies in *serenity, calm, and evenness*. This is *beautiful*. This is *good practice for the Choleric*.

The *love of the Sanguine* is *fond, likable, humane, and forgiving*. This is *good for the Melancholic*.

The *esteem of the Melancholic* is in *dignity and nobility*. This is *worthy of the Sanguine*.

The *esteem of the Choleric* rests in *graciousness*. This is *worthy of the Phlegmatic*.

The *compassion of the Choleric* is *courageous, supportive, and steady* (*focused*). This is *worth his striving for the Phlegmatic*.

The *compassion of the Melancholic* is *caring, kind, dear, and selfless*. This is *good for the Sanguine*.

The *interest of the Sanguine* lives in *openness, spontaneity, awareness, and perception*. This is *beneficial for the Melancholic*.

The *interest of the Phlegmatic* is in *factual statements*. This is *beneficial for the Choleric*.

Finding the Opposite Qualities in the Temperaments: A Poem

Sadness of the Sanguine
See it in his smile

Contentment of the Choleric
Watching all the while
Gladness of the Melancholic
Witty, lively, and
Good cheer of the Phlegmatic
Good will in arm and hand.

Alan Lindgren
August 18, 1999

Brief Characterizations of the Four Temperaments

In the SANGUINE the natural sensitivity and appreciation is for the realm of COLOR, whose life she loves. The element is the fresh AIR and out-raying and vigorous LIGHT. We find colors in the heavens in rainbows and at sunrise and sunset, flowers, and butterflies. The color specific to the Sanguine temperament is the warm, bright, and friendly YELLOW. The mood is a sunny morning. Physically the Sanguine is broad-shouldered, well-proportioned, and usually tall. The bodily system is the nervous system with the brain. The form of speech for the Sanguine temperament is the exclamation! Sanguines are mobile, flexible, and resilient, quick to forgive and forget. They have a surging thought-life with outer hobbies, outer interests. Concentration is paramount for this temperament with a short attention span. This is prolonged little-by-little by intentionally lengthening concentration on a line of thought or piece of music for a minute or so, then allowing oneself to flit from one thing to the next for a while to then return to the intellectual task or study once again. In this way, over a period of months and years, the attention span increases to half an hour, forty-five minutes, an hour, or more. Insanity is the danger of the Sanguine. Therefore concentration is the key for this temperament. The Sanguine's mobility can become solely an inner reality where the entire being is pointed to ever greater concentration but is never be diminished by weighty physical bearing. Indeed nothing of her beautiful spontaneity, flexibility, and resilience is lost in spiritual development rather only blossom but in a purely inner way. Their interest is the most beautiful of all the temperaments, open, aware, and spontaneous. The Sanguine child is like a bird, corresponding to the animal kingdom.

The CHOLERIC has the sense for FORM, GESTURE, and SPATIAL RELATIONSHIPS, as in the placement of furniture in a room and the man or a woman walking down the street. Esteem resides in the strong will directed outwards in what is solid and gestural for this bold, brave, and blunt temperament. The Compassion of the Choleric is supportive, strong, and courageous. The element is powerful condensing FIRE. The mood is the noontime or daytime sun. We find form in the reposing stone, in the mineral. The color for the Choleric is the focused RED. In the physical body the Choleric is compact and usually short. The bodily system is the blood in its circulation. The form of speech is the command. Cholerics are goal-oriented and assertive. They have the ego's certainty of its goal. They will accomplish what they set out to do. It is healthy for the Choleric to read biography, especially about individuals who have accomplished great things, great achievements such that he can say, I could never have done that. Learning about the lives of great heroes and heroines is very good for the Choleric. Repetition is therapeutic, performing mundane physical chores and tasks on a daily, weekly, monthly, seasonal, and annual basis, also rereading the same book each year for many, many years. Frenzy is the danger of the Choleric. Therefore ease and relaxation is key for this temperament. Will forces solely in the abdomen can be developed and intensified such that the greatest expansiveness and huge vagueness of soul expressed in a warm puffy physical body will never lessen them. Indeed they only grow more powerful as pistons firing in the gut. The Choleric is typified in the young man or woman. His is the kingdom of Man.

Melancholy men are of all others the most witty.

Aristotle

The MELANCHOLIC has an intuitive sense for THOUGHT and a natural interest in the craft of WORDS. The innate sense of compassion is expressed in words and the thoughts. Both are esteemed by the noble and dignified Melancholic. We encounter words and thoughts in the question, in the doubting human being. The element is lifeless EARTH. The Melancholic color is the complex, receding BLUE. The mood is the cooling evening with its long shadows and quiet thoughts. The sensory organs are emphasized in the Melancholic, who is lean, often wiry, and slender with a taut belly. The form of speech is the question?

Melancholics have physical bearing. They do a lot of thinking, especially about how others affect them. It is therapeutic for the Melancholic to be drawn out of himself in warm, friendly teasing, and happy jesting, for any kind of self-expression, soul-expresssion, passion, compassion, humor, conversation, talking, gesturing. It does her good no end to think on the lives of saints and martyrs, on the tremendous suffering of humanity, and of people in her own life. Madness is the danger for the Melancholic. Therefore openness and self-expression are keys for this temperament. The natural physical bearing and dignity of this temperament of thinking is not lost in spiritual development when the etheric body becomes enlivened to intensive activity visible in all manner of outer expression. Indeed the more expressive and outgoing the gifted Melancholic becomes, the greater her physical body develops as an organ of expressive, outgoing bearing, the dignity of the spirit in happy and joyous thinking and feeling, now humorous, now in earnest, but always in vitality and outwards expression. The Melancholic takes comfort in the cold, hard, lifeless, mineral kingdom.

All geniuses were imbeciles in at least one previous incarnation.

Rudolf Steiner

The PHLEGMATIC awakens in the TONE. He is therefore naturally musical. The animals and birds with their songs and sounds are much beloved by the Phlegmatic, whose love is of the most beautiful kind, serene and even. Interest is the gift of this temperament of sensuality and romance. This includes a favorite subject food, very much liked and always thought about. The element of the Phlegmatic is WATER that is very relaxing and expansive. The mood is nighttime and the sea with its vastness of liquid and undercurrents of feeling. It becomes easy for the Phlegmatic to become so comfortable that a kind of lazy lethargy can set in that requires the activation of the sleeping will to overcome. It is therefore healthy for the Phlegmatic to sit in a room with four walls and no other furniture until he gets so thoroughly bored with himself that he gets up and does something, takes action. Also being in the midst of a warm, loud, and lively group of people in whose company he will feel uplifted, rubbing shoulders with other personalities in mutual exchange and shared interest. The color is the abundant and contented GREEN. The glandular system is responsible for the corpulent expanding physical body of the Phlegmatic, who is overweight or even obese if he was not kept slender as a child.

The form of speech is the statement as a fact is stated. Phlegmatics have etheric ease—a kind of an inner life. They experience this in their feeling. Imbecility (idiocy) is the danger for the Phlegmatic. Therefore focusing out into one's environment and will-activity are keys for this temperament. My father, a tall and big Phlegmatic, practiced both. Driving along in the front passenger seat of the car, he would suddenly point to a large billboard and say, "That spelling is incorrect! It's supposed to be _____!" The tremendous ease and serenity of the Phlegmatic soul is not altered when the individual develops ever greater degrees of habit-transformation rather lives behind the mighty focus and will directed outwards. Indeed the more powerful the will of the individual grows in the hands and limbs, in the bones, the more beautiful the perfected pure and serene love becomes, apparent only where the soul is focused in light and love. The Phlegmatic understands the simple green plant. He is at home in the plant kingdom.

The Temperaments As Proof of Reincarnation

The four temperaments are the actual proof of reincarnation. There must be four and not three or six or any other number of temperaments. Again, this is because of the etheric body, which is determined by the person's relationship to his surroundings in his past life.

(Ordinarily we do not remember our past earth-lives because most people were not conscious during previous incarnations.) If she took an interest in many things, but only a passing interest, then she will be a Sanguine in this incarnation. If he didn't take much of an interest in anything, then he will be a Phlegmatic in this life. If she kept herself to herself in her past earth-life, then she will be a Melancholic in this one. If he faced everything head on in his past incarnation, then he will be a Choleric in this one. This is because the etheric body, which determines the temperament or habit-nature, is determined by one of these four relationships to the world during the previous incarnation. In our past earthly life, we created our temperament in this one. Our temperament now reflects this exactly.

If a person was conscious (wide awake) in soul in the previous life, then she will have the same temperament in all succeeding incarnations. Thus the spiritualization of the temperament grows great indeed. Rudolf Steiner, Christian Morgenstern, Günther Wachsmuth (1893-1963), and Manfred Schmidt-Brabant (1926-2001) were Melancholics. Elisabeth Vreede (1879-1943) and Jörgen Smit (1916-1991) were Phlegmatics. Michael Bauer (1871-1929), Ita Wegman (1876-1943), and Albert Steffen (1884-1963) were Sanguines. They and Marie Steiner-von Sivers (1867-1948) were all great anthroposophists. Gérard Klockenbring (1921-2004) was a great anthroposophist and Christian Community priest and Seminary principal. He and Marie Steiner were Cholerics. The exception to this rule is persons of the Venus destiny, in which case the temperament alternates between opposites (Choleric-Phlegmatic-Choleric-Phlegmatic;   Melancholic-Sanguine-Melancholic-Sanguine). We have the Melancholic St. John the Evangelist; Raphael (1483-1520), the great Sanguine Italian High Renaissance artist and architect; Novalis (1772-1801), the great Melancholic German Romantic Era of genius poet and novelist; he will come again as a Sanguine; then a Melancholic, and so on. We know these personalities have the qualities and habits of the temperament opposite their own to an extremely high degree.

Secondary and Tertiary Temperaments

Frequently, a person may have a secondary, even a tertiary temperament. This will come to expression in the body, habits, and behavior as well. But we should keep in mind that when it comes to practical treatment (see "Diet, Water, and the Four Temperaments." and "Practical Wisdom and Christ", above) and work on the temperament, whether it is with the help of the teacher or another adult in childhood or in our own hands as adults, we are always looking at the primary temperament.

There is one combination of two temperaments that is the hardest on the individual. This is Choleric and Melancholic, with either one primary. The other neighboring temperament combination is rather pleasant: Sanguine and Phlegmatic (again, either one primary). Opposite temperaments can be most fruitful, because the teacher or parent can bring out the secondary temperament, thus helping to balance the primary one. Here we have Sanguine, Melancholic secondary; Melancholic, Sanguine secondary; Choleric, Phlegmatic secondary; and Phlegmatic, Choleric secondary. As an adult the person with opposite temperaments can also work on this balancing, but on her or his part intentionally and independently.

A Balance of all Four Temperaments

It also happens that a person has a balance of all four temperaments. As with secondary and tertiary temperaments, one always predominates, but when there is the balance of all four, a beautiful harmony exists not found in any single one or other combination. A true balance is found in such people, and this is something special to be treasured. I myself know of two such personalities in my youth; one of them who still lives on earth is almost eighty. What greatness, and how she struggles! The greater in spirit an individual grows, the greater the struggle. In my far more modest way, my life has been all about struggle and hardship. But from this suffering, and sometimes real misfortune, have come the most beautiful flowers and fruits, mainly poetry/writing, but also sculpture, singing, and classical piano. My vocation is poetry. I am a gifted Sanguine with Melancholic secondary. Through much practice, I have developed Melancholic qualities to a degree beyond most of my temperament combination. That is how the qualities inherent in the temperament opposite one's own are developed: through much practice.

Female and Male in Temperament, Sculpture, and Painting

In sculpture and painting both, the classical female model or ideal is always a soft Phlegmatic and very beautiful. This is true for humans and immortals (Goddesses). We think of Galatea, the Nereid or sea nymph in Raphael's fresco *The Triumph of Galatea* (1512). The Marys of Raphael's several Madonnas, his *Madonna and Child* (*Madonna with the Book*) (ca. 1503-1504), *Madonna and Child Enthroned with Saints* (altarpiece, 1504-1505), *Ansidei Madonna* (1505), *Madonna del Granduca* (1505), *Small Cowper Madonna* (1505), *Madonna del cardellino* (*Madonna of the Goldfinch*) (ca. 1505-1506), *Madonna del prato* (*Madonna Belvedere*) (1506), *Madonna of the Pinks* (ca. 1506-1507), *La belle jardinière* (1507), *Niccolini-Cowper Madonna* (1508), *Madonna of Foligno* (1510-1511), *Alba Madonna* (1511), *Sistine Madonna* (1512-1514), *Madonna della tenda* (1514), are all Phlegmatic women as well. Raphael was a Sanguine.

The classical male model or ideal in art is a Sanguine for humans and a

Phlegmatic for God or Gods. We think of the Sanguine Adam and Phlegmatic God in Michelangelo's famous painting *The Creation of Adam*. (Michelangelo was a Choleric.) Sanguines love beauty. This is significant in light of the facts that Sanguines have well-proportioned, naturally beautiful bodies. Jesus of Nazareth was a Sanguine. He had the most perfect human body.

Melancholics tend to be slim with smallish waists and taut bellies (subdued etheric bodies). The Melancholic possesses physical bearing. Often Melancholic women are known for their legs, like the famous French can-can dancers at the Moulin Rouge cabaret of Paris, and countless fashion models.

Sensuality and enjoyment in the Choleric temperament of compactness is healthy. It acts as a balance to the characteristic focused will of the predominant ego that acts strongly formative. This includes especially eating and efforts at relaxation, but all the bodily functions accentuated in the opposite temperament, the Phlegmatic. This goes for the Melancholic temperament as well, which experiences such difficulty in attempts at relaxation, owing to the predominant physical body.

Phlegmatics and Melancholics of both sexes may have beautiful physiques and legs, athletic, toned, or graceful. Added height only enhances this fact. As the Phlegmatic is the sensuous temperament, beauty is as common in Phlegmatics as it is in Sanguines. We have seen this fact in art, sculpture and painting both.

Aristotle, the great ancient Greek philosopher, stated that beautiful women are always tall. This makes sense in consideration of many Sanguine women. However, many men beg to differ. All human beauty comes from suffering in the previous incarnation. Here we mean face and body both. But beauty may be solely of a soul nature, seen in the eyes. We pay far too much attention to the outer person and too little to the inner. Looks may be deceptive. It is the soul that is eternal. The face and the physical body, inferior, fugly, unattractive, homely, plain, cute, adorable, coquettish, voluptuous, attractive, handsome, or beautiful, that is an expression of the soul, perishes. In truth only the soul remains.

(Los Angeles?)/July 2010
Revised Los Angeles
October 9/11-12/23; November 14, 2014

Historical Examples of the Four Temperaments

Sanguines

King David (of David and Goliath)
Jesus of Nazareth
Lazarus
Raphael
Christian Rosenkreutz
The Count of Saint Germain
Mozart
Schiller
Ita Wegman, MD
Michael Bauer
Albert Steffen
RFK (Robert F. Kennedy)
Katherine Hepburn
Whitney Houston

Cholerics

Alexander the Great
Michelangelo
Benjamin Franklin
Johann Gottlieb Fichte
Napoleon (Choleric with Phlegmatic secondarily)
Beethoven
Vincent van Gogh ("Van Gogh")
Auguste Rodin
Edvard Grieg
Marie Curie
Marie Steiner
Gandhi
Paul Robeson
Marian Anderson
Picasso
Dylan Thomas
Valentin Tomberg
Peace Pilgrim
Barbra Streisand
Barbara Walters
Gérard Klockenbring

Melancholics

St. John the Evangelist
St. Thomas Aquinas
Leonardo da Vinci
Franz Liszt
Chopin
Novalis
Abraham Lincoln
George Washington Carver
Rudolf Steiner
Christian Morgenstern
Rainer Maria Rilke
Eleanor Roosevelt
Aldous Huxley
Günther Wachsmuth
Manfred Schmidt-Brabant
Barack Obama

Phlegmatics

Moses
Aristotle
Mary, the Mother
Mary Magdalene
Wolfram von Eschenbach
Shakespeare
Johann Sebastian Bach
Johann Wolfgang von Goethe
Franz Schubert
Elisabeth Vreede
Winston Churchill
Ingrid Bergman
JFK (John F. Kennedy)
Sidney Poitier
Rev. Dr. Martin Luther King, Jr.
Nelson Mandela
Maya Angelou
Bill Clinton
Elton John
Madonna

Seven Planets, Seven People:
Real, Living Examples of the Seven Destinies

The seven human beings described here are unnamed as, to the best of my knowledge, all of them are still living. My father Arne Lindgren (1918–1994), a Sun destiny, who is compared with the Sun destiny of this study, is no secret.

Moon

Several years ago I lived in the same apartment complex as a man who is a Moon destiny. He is a small person, short and slight, of very white complexion, and very quiet. He spoke to me and to any one seldom. He was often to be seen on the premises watering the plants with focused attention, patience, and simple care. I know he devoted a good amount of his time to painting, for his roommate, with whom I was close friends, invited me into the apartment, and I saw his desk with his supplies and what he was working on at the time. Early evenings when it was cooling off, and on more than one occasion, I saw him sitting there quietly engrossed in his art, for the apartment door always stood open and his desk was right there. His work was original and of interest.

He chuckles to himself frequently and almost inaudibly, clearly delighting in his naive belief in his sex appeal, and with which it is apparent he has much fun.

But he had a terribly bad vice, which was the consumption of large quantities of salt. The amount of salt he ate would have been harmful to a person of any temperament, but as he is a Choleric such consumption did him harm no end. He is also by nature already extremely greedy and jealous. He added so much salt to his food that I would not have been able to eat it (and I salt my food well, a Sanguine), and every day he bought a bag of salted popcorn, popped it in the microwave oven, added a lot more salt to it, and ate the entire bag.

In spite of this unhealthy practice with salt he is a harmonious and balanced little man, and he is very wise behind what is perceptible to the physical senses. In addition, his keeping to what he is doing, and not diverted by others, or frivolous, signify wise choices on his part. This is seen in his never mingling with those around him, rather he is wholly devoted to his daily activities.

He once said to me that a certain lady (who is also a Moon destiny) was very hard on him. He said this was good for him. He said this with quiet emphasis, indicating it had personal meaning to him.

Now he smoked cigarettes. He said his roommate, whom I have mentioned, told him it is wrong to smoke cigarettes. Again, he said this with quiet will, and it was clear he took the statement personally, and as something he dearly valued. When I said there is nothing wrong with smoking cigarettes, he repeated what his roommate had told him, agreeing with him. He remembered his roommate (who has since moved) in remembering what he had said to him. This stood before him as something that could not be altered.

Although I moved from the apartment complex a long time ago, I still see him often, because I live in the same general neighborhood, and he frequents the library where I work. He is literate for he takes the newspaper, sits down in a comfortable chair that is too large for him, and reads the news, keeping up with the political scene, which is but an immature 'interest' of his. I know he enjoys his quiet life, though in soul he suffers, because he is wise, not only within, but also to his self-created karma, which he safeguards jealously. He never 'acts out' but keeps his strong little will in check. He is a recluse of sorts for he always minds his own business and never socializes or reaches out to others, but he is not a true loner because he is not isolative. For all that he is a nice small man, assertive in his quiet, unobtrusive manner, and when he does say something, however brief, it is friendly, very concise, and contains intelligent thought. He is a good fellow and one cannot help but like him.

Mercury

I have a friend, a Mercurial destiny, about sixty-five, a big and tall man with a flabby belly, and rather dignified in carriage and demeanor. Balding (he now shaves his beautiful, well-formed head), he keeps his fingernails neatly trimmed. He is always clean and shaven. He is often to be seen outside at different times of the day, early morning until late afternoon. He walks slowly and deliberately, and I know he is in no little physical pain. Life is an effort for him, but it is apparent he is positive in his efforts.

He is a quiet man who speaks with great care and with distinction, using few and well-chosen words. He is truly virtuous and a perfectionist, imposing great discipline on himself in his thoughts, speech, and behavior. In addition to his physical pains, he suffers from negativity, which I attribute to his perfectionism. Where someone would make life unbearable for me, he says only that they are irritating. This is a good choice of word, I think, for that is his relationship to negativity that he experiences it to be irritating. In spite of the demands he and life place on him, he repeatedly asserts his small will, and in the most remarkable fashion, as you shall see.

There is one woman who is like a mother to him. She is probably younger than he, but as he is like a child, and she is wise and good, he frequently goes to her, ever ready and waiting to help her carry her purse or bag, or perform some other service for her.

I have observed him on numerous occasions repeatedly going up to strangers, asking in a manner that indicates he is making an effort to be friendly, for a dollar. When they give him a dollar, he walks away. When they do not give him a dollar but refute him, or turn him away, he peers down at them from his great height and, motioning, waves at them with a distinctive hand-and-arm movement, as though he were bidding his son or a dear old friend farewell. But instead of tears at the separation, he only winces and, having made what was for him a greater effort to be friendly, which is as with every gesture he makes deliberate and sincere, walks away the stronger for it.

Similarly, when he offers to buy someone he loves a bottle of water, or a cheeseburger, out of his own pocket, he makes every effort to communicate his well-meaning friendship. This is often with the woman in whom he finds motherliness. When she accepts he does as he has promised, and dutifully brings her the bottle of water or the cheeseburger he has bought for her. When she turns him down, saying she already has water, or has already eaten, he is frustrated for his good efforts made from purely good intentions, and goes away wincing with still greater efforts, the stronger for it. In this manner, he makes what are for him tremendous efforts, in repeatedly reaching out to friends and strangers alike, helping them as they him in a healthy exchange. This has a humanizing effect.

Now I will bring up something altogether different, but of real interest. My friend is simple, at a child's stage of intellectual development; this is a manifestation of his karma. I have already said he is like a child, and this is the case. But he does understand much that a child cannot, even showing insight, if not knowledge or brilliance. Frequently, when he says something to me, I respond with a few words. At once, he pays mention to what I have said in way of reply, passing off lightly his immediate grasp of what I have said, from his own standpoint, but with insight. For example, I might speak of what is supersensible, the divine. Then he says, "I know, the eternal." This happens time and again. It is as though he is ready with the answers, but he cannot have learned them; that is unthinkable. Yet they are mature responses, and he makes them without hesitation as though they were to be expected. It should be said his understanding of these and other things is at the level of a child, but nonetheless he has some general idea. He is intelligent.

My friend lives in a child's consciousness for karmic reasons he must suffer. As for progress, from his daily efforts and great self-discipline, he accomplishes much, far more than most, handicapped or gifted. But what is so interesting is that he intuitively senses the truth or essences of things from the standpoint of his genius that is as yet not incarnate in him and unable to because of malformed physical capacities. Not only this, but he readily puts this fine sensing or intuition into words, always very few words, tossing them off lightly as though it were a given. There is genius in this, beyond a doubt, but it is unformed, not rightly grasped, because the physical vehicle for intellectual knowledge is damaged, setting him back to the level of a child, developmentally. But he is intelligent.

There is something far more significant than my friend's intuition. This is his understanding of his own karma, if in general terms, then with genuine comprehension. I still see my friend frequently. We live near one another. Just the other day he asked me how to spell the word *BIOGRAPHY*. I had to spell it very slowly, the last half again yet more slowly, as it is an effort for him to write. Writing is a great effort for him, but in this case it was VERY IMPORTANT to have it just right. He is a perfectionist in his own right, so I understood his concern for the correct spelling. But he was intent on spelling *this* word in his special book. It is this word that is of significance, mind you.

I am convinced he senses there is a deeper underlying meaning for his suffering his lifelong handicap that it is karmic. He knows, insofar his mind can grasp, it is his karma, with which he actively works in shaping his own biography by his for him tremendous efforts. It is his karma, which chose (created) his malformed body (mind) before birth, for this incarnation as the way to gather life experiences for his eternal individuality, his spiritual individuality for learning during sleep and in the life between death and rebirth where he will be given renewed strength and fresh love for the next earthly life when he will realize his inner goal, his spiritual longing, which is perfection in Christ.

His handicap is temporary because it is limited to this lifetime, between birth and death. It is very significant in this incarnation and decisive for his biography, but for his spiritual development and entire destiny it is but one experience in a succession of earthly lives (reincarnations) going far, far back in time as he is an old soul. He is on a journey, on his own, individual path to Christ. This lifetime signifies the work he performs in these circumstances, outer and inner, by means of which he is writing his spiritual biography.

He does everything of his own volition, and nothing at another's bidding. He is respectful. Most he either tolerates or seeks to overpower with his personality. Many are they with higher education, well-paying jobs, and material wealth who take my friend utterly seriously, because he is in earnest as an independent personality in his intentions, something all-too-rare in our superficial society. Because of his special personality, great self-discipline, carriage, and sincere earnest attitude, he humanizes society where he goes. His human qualities are valued by many over any wanting in his intellectual development. What a special man and destiny.

Venus

I had a friend some fourteen years ago. We were roommates. He was of medium height and somewhat slender build, with rough features and hands. He was clean. Every morning he showered, shaved, and dressed in a fresh set of clothes that were always simple and that he looked good in. He moved about quietly and deftly, and in a contented fashion, at ease with himself and with his environment, both spatially and among people, slipping into a room or space and out again almost unnoticed, though I was always aware of his presence or absence. In this manner he went about his daily business. He was peaceful and amicable, and at the same time I found him unique.

He busied himself in the bedroom, listened to *Radio Disney*, his favorite radio station that played the same several songs over and over again, and made various objects out of Popsicle sticks and glue. Sometimes my friend went outside for a long slow ride in the neighborhood on his bicycle, a heavy 1-speed that required hard peddling. As it grew very hot where we lived, particularly in the summer when we were roommates, these bicycle rides must have been something of an exertion for him. But I think he enjoyed them as he enjoyed all things in his life.

He had a bad doctor, but my friend did not believe it, and when he demanded his doctor do something for him, he did so until the doctor did it. This was always to his favor. I once heard the doctor say that my friend was an extremely difficult patient. But invariably he relented and did as my friend wished, because he kept on him and would not stop talking about it until it was done.

In the bedroom my friend had a lilac-and-white *World Prayer Day* poster of medium size on his cabinet that he was fond of. I know this because he spoke of it once, and with candid love and simple faith. He was pure in heart and love, indeed that is what he was all about. I came to know him well, and I knew that he could do what few today can, genuinely pray. He was simple in his thoughts, but he was also gifted to know what lay in people's hearts. One could have no secrets with him.

My friend was by nature good with all kinds of people (he got along well with every one). He was always intent on everything he did, pursued his modest interests, reached out to all those around him, and, except when someone encroached on his inner space (mind), in which case he instantly became verbally fiery and outwardly alive, appeared completely protected in his world of quiet and contentment. He never once strayed from his virtues of heart and mind to which he was devoted with his entire being, soul and spirit. He possessed all of the virtues.

Sun

I have a friend who lived at our family home for one year after receiving his PhD and teaching for awhile, when he was out of work. During this time he put his master's thesis into book form. It was later published.

His bedroom was my father's former study, and my father's large desk was still there, likewise his recliner and the beautiful wood shelves he had made, stained, and put up on the walls for reference books and magazines, which were also still there. The medium-size room was a shady enclave, and my friend, like my father before him, looked good sitting there in the recliner. This was before the house was remodeled when my friend had to move out. (The furniture was all moved out and the floor torn up for the remodeling.)

My friend shares much in common with my father, and it seemed fitting that he occupy my father's study. Like my father was, he is a large man, big and tall and very strong. Also like him my friend is very manly and dignified, a true gentleman. Likewise he possesses great intelligence, with a sound scientific mind and a fantastic memory for facts. My friend is also highly knowledgeable, particularly in his own field. Like my father did, my friend looks warm, he has a big warm heart, and one feels his physical presence without or before seeing or hearing him.

He can speak and makes an impression in so doing, and he has a great deal of genuine interest to say, but most all of the time he refrains from speech. This seems intentional, for he is highly disciplined and an excellent man, again like my father. When he does speak he is rather modest, and he chooses his words carefully. (He has a *huge* vocabulary.

Once, after he had said something to me, he stated that a word he had just used he would never again (have opportunity to) use.)

My friend's genius is as great as his six foot three inch frame, and as solid and grounded in reality. Although he is fully cognizant of the many weaknesses and shortcomings of his lesser fellow human beings, in comparing himself with others he unfailingly places them and their human and spiritual qualities, abilities, and advantages before his own, then mentions to the side he has all of the virtues as though this were nothing of consequence. My father was similar regarding these things, for he was humble before God and men, and at the same time all-virtuous. It should be said he is aware of his intellectual capacities and strength (soul-with-spirit power), and of his deep heart qualities, which bears religion, something rare in our time. But he lets these things be felt in outer silence. He dwells in a nearly automatic condition of soul, except for his intellectual pursuits, which include the exercising of his fantastic memory for facts and language. This means that his great genius nature is latent in him; it is yet potential, but one may sense its greatness and the great strides he makes for progress in his still, patient, and daily efforts. He once said to me: <u>Patience is underrated.</u>

With his great heart and profound heart qualities my friend is enabled to pray, which I know he does. Once he said he would do so because of challenging inner circumstances I encountered at the time that I shared with him. My father also had the ability to pray and did so (quietly) in Swedish. Both my friend and father are special Sun personalities and destinies. They never met.

Of course they are very different men, with different biographies and lines of work. My father was a Swedish refrigeration engineer who came to America at age 36, became a US citizen, married my Mother (an American), settled down in the Los Angeles area where he raised a family, lived the rest of his life, and died. He bore great physical pain and discomfort his 75 years. He was a heavy, big-boned, and very physical man. His name was Arne Ragnar Lindgren, and he was a linguistic genius who enjoyed grammar. He read, wrote, and spoke—with correct pronunciation—twelve languages and dialects.

My friend is an American, born and raised in Japan of American parents. After graduating from high school in Japan, he went to Xxxxxxxx in Xxxxxx, Canada, where he attended college and went on to earn his PhD. He taught up there for a year, then came down to Los Angeles when we met as he lived in our home, which is how we began. (In addition to Japanese, he is fluent in written French.) My friend informed me "I have five to six good hours in me a day," meaning he can wholly concentrate for this length of time without pause. This is remarkable as he is a Sanguine. (Sanguines are noted to have a short attention span.) He once said to me with self-affirmation: I thrive on pressure. The Sun personalities and individualities are only equaled in self-discipline and all of the virtues by those of Venus, who exceed them in temperament transformation, but not in thinking work or personality strength.

(Now he is a professor at the University of Xxxxxxx at Xxxxxxxx. He gives his students equal treatment, careful not to show any favoritism as he is a fair and just man, and he also knows his duties and responsibilities as a professor, which task he performs rigorously and conscientiously. He is always well prepared for the lesson before stepping into the classroom. He frequently writes articles for journals and other academic publications, and he also travels for his research and to participate in conferences with other specialists in his field in which he is well-respected. Recently, he delivered a paper in China in Chinese. As spoken Chinese is different from spoken Japanese, he had to learn enough Chinese to do so. The written languages are nearly identical, so with his fluent Japanese, he can read ancient Chinese texts in the original. His third book is nearing publication. He was in Germany for his work recently.)

I used to visit my friend frequently during his year at our home. He is very good-natured and quite jolly, full of joy and life. This may seem odd for a man of his sheer size, but it is so. One rarely encounters an adult of such warmth and enthusiasm, and he is most cheery as he goes about his work and hobbies, which include baseball (his favorite team is the *LA Dodgers*), the TV show *The Simpsons*, Japanese *sumo* wrestling, and preparing fried chicken, which is his favorite dish that he makes from scratch. He also plays golf. That is another hobby and his exercise.

At the time he stayed with us we had a dog, a black Japanese Akita Springer Spaniel named Berta. My friend loves dogs and puppies, and he went out with Berta daily, taking her for a long walk. But my friend always said Berta took *him* for a walk. Indeed he let Berta take the lead, and only after a good long time took over and led her back home again.

He collected US copper pennies in change whenever he shopped for Japanese *sushi* (another favorite food) or what have you, and that he did not use in making purchases. Once I noticed he had created piles of these pennies twenty high in neat stacks on my father's old desk. He was carefully arranging them so that they stood there tall and balanced. (At all times my friend would sit there all warm-looking merrily occupying the space clearly enjoying himself.) The stacks of twenty copper pennies stood on the desk evenly in their equal number and weight, until one day my friend decided to take them to the bank to exchange them for dollar bills. These carefully piled stacks of pennies made a deep impression on me. One day I realized they were a picture for spiritual weights with which my friend and father are both endowed by God.

Jupiter

I had a therapist for a few years who remained my friend for several years after that until she went on to live and work elsewhere. I now see her seldom, if ever. She is a Jupiter destiny. Of average height, she is quite slender, narrow, and very warm. Her warmth is apparent in seeing her face and skin, and when shaking her small hand. She is attractive if not beautiful, with a majestic and gracious personality, visible in her reddish longish, thick, wavy head of hair. She seems always to be smiling, has a good sense of humor, and is most kindly disposed. She is almost constantly gesturing in lively and receding hand movements that will draw you to her, and her smile and entire manner are adorable.

Once, when I spontaneously mentioned this to her as we passed by one another (that she is adorable), she said with a laugh: You're on to me! She dresses well and appropriately, with some expensive jewelry, in keeping with her personal taste, and she retains her special human qualities, including her own special warmth, such that she doesn't entirely blend in with her environment, chemistry notwithstanding. The colors she most frequently wears, that I saw, were deep red and yellow-brown turtlenecks, and black slacks. So they were not bright or 'loud' colors, rather dark or 'earth' colors, though not colorful.

She looks as though she were standing in a small corner by herself looking about with interest and curiosity as to what is happening around her, though unable to see because she is within herself. She is a present and somewhat slow human being, and has the ability of drawing attention to herself without any bravado or outwards effort, while she is much more interested in learning your secrets from you. I was happy to share mine with her, and in this manner I found I was able to help her by enriching her inner life for her progress.

She once said to me during a session that I helped her. Accidentally I replied, <u>Inadvertently.</u> This cleared up any notion of my feeding her egoism. But I did help her, just as I have always done everything I could to help my fellow human beings. This is not for my benefit, but for the sake of the other, not that others profit, but for perception and learning.

We had very interesting weekly half-hour sessions, Tuesday late mornings. She was very attentive to what I had to say, and very astute in her observations, which she thought and did not speak. She kept up with my patter that regarded whatever I was doing during my week. This was centered on my work as a poet and writer, and everything that revolved around it.

My daily life was very full and active at the time as it has been for many years now. Whenever I said something of special interest she would invariably repeat it after me so as to 'get it' (she always 'got it' the first time), unless it concerned what was taking place at that very moment, in which case we both felt the real meaning of my words. Then silence sufficed. Those things I said that she repeated because they were of real interest to her are best described as wise thoughts.

For example, I once talked about the course of a typical day of mine. I said it was important for me I follow a schedule that I abide by (and that I impose on myself; I am my own boss), and that I keep to this structure of my time, but that the really significant things occur unplanned somewhere along the way. One must be open to receive such things. They are gifts by which I am frequently blessed, but they could not happen did I not dutifully pursue my goals within the framework of my daily and weekly schedule. Keeping to a schedule is important, however.

Another thought she found helpful, and that I 'knew', insofar a child can grasp, already at age seven, is that the process or journey is (at least) as significant as arriving at the destination.

Many are they who want to gain, for example, clairvoyance, when they are not yet novices. Many others want to achieve spiritual enlightenment when they are not seekers. But lifetimes are required before the soul is ripe and mature for the human being to be born to seek Christ, which signifies attaining or resolving his destiny in the only place possible, where it was formed: on earth. We make such decisions in the Spiritual World before birth, but only when we are ready. Other, also significant choices are made in the Spiritual World, for example with the Mercurial destiny described above. *Experience* is the important thing, experience and endurance or work, old souls (endurance) or young souls (work). The three old souls are Moon, Mercurial, and Venus. The four young souls are Sun, Jupiter, Saturnine, and Mars. So this kindly human being is a young soul: Jupiter.

Several years ago I saw my friend again. She said she remembered our sessions.

Saturn

I have another friend who is very good. A Saturnine, she is of compact but not small build, rather big-boned and really stocky, and of medium height. She is not beautiful but looks the picture of suffering. She dresses handsomely, is always clean, and keeps her shoulder-length frizzy brown hair that is turned white in places strictly straightened and tied up tightly in a bun, or combed out. She sits a great deal of the time all staid and pressed like a starched shirt, usually looking upset and terribly bothered by something she is hard at work on. But sometimes, filled with heartiness and good will, she suddenly addresses some one she loves who walks by, revealing her simple and good human nature.

Very feisty and extremely sensitive, she has had a hard life. On one occasion she told me as a child she was cruelly taunted and made fun of. Once she stated, "People suffer here", meaning she causes suffering. She knows suffering is significant that she also experiences, but she cannot have the conception it is karmic; it serves to connect us directly with Christ. At another time my friend, gushing over with joy, said of her daughter, whom she had never before mentioned, "She is such a good child!"

My friend is very slow and equally passionate. When provoked, which is seldom, as people caution to leave her alone, she lashes out vehemently in an instant, departing from her inwards and verbal rumination, which is how she usually sits, and for long periods of time. She is sensuous in her love of food, but disciplines herself in eating as she tries to in her behavior. She knows what she likes and dislikes in all things, to which she can be adamant or merely gloat, and she prides herself on her absolute decision. She boldly places herself into the space she enters, walking slowly, defiantly, and with resolution where she goes.

I have seen her knock someone out of her way as though she did not see them, and without apology. She likes to and easily exerts her will, but equally notices when another is bold and frank. She respects valor quietly and without question, but appreciates love above all things. She loves to embrace someone who is pure and loving in heart, and few human beings care as much as does she. She had skin cancer.

I am aware she is aware of everything around her and is genuinely impressed by strength and noble qualities. She seems a contradiction in human terms, awareness of others and all things in her environment, and blind to every one and everything because she is verbally preoccupied with her memories and chooses to ignore them. But it is in this manner that she builds up relationships and learns life's lessons, and that is a hard road because it is such a hard struggle for her, and by it she stockpiles new memories to add to her storehouse from her rich and meaning-filled past.

She knows I am a poet and writer; I gave her a few of my books. Once, after she felt bad for lashing out at me when I was trying to explain something, and I returned to her, earnestly and patiently taking the time to do so, she came up to me all grinning and smiles. She gave me a 'poem' she had written that she said she had learned from me. Although it has nothing to do with our conversation that prompted it, it is full of good feelings and enthusiasm, and I have kept it. One line that always stays with me is: *Begin the day with breakfasts of love.*

My friend says little to others but is usually circumspect, but when she does, initiating a conversation, she is always hopeful and expectant, eager for an exchange. When, on the other hand, she breaks into an existing conversation, she speaks with utter disregard to what has been said, asserting herself and what she has to say as though it were a given fact. Owing to her own ignorance and foolishness, in such a case she contradicts the facts, or else she states the obvious as though by her saying it she is superior. In the latter instance, she is simply showing forethought, which is intelligent, if adamant. By this I mean to say, although not very intelligent, she is not always foolish rather intellectual in her own right. But it is not her intellect that is striking about her, but her originality. She is, among many who are or who appear to be similar or identical, truly one-of-a-kind. Of course many human beings are distinctive. It is only that her originality is greatly pronounced in her. I believe this is because of three things: her being a Choleric, a Saturnine, and retaining and safeguarding her own particular quality such that no one may take it from her, however trying her life becomes. She will be herself, and she retains her past, from which she has learned everything she knows and come to know every one in her life.

At other times (frequently) she is genuinely repentant, and meekly addresses the other person with such sweetness that it is heart-rending. She feels easily disheartened and suffers, not only the pain of a hard and challenging life, but also from a feeling of depressing weakness. She tries to be gentle, but it does not lie in her willful nature. My friend loves to smile and laugh, which is warm, robust, and hearty. It is clear she is a romantic from outbursts of laughter at what some one has said about romance. But her humor is strange.

My friend is visually gifted in an active but subconscious manner; I saw her work—large colored pencil drawings covering the entire paper with color in strong, sure parallel diagonal lines—beautiful and interesting work, for example a dark green forest with a pure white dove in the center. Her favorite story she remembered from childhood is Hans Christian Andersen's *The Ugly Duckling* because the unlovely duckling becomes the most beautiful white swan. She knew that beneath her grim exterior lives a pure spirit, a dove waiting to be freed. She senses this in a simple, direct, and honest fashion.

She loves children as intimated, but also animals, and I frequently see her talking to the resident dog, a little Toy Poodle named Tinkerbell. "Tinkerbell! Hi, Tinkerbell," she always says with tender love. She loves to pick up Tinkerbell into her strong arms and cuddles the little dog with much affection, who seems pleased for the warm attention. Although propriety is foreign to her, she is a terrific human being, and I feel fortunate to know her.

Mars

I had another friend many years ago with whom I have long since lost touch when he moved away. He was an interesting man—a Mars destiny. He was of unusual build, medium height and disproportionate, with large hands and feet, long torso and arms, and comparatively short legs. He wore his blonde-brown hair beyond shoulder length down his back, and usually went about the house and yard barefoot. He walked and gestured in long firm, weighted strides, and with stirring motion, heavy and swift both. While he spoke (which he did readily and with eagerness or hope), he also gestured, and with animation. He would sit or lie down for extended periods, but never was able to relax. He liked to sit in his bedroom and draw in pen and ink in his notebook that served as a kind of sketchbook diary. He once told me he used to take long walks. He must have been in his late forties when I knew him.

From time to time he would come up to me, sharing something personal or that he cared about. At such times he spoke from his good heart. He was always sincere. Once he described a time in his life when he was severely depressed—for six months. He was so depressed he never got out of bed except to use the restroom. Had not a caring friend brought him food every day, my friend would have soon died from starvation, because he took no interest in life, neither was he motivated to care for himself or reach out to another human being. He dwelled in the depths of soul darkness. Such a depression is very hard and painful. Only strong souls are a match for them and, despite feelings of despondency and hopelessness, come back up into the world of light by struggle that for him signified efforts to relax, rather than physical or intellectual activity. He lay in bed for six months, with interludes to eat and use the restroom.

Although it is during such times the thoughts and feelings are normal and healthy, including thoughts and feelings of guilt, it is easy to understand the highs ('manic' phases) are preferable, when no thinking or feeling is possible. Of course there are times when the soul goes to neither extreme. These times reveal the human being best. However, it is a real struggle, as for every upswing, there must be a depression. This is a soul law: *What goes up must come down*. It should be said not all Mars souls suffer this illness. Henry David Thoreau, the 19th century American Transcendentalist, was one such Mars destiny.

At another time he enthusiastically showed me drawings in a notebook he had made many years earlier of Sets for live theatre. At the time he was living in Venice, California, where he worked on producing a play with a group of young people like himself. Venice is artsy. It is an art colony for sculptors, painters, writers, poets, actors, and others active in the art scene. Together with the stage crew, my friend was responsible for building the Sets, and he did the Set design himself. They were optimistic and joyous young people, and the experience was clearly the peak of my friend's life. It made him almost happy sharing these memories after so many years. He was fond in thinking back to this time. My friend could feel, not only the pain of dark depression, but the exuberance and light of fortunate experience. This was his joy.

One day my friend came to me. He needed to talk. He was dismayed. This is what he said. He had just had a telephone conversation with a close friend. His friend's baby boy had just died in a car accident. My friend looked at me for a moment with great sympathy for his friend. He communicated this at first without words. Then he said to me that what his friend was going through made his own concerns seem negligible in comparison. My friend was deeply compassionate.

As a young man he lived in Hawaii where he experienced a manic high. Once, when he was out walking along a road a ways from town, a group of men assaulted him. They beat him up brutally and left him by the roadside badly cut up and bruised. Though seriously roughed up, my friend walked back to town where he healed. He said this without any sign of concern for himself. Like the upswing in his mood at the time, it was just something he had experienced.

Then one time he was feeling especially good. He confided in me that he had been married to a Hispanic woman who was dear to him. They had separated. They had a daughter, a little girl. He saw her seldom. But every week he would sit down and write her a long letter to send her his good thoughts and let her know how much he loved her. He wrote her about what he was doing, what had happened the past week that interested him, little things.

There were other things my friend shared with me. Through irregular ups and downs he made strides in progress, mapping out his uncharted course throughout his emotional and eventful life. He couldn't form a cohesive picture or follow his own path with any clarity—he is no thinker, and even if he were, his thinking would not be autonomous, so he could not yet consciously know his experiences or possess Self-knowledge that results from Christ-knowledge—but like the other six destinies described above, he is nearly ripe for his inner goal. I was able to help him with clear soul perception (of Christ), and according to his planetary nature and temperament, as I did the Mercurial, Venus, Sun, Jupiter, and Saturnine destinies later on. The Moon destiny was on a different path than I could offer something. Had he lived in European Christendom (during the Middle Ages), this little man is a heretic, someone who does not understand why Christ is no longer to be found in the Sun but is, since the crucifixion and resurrection of Christ—the Mystery of Golgotha—the Spirit of the Earth, and who refuses to conform to Church dogma. I feel certain all seven of these special and dear people will reach their aim in their upcoming incarnation, for they have come so far through so much. What is the destination of the seven destinies attained, each by his particular route? The soul's spiritual awakening, the inner Bethlehem: the inner birth of Christ.

There are many paths, just as one's relationship to Christ is individual and personal. Each must find his own, individual path to and with

Christ. Without the gift of the faculty of spiritual perception bestowed on the soul's awakening to Christ, this must be in soul blindness, deafness, muteness; without the capacity to think sense-free, autonomous thoughts necessary for higher, deeper knowledge, divine and human, as some one who taps about in the darkness by the sense of touch alone. He who is a true seeker after the Christ-Being will know this about himself and make no other claims; this state of blindness, deafness, and ignorance in which he lives, he knows, is his sole spiritual knowledge.

But the seeker is on the right path, and he also experiences this as he nears his goal. It distinguishes him from his fellows already early on. For his soul is ripe and was born so. This is his true, inner guide, his feeling for the truth, which does not lie and cannot be deceived. As with pain and suffering, of which the original Saturnine woman spoke to me, and which was her own experience beginning in childhood, the feeling for the truth is personal. But also like pain and suffering, it is universal and objective at the deeper level. Not only physical pain, which can be excruciating, but also what makes two human beings close; both are undeniable.

As with deeper feeling, this pain and this suffering are connections; they are karmic. They connect us with one another as with Christ. We think of the wise Moon destiny, or the handicapped but disciplined Mercurial, both of whom shelter their karma: Christ within. Or again the powerful big-hearted Sun destiny, who is creative of karma. For without pain or suffering suffered there is no Christ, no karma for the destiny. Neither does reincarnation result in the actual incarnation of the higher, spiritual being, the eternal individuality, into the soul, heart, and body of the individual, in Christ. For Christ is the Lord of Karma, and in Him a human spirit descending takes hold of the body—legs and feet and hands—by the soul, and dearly suffers the heart in human closeness, after He awakens the soul. This is the meaning of human experience.

Los Angeles
2010/2011
October 11-12, 2014
Culver City, California
May, November 2014

Famous Historical Examples of the Seven Destinies
(Planetary Types)

Saturnine

King Herod
The poor widow (of Christ and the widow's mite)
Richard the Lionhearted
Saint Thomas More
Henry VIII
Martin Luther
Mary Queen of Scots
Shakespeare
Jonathan Swift (*Gulliver's Travels*)
Rembrandt Harmensz van Rijn ("Rembrandt")
Johann Wolfgang von Goethe ("Goethe")
Leo Tolstoy
Fyodor Dostoevsky
Victor Hugo
Honore de Balzac
Charles Dickens
Florence Nightingale
Edgar Allen Poe
Frederick Douglass
Abraham Lincoln
Samuel Clemens ("Mark Twain")
W.S. Gilbert ("Gilbert and Sullivan" operettas)
Conrad Ferdinand Meyer
Hans Christian Andersen
Paul Gaughin
Paul Cézanne
Auguste Rodin
Robert Burns
Gandhi
Eleanor Roosevelt
Pablo Picasso ("Picasso")
Helen Keller
Franz Kafka

Saturnine (continued)

George Orwell
Anne Frank
Ingrid Bergman
Dylan Thomas
Cesar Chavez (first President, United Farm Workers)
Michael Jordan
Al Gore
Michele Obama

Sun

Noah
Gilgamesh
Enkidu (Eabani, close friend to Gilgamesh)
Zarathustra
Pharaoh Akhenaten
Moses
Abraham
Isaac
Jacob
Esther
Rebecca
Sarah
King David
Aristotle (Plato's student) ("To know what to ask is already to know half.")
Alexander the Great (Aristotle's pupil)
Lazarus
St. Mark
St. Luke
St. Peter
Mary Magdalene
Martha
The Centurion (of the centurion's servant) whose great faith in Christ astonished Christ
Joseph of Arimathea (who gave his tomb for the body of Christ)

Sun (continued)

St. Paul (the Apostle)
Julian the Apostate
Theodoric the Great
Boethius
John Scotus Eriugena
Dionysius the Areopagite
Wolfram von Eschenbach (author of *Parzival*)
Meister (Johannes) Eckhardt (mystic)
St. Thomas Aquinas
Julianne of Norwich
St. Hildegard of Bingen
St. Mechtild of Magdeburg
St. Elisabeth of Thüringen
Matthäus Grünewald (painter of the Isenheimer Altar, Northern German Renaissance)
Giordano Bruno (pantheist, burned at the stake by the Church in 1600 for teaching reincarnation)
Christian Rosenkreutz, reincarnation of Lazarus (see Count of Saint Germain, below)
Jakob Boehme
Angelus Silesius (Johannes Scheffler) (mystic—"If Christ were born a thousand times in Bethlehem and not in thee, it were in vain.")
Johann Sebastian Bach
Count of Saint Germain ("The Count of Saint Germain has been the exoteric reincarnation of Christian Rosenkreutz in the 18th century"—Rudolf Steiner, lecture of September 27, 1911 [GA 130, p. 67]), also reincarnation of Lazarus; he had several incarnations between.
Rudolf Steiner, reincarnation of St. Thomas Aquinas, Aristotle, and Gilgamesh
Ita Wegman, MD, reincarnation of Alexander the Great and Enkidu (Eabani)
Maya Angelou

Moon

Confucius
Aeschylus

Moon (continued)

Homer
Virgil
Ovid
Sappho
Aristophanes
Pythagoras
Ptolemy
Socrates
Plato (student of Socrates, Aristotle's teacher)
Augustus Caesar
The Canaanite woman with Christ (Christ: *Let the children first have their fill, for it is not fair to take the children's bread and to cast it to the dogs.* The woman: *Yes, Lord; for even the dogs under the table eat of the children's crumbs.* Because of her faith in Christ, the demon was driven out of her son.)
Hroswitha von Gandersheim (AD935–AD973), German, first playwright and woman writer of medieval Europe, reincarnation of Plato (see Karl Julius Schröer, below)
Alanus ab Insulis
Geoffrey Chaucer
Giovanni Pierluigi da Palestrina ("Palestrina")
Edmund Spenser
Nicholaus Copernicus ("Copernicus")
Descarte
Tycho Brahe
Galileo Galilei ("Galileo")
Johannes Kepler ("Kepler")
Sandro Botticelli
Il Perugino
Leonardo da Vinci
Michelangelo
Blaise Pascal ("Pascal")
Carl von Linné ("father of modern botany")
Voltaire
Jane Austin
Molière

Moon (continued)

Benjamin Franklin
Louis Pasteur
Georg Wilhelm Friedrich Hegel ("Hegel")
Johann Gottlieb Fichte ("Fichte")
Johann Christoph Friedrich von Schiller ("Schiller")
Lord Byron
John Keats
Percy Bysshe Shelley
Johann Friedrich Christian Hölderlin ("Hölderlin")
Clara and Robert Schumann
Franz Schubert
Frédèric Chopin ("Chopin")
Karl Julius Schröer (1825–1900), German literary critic, Rudolf
Steiner's German and favorite professor, reincarnation of Plato and
Hroswitha von Gandersheim (see, above)
Vladimir Soloviev (1853–1900), Russian philosopher, mystic, and writer
(experienced the Divine Sophia)
Edvard Grieg ("Grieg")
Auguste Renoir
Claude Monet
Emily Dickinson
Rainer Maria Rilke ("Rilke")
George Washington Carver
Alexander Graham Bell
Thomas Alva Edison
Oscar Wilde
James Joyce
Siegfried Sassoon
Aldous Huxley
Antoine de Saint Exupéry (author of *The Little Prince*)
Alan Alexander Milne (author of *Winnie the Pooh*)
Elvis Presley
Marilyn Monroe
Drew Barrymore
Dr. Oz
Barack Obama

Mars

Aleksandr Sergeyevich Pushkin ("Pushkin"–much-loved Russian poet)
Vincent van Gogh ("Van Gogh")
Henry David Thoreau (American Transcendentalist, 19th century)
Ivan Bunin (1870–1953), popular Russian writer, Nobel Prize laureate
Farley Mowat (20th century and current Canadian humanitarian (with the Eskimos), animal rights' activist (with the seals), and writer)

Jupiter

Nefertiti
Cleopatra
Lady Mirasaki Shiruku
Eleanor of Aquitaine
Pocahontas
Wolfgang Amadeus Mozart ("Mozart")
Ludwig van Beethoven ("Beethoven")
Richard Wagner ("Wagner")
Jenny Lind
Enrico Caruso
Jussi Björling
Marian Anderson
Katherine Hepburn
Itzhak Perlman
Jascha Heifitz
Anna Sophie-Mutter
Barbra Streisand
Barbara Walters
Julia Roberts
Elton John
Whitney Houston
Madonna
Beyoncé Knowles ("Beyoncé")

Venus

Adam
Eve

Venus (continued)

Elijah the Prophet (Elias)
King Tutankhamun
St. Elisabeth
John the Baptist
Mary, the Mother
Jesus of Nazareth
St. John the Evangelist
St. Stephen
St. Francis of Assisi
St. Joan (Joan of Arc, "The Maid of Orléan")
Raphael (Raffaello Sanzio) (1483–1520), Italian High Renaissance artist and architect (see Novalis, below)
Novalis (1772–1801), German Romanticist poet-genius, reincarnation of Adam, Elijah the Prophet, John the Baptist, St. John the Evangelist, Raphael ("He will come again"—Rudolf Steiner)
Reverend Dr. Martin Luther King, Jr. ("Everything that we see is a shadow cast by that which we do not see.")
Peace Pilgrim

Mercurial

Hippocrates ("Walking is man's best medicine.")
Marc Antony
The rich man (of Christ and the rich man)
Emperor Constantine ("Constantine")
Erik the Red
Leif Erikson
Duke William of Normandy ("William the Conqueror")
Marco Polo
Prince Henry the Navigator
Bartolomeu Dias
Vasco da Gama
Amerigo Vespucci
Christopher Columbus ("Columbus") (Cristóbal Colón, Cristoforo Colombo)
Hernando de Soto

Mercurial (continued)

Ferdinand Magellan ("Magellan")
Hernando Cortés
Juan Ponce de León
Sir Walter Raleigh
Miguel de Cervantes Saavedra ("Cervantes") ("Our greatest foes, and whom we must chiefly combat, are within.")
Paul Revere
Garibaldi
Wilbur and Orville Wright ("The Wright Brothers")
Charles A. Lindberg
Amelia Earhart
W.C. Fields
Winston Churchill
Shirley Temple
Laurence Olivier
Nelson Eddy
Jeanette MacDonald
Spencer Tracy
Sidney Poitier
John F. Kennedy ("JFK")
Robert F. Kennedy ("RFK")
Dale Carnegie ("You never achieve real success unless you like what you are doing.")
Jack LaLane
Nelson Mandela
Bill Clinton
Hillary Clinton
Hugh Grant
Sandra Bullock
Jerry Seinfeld
Denzel Washington
Oprah Winfrey

Mortality, the So-Called Dead, the Child, and Us

The Realization of the Mortality of the Human Being

The experience of human mortality is one whose first knowledge belongs usually to the tenth year of childhood. Someone significant to the child dies, and it experiences this in a real and sometimes deep way. The child realizes for the first time the human being is a mortal one, that human life has not only a beginning but also an end. These are the two portals of life through which the soul must pass: the portal of birth and the portal of death. At the beginning of life we are fresh from the lap of God. In death we go in Christ.

Inner Questions

The child probably still senses its origins in the heavenly world and thus has some genuine if simple understanding for the pre-birth Mysteries of the human soul: the unborn. But what of death, which now presents itself with such absoluteness that the child encounters as an experience it, like all mortals, must know? Are their post-death Mysteries as well? Real questions may stir within the child's soul as one tries to come to terms with this solemn event that provides the key to the unknown.

If the human being is a mortal, what happens to me? What about my soul? I came from God before I was born. Where will I go after I die? Where did my friend/loved one go, whom I learned so newly died?

Helping the Child

It is good if a parent or other thoughtful adult takes this opportunity to speak with the child for whom this experience of mortality is a fresh one. It will be most receptive because the death of its friend or loved one is both actual and new. The words should relate to the child in such a manner that it understands. Philosophizing and the like will not do; mortality and death are deeper issues and not intellectual ones. Neither is the child intellectual. An intellectual approach to learning and thus teaching is senseless before puberty.

Let the child come to you. Welcome it. Explain you have something you want to tell it. The questions are not so important if one already knows what lives in the child's heart. One need only pause oneself for self-reflection before this profound event that is death.

If you have had a personal experience of losing a loved one, or a friend, with whom you were close in life, but that has had the opportunity to deepen within you following the event, this is a good beginning.

Human Responses to a Death

Many people experience a whole sequence of feelings and emotions or other responses following on such a loss. Many people first feel shock or disbelief. The reality of an event so deep places everyday life and its illusions into proper perspective. Our ordinary thoughts and feelings, all of our preoccupations are put in a true light by the actuality of death. Some people go about as though nothing of significance has happened. These people are in denial. Instead, they concern themselves with the will or estate left behind. They cannot or will not ponder the soul.

With some people the initial response is followed with a sense of anger. This is selfish but only understandable. How could you die and leave me here? One may feel abandoned by someone so close.

Then there are those who are overcome by grief. Genuine tears are wept. This is most human. We mourn for our dead whom we love, and who have now departed from this earthly plane of existence. Again, grief is a response to the human loss in death.

Some human beings take a more reflective position. They think about it. They are intelligent people and come to terms with death in this way.

Death. Death? This is an event that differs from all others. What does it mean? The true meaning it holds may dawn within the soul. As the flesh is mortal, so is the soul immortal. The eternal nature of the soul lives between the immortal and the unborn in the life between death and rebirth. The body is our temporary home for our earthly journey.

Closeness with the So-called Dead

After some time has passed, duration the individual and closeness depending, if one has allowed the experience or feeling or mood to deepen, to sink in as they say, and if one takes time in all quiet for remembering the friend or loved one as s/he was in life, an inner closeness may be felt that can be of even more help than was had when there was still the physical presence. This is unseen but all the more effective, from within.

A new kind of relationship can be tended, nurtured, and sustained if this post-death connection is made. A bridge is gradually built by our loving thoughts and feelings that connect us with our beloved so-called dead. Our loved one or friend looks down from spirit-heights to earth below and sees us, but it rests with us who remain here to make the connection.

Mortality and the Mystery of Death

We know that mortality is of the flesh. The soul, I, and personality that animated the human being in glance, gesture, movement, voice, touch, romance, speech, warmth; the soul-spirit part that is unseen that thought, felt, willed, loved, remembered, dreamed, imagined, intuited, was inspired—all this has fled. The empty lifeless shell is left behind: the corpse or ashes. The person we knew is not the body that is external. In this transition from what's seen and known into what's invisible and unknown lies the mystery of death.

Missing Our Loved One or Friend and the Bridge of Remembrance

It is by our remembering them with whom we were close that they enter into and help us, and we them. This is the bridge of which we spoke. Any initial feelings of loneliness are replaced by our missing them, their physical presence that signifies the closeness that we feel.

You can explain this to the child. It is human to feel close to someone, to love, to care. It is human to think about someone you love or care about, to miss them, to want to be with them. This is the basis on which and the way our relationship with those who have passed over is founded and continued. The child will naturally understand this.

Closing Words to Help the Child

It is important we are truthful with the child, that what we say is true. We may say the following words that speak simply and deeply to this topic:

When you learn of someone's death, always remember the person has gone on to other tasks in the Spiritual World (Heaven). We will all go there some day. The Earth is our temporary home. Heaven is forever.

Los Angeles
September 4-6, 2010
October 12, 2014

The Dead and the Living Presence of Christ

The dead with whom one was close in earthly life remain so in our remembering them. This is so whether they were initiated that is died with spiritual bodies or uninitiated that is did not have spiritual bodies on death. In the latter case, their presence is felt as warmth in the heart as in the former, only it is as large as were their physical bodies in earthly life. In the former instance that is they were initiated their spiritual bodies are large, even very large, and in our remembering them we can experience their presence from within, as is the case with the uninitiated, but extending beyond the confines of our physical skin out into our environment.

Our environment is of a spiritual-physical nature. Spiritual beings and processes are active in it as are physical beings and processes. This is true already in the plant and the earth, which have etheric bodies. Animals and human beings likewise have etheric bodies. In addition, we have astral bodies that include the soul members by which we feel. Human beings are also spiritual beings on earth as on the Other Side of the threshold preceding conception and birth and following death. It is this soul-spiritual aspect of the human being that continues after death. This is what lives on after a human being has died.

In our remembering a loved one or a friend with whom we had a close connection in earthly life, they are able to enter into and help us, and we them. These are the enduring relationships. It is important to know this. These special friends and loved ones live where there is no time or space in eternal realms of spirit. What this means is that they can be present in human beings and on earth in more than one place at the same time. This is so each time two or more human beings, at the same moment, remember the friend or loved one as s/he was in life.

However, in the case where the person who is remembering is consciously aware of Christ and therewith of the human soul and spirit, then the dead are able to work into the physical world in the physical body of the one who remains on earth. The dead lack a physical body as they are now discarnate, so they require a physical body in order for them to be active on earth. This is what the person who still lives on earth provides, the physical instrument that is otherwise lacking. This can only occur where the person who remains in a physical body is consciously aware of Christ and therewith of the human soul and spirit. Then, by this consciousness, the dead who are in union with Christ are able to utilize the physical body of the one still on earth. Then the dead can work into the physical world. But the dead are ever at work on earth in other ways, for example among the life of plants. We know this from Rudolf Steiner's work.

However, any person who was close to the dead in earthly life who can feel this closeness in their heart after the soul has departed from the body may experience the living presence of the dead, if in a dreamlike way. This dreamlike way is sensed though not yet conscious. It is sensed such that the person may say, "I feel close." This feeling is just as real as the feeling of closeness of a human being with whom one is in the same room, but it is with the soul who stirs within the heart. This enables the person to say, "I feel close (to my dear loved one or friend)."

Feelings tell the truth. Feeling a chill is unmistakable and undesirable. A warm feeling stirring within is unmistakable. It is this warm feeling that is felt in the heart by the person in the living presence of the dead that is with Christ. Those who are consciously aware of Christ and therewith of souls and spirits of human beings in earthly existence that is incarnate, or discarnate (who have departed from their physical bodies), they have the knowledge of the presence of Christ and the dead who are in their midst. This is also the case with human beings who are incarnate. This is the conscious awareness of Christ.

There is another instance where this experience of Christ manifests. This is in the experience of pain. The person who feels pain who is not aware of Christ has this experience of Christ as much as does the person who is aware of Christ, only s/he does not know s/he is connected to Christ in the experience of the pain. The person who is aware of Christ knows his/her connection to Him in the pain s/he feels. Then the pain becomes very dear. *All human suffering needs to be measured against the suffering of Christ on the cross.* (Virginia Sease)*

A human being who is suffering hurt or pain, even tremendous pain, who is not consciously aware of Christ may experience genuine consolation knowing that Christ is with them in their suffering. The human being who suffers even tremendous hurt or pain who is aware of Christ knows it is a Christ-connection that they experience the suffering of pain. If s/he thinks on this, recognizing this fact, then s/he may say, this experience is dear to me, because it connects me with Christ, Who suffered the greatest human pain and death, of whom I am now conscious.

It is the good powers, especially Christ, who show us the way forward in our suffering of hurt and pain. This knowledge has deep value to the human being. It is precious. It is very dear to us to know this.

If I possess vast material wealth, property, possessions, money, and all of the comforts and conveniences associated with them, but if I love no one but myself, I am empty, I feel nothing. All of this wealth means absolutely nothing without the experience of the living Christ. To the extent that I feel and that I love others, that I suffer and am capable of suffering pain and discomfort, that I love my fellow humanity, to that extent am I rich and large inside. This is the meaning of humanity that Christ is our humanity. There is much pain and suffering today. There is much humanity on our earth. The living Christ is present in many places on our earth.

Los Angeles
January 6, 2011
Culver City, California
May 30, 2014
Los Angeles
October 12-13/18, 2014

* Dr. Virginia Sease in no way endorses this volume or any study, story, or poem in it. *The Wood of Green* is published independently of the General Anthroposophical Society at the Goetheanum in Dornach, Switzerland, which the author recognizes.

On Meditation, Human and Divine

April 14, 2014
1:00pm
Los Angeles

Earlier today, I remembered I had had a special dream with my father on awakening the previous day. It's been awhile, but this is what I can remember:

I was with my father Arne; my Mother Margaret was nearby, I believe, but not so near as to be able to hear what we were saying. I believe my father was sitting. He was smiling, and he looked particularly good. I asked him at one point, how had he become so kind, what had he done to become so kind? He replied, unmoved but quite amicably, and without any show of self, that he was meditating. When I then asked him which meditation, he said, again unmoved and rather offhandedly, several. I then said (rather like a know-it-all), he should do only *one* meditation. He only kept on smiling, still unmoved, and warm and good. Then I continued (with my several notions) by telling him he could meditate in another language (from English, was what I meant). I was thinking of Swedish for him. Then I said *I* meditated in German. I said Rudolf Steiner had given us many meditations. He only kept on smiling. At one point thereafter, I awakened from my dream.

April 15, 2014
2:25pm
Culver City, California

In reflecting now on this most recent dream with my long-deceased father Arne (20 years, 2 January 2014), it seems to me he is already preparing for his coming lifetime, a significant incarnation. Those of us who knew him in his most recent earthly life may recall his being quite emphatic at times, making a point in his speech with much emphasis. He had a powerful heart. He was formative of much karma. I know that I have been carrying emphasis into my own speech whenever I 'put my best foot forward' with intention. This has long been the case; it's simply a part of my psyche; we often inherit various qualities from one or both parents. But my father has meanwhile changed, not yet on earth, but in the Spiritual Homeland by his practice of several meditations (not in an earthly language; in heaven it matters not what was one's nation of birth or were the language/s one spoke in earthly life).

I know from my practicing one meditation how effective it is; indeed, along with other practices and experiences, it brought me all the way to the Christ. Since this significant experience (my soul's awakening), I have continued to practice this meditation, and my capacity to concentrate for the duration of my meditating, with a period of gradually entering into the meditation, remains, even when I have not meditated for quite some time, which might be seen as a neglect. (The meditation I practice is a Western one given by Rudolf Steiner to a spirit-seeker who went to him for guidance. Anthroposophy, the international movement and Society founded by Rudolf Steiner, is for those on a Western meditative and thinking path. My father Arne Ragnar Lindgren was an anthroposophist from Sweden.)

The meditation my father referred to in my recent dream must be different in character from what those of us practice in a physical body on earth. But its effectiveness must nonetheless be a reality. Indeed, so far I am aware, a human being here (on earth) practices (does) only one meditation, for the reason it is most effective to do so. But my father said he is doing *several* meditations. This is not surprising when we think how different everything is in the Spiritual Homeland. It may well be the case, that the new kindness I saw in my father is a fruit of but *one* of the several divine meditations he is practicing. This would mean that there would be other benefits resulting from the other meditations he is doing at the same time. Time means nothing in heaven.

If I am correct in saying that my father already now is preparing for his next lifetime (which still lies far ahead as his passing was but 20 years ago; he lived to the age of 75 ½ years, and earthly lives are usually about 1,000 years apart), then these divine meditations he is practicing will really take effect in deeply significant ways, not only for his own future, but for all those who will receive the help of Christ through his presence and inwards activity, and for the future of all humankind, *on earth*.

My father made great strides in progress in this most recent incarnation of his. I and many knew this. I was always convinced he was almost ripe for the Christ-experience, which, in his case, will signify modern-day sainthood, and spiritual educator and leadership's gifts By this I mean to say, if I am not mistaken, he will begin his journey, his spiritual pilgrimage to Christ-knowledge that means Self-knowledge in his upcoming earthly life. So everything he is experiencing and doing in the Spiritual Homeland between lifetimes *now* is of utmost import for humanity. Just as his previous incarnations were the preparation for this coming one, this coming earthly life of my father will be the foundation for all subsequent ones, which will be still much more significant. So this dream with my father holds much more meaning than it may first appear to.

Alan Lindgren

Society and the I

Every ill or problem, and its healing or treatment or solution, is found reflected between society and the human I of every member of that society. So, for example, a major problem in our society is addiction, and this is reflected in and suffered by individuals within our society. At the same time, addiction as a problem suffered by individual human beings is reflected in the larger society, where it becomes a national and even a global issue. But if the ill is not addressed with human understanding, the problem will never be solved. Indeed it will be only compounded and carried over into other areas of life. There are several such serious issues at the personal and societal-national-global levels that are not being addressed. We think of technologies whose artificial sensations are causing irreparable damage to countless millions. Let us stay with the problem of addiction here.

One time in America making and drinking alcoholic beverages was illegal. This did not stop the market for liquor; it only went underground. As a result of the law, something known as bootlegging came into existence. Now the alcohol was produced secretly so that the authorities would not find out where it was being distilled. It was therefore given the name 'moonshine', as in, 'in the secrecy of the night', of the moon. So alcoholics, as well as moderate drinkers, kept on drinking liquor. The new law was not a good one. It created a crime where there had been none, and now those who wished to get help with their drinking problem could not do so, for fear of being caught for breaking the law. This period in U.S. history is called Prohibition (1920-1933).

Today we have the same thing, but with drugs, only it is much worse. The penalties for getting caught using hard drugs can include imprisonment, for peddling them much longer terms in prison. These laws have also created a drug ring, which is on an international scale as drugs are smuggled up from Latin America to fill the high demand for them in the United States. But the people continue smoking, snorting, and injecting the drugs anyhow, only now it is illegal with high penalties. The result is that the prisons are all filled and new ones are being built to accommodate the high number of people being punished for using and peddling drugs.

These are not criminals we are speaking of. They are people with serious issues they are not addressing in a healthy manner who instead are masking their pain or experiencing a temporary escape from their pain by taking drugs and 'getting a fix' or 'a high', or who are making profits on others by taking advantage of individuals with an addiction problem by selling them to them. So this 'crime' and its punishment is created by bad laws, instead of offering ready help to those who suffer, as is the case in Holland, where individuals who want help can walk into drug addiction help centers from the street. Further, entire lives are wasted behind bars, and the costs to confine one person in prison for one year are tens of thousands of dollars, higher than one year of university or college education. Many kids get involved with drugs at a young age. They get in with the wrong crowd and find the illegality of it somehow appealing, which is ironic. We know this is still the case with cigarette smoking. If we put higher funding into our educational system, and into job training and placement, instead of building more prisons, we would be doing a great service to our young people and for their futures. This in turn would be a big boost for an ailing economy as they would become productive, working members of society making a contribution.

What is at stake here? Entire lives of many souls, each of whom is irreplaceable.

Other societal problems include personal relationships, bad relationships where one party is abused in some manner. This could be physical, emotional-verbal-psychological, or psychiatric. It could be in a poor diet, medication, denying the person sleep. We note that much such abuse is under the supervision of a quack or a licensed professional, such as a physician, a specialist, or a psychiatrist. Present laws created to protect patients do not seem adequate in many instances. When the abused party is a child, we know the child's future may be lost. We mentioned another individual-societal problem: exposure to artificial sensations that cause permanent damage to the eye and ear organs, and the brain, and therewith to the human soul, which cannot be accessed without the organs with which to perceive, if indeed it is not deadened (unresponsive) from the effects already. Again, society is found in one human being at a time, here beginning in (early) childhood.

Where developmental disabilities are shockingly common today (once called retardation), and require special attention, mental illness is endemic in our society. Again, we know that such illness is suffered by one single human being, then simply multiplied millions of times. Mental illness such as schizophrenia causes homelessness. However, both developmental and physical disabilities, and mental illness, can serve the individuality of the human being as the means of gathering experiences that, together with others, prepare the destiny across lifetimes for its healing in the same incarnation it inwardly awakens on the Christ-experience. So these handicaps, hard as they appear to be, are not in vain. From this it is apparent, while societal problems affecting hundreds of millions of human souls are not being addressed that need to be, owing to the human, spiritual laws of reincarnation and karma, many do receive the help they require, if not in this incarnation in many areas and instances, then overall for the inner progress of the soul on its journey. This is highly complex, far more so than societal issues and their solutions, because of the vast and intricate web of world destiny of which each of us is one thread, but that the Lord of Karma, Which is Christ, knows to weave for the welfare of all and every one.

Reincarnation and karma are looked at closely in section 5.). This section focuses on various aspects of western society and its members: our common humanity, humanization in a dehuman society; the sacrifices and suffering the individual must be prepared to make and endure, and must make and endure, for his/her true freedom; and our spiritual I, the individuality in each one of us. Like the spreading of love, we stand at the dawn of a new Christianity. (See *Love (2)* next page)

Pay special attention to the first two studies in this section: *The Face of Our Humanity* (pages 397, 398) and *Human vs. Dehuman* (399-402) as they are by far the most pertinent. Additionally, they are succinct, which also suggests their content is significant.

Like the studies that have to do with the four temperaments in some manner, they address all human beings, here in western society. Unlike the temperaments studies, these two speak to our fundamental human being at a time in history when our very humanity is threatened by the wasteland of materialism and technology. This does not in any way diminish the importance for us to work on transforming our temperament by practices that cultivate the habits and qualities opposite our own to balance the inherent one-sided nature. (For the studies on or with content on the four temperaments, see those marked with an asterisk (*) in the *Contents*.) On such work rests all individual progress and therewith our contribution to society. However, it is also important to have an overview of our human situation and to keep ever in mind and heart what really matters. This is for other, personal choices that determine our very soul welfare, present and future.

Los Angeles
September 3-4
October 13/15/18/23, 2014

Love (2)

Within my heart essentially
My inner core is love
I sowed love's seeds within my heart
From wisdom up above
And see how beautifully love shines
My inner Christ, my love
I give thanks to dearest God
The Father-God above.

Alan Lindgren
Los Angeles
October 15, 2014

The Face of Our Humanity

What is the face of humanity today, the *real* human and natural reality? It is not to be found where we so often go, in the *virtual* dehuman and techno-reality of our own creation. We surf the Internet, TV channels, listen to iPods, CDs, watch movies, videos, DVDs, we surround ourselves and bombard our senses with virtual reality, with the deceptions of the Lie.

There, on the street, a poor mother is walking with her children, a homeless man is lying on the sidewalk or pushing a shopping cart, a homeless woman is looking for her next meal. Reality. There, above in the heavens, pure white clouds are slowly moving in the deep blue sky. Reality. At evening, the colors of sunset glow in all their feeling beauty, deepening from peach, rose, and pink to orange-golden and red until the sun sets at the close of a full day of her mighty works. Reality. There, little sparrows greet the new day with their songs of cheer. Reality. Here, all is right here in our midst, on our earth, in the heavens.

Here, an affluent couple drives with their three children, ages 3, 8, and 14, to the movies. Children who need physical play, art, and music, and the love, guidance, and support of their parents and teachers. Instead they play video games or surf the net. Reality. What kind of family life do they have, what kind of education? Questions. Our society. We go on making money, buying homes and expensive cars, living "The American Dream." Is it a dream, a façade, an illusion? Question. Are we living the American Lie? Millions of Americans live in poverty, in ghettos, in drugs and alcohol. There is social unrest. Crime. How can we go on like this, ignoring the homeless we pass by every day, denying our children their childhoods, missing the magnificence and wonders of nature, great and small? We make choices every day, and these our choices—each of our choices—together are what determine today, and tomorrow.

There is much human reality to be courageously suffered, and much

Reprinted with permission from Alan Lindgren, *By the Sunset there's a Door* (Culver City: Sun Sings Publications, 2002), 241-242

reality of natural beauty to be appreciated. The qualities of life, soul, and spirit, such as the colors and tones of nature, of painting and music, such as love and interest, compassion and esteem, these qualities cannot be measured. They mean nothing to the dead, analytical intellect of technology and cannot be registered as information or stored in a computer, yet these very aspects are our meaning and our humanity.

We are in danger of losing our humanity in divorcing ourselves and our children from nature and each other. We are at a risk like never before in all history. If we are to counteract all that is dehumanizing in our society, in our lives, *we* have to change, *we ourselves*. Freedom is not something *given* to us. It is an active *choice*. And there is genius and courage in this spiritual activity of freedom, of thinking.

In the past many traditions and customs gave daily life its wholesome meaning and significance and were handed down from one generation to the next. Now each one of us must consciously *create* a healthy relationship to the world. We can appreciate the beauty of our Creator's vast nature and tiny wonders, and get in touch with the daily, weekly, and seasonal-yearly rhythms of our sun, moon, and earth. We can look up at the stars. And we can be creative ourselves, developing and nurturing the artist in us.

We have made rapid technological progress, but genuine, inner, soul-spiritual progress of a human character is hard-won and proceeds quietly and steadily, regularly, unrushed, step-by-step, like the sun on her daily course through the heavens.

We may join the many special human beings in our midst who cherish in their hearts and souls all that is of value in our post-modern world, in humankind and in nature. They are our pulse-beat, our inner rhythm centers, our sustaining life-blood. Together with our loved ones and friends who have crossed death's threshold into the Spiritual Homeland, we form one great human family-community. Let us help each other, our children, our struggling humanity, taking time every day for thinking, feeling, and walking, for listening, learning, and perceiving, for meaningful suffering and inner growth. Then we shall help to make a *human* world on this our precious earth.

Human vs. Dehuman

The face of society has been changing more and more rapidly over the past one thousand to five hundred to two hundred to one hundred years, and over the past one hundred years even more rapidly, especially the past fifty, twenty-five, and ten years. Now *only four years go by for a radical change in the face or spiritual geography of the earth to occur. It is beyond human comprehension to determine whether the outcome will be for or against the progress of humankind. We are in the midst of both by far the greatest crisis ever to be faced by and at the same time the most tremendous potential ever to be offered humanity. The outcome will be the direct result of the combination of every single thought, feeling, and action of each person each day. It is therefore crucial what each one of us does, the choices we make in our personal lives. It really matters.*

The seamless technostructure becomes ever more integrated like a computer system in which human beings are mere units of information. Within this structure persons are treated like cogs in a great artificial machinery without regard to who the human being is or what he would strive to become, including the soul and spiritual qualities, character, and personality with which each man, woman, and child is endowed. We sense how easy it becomes to treat others as we find ourselves being treated in a fast-paced, hectic, and chaotic world, going, going, going without a real sense of inner purpose as to where we want to go. Yet, at the same time, we are aware of what we are doing, for we make decisions every day, even if this means that we blindly and passively accept and go along with what most everyone else is doing. Our true identity is lost in the shuffle. What is or was genuinely human and special is tossed around superficially in conversation in clichés and slogans like some meaningless commercial which we repeat because we lack the will to think of something original and genuinely interesting to

Reprinted with permission from Alan Lindgren, *By the Sunset there's a Door* (Culver City: Sun Sings Publications, 2002), 243-246

say to one another. We have become mindless and foolish with all our cleverness and intelligence because we simply don't want to make the inner effort to think for ourselves. After all, how much easier it is to let our government and corporate leaders, television and other media, and the current popular scientific theories provide us with our thoughts. Surely they must know what they are talking about. They are the "experts" after all. And aren't there experts for just about everything these days? There are seminars on how to conduct our lives, how to manage our time because we are so busy, how to make even more money, how to feel secure, how to relate to one another, how to stay fit and healthy, programs to follow to slim down. All we have to do is to do what we are told and everything will be alright. There seems to be something for every one and for every situation we could possibly find ourselves in. And there are countless pseudo-churches and spiritual movements, some of which claim they have the truth if only one will convert to their way of thinking or believing. Many so-called religious groups which are highly evangelistic promise salvation and warn again and again that world events, which *are* so tragic and the cause of so much suffering, are signs that the end of the world is near. Some of them schedule fund-raisers on television and countless "believers" pledge thousands of dollars, making a few "religious" leaders very rich. Few of all these groups and movements are genuinely religious or deeply spiritual. In the "New Age" movement, others adhere to what amounts to selfishness, eastern "self-health" and spirituality, which is but another self-deception. Yet people are looking for meaning everywhere, hoping to find it in wealth, technology, prestige, power, elitism, promise of salvation, a predetermined regimen ordained by someone else, and simple answers. People are insecure and deeply want to be secure in a world where material possessions and simple solutions have failed and will continue to fail because they cannot offer genuine security. There is so little love in the world, so little of what cannot be measured.

Aldous Huxley's *Brave New World* and George Orwell's *1984* have already arrived, yet people walk about as though nothing is wrong, instead pretending that life is better now because it is easier and more painless, so long as they are not reminded of the gravity of the situation, of the spiritual poverty and empty chaos and of the dear price of their own souls exacted by Mephistopheles in the Faustian bargain. Society, with all its outward abundance and the loud promises that we must only keep pace with the latest technological advancements, produce more capital, and earn more money and *then* things will be OK, is dehumanizing and dehumanized. But deep within, human beings are deeply afraid, for they know that the whole world seems to be caught up in all the excitement about nothing as they rush stressed out going nowhere fast themselves. Humankind is de-Christed and Christ is our humanity. The Christ experience, the most human of experiences, is the only experience which differs from all these empty promises and offers genuine help to human beings. Few are those who are willing to truly think for themselves and make wise choices in their own lives.

The world's problems are vast and manifold, and the answer to these problems is thus deeply complex, but on the other hand the solution depends on each person taking the time to "step out" of the "machinery" and the Lie, to work on his thinking, affirming what is good, right, and true, loving the inner Self and other human beings, and appreciating the great beauty of nature and each day, and the goodness of humanity wherever and whenever it appears. This means to be human and to suffer, for living in the Truth is often painful and uncomfortable. We must make some sacrifices and continually overcome our old selves, working on becoming our true selves positively every day and help one another whenever we can. Spiritual love is the love of the heart, and a loving, courageous heart is a blessing both to the person herself and to all human beings who share in this love. We share love with one another. Our good, warm thoughts are light-filled and contribute to the welfare of all humankind. It is a very good thing to think positively and creatively. There is much spiritual darkness as shadows in our world, but think how great and bright the Light must be to cast such shadows. There is much light today. We need to let our little lights shine radiantly and warmly wherever and with whomever we are. The Light in us dispels the darkness and grows stronger in the process. In this way, the darkness can *serve the Light.* We are living in a time when modern human beings must struggle with the question of evil (the darkness) in their own souls in order to actively choose the Good (the Light). This is our freedom. We are both individually and as humankind as a whole engaged in a real, earnest soul battle in our hearts and in our thinking in which all progress is hard-won and involves facing suffering and fear with love. Evil is more insidious today than it was during World War II with the extermination of six million human beings (twenty million in Russia were killed), although today men, women, and children are being killed in Syria, Afghanistan, and Israel without reason. Wars, fighting, armies, and weapons serve no good purpose. They are today completely unnecessary and without cause. We should not kill one another directly or indirectly. Evil in the modernized, industrialized, wealthy nations now takes the form of the Lie and deception through full cooperation— actually *invitation*—on the part of we "casualties." Whereas under the Nazi regime Jews, gypsies, the handicapped, the sick, and the weak were tortured and killed without feeling, today we "victims" *invite* the evil into our lives as pleasure and as virtual reality. The suffering and deaths of countless human beings was and is always identifiable. The Lie and virtual reality are far worse in that they *imitate* the human being and nature, in other words they present a *copy* of reality, which is in reality not human and natural at all, *artificially*, and would thereby desensitize and dehumanize human beings. Thus this form of evil is satisfied with nothing less than the human soul. It is not interested in inflicting physical pain and death, because the system Lie in actual people knows very well the soul is far more dear. One must therefore be either deeply good and unchangeably human, or good and wise as to what is really going on today if one is to work in a positive direction, and make real progress in a system which is ruthless in an often soul-less and chaotic world. Then one will find paths and places of 'real' reality where real and humanizing human beings appear, and where nature bestows her wealth of beauty and wonder. Then one will have good experiences and share love each day such that life becomes truly meaningful.

Human Change from Childhood and Youth to Adulthood: The Group, Society, and the I

We know there are clear stages in human development that happen in rhythms or time periods. One major rhythm is the 7-year. Each 7-year stage has specific requirements that must be met without which there are (dire) consequences.

We need only remember the time from conception or birth to the change of the teeth (7 years) that is the stage of early childhood when the physical body, needs, and development are central. For the small child, goodness in every manifestation provides the key: in routine of meal and snack times (nutrition), play, and naps/sleep, and in the adults in its life —working right into the limbs—, whom it imitates, all in which the fantasy life is active, works formatively on the developing organs during this time. Much joy and love are also essential to this special time.

In middle childhood (7 to puberty) the social element occupies center stage: the requirements of the child's feeling and temperament. Good habits are important, replacing the easy ones. The child's horizons should broaden to include adults outside its immediate family: teachers and historical personalities. Enthusiasm for learning and nature-experiences are most significant. Stability—the weathering of the storms of life in adulthood—depends on the presence of at least one loving authority figure during this period. To this childhood stage belongs 'education as an art' as we find in the Waldorf Schools. The adult must have had the religious in an adult as a child, usually a relative, such as a grandparent or a parent.

We ponder adolescence (about 14 to 21) when thinking and the critical intellectual faculties awaken with the ability to procreate and the capacity to form independent judgments asserts itself. The realization of spiritual potential in adulthood that is destined must have in key individuals at this time the active presence of the living Christ, which is embodied idealism.

Let us briefly consider the next stage, the transition into adulthood, from youth, that does not take place on the 21st birthday. It is a 7-year process, the ego's incarnation, 21 – 28. Consciously aware individuals sense this and must 'make room' inside for this process. The soul is still on the receiving end of life, but the independent personality makes its mark. Study, travel, and work experiences enrich the inner life and allow the individual to be active in whatever she or he is engaged in.

There are other changes in human life from those connected to or embedded in the rhythms and stages of development. By this is not meant any relationship or correspondence to historical or societal realities and influences. The effects of popular trends and norms to the *status quo* and upscale lifestyle with its comforts and conveniences, prestige, representation and anonymity, the many uses and abuses of technologies, the socioeconomic (class) standards and divisions come to mind. Although these influences have a considerable impact on many people, this impact cannot reach the inner recesses of the human soul and spiritual I. Those who define themselves by it have no possibility to develop along spiritual lines.

The only exception to this is when karma intervenes directly, but then the individual can no longer live under accepted pretensions, whether or not they stem from society, a group of any kind, self-protection, self-delusion, personal and social falsehood (deception, untruthfulness), mental illness that is an aversion to reality and health, or a combination of these directions. From this we readily see that the wealthy and upper classes are more susceptible to selfishness and the seductive attraction of the lie associated with money, property, materialism, and virtual-digital technologies (on a personal and group class level), while the poor and all who suffer a hard life are much less likely to lead false lives based on false premises to deny the truth of human experience felt in all suffering, because of the reality of their karma. The races and ethnic groups become human in Christ. This human-becoming in Christ comes from suffering suffered and always happens in individuals. We see the group-connection and, at the same time, the necessity of genuineness in terms of the individual's karma and striving.

Genuine and deeper changes are karmic because they occur in the destiny. This means they are an entirely personal matter experienced by the individual in the context of societal and socioeconomic differences and all outer circumstances, yet transcend or deepen within her or him in an act of personalization and individualization by the I from the differences defined by society and any group. These changes thus have a quality independent of common social influences owing to their personal and universally human nature characteristic of the human spiritual I (true identity). The general social influences become apparent and effective in most children already in middle childhood (7 years onward).

By high school age (adolescence) the differences defined by group identity permeate the social fabric and minds of many young people such that in adulthood the vast majority of the population can no longer make any real that is deeper changes. This fact is not altered by all the talk and claims about spirituality and religion that are largely empty as they have no basis in experience: the human soul and heart. This talk and these claims reveal something else entirely, directing our attention either to questions or concerns of the destiny, or to falsehood or illness. The latter include false worship (idolatry) and coveting (forms of self-seeking materialism (self-love) and selfishness), and the mood disorders of mood swings (especially mania) and pure depression (false spirituality and especially religiosity).

Yet many human beings today are dissatisfied with what society has to offer. What they are unwilling to see or think is that society cannot provide them with the inner endurance or work of their own *souls*, engaged in a individual soul *battle*, the gathering of life-experiences for the development of their spiritual I that alone effects genuine change that leads the human soul to the source of all striving, seeking, and being. Genuine change ultimately culminates in the full realization of spiritual potential during adulthood.

I must suffer the inner endurance or perform the inner work necessary for change; no one and nothing can bring about change in me. Beyond immaturity and adolescence that is childhood and youth (upbringing and education) awaits self-transformation. Adult self-education is the basis for self-transformation. Yet already in childhood and puberty we see the direction the individual person will take in life, outer success regardless.

The young person ventures out into the world where s/he can begin to endure or work in earnest—with much, some, or little self-application—make only moderate efforts, go about life with little genuine work or endurance and interest, or do nothing for her/himself at all. In childhood the fruits brought from the previous incarnation are manifest, which appear in a striking fashion from puberty and the late teenage years onward. We see then that all significant change results from the inner endurance or work of the spiritual I, which is performed in societal advantage or disadvantage. Independent initiative comes from within the soul and spirit, from deep within.

Most do not change in a profound way from when they were before the age of 18-19 years. Of these some do progress over the years, even significantly, even in great strides, for personal progress. This is their journey. This matters. This is important and essential for the present and future of the individual's soul. Others have not come so far but have yet opportunity if they engage in soul-battle with some discipline and virtue. This includes work on the temperament. This is their journey. But *every* one who would gain true worth in the sense of the realization of their destiny or potential—coming to know the Christ and therewith their higher Self—must go forwards the hard way else they go backwards the easy way. There is no standing still.

Changes for progress are always hard-won. They demand much from the individual and generally require long periods of time, many lifetimes to be made. Unlike change in the spiritual face or geography of the world that includes technological advancements, and that happens every four years, these inner changes take place according to the regular rhythms of the Sun planet, which we know are daily and seasonal-annual, but in terms of human life entire incarnations, and historically much slower.

Some few embark on a road of change filled with ever-new challenges encountered on uncharted yet wisely universal terrain that demands from them everything they can endure, muster, discern, sense, feel, remember, heal, or love. These individuals not only stay on course, they survive blows or hardship that would do in a less devoted or dedicated or determined soul, persevere when especially difficult or painful treatment, illness, or other experiences make themselves felt, work and walk onward when any and all doubts arise in the face of unfavorable winds. They follow their inner feeling for the truth that alone guides them and to which they alone remain true. Undeterred they reach their goal, whose approach makes clear or sure its achievement. Indeed all soul battle, endurance, struggles, and work to reach it are but signals of its inevitable attainment and serve to strengthen or empower the soul to this purpose that is predestined, because of their endurance or work.

Inner changes that are soul-spiritual are not given in the 7-year rhythms. They are fashioned from within in increasing endurance or creative soul-with-spirit deeds. Among the most significant is the transformation of one's temperament that is achieved only across many years of applied practice. The temperament is our habit-nature. We are accustomed to our second nature without any further efforts. So temperament is necessarily one-sided. Thus to transform our temperament means to take what comes naturally to us as behaviors and in relationships (life-habits) and to accomplish quite the opposite. We begin with our 'easy' habits, and we work on ourselves to establish habits that are good ones that require what lies opposite our nature. This is not easy. It requires years of application regardless of whether I am a Choleric, a Phlegmatic, a Sanguine, or a Melancholic. Yet there are specific practices we can take to develop ourselves in this area, our temperament depending. We work with ourselves, with knowledge of our temperament, and not against our all-to-human nature that would be but futile. All progress is founded on understanding. We briefly touched on forming good habits in the paragraph on middle childhood at the beginning of this study. For further and in-depth descriptions and help, please see the studies concerning the temperaments starred in the *Contents* (*).

Those who make real changes are met by those gifted with Christ. They receive the help they need when and where needed. They come to think and act in inner independence, when they encounter such a gifted individual as when they do not. They endure their karma or age-old suffering, or they achieve what they set out to do, and they accomplish much. This may be unapparent. This requires many earth-lives. They will care more deeply than the others. They work much harder. They endure more pain and suffering. They find satisfaction in their endurance or work, because they are on the right road in their soul-battle, and the rewards are good and self-affirming as they are hard-won.

This is their freedom. This is destiny. Freedom and destiny are chosen. For human beings, Christ is a choice who changes their souls forever, even as the soul who strives and seeks on the road to Him experiences genuine changes. This is the meaning of karma that is the destiny across many reincarnations.

Los Angeles
January 31/February 3, 2011
October 15/22, 2014
Culver City, California
May 13/15, 2014

Destiny and Society

While the problems and implications of the impact on individuals of society cannot be overstressed, it is symptomatic of the weakened sense of the human I (identity) today that the destiny, chosen or surrendered by the individual, is not considered, earnest in real gravity though it is. That this was not the case, for example in the Romanesque Period, the Age of the pilgrimages (ca. AD1050-AD1200), when the danger to the soul, and not the body, was recognized and occupied the place of primary concern, is not in the thoughts of young people and adults anymore.

We see the divergence in society, among all the peoples of the earth, of two groups: those souls who lose their way in either of two directions, and those who strive, do inner battle, and find their way. With the huge impact in the Western cultures, when we include such nations as Japan, of virtual and other technologies in their artificial sights and sounds on the human soul via damage to the senses—here the eye and ear organs—countless individuals are placed at risk from early childhood. Yet even here, the divergence mentioned above can be observed according to which group the individual, by choice, belongs: those who, more and more, give themselves, their souls over to virtual, digital, and other artificial realities in contrast to those who, wary of the effects the use of these technologies have on their perceptual (eye and ear) organs and therewith inner lives, intentionally turn away from them to fully engage in the real life and inner thought/imagination. Those who, before birth, have yet the possibility for salvation, chose parents or other childhood circumstances that will offer them opportunities in this direction.

Of course if one allows oneself to be seduced by the (system) Lie that pervades (Western) society at every level, which implies the surrender of the soul to lose all possibility to, going forward on its destined path, one day know the Lord of its karma, which is Christ, this seduction very likely includes the bombardment of the senses by virtual and other artificial sensations. For what is the Lie but a seductive imitation of reality, the reality of nature, human creativity, human feeling, human beings, and Christ? This seduction is ever-ready to accost those who will invite the Lie into their souls, which is a choice that leads to emptiness. The other direction a soul may be lost is to destruction by illness that is consuming emotion. There comes a point beyond which no recovery is possible any more. By this is meant emptiness and consumption by flagrant emotionalism both.

The path that goes to the fork that leads forward the 'hard' but only satisfying and secure way, is altogether different. This route, which the pilgrims in the Romanesque Period sought with all their souls, minds, hearts, spirits, and strength, results from positive choices. If I choose to embrace life fully, I will seek out healthy experiences, occupy my mind in intensifying work on my thinking, tend to my personal affairs and responsibilities that I know are crucial for my well-being, work on myself, which is to say on my temperament (see below), steer clear of bad that is harmful people and behaviors, set and pursue goals however modest they appear to be, affirm my suffering as deeply and personally belonging to me to my karma, perform positive, useful, and constructive work, study, map out my course inwardly, sometimes also outwardly, in short make *good* choices and decisions that protect my soul, my spirit, whereby my progress is ensured.

We live in an age of decline. This is witnessed all around us, even as it is demanding of and confusing for us. It is to be observed in the weather; all human and natural disasters; the world economy that, like the world climatic system, manifests regionally and nationally in different locations in various but inseparable and connected ways; at all levels of government; in social strife; childhood's fragile ecology; materialism and poverty (disparity, economic exploitation), hunger, illness, marginalizing and homelessness; prejudice/nationalism and militarism; the systematization and quantification of people, work, and education; the popular media; complacency; personal and national fears; insomnia, memory loss, anxiety, and nervousness; psychoses, neuroses, and addictions; antipathy; hedonism and the cult of the body; religiosity and false spirituality; and, not in the least, the ever-widening use of virtual and other artificial technologies. We know that these and other causes and symptoms are also interlinked.

Because of these great and complex problems, or at a deeper level, it is crucial what you and I do and do not do. The extent to which I contribute to society and to world progress can be measured by the degree in which I make good and beneficial choices in my own life.

Engaging in work on my temperament that is the habit-nature in daily practice is of immeasurable importance.

For the Sanguine this implies concentration in reading, writing, or musical-artistic practice that little by little lengthen her attention span. She needs to flit about sometimes like a butterfly until she once again comes to stay on one subject for a while. Crucial for her is to think her **I** herself, to receive impressions from what she sees and hears and loves, which leads her to reflect upon and quietly live and stay with the effects, with the inner effects of these impressions in herself, in her thoughts where they work on. In contrast to this are her outer hobbies and interests, which are superficial, but which may deepen. She needs to develop fewer or one lasting interest/s of her own choosing.

For the Choleric the challenge lies in practicing repetition, such as performing repetitive, mundane physical tasks and chores daily, weekly, seasonally, and reading the same book every year over many years. This is therapeutic. He needs to expend his excess will-force energy on small facts because they do not budge. And when he has gone too far, the Choleric needs to be faced with the seriousness of what he has done by one whom he respects. It is good for him to learn about great individualities and personalities who have achieved great things so that he can say of himself: *I* could never have done that. Hence, reading good biography is most beneficial.

The Melancholic will dwell on the depth of human suffering. This means immersion in the pain of humanity, learning about the lives of the saints and martyrs, human beings who have experienced hardship and hurt, also those in her own life, whereby she forgets herself in selfless compassion. This draws her out of herself. Important is much etheric liveliness, all manner of joy, happy teasing and jesting, warmth and frivolity, every kind of self-expression (factual, compassion, passion, humor, off-hand remarks *et cetera*), and good cheer, going outside into the fresh air and sunshine, and for invigorating and warming walks in the wide world, taking an interest in her surroundings: birds and animals of all kinds, stones, children and human beings of all ages, stars and the moon, flowers, clouds, rainbows, sunlight and big skies. This also leads the introvert from within outwards into the world. She needs to have caring friends.

For the Phlegmatic the events include sitting in an otherwise empty room with four walls to really *feel* his lazy boredom to resolve to get up and *do* something. Being surrounded by a group of friendly and loud people that is an awakening and uplifting experience brings this burdened, often heavy nature joy. Rubbing shoulders with other personalities in whose company he takes a warm, shared interest is ever welcome (brotherly love and camaraderie). Engaging in practical physical work, and walking with a purpose is healthy and positive. The experience of physicality in hand and limb is therefore important as by it the natural indolence is overcome with the efforts of will.

If I wish to be part of the solution to the many world problems and the healing of the many societal ills, I will join together with all those around the globe who do battle in their own souls, work on self-transformation, and who live in a right relationship to others in their immediate circles of activity.

What is this right relationship? It is one of two things, both of which involve suffering: the creation of karma in my relationships through active personal work, and the endurance of suffering in my relationships in disciplined contemplation. Actually, both call for discipline, and both are seen to be personal, for the journey of the destiny is always a personal one and at least some discipline is required of every one who will realize her potential and resolve her destiny that must be in the place it is formed: on earth.

Los Angeles
May 9-11, 2011
October 18, 2014

On the Soul Today

The inner-outer circumstances in society, and that present themselves to individuals today, pose direct dangers with clear consequences, bad or good, choices depending. Unlike in the poor, war-ravaged, and disease-infested nations, here in the West these dangers are not to the life of the body, to starvation, losing fortunes, jobs, housing, and vacations, because in many instances people—especially in upper-class society—are wholly preoccupied with their false materialistic lives, which are not only a product of the worldview that only what is material exists and there is no God, no soul, no spirit, but that make them complacent for their prized idle comforts and conveniences, so that they have everything material they could desire, or at least can obtain. This is a very serious condition, because it signifies disconnection from our divine source, one another, and Nature, and without these relationships we are nothing. True friendships, sometimes family connections, children, and pets, make all the difference in the world. Without suffering, there is no feeling, no karma, no Christ. It is all about humanization in a dehuman society. However, it is more and more common that those with little in the way of possessions and outer comforts also go down the road of inner emptiness and a pain-free existence, enhanced or created by the stimulus of sensations of artificial technologies, much as do their well-to-do or affluent co-citizens. The souls of people are at risk, and every one knows this, whether or not they kid themselves they would never do such a thing or that, "I know. It's so harmful. You see it everywhere," while they are hypocrites, or, "I need technology," or, "I couldn't live without it," or "I like it," then returning to their self-hypocrisy and cover-up that they are not among those who would ever bring their own souls into jeopardy.

Increasingly, people are making bad choices, and these choices have grave consequences that, at a certain point, are irreversible. It matters not if they say one thing and mistakenly or cleverly contradict themselves in the next moment. The point is, not the *what*, but the *how*, not the *content* (which may or may not be healthy), but the *medium*, the *sensation*, the impact on the sensory organs and therewith on the mind and sleep. For, as with food for fundamental physical health, so it is with the senses and the mind for soul health, which may lead to poor or lack of sleep and the eradication of all rhythm and sense of purpose. It is through this avenue of artificial reality, artificial sensory stimulation, that the soul is at stake, in one direction or the other, for real insecurity or true security, by way of personal choices. In the former situation there is dreaminess, mental instability, and illness, or the increased tendency to them; in the latter instance wakefulness, mental health, and healing.

The child has no say in the matter. Like their beloved pets, the children are at our mercy, and the very gravest dangers are the tremendous exposure on children to the virtual and other artificial sensations, when they should be protected from all harmful technologies altogether until puberty, and then under restricted uses. If a child is denied a childhood, it will not have an adulthood, period. Childhood is the foundation of adulthood. But as adults we do have say in the matter; we have *choice*.

There are still those who do not go down that road, who instead lead meaningful lives the *hard* but inwardly *rich* way. But the risk, not for the many for whom it is already long too late, but for those with an inwardly-rich past, is to slip through the cracks and lose themselves in this world of machine technologies with real consequences. They are the ones whose precious souls have not yet been lost to the vast nothingness of society, but neither are they protected from the seductive power of artificial technologies, which will be heeded at every hand. Many of these are more and more easy, inexpensive, and accessible to obtain, and you see people everywhere using them, so why not, it is very appealing, and besides, every one is saying it's very useful, actually indispensable nowadays. It would be backwards to revert to out-of-date ways. I must be up with the times and go for apparent opportunities that will, after all, make my life better, faster, easier. Do we ask ourselves what good is 'better', faster, easier? Why am I here? Why am I alive, and what am I doing with my life? What is my purpose, my contribution; what has personal meaning to me? What do I care about? What gives me worth? What about my soul that alone is worth real work, enduring suffering? Do I work, earn money, and pay the bills to work, earn money, and pay the bills, or do I do these things for progress and societal contribution, which go hand-in-hand? Am I learning lessons from the wisdom of life?

I am not speaking of clearly self-restricted uses of technology. So long I use the cell phone, the laptop, the Internet strictly for personal contact, business purposes, and as *tools* **only**, and not for any other reason, technology may serve a beneficial outcome. But the moment even these uses begin to replace direct human contact, time for close friends or family; nature-experiences (even in the city where the Sun shines, the clouds rain, or appear in beauteous white or in awesome color at sunrise and dear color at sunset, the trees and other plant growth make green and blossom of color, the little birds sing, the Moon shines, the stars sparkle, and the stones and buildings rest); reading non-informational literature (poetry, fiction, or non-fiction) from the printed page for pleasure or interest, and profound non-fiction such as anthroposophy for study; creator or audience of living art of a genuinely interesting and beautiful character, at that moment the insidious nature of these technologies enters the picture and very easily usurps more and more time and effort from the individual.

Why does this happen, seeing as the live experiences are so beneficial, inwardly rich, enjoyable, meaningful, and beautiful? Firstly, many are unwilling to make sacrifices any more, and if I do not give up harmful habits, comfortable or pleasurable indulgences, invest time and effort into something worthwhile, I will reap no inner rewards. Often there is little or no cost; no technological wonders are involved; simple presence, instruments, inexpensive materials, even attendance with attentive participation is all that is necessary. A major reason is that nothing is required of us to bombard our senses with artificial sounds and sights, which mesmerize, dull, or stimulate our minds, no inner activity. We become passive. Finally, we are as dead inside, so that when we turn off or leave behind the technology and are exposed to natural and human sensations, nothing stirs within, nothing happens. We think nothing, feel nothing, imagine nothing, inspire nothing, intuit nothing sense nothing any more. We are beyond help.

On the other hand, when we engage our senses and minds in good conversation, nature-experiences, and reading—all in a quiet environment—or are an active part of live music or art as audience or creator (listening or seeing), we must participate in the experience in a human or spiritual sense in order to get something from it. If we do this we find we are richly rewarded. There is opportunity; we must only avail ourselves of it.

There is much of interest in literature to be had at really low prices (often a book in new condition costs less than the $4.00 in shipping; this includes the best and most interesting books out there; everything is available for purchase online), and the selection is huge, your interests the limit.

There are always people who want only to visit with another human being without distractions; we must only seek one another out and take time for one another. Just doing what most every one seems to be doing won't do. How many today are lonely and in need of a friend, to help and be helped, to befriend and be befriended? Find a place, a quiet spot outdoors or room and share some quality time together. This could be in silence or conversation, with a snack or over a meal, reading a good book to one another, or just being together.

We mentioned nature-phenomena; they are just about everywhere. There would be neither daytime nor life nor food without the Sun, the Earth, water, plants, and clouds; neither nighttime nor soul nor animals without the ocean, the seas, the Moon, Venus, and the stars. We must only send out our souls through our senses to experience the wonders and beauty of Mother Nature.

Public lectures are given; many people are musically or artistically talented, even gifted, and often these fine individuals have experience and training in their medium. They are only glad to share their special work with an appreciative audience and often do so for little or no charge in an intimate setting with a small or very small audience. Discover and attend these events! Why, you'd think each performance would bring a packed house to hear what these intelligent women and men have to say on the subject of their expertise, experience their excellent live music, or see their genuinely interesting beautiful artwork. We are talking about real talent here, not some irrational, cynical, desperate expressions or experiments.

Then there are writers' and poets' groups, which meet on a weekly or other regular basis to read their work and offer helpful criticism to one another. Often talented and experienced writers and poets attend or lead these groups, and the humanity or spirituality present, while centered on the written word, brings about dear friendships based on common cultural interests and abilities, sometimes of a karmic nature. There are live theatre, workshops, and full participation in, not only drama, movement, and speech; but also writing, painting, sculpture, singing, and dance, to mention a few. Eurythmy, a relatively new art form of *visible speech* and *visible song* that is in gestures, is deeply therapeutic, pedagogical (for children), and for performance. (see page 324)

With the informational and connective technologies, we really have no excuse to not locate these inwardly rich offerings and experience them live that is in person. Then technology serves a good purpose, brings about meetings and gatherings for people united by common interest, desire for humanity, and the willingness to make personal connections. Of course, word of mouth remains the major means for us to meet and connect with one another. The printed word announces gatherings, concerts *et cetera* as well. Or a combination: Why not post news regarding an event over the Internet, in printed format, and by word of mouth? And this is done. However, technology actually separates human beings, because too often its uses replace coming together for actual visits and sharing in the company of one another.

Open the curtains, the blinds, the windows; let the sunlight in; step outside and feel the breeze on your face, the soft rain, the freezing magical snow, the warm rays of the Sun. Look up and gaze at the pale Moon, twinkling Venus, and the still stars at night. God speaks through Christ in Nature. Hear with the prophets, poets, and philosophers. Sophia the Spirit sings through Christ in Heaven. We are men, women, and children—human beings. We are souls—spiritual beings. We are realists. We are idealists. We are young. We are old. We are human. We are spiritual.

The dangers we face, societal and individual both, are real and great; the opportunities are equally great. We are, for the first time in history, truly free. Today is the Age of Choice and choices. In a very real sense, it all boils down to saying "yes" or "no", to what we do and do not do. This applies specifically to technologies and their uses, but it encompasses all personal decisions for worse or for better. Habits are very important. Here we have the four temperaments. This is developing the qualities and habits *opposite* one's own. We can only work with our natures; force brings no results.

The Sanguine with the short attention span gradually lengthens hers over time by daily concentrating slightly longer than is comfortable. Receiving impressions and allowing them to sink in to really live with them for many years is important. Going from outer hobbies and interests to deeper lasting interests by concentrating in one or two fields of study or in painting or musical composition or performance through faithful and disciplined practice is necessary over the years. The Sanguine chooses her own interest. It is important for this work to be done in a quiet environment *without* the stimulus of artificial sensations.

This means both visual and auditory stimuli on this aware and open nature. Otherwise the senses are damaged, the mind hyper-stimulated or mesmerized, the soul deadened. This leads the soul into a condition from which it cannot recover, sometimes insanity, which is no attention span, the direct opposite our aim. The Sanguine has the most beautiful sense of interest, spontaneous, open, and aware, and she notices and loves lovableness and beauty. She has a natural and profound appreciation for light and color phenomena. The Sanguine naturally imagines. Where the intuition of thoughts is innate in the Melancholic, the imagination of colors and color and of beauty is inborn in the Sanguine.

The Choleric with the strong will directed outwards expends her excess will-force energy on small facts, facts because they will not budge. Performing small, ritual, mundane physical tasks and chores repeatedly is therapeutic; repetition is a key here. The work performed must be physical to receive the benefits. If the individual sits at the computer or otherwise engages himself with artificial sensations, the soul faces nothing, experiences nothing real, when he requires the healthy contact of reality to face the world and receive human and physical impressions. Artificial sensations dull the sensory organs so that the by-nature strong will has nowhere to go. This can lead to frenzy or emptiness and desolation or anxiety or nervousness. Reading the same book once each year, for many decades is healthy. We note repetition again. Reading biography is especially good. Learning about the lives and accomplishments of heroes and heroines, great men and women, those greater than oneself such that one can say, *I* never could have done that, is good. These several beneficial practices all aid in relaxation. These must be hard copy, physical books, and not Kindle or e-books. The Choleric has the most beautiful sense of compassion, strong, supportive, and courageous. He has natural dignity, and his good will is absolute. He requires contact with others who possess self-regard, strength, and knowledge, and he knows when his deeply human sense of dignity is offended. Respect is the key to the Choleric, self-respect and for others, for specific qualities and strengths such as wisdom or perceptiveness or knowledge or physical courage and power, and for those superior to oneself. He has a natural sense for objects and spatial relationships, such as the placement of furniture in a room and the human being walking down the street. The Choleric intuits forms and spaces.

The Melancholic has other needs. Learning about the great suffering of humanity, of the saints and martyrs, and of the people in one's own life, to forget oneself in selfless compassion is essential. Abundant selfless love is expressed by this otherwise egoistic nature. In thinking obsession to the extreme, she might go mad. Compassion and all soul-expression are essential for the social participation, interest, and health of this deeply sensitive nature. Taking an active interest in others, culture, and nature/the environment is a key, passing interests as well, learning hobbies, noticing flowers, butterflies, rainbows, cultivating a sense of humor, passion, compassion, matter-of-fact-ness, touch, gesture, glance, word, voice, every kind of outwards expression is important for this introspective thinker. This self-expression and interest must be personal and natural. Not with technologies but in life, and with human and natural sensations, is experience meaningful and progress made. The auditory technologies are particularly harmful for the Melancholic: the iPod, headphones, music websites, CDs, DVDs, *et cetera*. The soul goes from looking inwards to outer seeing and expression, opening up a wide new world, or at least affording a healthy glimpse and experience. A true friend or partner is so important. We all need true friends, but for the Melancholic this takes on a particularly personal significance. This special nature has the most beautiful esteem, dignified and noble. She has a natural sense for words and thoughts, which she intuits.

The Phlegmatic, who is perfectly contented relaxing and doing nothing else, needs to get up and do something. Physicality is the byword. Walking and working with the hands are positive. Beware of the machine technologies, also for another reason: The Phlegmatic requires the healthy rousing from his slumbers from natural and human engagement such as taking a walk, camping, gardening, carpentry, singing, speech, spending time with (a) good friend(s), being a part of a loud, lively group of peers in whose company he will take a warm, shared interest. This is set in contrast to staring at the television or sitting at the computer for hours of endless monotony. We learn from Rudolf Steiner that every genius was an imbecile in at least one previous incarnation. Where imbecility (idiocy) is simply the Phlegmatic temperament in the extreme, becoming lost in the auditory and visual stimuli produced by artificial technologies that do permanent damage to the ears and eyes and therewith the mind bring about, beyond imbecility, a condition from which no genius can arise, but only soul dissolution. We need to be kind with our Phlegmatic friend or loved one who feels so burdened. He likes food and is the natural sensuous romantic, so we must watch that he doesn't overeat as a weight problem makes him feel only heavier inside. This most social of the temperaments is the multifaceted genius, yet he feels himself to be a failure owing to his sense of carrying a burden. Encouragement is positive showing only understanding; it is this attention required by this temperament of the most beautiful love, serene and even. He cannot be directly influenced by others, rather considers everything placed before him with indifferent survey whence he finds his evaluation and forms his own judgment. He thereby goes from apathy to contribution, from dullness and laziness to active interest. It is by means of this his worthy voice is heard and his unique personality appears singular among other personalities. He is by nature musical and awakens in the Tone world. He can sit at the piano and, note followed by note, create a perfect simple melody, harmonious in itself. The Phlegmatic is inspired by the songs and sounds of singing, music, and Nature.

Many today are or remain passive or go along with the crowd. Every one else seems to live by technology, work to work, live to live, eat to eat, make money for property or wealth. So I have every reason to do the same. After all, no one else seems to be questioning what they're doing. Besides, I like my lifestyle, at least I don't want to make the effort necessary to change my ways. But inside their souls, whenever they pause from what they're doing or rest their minds on a thought or take a moment for self-reflection, these people know this is a lie or that it leads nowhere. What is popular is likely untrue and does not serve real progress and the Good, individual and societal. Being true to oneself that signifies finding one's own, individual path in life is the only way that is meaningful, real and ideal. But most people don't consider these issues, or if they do, do not act on them. They make no changes; they do not progress, or only very little.

If these same individuals would get a copy of Aldous Huxley's 1931 novel, the prophetic classic *Brave New World* (first published in 1932), go to a quiet place, and read it without distraction, they would be encouraged to really think through their situation, possibly make some life-determining changes that would actually save their own souls. It is also important to take time out every day for self-assessment, to look at where one is going, if any adjustments or redirection should be made, and to then implement these changes in a concrete fashion.

One thing is certain, this would give them pause for thought, which, if heeded, *might* encourage them to exercise great caution, perhaps turn around before it is too late, not for a society at risk, which is ridden with so many problems, but for their own souls. Here it becomes apparent adult self-education provides the key, which means real self-questioning and thinking applied, not to otherwise beneficial wisdom, cleverness, or talent, but for real positive personal change.

Los Angeles
June 19-21, 2013
October 18, 2014
Culver City, California
May 30, 2014

Freedom: On Being 'Different'

Under Hitler's fascist regime in the 1930s and '40s, not only were those who were different from the Aryan 'norm' marginalized as is often the case socio-historically, they were driven out from Germany and its axis powers under certain death. This fact is apparent in the extermination of six million Jews in the concentration camps. (Hitler was short with dark hair and brown eyes. His grandmother was Jewish.)

But there were other marginalized groups of human beings whom the regime sought to wipe out or to drain of all inner qualities in the holocaust, which make us particular, human beings. The gypsies, the weak, the elderly, homosexuals, the disabled, and the mentally ill were among those put to death in the German camps.

Unhealthy and irrational conditions that marginalize people and send them into extreme poverty, homelessness, and hospitalization; disabilities and illnesses can be decisive in karmic significance, so long their suffering is endured to eventual healing and redemption. Here we usually do not see their deliverance until future incarnations.

Under Hitler, true culture was also banned, and those who sought to pursue their cultural vocation in freedom as artists, writers, teachers, professors, scientists, and centers of religious life in Germany during WWII were sent to the concentration camps, joining the Jews and the other 'different' people there. Hence, just as many Jews fled Germany to escape death, many of these gifted, creative, and intelligent individuals left the country to practice their calling in cultural freedom.

Because it fostered freedom of the human spirit, the Waldorf School in Stuttgart was shut down, but the students spray-painted "WE WILL RETURN" on the outer walls of the school building. Indeed, immediately after the war, former teachers and students did return, and by their initiative this first Waldorf School began afresh with next to no resources other than their sacrifices and enthusiasm.

The Christian Community was likewise banned by the regime, but the main sacrament, the *Act of Consecration of Man*, was carried out by courageous and wise priest-pastors secretly in private homes. Had these brave men been caught, they would have joined many of their colleagues imprisoned in the camps. Emil Bock, the first Erzoberlenker (archbishop) of the Christian Community, was in a concentration camp throughout much of the war where he made translations of the New Testament from the original ancient Greek into modern High German. Because Bock's aim was to capture something of the power of the three great languages of antiquity—Hebrew, ancient Greek, and Latin—in modern German, which in a sense is unattainable because our modern languages are all weak in comparison, he made three translations. Bock's third translation is effective, as is evident on an artistically-spoken reading, especially the great Prologue to the Gospel of St. John.

We mentioned that German writers and artists had to leave Germany if they were unwilling to conform to the artificial constructs of fascist ideology, or else they too would have been sent to the camps. Two such writers came to Los Angeles, Thomas Mann and Berthold Brecht.

From these examples, we can see that Hitler's aim was, not only to wipe out human beings who were different from an Arian German 'norm' that did not include himself, but more than this to destroy the soul of the true German people. To this end, all German culture had to be eradicated. At the end, although he came close to achieving his goal, we know the German folk soul lives on unbroken through WWII and the present time. This is actually visible today, not in the annual beer-drinking Munich Oktoberfest in Bavaria, German politics or universities, or in any other German academic, political, or traditional activity (all normative), but in genuine German culture that has real soul-spiritual roots as we have in anthroposophy and the Society, in the following examples:

Waldorf education, special needs education, pedagogic (in the Waldorf Schools) and curative arts, anthroposophically-extended medicine, eurythmy, veil painting, Sprachgestaltung (speech formation), singing, music, sculpture, organic architecture, artistic phenomenological (Goethean) science, bio-dynamic agriculture (farming and gardening), business, banking, the Christian Community, all of which thrive in real terms, in actual Waldorf teachers, students, and schools; special needs teachers, students, and schools; anthroposophic doctors, nurses, patients, hospitals, and clinics; eurythmists (eurythmy troupes) and eurythmy performances; veil painting artists and their work; curative eurythmists, their patients, and curative eurythmy; watercolor painting therapists, their patients, and therapeutic watercolor painting; pedagogic (Waldorf School) eurythmy teachers and their pupils (Waldorf students); pedagogic (Waldorf School) watercolor painting teachers and their pupils (Waldorf students); bio-dynamic farmers and farms, gardeners and gardens; Goethean scientists and scientific research; businessmen and businesses which practice economics founded on the anthroposophic knowledge of the human being; Christian Community priest-pastors, communities, churches; the German branches of the Anthroposophical Society and its members, the German anthroposophists.

There are hundreds of Waldorf (Rudolf Steiner) Schools in Germany which have long pupil waiting lists, dozens of Waldorf Schools and establishments for special needs children, dozens of anthroposophical hospitals and clinics in high demand, organic architects, several eurythmy schools and professional eurythmy troupes, hundreds of eurythmy and painting practitioners and teachers in pedagogy in the Waldorf Schools and curative (therapeutic) work, many sculptors who use the anthroposophical approach, dozens of very talented and gifted anthroposophist musicians, many students and singers in the School for Uncovering the Voice in Hamburg ("die Schule der Stimmenthüllung"), dozens of fully-trained speech formationists, hundreds of fully-accredited bio-dynamic farms, dozens of scientific researchers and teachers who use the Goethean approach, dozens of Christian Communities, as many branches of the Anthroposophical Society with their anthroposophists, businesses and banks practicing anthroposophy in economics, and many dozens Rudolf Steiner libraries and bookstores, all in Germany today. (The Singing School, which teaches the *School for Uncovering the Voice* method, is in Finland. Students are taught in English. German and Finnish are also used. After four years, the fifth year of study focuses on one of three life-directions: performance, pedagogical, or therapeutic.)

In addition, there are the many seminars, for example in Stuttgart, the Christian Community priest seminary, the Waldorf teacher seminar, the Eurythmeum (the Stuttgart eurythmy school), the Waldorf kindergarten seminar, the anthroposophical arts youth seminar, the Rudolf Steiner House. Hamburg now has a Christian Community seminary. Veil painting artists learn the anthroposophical approach in German cities, while in other European and non-European lands other seminars and schools instruct students in these and other disciplines, while schools, hospitals, clinics, farms, gardens, businesses, banks, artists, Christian communities, Steiner libraries and bookstores, and local branches of the Society thrive. Thus Europe and Germany in particular is full of creative activity where much learning and practice is happening. In America we also have places where such cultural activities are happening. They are not well known by non-anthroposophists as in Europe, but many are they who are helped and whose lives are enriched. Some human beings are practicing their vocations in an entirely individual way. Many of these creative human beings are gifted, something often overlooked but of tremendous value in our time.

In communist societies, free culture does not exist, or it must be carried on (practiced) in careful ways, which are wisely protected by close connections with insiders within the system. This was the case in East Germany before the Iron Curtain came down in the Soviet period, which means under this brand of communism. There were not only Christian Communities, but a seminary for the Christian Community as well. This was only in East Germany. The Christian Community was the exception, because such cultural practices as eurythmy were prohibited in East Germany altogether as in the rest of the Soviet Union.

In earlier periods of Russian communism, the Marxist government was much more severe. In the 1930s the pogroms were carried out against, not only Jews, but also creative spirits such as writers were forced to emigrate or put to death. During WWII under Stalin, twenty million Russians were cruelly murdered. This left just as deep a mark on Russian history and the Russian people as did the deaths of six million Jews on German history and the German people. Later torture was also common. We think of Siberia and the Russian writer Alexsandre Solzenitzschen who was forced into exile when he did not bend to torture and had gained world renown as a writer.

For years, communism in China was no more benevolent. The Cultural Revolution in the 1960s and Tienanmen Square in particular is an especially horrible period in communist China. Thousands of professors, teachers, students, artists, scientists, and individuals who professed their religion or who were centers of religious community were imprisoned, tortured, or killed. Cuba under Castro is another example of a communist regime where official torture and punishment by death for the exercise of cultural freedom have long been commonplace.

More serious in the current world situation is North Korea's "European fascism" that is closer to the fascism of Hitler and his cronies, and in Italy under Mussolini, than it is to Japan's fascism, during WWII. The State rule is under the personalities of men in a family, father to son down the generations, which will inspire absolute obedience of all North Koreans through fearsome charisma. North Korea today experiences poverty and hunger as severe as very poor African countries, and those who do not conform to the State's fascist ideology live in Labor Camps, which include the children born there. About 50,000 North Koreans are forced to a life of hard labor in these camps, and whoever challenges the harsh rules is tortured to 'straighten out'. If they fail to conform they are either executed or imprisoned within the Labor Camp.

I recently saw a propaganda film clipping of North Korean soldiers marching, which looked strikingly similar to a film clip I saw many years ago of drummed up Nazi soldiers on the march, only much more so, if this is possible. It is really bad, like George Orwell's *1984*. But in the 21st century everything is far more more severe. Disparity separates the classes more than ever before.

We must understand the position of the Korean people, who were the Koreans of one land since divided by political and military powers (China and the United States). Their suffering is tremendous, their hunger and the fear they live under is extreme, to say the least.

The Fabric of Technology and the Spiritual Wasteland of Materialism

The answer to the question "Who am I?" implies the answer to the question "Who is Christ?" These questions must be asked, and answered, by every human being, for without them there can be no true freedom, neither can there be realization and resolution of the destiny.

In 'free' Western society other forces are at work, which are highly seductive as those who conform do so without outer compulsion. Selfish gain (property, profits, capitalism) separates the few, who live in idle luxury on capital produced by those who do the work, the majority, who perform the strenuous labor—sometimes two or three jobs at once—for so little income they often cannot make ends meet for the family. Complacency because of comfort and convenience makes these rich individuals capitalists, such that they invite the seduction of the system into their lives. Their materialism is not only in conception (thinking that what is not material does not have existence), but in lifestyle as well. Hence the lie of the system and materialism is both insidious and selfish. Materialists love no one but themselves.

But our souls are in grave danger, because the system lie will remove suffering, rendering us empty, meaningless, purposeless. Technology plays a large role in this, one that stimulates or deadens the senses and the mind even as it mesmerizes, separating souls from suffering one another. The poor are neither protected as many live an empty, if impoverished existence, although such conditions as homelessness may create genuine suffering and hardship that keep the soul safe.

For those who have opportunity today, the cultural life, which expresses itself in society, is given fresh life and fresh impulses from the spiritual world in human beings and their cultural aims in many places on earth. Poor, upper class, or rich, we must each be 'different' despite all efforts for marginalization, threats of torture and death, and not least the forces of popular conformity, make some sacrifices, take courage of heart with the accompanying suffering, and stand independently in inner freedom, which no regime, government, or system may influence or alter.

From the examples given, it is plain we require our cultural freedom to carry out our tasks in outer life, but to stand in independent inner freedom we depend only on our own courageous, independent, ethical thinking, feeling, and good will which no one or institution may influence. This is responsible ethical individual 'anarchy'. This 'being different' is our 'Western dissidence' that we do not conform to any standard, accepted or rebellious. Instead, we maintain our true, inner course, good, clear, reasonable, healthy, and virtuous. We are free men and women who stand in Christ, and death itself has no power over our choices. We choose our own path and future, and all responsibility falls on our own heads. Who is Christ? His only true name is 'I AM'. He who does not know this, does not understand this, or calls Him by another name knows absolutely nothing about Christ. Self-knowledge implies knowing Christ, the 'I AM' within. This is the answer to "Who am I?"

Los Angeles
July 22/24-25, 2013
October 18/22/27, 2014
Culver City, California
May 30, 2014

Culture, Politics, Economics

The three great ideals of the French Revolution were Liberté, Egalité, é Fraternité: freedom, equality, brother/sisterhood. These are three distinct realms in the human makeup, relationships, and societies. Human beings can, and should, ever and again, apply them at the personal level, then at higher ones.

At the personal level, freedom is thinking's true realm and therewith the pursuit of adult self-education. Here, I am free: in my thinking activity, contemplation, meditation, and study. This is the practice of our essential spiritual freedom and varies according to the inner progress of the individual. Here, we are unequal but should share our gifts with others less gifted.

Equality is shown in all personal and impersonal relationships in common agreements and meetings. If we have agreed to meet at such-and-such a place and time, and I am unable to (something unexpected may have come up such as illness or a death in the family), it is my responsibility to contact you to 1.) cancel, 2.) reschedule, or 3.) take a rain check. Here, we are equals, differences in inner development or lack thereof regardless. We are peers, colleagues, friends, lovers. We share in love and human feeling.

Brother/Sisterhood at the personal level signifies one human being who is able helping another in need of his help without thought or action for compensation or even recognition. The best illustration is Christ's parable of the Good Samaritan. Here, we are brothers and sisters in the human family and God is our Father. We lend a helping hand. We work. We till the soil. We garden. We farm the earth. We exercise intentionality. We show one another our good will.

At larger and higher levels, freedom extends to all culture: education and instruction, schools of all kinds, all learning, the arts and sciences, the religious life. These are individual freedoms that serve the inner development of the soul, so essential to the modern human being, we who raise ourselves up above the animals with their drives and are only a little lower than the angels in our thinking.

Equality at the higher level is the body politic: one citizen, one vote;

electing representatives who serve the public interest. Our governments have grown too fat; they need to be slimmed down to the task of legislation. Put an end to the excessive bureaucracy; cut the red tape.

Brotherhood in the larger sense is economics that is global. There is one world economy. Since 1900 (1898) there are no longer separate national economies that therefore had to be defended. Wars, armies, navies, air forces, weapons, bombs, missiles, tanks, military ships/aircraft—all are entirely unnecessary, wasteful, and senseless. There is now one world economy. We are truly in this together. This is the great brother/sisterhood of humankind. The Sun shines on all humankind. Like the Sun, world brother/sisterhood is cosmopolitan.

The Threefold Social Order of Rudolf Steiner is based on the objective knowledge of the threefold makeup of the human being seen in the three French ideals discussed above. This is not a system of society created by a social scientist or reformer. It lives within the very nature of the human organism. We have the head: thinking and culture; the heart: feeling and love and politics; and the hand or limbs: willing and economics. This threefold human makeup is separated into its three constituent parts, and each is given independent life for the well-being and health of the whole organism, the human body and human society. There is nothing random or experimental in threefolding society, just as we human beings live, experience, and act in a threefold manner using our heads, hearts, and hands as whole people. Threefolding was successfully practiced in the Philippines on a national level. It works.

Culture must be free. The State should not interfere or overstep its position of running governmental affairs. The cultural life, including education (schools, colleges, universities, self-tuition), the arts and sciences (including research), and religious communities, must be autonomous. In communist societies, teachers, artists, scientists, and religious leaders are regimented under the State. They cannot practice their calling. Culture is unfree. This is a misnomer. Autonomy in thinking as in culture signifies individual freedom and independence of the human spirit.

Politics must render each citizen her/his equal rights protected by governmental law. Rights are not freedoms, they are a given, and every one may enjoy them so long s/he does not infringe upon the same rights for others. As private human beings in feeling and love, we are equal. In the political life, each citizen may cast his/her vote in the electoral process. No one is disfavored, no one favored. Life is fair and just; so should legislation be fair and just. The laws of the nations should be fair and just. What is friendships and relationships at the personal level, community at the local, the political life is at the national.

The economy is global, as we have noted. It should not be regulated by governments or the vested interests of nations, corporations, or individuals. Regionally, consumers and suppliers should meet on a regular basis to clarify the demand for products and services is supplied with neither excess (waste) nor want (deprivation). Quality means value. Mass production aims at high quantities but at the expense of quality. Actual value decreases. There is waste because of excessive production. Every one loses.

Higher quality means investing in human-creative, close attention, time-consuming, even handmade work; but a tremendous, immeasurable increase in value results. Ordinary products last far longer and perform much better because they are made to last and to do good work. Services likewise have higher standards because there is more attention given by human beings instead of machines, which continue to serve a useful purpose in their own proper place but do not replace people. Every one benefits. Every one profits because of the actual higher value. At the personal level, economics also includes human care, compassion, personal visits, handmade gifts, handwritten or typed letters, what is truly human. We take time for one another because we are precious to one another.

Human beings are no longer treated as commodities in the work force. Dignity returns to human work. In businesses and companies, the workers—from the janitor to the president—each have their turn at every job on a rotating basis. Every employee gains firsthand experience and thus appreciation for the work involved in each task, all of which are necessary to run a company. If the president of a company does custodial work cleaning the toilets, he will not shun the job. He will find dignity in it. If the custodian fills the office of the president of a company, he will know the responsibility of the job, and it will no longer be something beyond his scope. He will learn to exercise leadership abilities. There are actual companies, which put this into practice.

Economics is all about relationships: between a company's employees, between consumers and suppliers, between economic entities, between benefactors/philanthropists and donations/endowments for schools, institutions, the arts, the sciences (research), and religious communities. Money must circulate for a healthy economy. Healthy, viable businesses must turn a profit else they are poorly run or operate at a loss. But these profits must not make the few rich or richer, rather they should go to fund cultural endeavors, which run at a loss, but which bestow spiritual riches on humankind and are an intangible, spiritual investment in the world's future, much as a good education is a wise investment for the future of the child or young person, who will benefit society as an informed and productive adult.

Education is life for the human spirit and good for the economy. The same is true with medicine and therapeutic artistic work and the patient receiving the treatment, and with pastoral care and human souls in the community cared for by the pastor/priest. The entire world is within each and every human soul. In the case of religious tending, the help of Christ, the benefits are intangible but are more valuable than any other form of work.

The services, such as public transportation, should break even, neither turn a profit nor show a monetary loss. Hence, they are services. Libraries and parks are not services. They promote education and culture in the wider sense and should be entirely funded by business profits.

This gives the reader a sense for the Threefold Social Organism called threefolding. The studies in this section emphasize culture, past and present. There are two studies each, which relate directly to the political life and to economics.

Los Angeles
September 3-4, 2014

East and West: Asia as the Morning Land, Europe as the Evening Land

There are very beautiful words for Asia and Europe, and for Asian and European, in the German language. Asia, whose common name is *Asien*, is also called *das Morgenland– the land of the morning* or *the morning land*, and Asian (= *asiatisch*), *morgenländisch–like the morning land*. This derives from the Eastern continent – the (Far) East, because the Sun rises in the morning in the east. All we need think of is the Orient, another word in English for Asia. Orient derives from *oriens = east, where the sun rises,* literally *"rising"; oriri = to rise* and *orior = rise–* all from the Latin.

Europe is commonly called *Europa* in the German language, but also *das Abendland–the land of the evening* or *the evening land*, and European (= *europäisch*), *abendländisch–like the evening land.* Similarly this derives from the Western continent–the West (Europe was the western world before the settlement of America by the Europeans), because the Sun sets in the evening in the west. We need think only of the Occident, another word in English for Europe and the western world (which includes America). Occident derives from *occidens = west, where the sun sets,* literally *"setting" or "falling"; occidere = to set (used of the sun)* and *occido = fall; set–*also all from the Latin.

Thus Asia, in a beautiful way, is the continent or land of the morning– the east, while Europe, also beautifully, is the continent or land of the evening–the west. To express these special geographical regions with their profound spiritual roots, rich cultures, customs, and traditions, in terms of morning and evening, sunrise and sunset, dawn and dusk, is indeed beautiful imagery or thought.

There are four root races. The earliest is the black race, the African peoples of today. Their origins were on Lemuria, the continent where the Indian Ocean is that God destroyed by fire because of their wickedness. On Lemuria young men had to go into and fall in battle and young women had to see the young men die. From these experiences human beings developed the virtues of bravery (courage) and equanimity. Next is the yellow race, which are the Asian peoples. They originated on Atlantis, the continent where the Atlantic Ocean now is. Atlantis was destroyed by water, by the great Flood that is related in the traditions of all the ancient peoples: the Jews, Irish, Ancient Greeks, and Chinese, to take four examples. This was a great deluge described in the Old Testament (the Torah) as the Flood of torrential rains that lasted forty nights and forty days.

Good Noah and his extended family, and two kinds of every animal, were spared from death to settle and repopulate the earth. This took place because God favored Noah, while He was furious with the rest of humankind for their debauched ways. While Noah was building the huge Ark according to specifications given him by God, the rest of humanity, who were about to be drowned, only laughed and jeered at him and at his explanations in answer to their taunting him as to what he was doing and why he was working on the Ark. They were busy cajoling and partying and cared not a bit about their own future.

God made a promise to Noah that He would never again destroy the people of the Earth. He will keep His promise, for our current Epoch, the post-Atlantean, will be destroyed by the war of all against all. This will not be for some time–thousands of years–and much work is yet to be done, much work for salvation, and it will be followed by a New Age of peace forevermore. Then humankind will have other tasks. On Atlantis the atmosphere was different; it was thicker than it is today. It was between air and water. This enabled a technology of the Atlanteans to harness the power contained in (plant) seeds to fuel flying machines.

The third root race is the white race or European peoples, who are all descended from Noah and his family. We know that Europe is a special place, in our time, for the past, as for the future. European and Western culture (dating to Ancient Persia; Mesopotamia, Chaldea, Assyria, and Ancient Egypt; Ancient Greece and Rome (antiquity), and European Christendom (the Middle Ages); followed by the Scientific Revolution, the Renaissance, the Baroque, the Romantic Era, Anthroposophy, on into the future): architecture, sculpture, drawing, painting, music, poetry, drama, literature, dance, eurythmy, romance, the sciences, religions, and spirituality (including Christianity); and education, as well as practical endeavors and aspects of human life; was and continues to be extremely rich in goodness, beauty, and truth: religion, science, art, and Christ.

Novalis, the huge poet and novelist genius of the German Romantic Era (see pages 451-456), gave a speech *Die Christenheit oder Europa* (*Christendom or Europe*). From the title one can see he equates Europe and Christendom through his own time. He outlines European culture from its beginnings into the late 1700s, while showing the influences of other streams, and the impact of historical events such as the Reformation and Counterreformation, and the Scientific Revolution, on European culture. This talk is of deepest interest to the student of European culture and history, and it is as beautifully and poetically written as it is profound, insightful, and fascinating, as are his two novels. Novalis's work does not only look back, historically speaking, to address the people and culture of Europe of his own day, of which he is the loftiest and largest figure. It also looks clearly and prophetically into the future of humanity and the Earth as we find in his wonderful fairy tale he wrote into his novel *Heinrich von Ofterdingen*. As Novalis's poetry is untranslatable in the sense that much that is of essence is lost in the attempt, and his prose suffers in translation as well, learning German for the sole purpose of reading his work is well-warranted and richly rewarding. Fortunately for the student of Novalis, this rarest of geniuses utilizes the simplest German, notably in vocabulary, which signifies his astonishing creativity and talent with the language, especially in light of the spiritual depth and height of his work.

The fourth root race is the red man of North America, which region the United States in particular occupies today. The Native Americans were dying out before the Europeans set foot on the American continent; this wise old people who have suffered so much at our hands.

Africa is the continent of childhood (Lemuria). We were all Lemurians. In this sense 'we all come from Africa'. For this reason all children are spiritually connected with the black peoples with their beauty, vitality, color, and spontaneous joy. Asia is the continent of youth (Atlantis). We were all Atlanteans. In this sense every young person is Asian. All youth are spiritually related to the yellow peoples in their idealism, sensitivity, spirituality, and symbolic love. Europe is the continent of middle age (post-Atlantis). We are all post-Atlanteans. In this sense every human being living to be middle-aged is a European. All middle-aged human beings have a spiritual relationship to the white peoples in cultural interests, pursuits, diversity, and the quest for knowledge (life and adult self-education). We have the powerful, worldwide impact of Europe and the West. This has not only an adverse, injurious side (most of us are aware of the tremendous damage we have done and continue to do in waging wars abroad; enslaving and exploiting whole peoples; and polluting the environment). The influence is not only spreading the terrible wasteland of technology and materialism, the worst reality of western civilization. It is one of increasing cultural consciousness and the sharing of culture (cultural diversity) through the migrations, travel, immigration, and education. This includes world religions and Christianity, which is for all humankind as it is truly cosmopolitan. The positive, necessary side to colonization is Paul's Damascus experience of Christ for all the world's peoples. America is the continent of old age. In this sense every old and dying person is a Native American. All old and dying human beings are spiritually related to the red peoples in their natural life-wisdom, suffering, illness, and death. Where the red man lived in harmony with Creation and experienced the Great Spirit in the Tree, the River, the Eagle, the Wind, which was deeply wise, we will learn to live in harmony with and experience the Divine in one another and in Creation, farming, and gardening. We are slow to this, but like most human beings who live a good and long life, wisdom is part of growing old and dying: preparing for the life between death and rebirth.

Los Angeles
February 17-18, 2010
October 18/22, 2014
Culver City, California
May 9-12, 2014

Johann Sebastian Bach: German Baroque Genius and Master Composer

Johann Sebastian Bach (25 March 1685 – 28 July 1750) is the master of contrapuntal music. He explored every possibility of polyphony. His polyphonic works are uniform in rhythm and entire as whole compositions worked out into every detail. Thus they are only apparently easy to perform, because his music is the most difficult as every note is exposed, allowing for no flaws, unevenness, irregularity, or any other imperfection. Even his simplest pieces for 'beginners' (such as *Little Preludes for Beginners*) are small masterpieces far from the diet of the struggling piano student as they, too, are exposed and partake of the complex. As his music is evocative of human feeling (of the heart), in his sacred music we experience the most profound religious feeling. We think of his Christmas and Easter oratorios with their solos and choruses.

In his more advanced compositions the high degree of complexity appeals to musical genius. There is a formal technical structure that underlies the deepest feeling evoked by his music. Even his most complex works retain utter soundness of mind in their regularity of rhythm, melodic lines, and harmonies (the 'voices'), because they are grounded in the profound religious genius (the human heart) and not the offspring of the erratic brain that may show brilliance but often exhibits illness, common to many artists and scientists today.

Bach as a Universal Composer of the Present Age

In Bach we have the twin characteristics of our cultural epoch: the most developed general qualities and the specifics that bring attention to every detail. The overall effect of Bach's *Preludes, Fugues, and Fuguettas* is either enormous (the great organ *Fugues*) or harmonious in the feeling, earnest, complex, tasteful, pleasing, and clarifying (the *Preludes* and *Fughettas*). He composed *Cantatas* and *Motets* as easily as *Songs* and

Arias, and *Sonatas* and *Chorales*. His music was composed out of the chest organization, the rhythmic system of the heart and lungs. Hence his 4/4 time and the warm human feeling qualities we experience in his works. However, as he was wide awake, the quality of clarity and purity in the tone is ever-present. Hearing is a thinking sense. But Bach's are not 'head' tones. His mind-soul was clear and wide-awake, as stated, but as a man and a composer, he was of the heart, hand, and mind, and not only 'above the shoulders'.

Bach was equally master of sacred and secular music. He dedicated all of his compositions to God. Sometimes Bach incorporated his earlier secular works into his religious music as he did in his *Christmas Oratorio*. Among his *concertos*, his *Brandenberg Concertos* are the most famous, wonderfully beautiful masterpieces of fast *tempo*, harmonious and highly complex. His *Christmas Oratorio* for instrument and voice may be the dearest religious music ever composed. In this great work are warm and lovely solos for the four voices, for example the simple alto *Jesu, mein Liebster*. He did not 'show off' his genius when the simplest solo is suitable and conveys the deepest feeling. J.S. Bach gave us all four Gospels in his *Passions* and *Oratorios*. One of his pieces is considered the hardest for keyboard, unplayable, because of the perfected technique and technical skill it demands. This is his *Chromatic Fantasy*. Yet we have seen Bach's genius includes the aspect of simplicity of his temperament: the Phlegmatic. This is no contradiction as other Phlegmatics are also very great (Shakespeare, Goethe), and complex as well (Aristotle).

In the past century, several great Phlegmatics have lived or still live. Like Bach, they are all Christ-Sun initiates. We think of the Dutch mathematical and astronomy genius Elisabeth Vreede (1879-1943) and the great Norwegian educator Jörgen Smit (1916-1991). Both thinking giants were on the Executive Counsel of the General Anthroposophical Society at the Goetheanum in Switzerland* and equals to J.S. Bach.

Owing to the validity of its universal nature, Bach himself cared not on which instruments his music was played (except for the organ *Fugues*). Indeed his work is ideally suited to the piano that had not yet been invented when he lived. It was usually played on the harpsichord that is uniform in tone and sounds tinny, but because of the great variety of sound that can be produced on the piano (approach, touch, and ear depending), Bach's keyboard music is far more varied, beautiful, and richer when played on this instrument than on the original harpsichord.

Bach's musical work, like the man, is profound and complex. Its unity comes from its heart-nature, which is also the source of its complexity. The greatest and most complex geniuses are of the Sun planet, the planet of the heart. To them belongs religion. Thus we have in Bach, not another genius, but the genius of the scientific mind that springs from the same source as religion: the human heart.

Music is an art form. Along with architecture, it is a thinking art form because of its thought structure (hearing is a thinking sense) and highly complex possibilities. These complexities may be methodical and regular, however, which we find in the music of this Baroque master.

J. S. Bach: The Greatness of a Master

No one equals J.S. Bach as musical genius. Few even approach him. None match his even temperament and regularity that resulted in the steady production of works of genius—on a weekly basis, on commission—for many years. Yet he stated that any one who worked as hard as he did could be as great a composer. We must keep in mind that he was fantastically self-disciplined and a perfectionist who had attained the first level of perfection, rare in our time and outstanding in any time. Bach had the *capacity* to work so hard and produce such music. He was a great One, one of the first in history.

The music of J.S. Bach pleases the inexperienced listener, satisfies the most developed musical taste, and enriches the ear of the genuinely religious heart with the profound tonal experience of the spiritual essence of Sun of Christ. Johann Sebastian Bach of the German Baroque is the unsurpassed master. His music has universal appeal.

Los Angeles
2010
Culver City, California
December 4, 2014

* No one on the Executive Council of the General Anthroposophical Society at the Goetheanum in Switzerland endorses this volume or any study, story, or poem in it. *The Wood of Green* is published independently of the Society and the Goetheanum, which the author recognizes.

Prophecy and Christianity in the Art of
Raphael and Novalis

A wonderful aspect of the art of the great artists, such as the paintings of Raphael (1483-1520) and the poetry and poetic novels of Novalis (1772-1801), is in the works where what is contemporary to their culture dresses or clothes the subjects or content that is timeless or historical, and/or that belongs to the holy figures of Christ's life. We think of the Marys of Raphael's many Madonnas who are young Italian noblewomen of his day in the costume of the same.

The German of Novalis' lifetime is slightly different from that of our time. When reading his novels this can be discovered in a few words that become very dear to us, as do Raphael's Marys, because they are used by Novalis.

The word for *approximately* in today's German is *ungefähr*. This has changed from the German of the Romantic Era of Novalis that was *ohngefähr*. How rich in spoken vowel sound depth and color is the first syllable of this word Novalis uses on occasion in his novels!

Simplicity in terms of vocabulary size characterizes Novalis' German. But what wealth of sound and tone pour forth from this master's poetic pen-lips that alone can carry the inexhaustible spiritual perspectives fathomed only by the adept contained in the in-flowing flood of his pulsing words in long sentences, line upon line of them like a rolling river. One must 'breathe in' these ever-ongoing long sentences of inwards-flow that pulse in inner feeling rhythms with the power of Novalis' great Christ-love.

Novalis' German is the most beautiful of all time. It has the capacity and the power to heal enmity and discord. Ill feeling and dissonance resolve in the divine peace of heaven-touched earth, and only love remains.

I know this from personal experience as a student at Pomona College in an upper division German course. The class met from seven to ten o'clock Monday evenings. This was the autumn semester 1985. The professor called on me to read a passage from Novalis' work. During the break a student came up to me who was severely physically disabled. When she walked, it was with forearm-crutches such that she jerked about. She resented her handicap. She owned a specially modified car so that she could drive for independence. Yet she was a very pale and soft-skinned Phlegmatic, and there was something very delicate about her.

She had studied a year abroad in Germany. She said she had borne ill will against the German people for what she had believed was their unfair treatment of her for her handicap. Then she said when I read Novalis' words all of her animosity melted, and she felt only love for this language and its people.

She was transformed by Novalis' German. I had been true to Novalis in my reading. I had read Novalis with the spiritual love and beauty of his German that streams in feeling and imagery into the poet. This in-streaming is healing. What is Novalis' own innate, creative wellspring that will also stream into us? It is Christ. We can also experience these deep-working healing qualities in the paintings of Raphael. It is not possible to truly see an original Raphael without undergoing an inner transformation. If every one could see the paintings of Raphael in this way, there would no longer be any crime.

I recall my class teacher Noah Williams III at the Waldorf School Highland Hall have us copy down words close to these on Raphael's paintings for our main lesson books during main lesson period in the mid 1970s. I was twelve or thirteen years old at the time. The main lesson subject was Renaissance art. We learned that of the three greats, Leonardo da Vinci the artist of thinking, Michelangelo of will, Raphael the artist of human feeling. This is true. But with this human feeling is the beauty-love of Raphael's planet Venus. These are essential qualities in every painting by Raphael.

We know the arts are by nature therapeutic. Doing art is healing. This is implicit in the process or immersion of the soul in creating what is beautiful. Rhythm can be one element in this. So can warmth and movement. So can light and color, tone and speech. But when we are allowed to experience a work of art at the level of Raphael or Novalis, then something much higher than our ordinary experience enters into and helps us. It is this qualitative experience that we find in the work of Raphael and Novalis. Our souls are lifted up to the heavenly even as we are touched and warmed in heart in our feeling. If we allow it, this experience is transforming.

Like the pulsing Christ-love in Novalis' poetry and poetic prose, the profound and tender inner qualities that can be experienced in the compositions and colors of Raphael's lovely and wondrous paintings are innately healing. Such is the beauty, love, pure feeling, and mercy of his art. This is one significant attribute of the art of these two historical figures: healing.

Another aspect is vision. We know that both of these men were visionaries. They were also masters, each of his art, to portray what they saw by means of spiritual perception in the chosen medium. In Raphael it was in the language of color and line that he revealed to us what he saw. In Novalis it was in words, in the language of imagery, of poetry that he will open our inner eyes to see with him.

Because of their spiritual stature, these men viewed, not only the rich and meaning-filled past, extending back to the time when some human beings still resembled the archetypal image of God ("*Wo manche Seinem Urbild glich*"), in which they had fully played leading roles (this personality was Adam, the first man), through the great prophet Elijah, John the Baptist, and St. John the Evangelist, but the present—their own day—and the *future.* This individuality has always been the forerunner of Christ. This is the role of prophet. Let us briefly consider Novalis.

The prophetic vision of his work, best portrayed in Novalis' fairytale in his novel *Heinrich von Ofterdingen* ('*Henry of Often Things*'), is not only painted for the reader in his wonderful pictorial language. As healing power that will take effect in humankind as a whole historically in the coming millennia, this prophecy is active in the very qualities of his writing and language that already changes readers today.

The great prophets beginning with St. John the Evangelist, possess the power, not only to foretell the future, but to move us to that time and to those happenings. Reading the future in the present moment also contains the impulse that sees to it this future occurs. This is in addition to the height and depth of the knowledge of the seer.

Christianity, which is the very beauty, love, and substance of the lives and work of both artists, is made known to us in Novalis' eternal poetry, for example in his *Geistige Lieder* (*Spiritual Songs*) and his *Marienlied* (*Mary's Song*). In the latter, the Mary motif, found in color and figure in Raphael's beautiful Madonnas, returns, this time in the imagery and concept of language, of poetry. Here is Novalis' *Marienlied* with an English prose translation by this author (by me):

> *Marienlied*
>
> *Ich sehe dich in tausend Bildern*
> *Maria lieblich ausgedrückt*
> *Doch keins von allen kann dich schildern*
> *Wie meine Seele dich erblickt*
>
> *Ich weiß nur daß der Welt Getümmel*
> *Seitdem mir wie ein Traum verweht*
> *Und ein unnennbar süßer Himmel*
> *Mir ewig im Gemüte steht.*
>
> *Novalis*
>
> *Mary's Song*
>
> *I see you in a thousand paintings*
> *Mary, lovingly expressed*
> *But none of them can portray you*
> *As my soul sees you*
>
> *I only know that since then*
> *The tumult of the world fades as a dream*
> *And an unnamable sweet heaven*
> *Stands eternally in my soul.*
>
> *Novalis*

We know from Christ's words, spoken to Mary and John as He hung on the cross, of the relationship formed between these two holy persons, commanded by Christ. ("Woman, take John as your son. John, take Mary as your mother.") We sense this relationship in Raphael's Madonnas where the infant John the Baptist is present, and we experience this in Novalis' *Marienlied*, cited above. We see that the Raphael-Novalis individuality is the same as the Adam-Elijah-Baptist-Evangelist individuality.* For Raphael, and for Novalis, the events of Christ's human life were more than historical realities. They were personal experience. Their art is thus the rarest of all art. It has meaning of a higher and deeper nature springing from personal experience.

This is actually visible in Raphael's colors. We think of the red blush of Mary's cheeks seen in his *Madonna with the Book* on exhibit at the Norton Simon Museum in Pasadena, California. We recall from Novalis' *Marienlied*: "*ein unnennbar süßer Himmel*" ("*an unnamable sweet heaven*").

There is a tenderness in Raphael's Madonnas and in this verse that belongs to the work of no other artist or poet. This is because of the evangelist-artist-poet John-Raphael-Novalis, who will come again. (Rudolf Steiner) The Mary and the Christ Infant Jesus in Raphael's last Madonna, the *Sistine Madonna* in the *Gemäldegalerie Alte Meister* in Dresden, Germany (finished ca. 1513-1514), is the loveliest and most tender painting of all time. Not only the figures and the skin tone (color), but the eyes of the Mother and Child show this love and this tenderness.

Christianity is an ongoing spiritual reality or ideal process, whose substance streams from the future into the present. As such it speaks to human beings in each era. Christ is the Word who was in the very beginning. (The Prologue to the Gospel of St. John) But He is also the Spirit who comes to us from the future. Without His grace coming from the future, everything would stand still or crumble. What has been would be, and all would be old and older. But with God's Grace and Truth, which is Christ, newness streams to us from the future. Each morning is the birth of a new day. The night of peace and the rising sun makes it so. The outer wisdom of physical Creation of the Past is becoming the seeds of internal love of soul and spirit for the Future.

(from *Die Geheimwissenschaft im Umriss* by Rudolf Steiner (*An Outline of Esoteric Science* or *Occult Science:An Outline*), 1909)

Prophecy sees into the future what shall come to pass with the power from Christ to effect the change. Christianity is born from the future anew in each present moment, reaching back to the physical birth of Christ in Bethlehem when Divine Love (Christ) was born in Jesus. The child of this birth, become *renaissance* or *rebirth* in Raphael's work during the Italian High Renaissance, is portrayed with the greatest and simplest, yet into every detail, love and beauty in his singular Madonna compositions.

With the prophets we glimpse into the future what shall be. In Christianity we evolve with the world. In Raphael's final masterpiece, *The Transfiguration*, displayed at his funeral, prophecy—in the figures of Elijah and Moses, and Christianity—in the transfigured Christ, appearing in the blue-white clouds, are both present.

The art of Raphael and Novalis is prophetic and Christian, for these men were great prophets pointing to the future coming of Christ, and they are forever joined with Christ in the world's evolving. They portray their prophecies, and they portray the timeless motifs from Christ's life, in themselves and in their own cultures and eras, each in his chosen medium: Raphael in color and line (oils and fresco), Novalis in words (in the German language of his day). Through their beautiful work, we love the Italy of the Italian High Renaissance and the Germany of the German Romantic Era, two periods of tremendous, abundant, and wonderful European cultural blossoming.

Los Angeles
January 10/12-17, 2011
October 19/22, 2014

*See GA 238: *The Last Address of Rudolf Steiner, Dornach, Michaelmas Eve, September 28, 1924*

German Romanticism:
Motifs in the Romantic Era (1798-1832)

The themes or motifs of Romanticism are several. Among the most significant are idealism, symbolism, love, feeling, beauty, nature, and individualism. They are in no particular order.

The German Romantic Era Time Period

The German Romantic Era in literature is usually considered beginning in 1798 and ending at Goethe's death in 1832. However more generally Romanticism began in the 1770s and extended (in music especially) into the late 1800s and even early 1900s. In this study we are looking into the Romantic Era of genius particularly in the written word that appeared in Germany during the brief period cited above, with mention of England where Romanticism began earlier but ran parallel.

Idealism in Romanticism

Idealism is the philosophical view cherished by geniuses of the era. The ideal philosophy of the German Romantic philosopher Johann Gottlieb Fichte (1762-1814) is so ideal that for Fichte ideas alone were real and outer, physical reality paled to nonexistence.

Symbolism and Romanticism

The symbol that came to symbolize the entire German Romantic Era (and in England as well, if we look at the literary scholars) is from the huge German Romantic poet Novalis's novel *Heinrich von Ofterdingen* (1799), *die blaue Blume* ("the blue flower").

Beauty and Art

In *Ode on a Grecian Urn* (1819), Art is portrayed by the English Romantic poet John Keats (1795–1821) in the well-known lines:

'Beauty is truth, truth beauty,' that is all / *Ye know on earth, and all ye need to know.* The latter part of this is an oversimplification; the first five words that view truth as beauty and beauty truth is a description of the arts: what is true is given in the form of beauty, rather than in its original condition of truth as it is sought in philosophy (and the spiritual science of anthroposophy), in the direction given by lucid thinking.

Nature and Romanticism

Nature is also a key motif in Romanticism, an idyllic setting for love, for romance, not between lovers, but the romantic and Nature Herself, where today She has become all but lost in the vague distances of an imagination that is removed from Her real source: the beauty, reverence, joy, wonder, and revelation of Creation.

During the Romantic Era natural beauty was an integral part of the human experience. Human beings were still quite at home in the beautiful scenery of untouched Nature, where today human souls are as soiled by corruption as Nature is by encroaching civilization in tourism and pollutants, and human minds seem as untrue to real life as virtual reality is a deception of the healthy sensory world.

Although those people who still read the literature of the Romantics encounter the recurring theme of Nature, few truly appreciate the beauty bestowed by Her on the creative works of the Romantic poets. For those who learn to see supersensibly, Nature returns in Her awesome, dear, and wonderful beauty, now in a new way: through Christ.

Romanticism and Individualism

The really big Romantic geniuses and the lesser but equally genuine ones were all individualists. As Johann Wolfgang von Goethe, the great German Romantic poet, scientist, novelist, dramatist, color theorist, painter, and more, writes: *Individuality of expression is the beginning and end of all art.*

Each contributor to the beauteous culture that flowered and flourished in Germany and England during this brief time period is characterized by his place in the context of the whole of Romanticism and by his unique and inimitable quality both. Thus even the lesser and least romantic geniuses made irreducible contributions to the cultural life that cannot be found elsewhere. So it is with each individuality through the Ages. Each one has his own quality, special flavor and fragrance, coloration and warmth or coolness.

Feeling/Religion and Novalis

Novalis, who is by far the greatest poet and novelist of all time, wrote of the 'poet-priest'. For him poetry was not only romantic, it was a sacred art, an expression of the poet's personal religious and spiritual life. We feel the pulsing Christ-love in the feeling in his novels, where the long sentences and ongoing flood of words must be taken in ('breathed in') by the reader in a single inflowing and warm rhythms. This is a deeply stirring religious experience additional to the profound ideal (spiritual) content of his poetry and poetic novels. The poet is the priest.

Feeling and Goethe

Goethe was not a Christian but a pantheist who affirmed the existence and power of God. His poetry is all romantic in the sense of German Romanticism and as this word has come to mean today. (See following section, *Minne and Romance*.) Differently from Novalis, Goethe shaped German Romanticism. His death in 1832 marks the end of this cultural-historical time period, so closely are he and his work aligned with it.

Minne and Romance

Romance as we know it today did not exist prior to the Romantic Era. It is a direct offspring of Romanticism.

Courtly love first developed in castle life between queens and nobility of lower rank in Medieval France around the time of the First Crusade

(1099). Eleanor of Aquitaine brought courtly love to the 'courts of love', first in France, later to England. The term 'courtly love' appears in the literature of the time only once in the late 12th century (*cortez amor*, Provençal). But in both Provençal and French the expression *fin'amor* ('fine love') is common, in German *hohe Minne*. This is the same as what we refer to when we say 'courtly love' today. All the authors in the Middle Ages write of it: Chaucer, John Gower, Dante, Marie de France, Chretien de Troyes, Gottfried von Strassburg, Malory. Courtly conventions can be found in the medieval genre of the lyric, Romance (not to be confused with later 'romance'), and allegory. The Provençal poets (11th century) of the lyric who espoused courtly love were the troubadours and trouvéres. In Germany the poets were the Minnesinger, such as Walther von der Vogelweide and Wolfram von Eschenbach.

The favored poets were known to travel far and wide to the courts of courtly love as wandering minstrels, singing their love-poems. They suited what the German's called *Minne*, a word that no longer exists in the German language. (See above) But *Minne* is still retained in modern German in the name for these poet-suitors: the *Minnesinger* (*Singers of Minne*), in French the troubadours. (See above)

Thus (suiting) *Minne*, found only in the German language in a brief historical period, was a kind of predecessor to romantic love. Yet the romance that captured the imagination of Germany and England, and therewith all of Europe (even reluctant France was finally won over), during the Romantic Era, encompasses much more than romantic love, which again is something new in human and historical experience, not found in the *hohe Minne* or *fin'amor* of Medieval Europe. Romance in the sense of the Romantic Era began with romantic love and ever returns there, but it reaches out to embrace everything within the artistic culture of this special time, particularly in the written word.

Romantic Love as a Symbol for Spiritual Love or Communion

This includes the spiritual heights attained by the spirit-seeking human I or self or ego, the German *ich* ('ich'), that is the member of the human being of individualism, filled with the genius or spirit self or higher Self or higher I: the source of all idealism, the highest ideal of all, which is Christ. In this context romantic love is a symbol for the relationship between the human soul or self that will be married to Christ: the human I to the *I AM* that is the only true name of Christ. This is the highest, loftiest love, the love of the divine felt in human hearts who are lifted up to commune with Christ: the human soul-spirit with the Christ spirit. The true spirit-seeker is the seeker after Christ.

Sacramental Communion

The experience of sacramental communion is present as well, where Christ descends into the elements in transubstantiation: the Bread and the Cup becoming the flesh and blood of Christ eaten and imbibed by the human being who hungers and who thirsts for Christ Who died for us, whose body is broken for us and for our salvation, whose blood is shed for us that cleanses and purifies us. We are part of this process in baking the bread from the grain and crushing the grapes for the juice. (Novalis writes: *The human embrace is a sacrament* and the cliffs and waters of the Earth are Christ's flesh and His blood.)

This Romanticism is also pure in essence, pure in the feeling, in the heart. Then the heart joins the highest aspirations of idealism, spiritual love. (This was also the ideal of *hohe Minne* or *fin'amor* that love lifted up the heart so it was of a higher, spiritual nature. But at that time in history, consciousness was younger. Humanity was preparing for the ideals of Romanticism as found in Germany at the turn of the 18th century, appearing in an earlier form in Medieval France and England, and especially in the region where Germany is today. The German poet, Minnesinger, and knight Wolfram von Eschenbach came closest in his true legend of the first millennium (cast in the imagery of knighthood, honor, nobility, and the suiting *Minne* of his own day, and written in *Mittelhochdeutsch* (Middle High German), during the early part of the 13th century), the epic poem *Parzival* that is a forerunner of modern consciousness.)

The Romanticism of Goethe

The great German dramatist (*Faust*), novelist, poet, and scientist Johann Wolfgang von Goethe (1749-1832) (Goethe's scientific work equals his masterwork *Faust*) was romantic in the modern sense by nature. This is clear on reading his poetry, his novels, even his *Faust*. So Goethe epitomizes what we have come to know as romance. (Shakespeare the man and sonnet writer was also creative in the 'art form' of romance, although it did not exist until almost 200 years after his death.)

Christ as the Spirit of Romanticism

From the rich imagination of Novalis, that serves his conceptual work (his poetry, novels, and his Europe speech are conceptual in this sense, but Novalis' ideas for his planned encyclopedia are purely conceptual), Christ is the spirit of true Romanticism. Not only the love of the young Heinrich for Mathilde (there is also another girl next to Heinrich who is a romantic, but he is not interested in her) in his novel *Heinrich von Ofterdingen* (*Henry of Often Things*) (Heinrich represents Novalis in the novel), but in actual life Novalis experienced the loftiest love for the young Sophie von Kühn. After her early death Novalis, in deepest grief, went to her grave site where he experienced her soul in the spiritual world. Then he wrote in his journal every day an entry on Sophie's spiritual journey, until one day Novalis' entry reads "Sophie = Christ". Such a love as Novalis felt for Sophie was a communion, one which resulted in a perfect union with Christ. Christ is in each motif of Romanticism: idealism (the Christ-idea, Christ-concept), symbolism (the blue flower), love (Novalis' love), feeling/religion (Novalis' heart), beauty (Novalis and Sophie), nature (Christ experienced in Creation), and individualism (the I-cosmos of love): the Christ of romance has its roots in this rare cultural-historical period of European spiritual life.

Los Angeles/(2010?)/October 22, 2014

Simplicity: A Contemplation in Art and Nature

There is a beauty in simplicity that cannot be found in the complex. A composition, if it is to be beautiful, must be based in a few lines, deftly and masterfully drawn lines, but equally simply, unbroken. These lines must remain unchanged through the completion of the picture, intact in the final composition as a melody in a symphony, or a *leitmotif* in a masterpiece of classic literature, such as a dramatic work or novel, a saga, legend, epic, or other tale in prose or verse.

Again in the arts the human gesture in sculpture comes to mind: serene repose, gentle supplication, feminine demure and loveliness, masculine strength, stance, and readiness for swift action, athletic or heroic stature, modest chastity, childlike naivety, aged wisdom, somber earnestness, weighty tragedy, comic relief, playful humor, thoughtful contemplation.

The human form is typically the classical and beautiful corpulent Phlegmatic (for God, Moses, Eve, Mary, Venus-Aphrodite, female lovers and most female figures, robed or nude) or broad-shouldered and well-proportioned Sanguine (for Adam, Christ, boys, athletes, male lovers and many male figures, clad in garb or nude). Michelangelo's *David* in Florence, his tender early *Pietà* (1498 – 1499), housed in St. Peter's Basilica in the Vatican in Rome, and the *Venus de Milo*, discovered in Greece in 1830, in the Louvre in Paris. These classical types are also found in painting. Consider Raphael's *The Betrothal of the Virgin* (early 1500s) where he masterfully uses perspective, and Michelangelo's *The Creation of Adam (God and Adam)*, a fresco painted on the ceiling of the Sistine Chapel ca. 1511, in the Vatican. With the highest concentration of Western art in Florence and Rome (*the Italian High Renaissance*), many examples of these classical types are to be found in these two cities.

The different cultural eras in art each have key elements that define their style and determine the architecture of the place and period. We have the wall, arch, pillar, pier, nave, choir, column, capital, vault, and portal of abbeys, churches, and cathedrals in the architecture of the Romanesque and Gothic periods. In fundamental design, simplicity provides the basis for and common denominator in these and other architectural elements.

The Romanesque arch is so named because it has its origin in Roman architecture. It is semicircular or rounded. The word "Romanesque" came to be used to encompass an entire historical period (ca. AD1050-

AD1200).

Romanesque building is very regular and symmetrically planned. A massive solidity and strength characterizes its walls and piers. The interior spaces in Romanesque churches and abbeys tend to be very dark, because the structures supporting the Romanesque arch must be heavy for physical reasons, disallowing large window spaces. These buildings are solemn and secluded in mood, lit by small windows and candlelight, lending the feeling of cool and restful quiet or austerity in simplicity. Yet they are often of great beauty, and some Romanesque churches have huge interior spaces.

The Gothic arch found in the next period (AD1140-AD1500) comes to a point. (There is a transitional period when both Romanesque and Gothic architecture coexisted, the same period as Early Gothic, see below.) This simple change brings about an entirely different spatial experience. It determines other architectural elements in design and building, which in turn alter the architectural experience. This is owing to the arch bearing greater weight. Gothic architecture divides into three distinct periods: Early (ca. 1140-1200), High (1200-1300), Late Gothic (1300-1500s).

Gothic cathedrals typically have ribbed vaults and flying buttresses that are supports external to the interior spaces. Stained glass windows are another feature. All of these factors bring much light to inside the buildings and give them majesty. They will soar vertically, upwards to heaven with each succeeding cathedral exceeding the previous one in length and height to the glory of God. The experience of light in the interior is thanks to the pointed arches that require little material support, allowing for great height and huge stained glass windows typically found in these beautiful cathedrals.

With the overall experience of unity and simplicity or singularity, owing to the fundamental architectural elements, the men who designed these great church and cathedral structures were a few extremely gifted and knowledgeable master architects brought in from great distances, and the men who built them were highly skilled master builders.

There were masons who knew how to cut perfect stone bricks of irregular shape for the intersecting arches in the Gothic cathedrals. Along with the other, regular bricks, these stones had to be positioned, each in its place, in the erection of the structures. Other men specialized in making the stained glass using a secret recipe that has been lost to us.

Especially the red and the blue stained glass are very beautiful. The leading and installation of these windows called for yet other skills. *

Romanesque and Gothic architecture has its heart in France, although it spread abroad, particularly into Italy, England, and what is today Germany, where the buildings developed their own styles.

Architecture is notable among the art forms because of its inherent functional qualities that must take purely physical laws into consideration. In (large) sculpture the latter aspect also comes into play.

Considering any art form, we always turn our attention to an underlying principle or lawfulness, present and active in the work, that manifests in endless possibilities according to the artist and the outer also inner circumstances, but that does not change.

The true master is the artist who has found complete freedom of expression, to hear, think, imagine, intuit (see, touch, breathe, romance), move-gesture, or speak in utter self-discipline, adhering to these laws, with perfect ease in the chosen medium and in the genre. Rigorous discipline and mastery of technique enable complete and unlimited freedom to create. The German Baroque composer and uncompromising immovable master of polyphony Johann Sebastian Bach (1685-1750) is exemplary of this. (See my study on J.S. Bach, pages 441-444.)

Artistic faculty must appear easy and does so for the reason that a level of creativity has been attained that is higher than sheer work or will, belabored repetition, or dead and dry intellectual cognition. Aesthetic-spiritual artistic ability, vision, and experience are of a soul nature, above the constraining confines and heavy drollery of the daily ordinary-necessary. One must be so fluent in the 'language' or technique that there is no awkward hesitation or unsightly flaw in execution.

The forces at work in natural creation are guided in a similar fashion in the development of the innumerable individual phenomena of nature. They must follow natural laws, just as the composer of the *Prelude* or *Cantata* must work within the structure or laws of these musical forms.

Mother Nature 'plays Her children'—every animal and stone, plant and cloud, meadow and insect, hill and valley, lake and wood, river and mountainside, stream and pebble, petal and dewdrop, twig and leaf, raindrop and snowflake, sunbeam and moonbeam—according to the laws (Will) of God in the endless variety, combination, and instance of nature 'events' in each time and place where they locate and transpire.

Therein is our joy—in the joy of natural creation, of God's Creation, just as our joy in human creation is found in the diversity, talent, skills, and craft; experience, gifts, and individuality of expression of human artists. God knows to make use of the simple in His Work of Creation, whether in grandeur or the minute, even where the greatest care and attention has been given to precision and detail. A rainbow is ever an arch of colors seven, fair and beautiful. A snowflake is invariably hexagonal, though each single one is unique and marvelously detailed. A landscape is always in accord with itself neither does any feature stand out or alter this. Each part, in the broad whole spread out before us, illumined by the glorious sun, plays its role, whether lesser or greater. So it is in the myriad stars beneath whose stillness we stand each night, looking up with reverence and awe at their beautiful citadel. Fair Moon shines brightly, and we see lovely Venus twinkling.

All beauty partakes of simplicity, else the beauty would be lost in the confounding, unseemly, stimulating abundance of complications that give the eye no rest, the ear no even measure and familiarity, the mind no peace, the heart no meaning, sense and soul no love, the hand no grasp, the limbs no tempo for rhythm, the whole man no unity.

We require the simple for our common understanding, as the warmth of a fire and a blanket to warm our bodies and hearts to feel good after exposure to the numbing cold of a freezing blizzard, or the soft breast and loving kisses of the mother when the small child is crying, upset by something disturbing its feeling of safety and peace. The distraction and confusion of taxing noise and restless chaos are quieted and stilled in the presence of the Sun and the embrace of the Mother, and we return to our selves, who we are and who we will become, once again.

Los Angeles
January 22-25, 2011

Additional reference

* Gardner's *Art Through the Ages* (© 2004 by Wadsworth Publishing Company)

Homogeneity, Diversity, Cosmopolitanism, Culture, and the Individual

Today—at the local level, among the people—you still have the classes, partially figured by ethno-religious demographics, and this demographic grouping of people is responsible in part for the cultural milieu of the place. People look for personal sustenance found outside of their immediate family or other birth circumstances so essential in our time and in the time to come, but often we find the situation that prevailed from the beginning of our post-Atlantean epoch, where people still live in homogeneity within the bloodline and with which they content themselves. This is particularly the case in the internal communities of the larger cities in America and elsewhere. For example Jewish, Russian, Ukrainian, Indian, Persian, African, Latino, Korean, Chinese, or Filipino. Further, sub-groupings include Jewish Hasidim, Jewish reform, Jewish secular; or Salvadoran, Nicaraguan, Honduran, Colombian; or Kenyan, Ethiopian, Somalian; to take a few examples. Of course it goes without saying these communities prevail in the country of origin itself. How strange it would be if no Swedes lived in Stockholm, Göteborg, or Mälmö; and if no Austrians populated Vienna, Salzburg, and Innsbrück! It is when work and study circumstances, and immigration, bring about combinations within a given place that these separations cease. Connections, new or karmic, are made or continued. However, even then, home often remains homogenous.

But today it is much more common than ever before for people to build friendships and relationships that are creative of, we might say, 'personal diversity'. In such a situation the old, homogenous patterns break up and new, interesting patterns appear. These new patterns arise in freedom. No model, no traditional structure exists for them. We find this especially among young people, who are naturally open to such possibilities, while they also lack the experience of the years. They are creative of lives of experience new to the world. With international study and work opportunities, which many pursue, where another language from one's Mother tongue is learned and spoken, a global community comes into existence. The entire world is connected in real human beings. Because of immigration over the past several centuries, whole populations in a country or region are mixed. Those who remain in the 'homeland' are also connected in real terms. We are all united.

This is owing to the colonization of continents and places in continents by the explorers and colonialists, otherwise looked at in such a negative light, because of the oppression suffered. But we can see the positive and necessary aspect to colonization, because it brought about the circumstances for all the world's peoples, for all human beings of every folk group to have the Damascus experience, the soul's awakening. Otherwise, only Europeans would have had the possibility for salvation. This is not the case: Christ came for all humankind; He is the great Sun-Being; Christ is cosmopolitan in His very nature. All the world's cultures are being enriched by those who are giving inner birth to Christ, are experiencing their inner Bethlehem. This means every continent, excepting Antarctica where few scientists live the year round.

Both at home and abroad, all of the people of a given place partake of and contribute to the culture. This culture is one in which human contact is made in some manner followed by the cultivation of human relationships in real terms. In contrast, uses of technologies isolate human beings. So long a human being breathes, s/he requires human connections and exchanges. We cannot make it alone. This can be verbal. It is always in person.

A good analogy to the diversity patterns within a place is different tables in a restaurant or café. A different ethnic group is seated at each table, while all of them are filled in the same room. As you walk about the room you hear many languages and dialects spoken. It's a small world. Again, many today have bridged these differences so that individual tables are also mixed.

The above insights regarding technologies apply to another and specific cultural phenomenon: music. Live performances and audiences are irreplaceable by recordings and their transference. More and more, individuals perform and listen to, not live music, but recorded. People frequently have earphones in their ears by which they listen to downloaded recordings on their iPods or music websites, to take two examples. CDs produce a chilling, artificial sound that exactly replicates the original, but that other than this replication shares nothing in common with the live performance. Headphones do the same thing.

Music is an international language. Where such genre as Country Western and Gospel are normally performed and listened to by their particular exponents, the native genre of the many kinds of folk music can be played/sung/danced and appreciated by any one. Here is diversity at its best. Modern forms that are recorded, sometimes altered by technologies, are harsh and damaging in sound and decibel or they are without boundaries, by definition, but equally nonspecific and so popular. No one in particular feels addressed by these modern forms such that they enjoy wide popularity much as does film ('Hollywood'). Classical music is universal in the highest sense and thus cosmopolitan for performance and audience. Quality and qualities are both inherent in this genre. So it is with the individual. What we have said regarding music applies to each one of us.

Los Angeles
November 11, 2012
Revised October 25/27, 2014
Revised and edited Culver City, California
November 13, 2012
May 13/15, 2014

Jung's Worldview

In *Man and His Symbols* Carl G. Jung denies any divinity or divinities, neither does he find any deeper human purpose, which initiates in freedom from inner-guided direction. Belief in God, Christ, or spirits is seen as merely filling a need without which the human being experiences life as unbearable, plagued by uncertainties, anxieties, neuroses, and bodily and mental diseases—all that cause pain, confusion, and torment—and the realization of the reality of death. He extends this view to all of society—and justifiably so—because society is made up of individuals who suffer from the same ills and ailments, take solace in the same comforts and face the same issues, including human mortality. Thus Jung acknowledges everything symptomatic in human life and experience, which is reality at one level, but he never finds—or seeks—any real meaning behind or beneath these symptoms because of his completely materialistic views. For Jung there can be no soul, immortality, or spiritual world. This is not limited to *Man and His Symbols* but is valid for Jung's entire world-conception.

How does he explain the presence and activity within nature, human beings, and society he says is only attributed to the divine and the human soul because it is our nature to seek after and supply answers that will satisfy our inborn needs and quest for a soul and immortality? He says age-old symbols have been given meanings that connect the human psyche to divine and immortal sources, when, in fact they are the product of the unconscious will and the dim realm of dreams. He says it is our task today to reflect on these symbols and their 'actual' meaning, defined by his psychology, for our understanding from a modern perspective of man, society, and the individual.

Jung is smug in his intricately worked-out worldview and the detailed explanations he offers. He supports it with sketchy historical accounts of minor little-known or only-known-to-him individuals, a few well-known personalities and leading figures, including lofty spiritual and religious personalities, and popular sociological views, but gives them a purely materialistic that is external, spiritless, soulless, and lifeless treatment, for Jung is an avowed materialist, not in lifestyle that is outwardly, but in his deep-seated belief and outlook. He is wholly trapped within the confines of his own belief system (psychological materialism). He does consider an inner aspect of the human being, seen in the psyche, as real as outer nature that is physical. This psyche is animal-like and impenetrable. It is without soul and therefore cannot be illumined (by soul-light). In this system he has created there is no possibility for true development.

Real inner, personal and world progress is enabled by the development of human consciousness, thought, and therewith freedom, which are all spiritual, in conjunction with the sacrifices and deeds of the progressive powers, great and lofty spiritual beings above man, Christ foremost among them. The Mystery of Golgotha—the crucifixion and resurrection of Christ—is the central and pivotal event for all history, evolution, and time. For Jung it meant nothing; it had no significance because he was an atheist in a world populated by sick, distressed people with no possibility for healing from their illnesses or redemption for their souls, because he did not grant human beings souls. Without Christ, human sickness cannot be healed. Christ is the great Healer.

Jung offers one conception of man that is spiritual because thinking is a purely spiritual activity of the soul, and thus all world conceptions are spiritual, which is his Jungian psychology. It is inherently extremely limited and untrue; it cannot be otherwise. He possessed a strong and devoted intellect, a disciplined mind, and other worthwhile virtues, but he applied his entire will and intellectual faculties to an inner psyche and its thinking conception as narrow and untrue as his scope of understanding and dim vision.

Jung groped about in the darkness of the unconscious and in the dimness of dreams and found only symbols as they appear in human tradition and the dreams of individuals and on which he reflected. He believed this determines the limitations of our knowledge of man and constitutes our entire purpose and task today. Any 'development' is merely improvements in the interpretations of symbols in dreams and their particular meanings in individual cases by the advancement he believed took and continues to take place in the human capacity for reflection. In Jung's view, by reflecting on dreams and their symbols, individuals find relief from their symptoms. This identifies and connects individuals, therapist and patient, both. These reflections are defined by his materialistic psychology. Jung's psychology is extremely complex and detailed. However, what is essential about it can clearly be described in a few concise pages.

On the one hand, the power of inwards reflection (spirit-inwardness) seen in human beings of his destiny—the Saturnine—is revelatory of Jung's soul-spirit constitution. On the other hand, it is telltale of the 20th century human situation that regresses into the grips of dark materialism that with our era is on the decline and from which millions of souls are emerging into the age of light in which we are now living that began in AD1900. Jung was behind his time and left us with one of many materialistic explanations that do not and cannot satisfy the post-modern soul seeking after the Christ.

Man has developed over eons of time, not only on earth over great changes in the Earth and its atmosphere, and in the evolution of the human body and consciousness (as a spiritual ego), but long before our present earth-stage: as a physical being (beginning with the first, Saturn stage of planetary evolution), a living (etheric) being (beginning with the second, Sun stage of planetary evolution), and as a soul-being (beginning with the third, Moon stage of planetary evolution just prior to our earth), and endowed with an I (on our present, Earth stage of evolution). We will continue with our development, both on earth and throughout the coming three stages after earth, but jointly by our own sacrifices and not only as the result of the sacrifices of lofty powerful, wise spiritual beings as was the case up until now. We must make sacrifices to help one another through perception, later the animals by great love.

Since the Mystery of Golgotha—the crucifixion and resurrection—Christ has coexisted with our development as a spiritual essence in the Earth and in each one of us who awakens in Him. Hence history and evolution are entirely different from the way they were before Christ's human life, while the divine beings or God (the hierarchies or heavenly hosts of Medieval European tradition, the gods and goddesses of the mythologies) have been ever-present and -active in our evolution from the beginnings of time. Indeed, humanity would not exist without the many great sacrifices of these exalted divine beings. The Christ-Being is above them all.

It is easy to see the materialist (and Carl G. Jung is but one exponent of this worldview) cannot grasp the evolution of man's oldest member, the physical body, let alone our higher, spiritual members, and the significance of the divine beings—with Christ's unique and central place —in human and world evolution.

Los Angeles
October 28-30, 2012
May 24, 2014
October 25, 2014

The Dawn of the New Age

If you wish to know a people and their language, with the exception of anthroposophy* and anthroposophical initiatives (including the Waldorf Schools, Camphill Villages, bio-dynamic farms, anthroposophically-extended medicine (clinics, hospitals, and practices), the Mystery dramas of Rudolf Steiner, speech formation, and eurythmy), and you seek them in the 20th century, you will look in vain. For the blight of competitive egoistic materialism, technology, and general apathy, on the one hand; and unspeakable genocides and wars, and natural disasters, on the other—which are but two sides of the same coin (we are inseparable neighbors, near and far), has cast its shadow over the entire earth, so that only the inner birth of Christ by His great Light has begun to awaken human souls from beneath and behind this condition of decline and degeneration, and in the vast spiritual wasteland where many souls wander hollow and without purpose or meaning.

But as recently as the wondrous cultural Era of German Romanticism in poetry, novels, philosophy, and science, which began to blossom in the late 1700s and ended with Goethe's death in 1832, the European peoples (folk souls) and their languages were infused with the life, richness, and beauty of the spirit beyond compare. Earlier there were other great European cultural periods as we have in J.S. Bach (1685–1750) and the music of the German Baroque, the Italian High Renaissance in architecture, sculpture, and painting in the 1400s and 1500s, the Gothic period with its great cathedrals 1140–1400, and the Romanesque period with its churches and the pilgrimages (1050–1200).

In our time, in the 20th and especially 21st centuries, something entirely new is being born. More and more human beings are privileged to have the experience of Paul before Damascus, to witness Christ come in etheric form by way of higher, supernatural senses, the eyes of their souls opened. This great event, which is transpiring beneath the surface and behind the appearances of society and of life the world over, has not merely passing significance that is exoteric, but eternal in time or esoteric significance. Then the Reappearance of Christ in the Etheric— Christ's human mission was fulfilled in Jesus of Nazareth with the Mystery of Golgotha some 2,000 years ago—is repeated for ever-greater numbers of human souls in key human beings and nature-phenomena. This is the deep renewal which results from the soul's awakening of the Damascus experience and is the source of inexhaustible inner refreshment, healing, strength, and nourishment for many, without which humanity would be unable to live, but by which those souls touched are profoundly enriched and enlivened now and in future. The font of Christ is thus both deeply human and Nature, and both are indispensable sources of strength and meaning for spiritually-awakened souls: LIFE is LIGHT and LOVE. This is the inner HEART and WORD, the MEAL or COMMUNION of CHRIST, Sacramental and Spiritual.

Los Angeles
November 23, 2013
Culver City, California
February 7
Revised Los Angeles
February 12/August 21/October 25
Culver City, California
April 2, 2014

* Neither this nor any study, story, or poem in *The Wood of Green* has the endorsement of the Anthroposophical Society, which the author recognizes.

Sense and Culture in the New Age

The Sense of Norms: A Legacy from the Past

How to make sense of seeming non-sense? The norms of family life and society, which seem to have less and less substance, not only 'at home' but in such places as boarding schools and foster homes, and earlier in convent homes and orphanages, or in life in homeless shelters and missions, *are* the sense, which structure in shelter, food, and routine (waking times, mealtimes, 'out' times, bedtimes, studies, and other duties) provides. This is necessary for children and adolescents, for without them the bodily constitution weakens, falls ill or fails, and the inner life has no basis for adulthood, lacking stability and protection in childhood. Where norms can be viewed as external and class-dictated or demographic, with the wise traditions, which once gave meaning to life in the household, foundation in childhood for maturity, and one's proper place in the world, we see that our norms are merely what remains from traditions in former times, watered down and weakened by generations of industrialization, and far more serious now with the machinations of technologies.

Past Tradition, Present Self-Reliance

The wisdom of tradition meant that there were expectations for each and every one according to social standing, whether landowner or peasant, tradesman or craftsman, clergy or congregation, monk/nun or laity, breadwinner or homemaker, parent or child, ruler or subject, nobility or commoner. One did what one's father and father's father did before one, or what one's Mother was taught by her Mother. Today we must create order in our own lives and in the lives of our children, and fashion what is beneficial and useful from what is available to us. We find more and more we must be self-reliant. However, childhood remains the ground on which we have to stand in maturity. The children are at our mercy.

The Small Child

Humanity will speak. Where the support of adequate structure provides the framework for growing up and the foundation for adult life, it is the people who populate one's world, people real and imaginary. Little children know the difference, and an imaginary parent or friend does not fill the need for an exemplary or real one. The small child needs real people to look to and with to play, as for it imagination *is* truth. (Real people are within the child's imagination.) Play is important for children, who know this, though some are denied play, disallowed to play, to be children! Then the fantasy world is limited solely to inner places and cannot be expressed with simple toys, creative endeavors (such as drawing pictures), and with Nature.

The people, places, and things in the small child's environment, whether or not it is allowed to play, take on imaginative life. It is therefore extremely important that it experience solely real reality—real people, the natural world, and simple toys (such as balls, wood blocks, dolls made with a piece of wool tied in a cloth with buttons for eyes)—and not virtual and other artificial sensations from technologies (sitting in front of computers, TVs, watching DVDs, and playing video games; or hooked up to headphones, iPods, and CD recordings that bombard the eyes and ears with their imitation sights and sounds, thereby stimulating and numbing the child's senses and mind, in place of the needed healthy, physical and imaginative play.

Innate Affinities in Childhood and Adolescence

Everything in the small child will experience real and good reality through imagination, in the middle-aged child beauty through art, in the youth truth through independent observation. We must only provide it with love and ample opportunity. This doesn't have to be costly; simplicity is, in many instances preferable to involved and advanced tools and supplies. We have already mentioned plain toys for the small child's imaginative life. However, one will try to obtain quality materials for the children to work with:

> Beeswax candles and colored beeswax (First Grade); wool and felt for crafts (First through Third Grades); watercolor paper, pigments, and brushes (First through Twelfth Grades); good large crayons and colored construction paper (Preschool through Fifth Grades); wood straight edges and board for drawing (Third Grade on); triangles (Sixth Grade on); quality colored pencils, ink cartridge pens, and blank notebooks for subject books (Sixth through Twelfth Grades); recorders (wooden flutes): pentatonic (First through Fifth Grades), soprano or alto (Sixth Grade on); orchestral instrument (Fifth Grade on); prisms for physics of light and color experiments (Sixth Grade); good yarn and needles for knitting: large wooden needles (Third through Fifth Grades), metal needles (Sixth through Eighth Grades); quality sewing cloth, thread, and needles for sewing (Eighth Grade); excellent compasses for geometric drawing (Eighth Grade on); nature substances/elements for chemistry experiments (Seventh and Eighth Grades); a real human skeleton for anatomy (Eighth and Ninth Grades); copper rods and cotton robes (blue for boys and pink for girls) for eurythmy (all Grades); quality wood, wood chisels, and mallet for wood carving (Eighth Grade); copper plates, metal compass, shears, points, and hammers for metalwork (high school); …..

Adults and Teachers: Early and Middle Childhood

Again, until puberty, it is the kind of teacher/adult who makes or breaks the child's education and not what s/he knows. If the Waldorf method and curriculum ideally meets the child's needs for learning, then the good adult and teacher is a loving authority figure the child looks to with love and veneration/admiration. Middle childhood is the life stage of reverence for adults, God in His Creation and the child's own efforts in creativity—beauty—and when the temperaments requirements must be met, just as early childhood is the time of imitation of goodness in adults and examples and imaginative play.

Adolescence: Requirements None to Soon

In high school the teachers should embody the ideals of youth and know their subject as experts in their field of learning. The adolescent requires expertise as s/he prepares for the 'real world'. Before puberty any education geared directly towards mature life does only harm. The adolescent will have ample time for intellectual training and to develop technical skills. Indeed the critical thinking faculties and intellectual prowess of the young person will develop more readily and quickly when the intellectual approach to learning waits until puberty because the adolescent has been duly prepared through a thoroughly child-oriented education, and not crammed with information before s/he was ripe and ready. Treating the child like an adult only deprives it of a healthy childhood, while education as an art as we have in the Waldorf Schools nourishes the growing soul of the child just as wholesome nutrition does its physical body. We must provide the child with its needs, outer and inner. When the needs of early and middle childhood have been met, then the young person will be ready to prepare for adult life with its demands and experiences. S/he will be strong enough to weather the storms of life as an adult if there was at least one loving authority figure in his/her life during childhood's middle years. (Rudolf Steiner)

The Sense of Tradition in Europe

In Europe and elsewhere, the people retain the sense of tradition and know, to a greater or lesser extent, what society expects from them.

There are clearer distinctions for example in Europe than in America between the roles played by men, women, and children; schooling, training, and employment for the various practical vocations and intellectual professions; the work ethic and leisure activities, working months and vacations, 'ordinary' days and holidays. These distinctions are a legacy from former times, centuries when the Pope (Church) stood above the king and the people knew their place in the larger picture, in the feudal system. Common faith served to unify every one, while who one was (or believed one was)—one's role or place in society—was a given, was simply inherited.

Decadence, Decline, and New Birth: The Time of Christ and Culture in the New Age

It is easy for us to identify the decadence and decline of our own Age. Like Ancient Rome, we are experiencing the final centuries of what was once, in periods of great cultural flowering, glorious. These periods have since wilted and died away, giving way to increasing materialism in thinking and lifestyle.

But just as 2,000 years ago the Christ was born a babe in Bethlehem, so now something entirely new is being born, and in just as modest and quiet ways as the holy Child was then.

If we 'pay our taxes to Caesar' by following external laws, then those who have chosen and are chosen also follow an entirely inner law, one of the essential Sun Spirit Christ of ethical anarchy, and do not need to break laws because they live in accord with the world, with the inner human being, with the divine. Like the early Christians they bear their crosses—now inner—on which they are crucified and die, their souls to rise from the dead. A new culture appears in many places, here then there, not as a norm or an expectation from without, but one of the Christ at work from within, which sacrifices, which suffers, which works, which prays, which dies, which loves, which forgives, which embraces all who will come to join in the work of salvation.

There is no need for norms here. The old and wise traditions are replaced by sound practices carried out with real conscious insight. This new culture nurtures the children, loving, caring for, and protecting them during the formative years; meets the youth, who seek after Christ in their unerringly-sensed idealism; supports and encourages the adults, whom are treated as equals; and guides all with wisdom according to age, temperament, country, destiny (planetary), and individual needs.

This is the time in which we are living, not the Rome of Augustus Caesar and the human life of Christ; not the Church, saints, heretics, thinkers, and the feudal society of Medieval Europe; but the world over: the dawn of a new Christianity, the Age of great Light. The new culture is an intimate one provided, not by birth or inheritance, but by meeting individual need. Those doing the work or enduring the suffering who therefore need help receive it. Each receives help according to his/her own endurance or efforts. Each has her/his own individual path to Christ to pursue. The Christ is genuine and singular. It rests with each single one. This is the new culture. This is sense in the New Age.

Santa Monica, California
2012
Los Angeles
October 25, 2014

Politics, Leaders, Nations

In 'politics', by which is most frequently meant Washington in the nation (U.S.) or Sacramento in California (both here in America), to take two examples, we usually indicate money- and partisan-powered campaigns, special interest groups, political strategies, smooth politicians—better-stated a significant branch of the system Lie, which permeates our society at all levels, that is intimately connected with the other branches of this system: the military machine, the big corporations (international), the popular media (television, the major newspapers, most radio), and countless people locally everywhere, and thus something inherently corrupt, if not evil, because all systems are so.

But there is something deeply significant that is missing in these assessments. While political analysts and many other highly intelligent individuals inform themselves on and study, not only tremendous amounts of data and other collected information, but also complex government policy on foreign affairs, war, the economy, the judicial system, employment, education, health care, welfare, energy, and other governmental departments and positions on rights, such as same-sex marriage, these individuals are further from understanding the essential aspect of government and nations than a simple constituent may be: the people or folk as a group and the leaders who may represent them.

Seen from this standpoint, the position of a candidate or elected official on one or more issues or platforms is not necessarily essential, although we know some one may choose a wrong or a right whether s/he is a voter, candidate, or elected official. Time is required for the laws of Christ to change the governments. Real progress is slow, although there are turning points, transitions, and transformations when something new is being born and growing up.

But a candidate and/or elected official may voice the soul of a people, and this quality may put him/her into office if the people are free to vote because the people recognize this, despite the superficial elements of politics that appear everywhere on the surface of life. Such a leader will invariably do good; s/he will be inspired by something greater than an individual person or any party or other sectarian group. Instead merely of a candidate's election because s/he is 'the lesser of evils', the folk soul of the nation will place her/him into the position of political power to work for the Good, which is Christ. This is the true body politic, the political life of every nation that will serve its people.

The candidates and elected officials who are called to office and truly inspired to lead not only take a stand on various issues; they are part of the change that heads towards the approaching future with a power that comes to light with them. This is necessarily followed by temporary set-backs in regressive politics under the uninspired leadership of others and losses at the national and societal levels but will in future emerge as part of the "symphony of nations of brotherhood and love". (M.L. King, Jr.)

Indeed we saw this political power wielded by the great Reverend Dr. Martin Luther King, Jr., not as the president of a nation but as a leader of national proportions. The progress effected under King's leadership changed America in lasting and far greater ways than any president of any nation has ever done before. King was awarded the Nobel Peace Prize in 1965 and assassinated a true martyr in 1968. In King we gain some kind of a sense for what is to come during the sixth and next post-Atlantean Era: the Slavic (AD3573-AD5733).

Examples of elected true national leaders include Abraham Lincoln (1809-1865): 16th U.S. president (1861-1865 (assassinated)), John Fitzgerald Kennedy (1917-1963): 35th U.S president (1961-1963 (assassinated)), Václav Havel (1936-2011): 9th and last president of Czechoslovakia (1989-1992) and 1st president of the Czech Republic (1993-2003) (the Václav Havel Prize for Creative Dissent "will celebrate those who engage in creative dissent, exhibiting creativity to challenge injustice and live in truth"), Nelson Mandela (1918-2013): president of South Africa, the first ever to be elected in a fully representative election (1994-1999) awarded Nobel Peace Prize 1993, and Barack Obama (b. 1961): 44th and current U.S. president and 1st African-American to hold this office (2009-present) named Nobel Peace Prize laureate in 2009. There may well be others I am not aware of.

Los Angeles
November 8
Revised and Edited Culver City, California
November 9, 2012

Obama's Berlin Speech Sounds a New Tone

Barack Obama won the sympathy of the German people in a speech he gave in Berlin on July 24, 2008 during his campaign for the presidency of the United States. It is true he has proved no different from the other U.S. Presidents regarding U.S. involvement in wars. But it is also true that in this speech he spoke the following words never before heard from a U.S. President or presidential candidate:

> Now the world will watch and remember what we do here – what we do with this moment. Will we extend our hand to the people in these forgotten corners of the world who yearn for lives marked by dignity and opportunity; by security and justice? Will we lift the child in Bangladesh from poverty, shelter the refugee in Chad, and banish the scourge of AIDS in our time?

> Will we stand for the human rights of the dissident in Burma, the blogger in Iran, or the voter in Zimbabwe? Will we give meaning to the words "never again" in Darfur?

> Will we acknowledge that there is no more powerful example than the one each of our nations projects to the world? Will we reject torture and stand for the rule of law? Will we welcome immigrants from different lands and shun discrimination against those who don't look like us or worship like we do, and keep the promise of equality and opportunity for all of our people?

This may be seen as mere rhetoric, and indeed it is words from a speech of a political nature whose purpose was a political one. But one cannot but recognize that its tone is a different one from all that came before it and that, in spite of the references to democracy and freedom, so empty from many decades of meaningless use, it sounds the responsibility of the western nations and embraces the entire world, including the poor and the marginalized. And the people of Berlin who were gathered there and heard this speech felt this, and they were responsive.

Los Angeles
2010

Encounters

It is a law of human life that whatever we put into it, we get out of it. If we invest nothing, we get nothing. If we invest something, then we get something. If we invest all that we have into life, then we receive a great deal from life. These investments are not material ones; they are of the soul and spirit that is inner. But they take place on earth while we are in our physical bodies. Thus they may be practical. In every case, they are put into practice. So there can be no hypocrisy in the actual spiritual life. This is because the real spiritual life is *lived.* Conjecture means nothing. Living is everything.

This applies to every one equally. Life is fair. This investment necessarily involves suffering because we fully live it, but if we ask ourselves whom this suffering belongs to, we will find the answer that it belongs to human beings, ourselves and our connections. For it is personal. We see the connection: The application of our efforts in life (investment), the progress we make from these efforts in life (returns), the suffering we and those with whom we are connected experience and thus our learning along our way in life (profits). All three are objective in this sense and at the same time personal to our experience; they are intimately bound up with 1.) who we are or have already become across reincarnations up to the present moment, 2.) what we will become beginning the present moment, 3.) our destiny, which is these first two: our being and becoming.

Our suffering makes us rich inside. We feel it. By this inner experience, we learn what life has to teach us. Life is the best teacher. Life is a very wise teacher. If we pay attention, do not stray, and are virtuous, life corrects us. Even if we do not, so long we endure or work our own soul battle that is our path ahead, then life corrects us over the course of reincarnations. If we orient ourselves according to this wisdom, then we progress surely and undeterred on our way ahead. There will be suffering and obstacles, but they will not defeat us, rather in encountering them, we will grow stronger.

A good analogy is the darkness to the light. The light is strong in its very essence, stronger than the darkness. But when it encounters the darkness, it grows even stronger, and in the process greater, sending the darkness away. This is true in us, in our souls. The light in our souls is stronger than is our soul darkness. But we must suffer the darkness of our souls with our little inner light for learning and progress. This is for our inner growth, our spiritual development. This is also our inner human, soul battle.

So it is with the obstacles life throws our way. In our encounter with them, our own, inner strengths or qualities are put to the test, but because we call on their true source within us for help and guidance, we receive the help and guidance we require for our continued journey, and we find we are the better for it. We have taken an important step forward, and the obstacle that life had thrown our way has been met with idealism and wisdom or love or reason and independence for our journey forward, or thrust aside with passionate inwards forces or heart-power or our individual struggle or assiduousness while we are not misled and retain our warmth, making room for the gradual but sure inner growth or development of our spirit. It is our soul, which has suffered the darkness or obstacle, and it is our eternal (spiritual) individuality, which has gained from this soul experience, which has learned and thereby prospered.

Neither do the fear and terror coming from out of the future get the better of us. We face the future with complete equanimity, trusting in the ever-present help of the spiritual world, of Christ, with no security in existence. We discipline our will, and seek the awakening from within ourselves, every morning and every evening. (Rudolf Steiner)

All of this is inner. It is invisible to the outer eye, but it is very real, even more real than outer reality, because it is creative, whereas outer reality has already been created and thus has only existence, a finished product, as it were. But that in us, which is creative, gives birth to something new, which changes the world. This is real power. This is the inner sun power. The world creative spirit is powerful. It not only changes the world. It changes those in whom it is active that they become part of the process of world-change.

Christ is the great Sun Spirit. God creates through Him. God created Nature without through Christ the Sun-God. God is creative in human creativity through Christ within. That is why human creativity is beneficial, not only for humankind, but also for the angels. We become co-Creators with God through Christ.

But creativity necessarily involves selfless sacrifices, which implies suffering. This is for learning, as well as vocation. But it is also that we help one another, for our human relationships. *Again and again we will find, when we reach out and help another, we learn from this person what they have to teach us.* So it is, in helping we are actually helped more. Those whom we suffer and make personal sacrifices for teach us more than they could ever learn from us. The teacher is the best pupil.

Our suffering makes us rich inside. We feel it. It is undeniable. It confirms our efforts and progress unmistakably, while it affirms us and what we are undertaking. More than this, it is dear to us. This is its personal meaning for us: suffering is precious. We may choose to create and endure it. This choice can only be made in freedom. Then we embrace our suffering because, finally, it is everything that we possess within. But we cannot wallow around in our suffering. That would lead us nowhere. Only when our suffering is part of our journey and thus of our destiny does it become our trusted companion and ally.

Along the road we encounter like-minded or -intended individuals. As we have described, we help one another. Such encounters are a blessing. Each is an exchange between two individuals, which transpires in freedom. Only in freedom can we truly meet one another. Such meetings or exchanges are personal because in them we cause suffering and suffer, but at a higher level they are supra-personal because they are not under the sway of feeling rather objective. Such is the personality, earthly and divine.

There is something crucial and much-neglected today when logic and reason are often pronounced that will I bring to your attention: Feeling solidarity with someone in direst need. Solidarity connects us with the poorest, most neglected human being. As Christian Morgenstern writes,

You explain, don't feel social, you dislike your fellow human beings almost more than you love them. Good. I expect from you neither social feeling nor honoring the "least among you". But if you see a hungry dog next to you, you will share your food with it, that goes without saying. I expect only that you feel with your fellow human beings as you do with a dog, namely: When in direst need: solidarity.

Only on earth can two destinies cross paths and make connections. It must be willed by both individuals else it does not transpire. But when the exchange has been made, love has been shared. God is at work on earth only in human freedom. This is the meaning of initiative-taking. When we do this our shortcomings are pardoned. These shortcomings are our all-too human side. It is the genius in us gifted by God and at work in human initiative-taking. Christ is our genius. By this we mean His Name not our lower self or individual nature. Christ is the 'I AM' in us, our true individuality. Christ is also our brother, the personality or Divine Will. Martin Luther King, Jr., spoke of "the sacredness of all personality". Again, in feeling solidarity with our brethren in direst need we cannot be complacent. We reach out and help the other.

If we take initiative we will invariably be rewarded (not in business and commercial profits, which is what real thieves do because they love only themselves and take more than their share), because when we do so we encounter our human brothers and sisters in mutual exchange. This is economics at the personal level: helping and being helped. It is simply matter-of-fact because a divine law works in true, selfless economics. This is the law of gift-exchange between two individuals in freedom. God is at work between human brethren who help one another (fraternal relationships). Both parties depart blessed. So is has been.

Los Angeles
December 2-3, 2012
October 25/29, 2014
Culver City, California
May 9, 2014

Value

The Price of Mass Production and Waste

We may believe mass production is good for the economy and saves money because it produces more goods and the cost of production per unit decreases, but we have two other factors to consider: value and waste. If we are willing to spend more initially on producing and purchasing quality goods and services, their value will be higher. They will be worth more to us. This is their actual value. When production exceeds real need and supply demand, as is frequently the case, there is a tremendous waste of natural and human resources, and the economy becomes inflated. Money is worth less. So we have to ask ourselves: what is the price of quantity at the expense of quality?

The Cost of Excess

When there is excess somewhere, in another place there will be too little of what is needed. When there is great waste in one place there is great poverty and hardship somewhere else. When work, time, and money are poured into sheer quantitative production, goods and services suffer qualitatively, even as there is waste.

Ultimately everyone loses. The economy is inflated, while the standards of goods and services are lower because the quality is lower. When the standards go down, people want more of and expect less from these goods and services, even as they have less worth, a lower value. People want more things and demand 'faster and better' services because they have less value, less meaning to them. People consume for consumption's sake. They jealously devour in spending money what they are lacking in quality, in their spiritual lives, in nourishment for their hungry souls. They want more because they are not being nourished. More means less. It is downhill. Meanwhile, because of this wastefulness or overproduction in one place, the poor want for even the basic necessities. They know how to value every small thing. They struggle with next to nothing and care for one another, as best they can.

Investing in Quality Goods and Services and in the Cultural Life

When human beings invest work, time, and money in the spiritual or cultural life (education (children's education, higher education, and continuing education or self-education), the religious life, the arts and sciences) and in quality goods and services, value *increases* accordingly. The economy is strengthened. Money has a higher value, is worth more.

Less is More

Purchasing the same item when one has worked hard has more meaning. A meal tastes better. One is really hungry. It satisfies. Human need remains the same, but human beings are now being nourished, spiritually *and* physically. They no longer seek in quantity what was lacking in quality. They consume less yet feel they have more. They enjoy what they have and want to share, to help more. They want for themselves only what they truly need because it is enough. Where there's less there's really more.

Cost-Efficiency and Meeting Human Needs

Production should meet real human need. Now the resources left over can be directed to those who truly need them: children loved and cared for, receive a good education, likewise our youth and young adults; the elderly are assisted in their daily living; the poor, the homeless, and the mentally ill are given shelter, food, clothing, work opportunities, and job training/placement; new cost-efficient, non-pollutant technologies are developed and produced. This in turn creates new jobs. Labor-intensive bio-dynamic agriculture and gardening heals the earth and gives human beings highest quality foods. Communities for the handicapped realize that society is only as strong as its weakest members.

Those working out of the spirit are to be especially valued. Without their contributions nothing would have value. Spiritual abundance bestows the blessing of cultural riches on mankind. This includes the selfless work of priest/pastors, rabbis, and imams who are genuine centers of religious community who provide pastoral care for the souls of those in the community. This includes our nurses, doctors, therapists, teachers, and artists who serve society according to their field of work. Those working with ideas and Christ Impulses from anthroposophy also work out of the spirit. These ideas are bearing fruit in medicine, art therapies, agriculture, finance, education, and special education, the religious life, architecture, sculpture, painting and drawing, singing, music, drama, creative speech (speech formation), and eurythmy.

Like the education of the child, the genuine religious life is an investment, not a tangible one as are trade schools, but for the growing soul of the child for its future and the soul in need of Christ for her/his future. Ultimately, every one should be included, because all human beings have needs and requirements, and each one of us can have worth, present or future, development depending. Each thing is appreciated and supported according to its actual worth. Everyone wins. We have the resources. We need only put them to work in the right way to make the economy healthy, the world a more human place.

Work in industry and all labor should not be reduced to a commodity rather workers should be treated with dignity. Continuing education courses and educational periodicals should be included in workers' benefits, as well as care for their children. These children should receive an education of high quality as every child.

Economic Relationships and Value

We see the positive relationship between human work, quality, and value, also between work, time, and money invested in the spiritual and in higher quality goods and services, and the economy; and conversely between excessive quantitative production and consumption for the few, extreme poverty for many, and the economy. Money does not remain constant in value. We know this because of the facts of inflation, depression, and recession. Therefore money should be devalued and revalued according to economic conditions and laws.

NOTE: Some of this study is first-published in this volume. A large portion was published in an essay by the same name ("Value") in *The Courage of the Flame* (Culver City: Sun Sings Publications, 2002), reprinted with permission from Alan Lindgren.

Reincarnation and Karma (Destiny)

Karma (the destiny) is shaped from the first incarnation, beginning when the individual soul had no karma, through every reincarnation to the present one, but extending into all future incarnations, insofar what has already been formed must still be endured, new karma may be formed, and all this is resolved. But for this to happen, the individual soul must bear within it forces, which have the capacity to create and endure karma. These are the inner I-forces, integrally linked to the sense of identity, and are essential to the destiny, to the soul, for without these special I-forces the possibility for salvation is missed. Many today are deeply afraid of this, while others do soul-battle, however great or small.

Karma is always a blessing, as we shall see, either an indirect one, when suffering is involved such that it is undesirable from our human, earthly perspective, or a direct blessing of welcome and love from human kindness. But when we refer to karma, we usually do so in connection with some form of suffering. This is because destiny (karma) is always felt, not in comfort and convenience, rather it requires soul-battle that is *not* easy. Of course, there are different 'places' the soul or destiny traverses on its inner journey. This means life does not always give us the same measure of karma. Additionally, individual souls have various degrees of misfortune and fortune, karma depending. This shows why some human beings suffer extreme hardship and want, while others experience benevolence and the blessings of cultural experience. This also depends on a specific incarnation.

Again, simply because some one is not poor and enjoys a beneficial cultural background does not imply s/he does not do inner soul-battle. Indeed the most cultured souls have or have had the greatest hardship; because their faculties, talents, and gifts result from refined previous abilities, which implies inner progress through the requisite suffering. Further development requires ever greater suffering, so the greatest geniuses suffer the most. These human beings often receive an excellent education, have a gifted teacher, and a good childhood. From this it is apparent that, while both ordinary or crude and gifted souls may experience misfortune and tragedy, or know good fortune and joy, soul-battle and sacrifice is essential to all progress. Without these twin activities no destiny can find fulfillment, realizing its potential.

Like reincarnation, karma is a human, spiritual law. It is experienced in three main distinct areas: in karmic relationships, in vocation, and in illness. Without karma, there is no connection with Christ, just as without karmic relationships, those close human connections that are suffered, Christ is not present in the relationship. Let us look into these three areas. Later, we will consider other kinds of karma.

Closeness signifies feeling between the two souls where one suffers the other, or both suffer and rejoice in the other. These relationships, formed on earth, carry over into the Spiritual Homeland on the Other Side of death's threshold where they continue in another way, then into the next incarnation/s or earthly lives, where they find resolution. But there are also new karmic relationships forming all of the time, necessarily on earth where they come about and are resolved. Karmic relationships are the close ones that really matter. Like the reality pain, karma is undeniable.

We know there are different kinds of pain and suffering a human being may experience. Pain may be of a physical, bodily nature, although all pain is suffered by the soul. This could be a toothache, headache, or stomachache, for example. It could be acute back pain, sclerosis, arthritis, or gout. These, too, are karmic.

There is also emotional pain, which can be experienced as just as hard to bear, but differently, as it is only within the soul. For some, depression, rather than being a sign of weakness or emptiness, is the recovery from a manic high and is experienced suffering inner pain and guilt in the darkness of soul depths. This is an example of emotional or direct soul pain. But for those who suffer this illness, who are strong souls, through much inner sometimes manifesting in outer, struggle, they come out of these depths of soul darkness and back up into the light of cheer and good fortune. Their struggles do not cease at this point, however. They are only not suffered in soul darkness, rather in more normal, regulated circumstances. Owing to the typical imbalance of these destinies, however, their lives are sometimes something of a roller coaster.

Other emotional pain is experienced acutely in the mind as the grief of self-hatred. This is extremely hard to bear. Often, this experience continues for years. Only the Christ is the cure. Because of pain, physical or emotional, some human beings consider suicide an option. They do not realize that in taking their own life they would only compound the existing pain they sought to escape from with suffering far worse, indescribable. If every one who contemplated suicide knew this, they would never go through with it. Those relative few who do must also forgo the experience of being ushered across death's threshold by Christ, which is the case in every kind of death that is not suicide.

Some perfectionists suffer negativity, while others who endure more find it only irritating. Then there are those who are equal to the perfectionism they demand of themselves. They are not subject to negativity at all. But these very individuals who will achieve or have achieved levels and ever higher levels of perfection must endure by far the most terrible suffering: that of a saint. They take this suffering into their hearts in utter freedom, with the insight it belongs to them as their karma and to no one else and that they must fully suffer. This may include tremendous physical pain, but it is always heart-suffering lasting many lifetimes over which it becomes ever greater and more intense until the end of the Age when final healing of all sins and ills shall take place.

Heart-suffering is the dearest, because it is located where the inner Christ indwells. All human beings whose souls awaken in Christ gain an inner heart and with it this dearest suffering, if only for a time.

Illness is another kind of karma from karmic or close relationships. It, too, is suffered and can be physical or emotional, as described. We think of diabetes or cancer, both of which can afflict all seven destinies, similar to a sprained ankle, broken leg, stroke, or concussion.

Where all illness belongs to the destiny that is is karmic, some illnesses are karma-specific that is each belongs to only one of the seven destinies. Five such illnesses are head-metabolic. Where medical science, and psychiatry in particular, calls them the mood disorders, they are actually head-metabolic because of imbalances in the lower and upper systems of the human body and soul. We have already mentioned one of these that is experienced as mood swings. Psychiatry calls this disorder bi-polar. This is the Mars destiny. Another is experienced as fragmented thinking. Psychiatry calls this schizophrenia. This belongs to the Moon destiny. One destiny suffers from paranoia and negativity. This destiny is proud they are not 'mentally ill', yet paranoia is not healthy and can lead to irrational thoughts and behavior. This is the Mercurial destiny. Another illness is pure depression. It can affect two of the five destinies, each from its own direction, but it is essential neither succumbs or the inner situation is hopeless. These are the Saturnine and Jupiter destinies. The final two destinies cannot be mentally unstable or suffer from any mood disorder/head-metabolic illness. The illness belonging to the Sun destinies is centered in the rhythmic system and the heart especially because it is there the suffering becomes tremendous and must be endured for several or more lifetimes. The illnesses of the Venus destiny are not karmic in the sense of the other six because they are blameless. (see, below) Hence they are adoptive and redemptive. Now we have all seven destinies and their illnesses. All illnesses can be cured, but they must be suffered first, even until and including death. This is because of the karma of the illness.

The inner Christ is the final cure to illness. I knew an older woman born with grand mal seizures. Growing up she had three seizures every day. By the time I knew her (she was in her late 60s or early 70s at the time) she had not had a seizure in three years. She told me Christ was healing her. But she had to fully suffer her illness, that in her case lasted her entire life, for the healing to take place.

The purpose of illness as all suffering is karma: to balance past deeds for harmony to return to the world. I break off a branch from a tree. I have altered the world because of my deed. It bears the stamp of my I on it. Decades pass, a whole lifetime. It is no wonder we have forgotten. But I am as deed in the world. Something happens to me that is undeniably personal. I know it. My deed has found me. I must receive it back. Karma has happened. The experience of memory inside is what has come to mean to us personally in our past. Can we see how from without what we did as action equally relates to us personally and must find its way back to us in future? This is karma. Karmic relationships, illness, and vocation, which we will discuss next, carry over from previous incarnations as well.

Vocation is the third kind of karma. Not merely the person's employment —although we may suffer our karma in carrying out our job-task—it belongs to the destiny and is necessarily suffered. Of all artistic souls, composers and poets suffer the most, but the poets more than the composers. Composers and poets are so by vocation. Nursing, too, can be one's vocation, as can social work and teaching. The priesthood of the Christian Community, the movement for religious renewal, is the vocation of its priests/pastors. Vocation spans at least two incarnations with its roots or first practice in (a) previous one/s carrying over into the next lifetime.

This points to something else of great import in all karma, namely, the periods spent in the spiritual world between incarnations. What takes place between embodiments of the soul prepares it for its coming earthly life. Thus, my experiences, deeds, and relationships in one lifetime are arranged together with Christ, the hierarchies, and those with whom I have become closely connected (when one or both have suffered the other) in the spiritual world so that their karma can occur or be carried out. However, one or more incarnations can be skipped for a karmic relationship to resume. In the instance of the suicide, certain specific laws apply. For example, soul qualities from the one lifetime reappear refined in the following one. Again, the suicide in the following incarnation manifests as a closeness to Christ. As the suicide forgoes the experience of Christ ushering the soul across the threshold of death, this closeness in the next incarnation could be seen as karma to balance this out. Karma always restores balance, to individual souls and to the world both.

(The Christian Community is neither Catholic, Protestant, nor Orthodox. It forms a direct link from the first Christians through the decline and fall of the Roman Empire; the Dark and Early Middle Ages; the Romanesque Period; Early, Middle, and Late Gothic Periods (the High Middle Ages); the Italian High Renaissance, German Baroque, and German Romanticism. This means simultaneous to the Scientific Revolution and the gradual entrance of materialism into human thinking and lifestyle, irreconcilable with Christ.)

Let us briefly look into other kinds of karma. There is the karma of untruthfulness. Untruthfulness also has specific consequences and repercussions. Everything surrounding birth and death can be karmic as it brings about significant life-circumstances. The country of birth is karmic: where the soul is born. This is for karmic relationships. When an individual immigrates this is for his/her karma and for the same reason. Childhood is deeply karmic. Instead of seeing childhood experiences as determining who the child, later adult, is, it is the other way around. Before birth, the soul chooses to have significant experiences and, together with hierarchical beings and Christ in particular, arranges the outer circumstances that will bring about these experiences. Thus the destiny, shaped in previous earthly lives, must undergo the significant childhood experiences in this one. They are karmic.

We choose our parents. We either get first choice or second best. There is the karma of displacement or orphanhood, or the death of one of the parents during childhood bringing about half-orphanhood. The experiences of an orphan are entirely different from those of a child raised by both parents or even close relatives. This deeply affects the soul—perhaps going from one foster home to another. Education can be karmic. Though not for every child, a Waldorf education can be karmic: necessary for the destiny. Or a certain teacher may be in the child's life for its destiny, also the subject taught. The death of every human being that is not a suicide is karmic because death is deeply significant for the destiny. We note the really significant human experiences are karmic and not the non-essential ones.

The laws of destiny are highly complex. We should pay close attention to details surrounding key experiences in the person's life as they are highly telling. Not the details as such, rather what is of outstanding interest in the biography. We think of an extraordinary meeting between two human beings who spend the rest of their lives together who have a karmic relationship, or how one human being who is of deep significance in the life of another comes into contact with them, or an unusual circumstance of how some one contracts a fatal illness, or the situation surrounding an accident where some one is badly injured or killed. As in all human experience, it is important to pay attention where karma is concerned.

An elderly woman who lived in London I was fortunate to know lost one eye at an advanced age. Otherwise, she remained healthy her entire life. At age 95 she was hit and killed by a car in the far lane of a major street she was crossing at the light. (We shared a meaningful correspondence. I always recall her beautiful handwriting. Her writing was perfectly even as though she were writing on equidistant parallel lines. Of course, she was not. It was her eye-and-hand together, by which her writing was so beautiful and so evenly written. We wrote one another in the German language. She was a German Jew and a genuine Christian, so especially my German poems were dear to her. I sent her an inscribed copy of each of my books as they were published. I knew her through her son-in-law, my second best and dearest friend. We met only once.)

All beauty comes from past suffering. This could be a beautiful face or soul. Goethe (1749-1832) writes: *Colors are the deeds and sufferings of the light.* When we consider this light may be sunlight or soul-light, the colors may be physical or soul colors, or even spiritual colors. Pure colors are beautiful.

We need to recognize the precious nature of all pain and suffering, because it serves to connect us directly with Christ, even for those not consciously aware of Him. We call to mind the suffering of Christ in the man Jesus the Three Years, the most excruciating of all. All pain and suffering needs to be measured against the suffering of Christ on the cross. (Virginia Sease)* Like all Venus destinies, the future, present, and past martyrs, Jesus of Nazareth was always pure. His destiny and suffering were blameless. Unlike our karma, which is earned, the suffering of the Venus destinies is innocent and redemptive. Like Jesus of Nazareth, their karma and suffering is a mystery to us. God favors the Venus destinies.

Christ is the Lord of Karma. He works in the infinitely-complex threaded pattern of the karma of all humankind, in the billions of earthly lives of all human souls down through the Ages, past, present, and future. Christ is the essence of and key to each single one, and to all of humanity. Humanity is found reflected in each destiny, each human being who suffers is humanity, and Christ is all our humanity, the humanity of all karma or destiny. The extremely complex web of destiny is beyond human knowing.

The studies in this section connect the human spiritual I (reincarnation) and/or soul (karma, the destiny) on the soul's journey to and with Christ. They give the reader an overview of reincarnation and karma and their relationships in human experience and life for the single soul and human destiny as a whole. The last study shows how the need for Christ equals the help of Christ in each instance. The section opens with three well-known examples of karma. My significant poem *Destiny* is on page 504.

Alan Lindgren
Los Angeles
September 3-4/6-8
October 26, 2014

* Dr. Virginia Sease does not endorse this volume or any study, story, or poem in it. *The Wood of Green* is published independently of the General Anthroposophical Society at the Goetheanum in Switzerland, which the author recognizes.

Three Examples of Karma

Often a human being, and with good reason, wishes he or she had been born white, a man, not physically, emotionally, or mentally disabled, had never experienced abuse or hardship, pain, suffering, or illness. Sometimes a human being, in experiencing the suffering which being different or disabled has brought, devotes her life to service, turning the obstacles into learning and growth, even though this hardship is so undesirable. We think of Helen Keller. Sometimes a human being embraces her difference and all of the suffering endured because of it, and forges her indomitable spirit in the fires of human experience with courage and love under incredible odds, triumphant and creative, an example for us all. We think of Maya Angelou. Sometimes a human being, from the depths of oppression experienced from being different, rises up to spirit-heights to champion all human dignity and freedom, a beacon light for black and white, brown, yellow, and red; women and men; physically, emotionally, and mentally challenged and not; abused and not abused, for all human beings. We think of M.L. King, Jr.

It is essential for us to come to the realization that human differences enrich both the different minority and the different majority, that the Jewish experience, the Black experience, the Woman's experience, the experience of the physically, of the emotionally and of the mentally challenged is a deeply *human* experience, an experience whose often painful and unfair treatment can become human strengths, qualities, and goodness which *all* of humanity can learn and benefit from. We need to know *each human being is the final minority, a one-of-a-kind, unique child of God.* We need to affirm our own humanity, in ourselves, in our children, in one another.

The price of human suffering is indeed a very dear one. Jesus of Nazareth paid this price for our salvation, and the many saints since His Life, Death, and Resurrection have taken up their own, personal crosses and followed after Him in selfless sacrifice. They have done so not only for their own salvation, but also to serve the world with courage and love that each human being might experience knowledge of Christ, His healing Word, Heart, and Light in full consciousness. They spread His love among us. This is their work, their suffering, and their joy. These recognized and unrecognized saints and martyrs are women and men, black and white, yellow and brown, disabled and not disabled, and they all of them know the deepest meaning of suffering, joy, and love. Whether or not we can be like them and join their ranks, we can at least take heart with Maya Angelou, Helen Keller, and Martin Luther King, Jr., and with countless others known and unknown, and do our own part in God's Great, Good World Plan.

Each one of us partakes of what is universally human, going back to our common Adam and Eve, and then through the Christ, Who became human in Jesus of Nazareth, can find the Divine. He came for *all* humankind. Each one of us is both utterly unique, and also a sister or brother in the *one* human family. We are individuals, but more than that we are human beings inextricably interwoven into the fabric of all human destiny. Each individual destiny thus relates to other individual destinies through karma as part of one great destiny, the destiny of humankind. Christ is the Lord of Karma. He is always at work in karma and in each one of our personal destinies maintaining harmony and balance. We need only seek and we will find Him, for He finds those who, striving through every struggle, hardship, illness, and challenge, would receive His Help. We know this. This is our faith, the faith of those who came before us, and the faith whose works, together with hope and love, shall change the world.

> *All of my work is meant to say, "you may encounter many defeats but you must not be defeated." In fact, the encountering may be the very experience which creates the vitality and the power to endure.*

Maya Angelou (1928-2014), poet, writer, performer, teacher, producer and director.

Originally published as an essay, "On the Human Experience", in *By the Sunset there's a Door* (Culver City: Sun Sings Publications, 2002), 247-248. Reprinted with permission from Alan Lindgren

Destiny, Christ, and the Single Soul

What is destiny? The word 'destiny' is one often used today. It can be said it has gained popularity in common usage. I know a young woman by the name of Destiny.

Even as it is liberally utilized, its true meaning is not clear or understood to most people, and this is reflected in the way the term is used. To give a good example of this in America, where there is much experiment and talk about 'consciousness' and 'spirituality' (commonly associated with the 'New Age' movement), we often hear that President Barack Obama is 'destiny's child'. This intelligent man plays a large role in the ever-emerging and developing history-in-the-making of America. He is a good public speaker. But what does it mean when people say that Obama is a 'child of destiny'? Do people really understand this phrase that is so lightly tossed about?

These people, who may well be you or I, our friend or next-door neighbor, our colleague or co-worker at the office, do not know what destiny is. If they did know, they would understand that destiny is karma. Can Barack Obama—or any one—be a child of karma? Does this even make sense? Would my friend's parents have named her Karma?

President Obama has a destiny, because he has karma, so long he wisely suffers it. This is not a given, however, especially in light of the fact that he is in the most prominent position in the world so that he is especially subjected to powerful dehumanizing spiritual forces that place great personal demands on his soul.

Only those creative of their karma, or who insist on suffering it for the preciousness of their irreplaceable souls, pave the way and travel the distance, the inner journey in earthly life that, over many incarnations becomes the destiny. In the big picture, karma is the destiny.

When I say, for example, 'This is my destiny'. I could equally well say, 'This is my karma' I must suffer or endure. Karma includes sorrow and true inner joy, felt hope, the grief of loss, the tenderness of solace and comforting (when we suffer, ail, or endure illness or heart-suffering), all kinds of pain and hurt. In other words, all those experiences that make the destiny, for karma (destiny) is felt; it is the inner road or path that is traveled on earth in real times and places that involves human feeling and mental experience, that makes itself felt in human life. But many people today do not want to feel, or anything but fleeting pleasure.

Deaths, accidents, relationships, and meetings that signify true feeling and necessitate or cause painful or uncomfortable experience, transitions that involve hurt or suffering, physical or emotional, these are also karmic that is part of the destiny.

No one is a child of destiny. We have a destiny that belongs to us and to us alone, and if we actively choose it, or endure it contemplatively, then we will fulfill our destiny, which is the same thing as realize our true human and spiritual potential.

As with freedom, destiny is a choice. Either we find, create, or suffer it, or we lose it. If we lose it, we will be lost because we will lose the possibility to come to Christ to know Him and thus our own souls, life, and true meaning. If we create or suffer it, we will find (know) Christ who can always find us.

This is very earnest, for those who are sad and who rejoice, for those who weep and who delight in humor and fun. It is earnest for each single one of us, and 'deep down' we know this, every single one of us.

Our karma, our destiny is singular. Although there are seven destinies that are the planetary types, each soul-spirit or individual, in the body, has his/her own destiny or karma to create or endure and to suffer. Thus it is intimately bound up with the human core: the spiritual ego or I.

We sense the gravity of karma in our lives, today when so many take wrong paths, surrender their souls to the powers that be, and allow themselves to be seduced by the lie in its many forms that approximate, copy, and imitate Nature, creativity, human beings, human feelings, and Christ, *artificially*. This is in technology and people both. We think of several different versions of the same photograph or recording.

If I lose what is most precious to me, which is my soul, my destiny, then what is left? Then what is left that belongs to me? Nothing. Nothing of genuine worth is left me. Money, material possessions, property, power, prestige, excessive or rampant pleasure, blind emotion, criminality, the dark occult, these things are either empty by themselves (they have no soul), or they can consume the soul in illness beyond human recognition. Yet many are they today who go in one of these two directions, which means that is what they have left after they have lost their karma.

At death every lie, every mindless exercise, every pointless (empty) existence, every falsehood, vice, destructive life, every harm comes to an end, loses its gratification, loses its deception, loses its power. For at death the truth stands clearly, unmoved, unchanged, and alone, and everything is revealed for what it is (according to its true nature), measured against the truth. This can happen in life on earth in the presence of some one deeply human, in whom Christ indwells unmoved.

If human beings live their lives in accordance with the truth of human and spiritual experience and behavior, or not far a-field from it, they will find themselves with their Christ, for He is the truth. They will have good deaths for a good afterlife.

Some people do. They have a destiny. When they return to earth in their next incarnation, they have the opportunity to continue their soul journey in a new physical body to one day come to Christ. Then they will have made the decision, before birth, to realize their destiny, to find the Christ, selflessly serve their fellow human beings, suffer the karma they have created, or resolve their age-old suffering that is their destiny (karma), for the work of Christ on earth.

The reception of the spiritual sun essence will transform their hearts in Christ, and they will know Him, He who is the Saviour of humankind.

All of their losses, suffering, and endurance, all of their work, all of their striving and struggles, all of their looking and listening, all of their dreaming and hopes, all of their helping and, finally, their seeking, will lead them to His grace, and they will have found the true meaning of existence, the essence that will shine as an inner sun in their hearts and souls, which is a drop of the Christ-sun essence in them.

Christ is the Good Shepherd, and we are His sheep. He protects us. When we abide in Him, He abides with us, for He is faithful and good to us, merciful and kind. Let us be faithful. Finally, faith is very simple, for the artless as for the complex thinkers. Those who keep faith, they trust in life's wisdom. It is in this relationship to the wisdom of life that we are safe in the Divine, in the ever-present help of the spiritual world.

Los Angeles
April 22-23/June 24, 2011
October 15/26, 2014

Destiny: A Poem

My body and my soul are separate
Indeed they always were
But when my soul the Christ appeared
My soul with Christ suffered
My body housed this soul of mine
To nourish from the Earth
To strengthen from the Sun above
My soul my body thanked
But ever separate remained
My body does express
My soul that within does dwell
My destiny on Earth.

Alan Lindgren
Los Angeles
October 15, 2014

Reincarnation and the Destiny

The continuity we think of throughout life, from conception or birth through physical death, and all of the transitions from waking life to sleep and from sleep to waking life, should not be viewed only within the apparent boundaries of a single lifetime. Just as we awaken from a night of sleep into day to then fall back asleep again after a (full) day into the night, to once again awaken from sleep back into waking life, so do we go from the spiritual world (=heaven) into one earth-life, then back into the spiritual world, and then back to earth into the next earthly existence again. This is a kind of divine-earthly rhythm between heaven and earth, back and forth, necessary for the destiny on its journey to and with the Christ. We gain from one lifetime what we are able to; so long we head in the right direction and learn according to our karma (destiny).

Each lifetime or incarnation bears its fruit. This fruit is the karma of and everything we have learned during that particular earthly life. Then we return to the spiritual world for a usually long period of time measured by the passage of time on earth—about 1,000 years—(in heaven there is no time in our sense; all is eternal, with neither time nor space as we know it on earth) where we bring everything with us from the earth existence that can be brought over. All of our close human connections and relationships that were suffered on earth continue on after physical death in the spiritual (=heavenly) world or divine life. All those qualities essential to our being, soul qualities that are inseparable from who we are as souls, these, too, we bring with us over to the Other Side of death's threshold. Through karma, across many lifetimes or incarnations of the soul, these soul qualities are refined. If I have an artistic soul, then these soul qualities reappear in this earth-life, but refined from my suffering. In Christ, on the soul's awakening, all soul qualities refine much more than was previously possible. The physical body itself undergoes changes, especially the face (countenance, the features). All these changes, inner and outer, continue as the soul develops. This is because of the activity of Christ, of His 'I AM', in the spiritual individuality that has incarnated into the lower human sheathes.

Human suffering serves the destiny in its development that is progress in various ways. It binds us together in the single tapestry of the destiny of all mankind. Thus my suffering you or your suffering me or our suffering one another connect us, whereby we are related, not necessarily in familial relationships, but always in the deeper, human sense. Our suffering also determines our task in one earthly life, which can be our vocation. All vocation is so because it is suffered. This is what makes it vocation is that it is must be suffered to be fulfilled. Other tasks/jobs can also be suffered whereby they fulfill the purposes of the divine beings of destiny. Christ is foremost among these beings. Thus karma is under the guidance of Christ, for He is the Lord of Destiny or Karma. The illnesses and other experiences of suffering, including accidents and death, are also karmic or part of the destiny.

We choose to experience our karma before we are born, because we know that it is spiritually lawful, and that we require these painful and, from our limited earthly, human perspective, undesirable experiences on earth to know Christ, to become human for our destiny. Our lives are ruled by the karma we have brought with us from previous incarnations. Every illness, each blow, every loss, every deprivation, all pain, accidents, and our final death, we choose to have these experiences in our coming earth-life before birth in the spiritual world. There, from the higher perspective of eternity together with all good beings, which are the progressive powers, we are aligned with progress that can only take place on earth. Everything of significance exists in the spiritual world prior to physical birth. All important decisions and possibilities are made there.

Rudolf Steiner (1861-1925), the great Austrian seer and thinker, spoke of the transmigration of souls in his work on reincarnation and karma. It is best to read his words directly, however, I will mention that souls who lived in Europe in the first centuries after Christ were sometimes reborn in Asia, though not always. There are others: transmigration from Asia to Europe, and others involving America. Although a person may be born and live all or most of his/her life on the 'new' continent and land, what sometimes occurs is that (a) key experience/s occur/s in the 'old' country, while most of the lifetime is lived in the 'new' land.

To take an example, an individual may remain and find everything s/he requires for her/his destiny (development) within a 10-mile radius from where s/he was born during this incarnation. This could be Glasgow, Edinburgh, Liverpool, London, Lyon, Paris, Hamburg, Berlin, Florence, Rome, Athens, St. Petersburg, Moscow, Tokyo, Manila, Sydney, Boston, Houston, or San Francisco, for example. Another human being, born in the same location, is drawn to another continent and language for karma, to realize the aims of the progressive powers and fulfill his/her destiny during this incarnation. This is especially for karmic relationships. This could be America, in the examples of European and Australian cities, also Latin America, or Europe and, say, Germany or France, in the examples of U.S. cities.

This is so because of past earth lives. In the first instance, those individuals who play key roles in the destiny are all living or working within the 10-mile radius of this soul's physical birth that is the meetings and experiences are arranged to take place there. In the second example, the soul has a deep connection to others in other lands, from past incarnations, maybe elsewhere.

I had a friend who never left the Westside (West Los Angeles, Culver City, Venice, Santa Monica, Mar Vista, Palms) her entire lifetime, except once as a teenager on a train to and from Chicago for a week. The entire time Ida said to her father: *When are we going back to Los Angeles? When are we going back to Los Angeles?* She found everything for her destiny right where she was born, every true that is karmic relationship. She never left, except for this brief inconsequential period. Her Christ-work kept her where she was born. Ida died in 2004 in her early 70s.

To take another example, I know a gifted woman from El Salvador who came to Los Angeles where her destiny is working itself out. She had to leave her country to experience her soul's spiritual awakening in another land and language. Her (American) English is superb. She has karmic relationships with other immigrants from El Salvador in Los Angeles.

A third example is a good friend of mine who is a Brit. He was born and raised in England where he went to the same Waldorf School with his future wife. He earned an MA in physics and mathematics from the University of Edinburgh, Scotland, at age 20 when he immigrated to the United States, settling in Spring Valley, NY. His wife later joined him there, and they now have three grown sons. His house remains in Spring Valley, and he has lived and worked in New England since he came to America in 1962. He was a teacher for thirteen years, with students ranging from first graders through college age. A Certified Public Accountant, he holds an MBA in finance from the Stern School of Business at New York University. He spent eleven years at J.P. Morgan, the Wall Street banking investment firm, where he was a Vice President, and was Executive Vice President and Chief Financial Officer of a bank in Pennsylvania. He is 72 years old. This highly intelligent and diligent man has spiritual roots in Europe, but his destiny brought him to America where he has spent most of his life. His immigration was most matter-of-fact. He has lectured in Europe, but most of his karmic connections are with Americans. Like the woman who never left the Westside and the woman from El Salvador, he consciously pursues his karmic relationships. These three individuals are all gifted.

America is a special phenomenon in terms of the destinies of different peoples. Many souls of all the folk groups either have been born here or were born in other lands to later immigrate here. My father Arne is an example of the latter. He lived most of the first 36 years of his life in the country of his birth: Sweden, coming to Los Angeles in 1954 where he settled and died in 1994 at the age of 75. Again, his karmic relationships, which means those formed in past earthly lives, brought him here.

I am a fourth example. I was born and raised, and have lived all but 3 ½ years of my life somewhere in the Los Angeles Basin of the Southland. I am 52 years old. After high school, I paid for and made a 5-month trip through Europe where I had very disorienting soul experiences. In The Hague, Holland, I encountered a man, who is key to my destiny. He was there for me in moment of crisis. This exceptional man is a Sun destiny.

A few weeks after that I met a priest of the Christian Community in Denmark, who played a vital role in my destiny. (At that time all priests of the Christian Community had their training in the German language at the Seminary in Stuttgart, Germany, with very few exceptions.) At the time I spoke no German, but I felt more deeply during my stops in German cities on this trip. Although I did not feel comfortable in Germany at this time, a deeper feeling lived in my heart when I was there. With one woman who briefly took care of me it was also a deep consolation for me. It was a warm, inwards feeling I knew in my heart. I also experienced this feeling staying with a family in Vienna, Austria. In no other land in Europe did I feel this way, not in Sweden (with my Swedish aunt), not in Holland, nowhere else. It was a young German woman in Hamburg who directed me to this priest. That is the only part she ever played in my life. There was no other connection than her connecting me with him.

This Danish Christian Community priest was very warm and hospitable. He welcomed me with open arms. We shared a lighthearted but joyous few days in Copenhagen together, but for one statement he made:

I have never been to America, but I have a Scandinavian friend who has, and he has told me that for Americans, as for Scandinavians, it can be valuable to have an experience in Germany in the German language.

I was 18 years old.

I remain in touch with him. All of these years he has been pastor in Copenhagen. He is moving next door to the main residence as he is soon to be 70 years old and senior priest, and a young Danish woman who is entering the priesthood will be taking his place. He is a Sun destiny.

After returning to the United States and Los Angeles, I proceeded to become very ill very rapidly. It is apparent this disorienting trip and my quickly becoming ill were necessary in order for me to turn around and get better. There can be no healing without suffering illness. After this, right away I recalled the Danish priest's words. At once I went to nearby UCLA (University of California at Los Angeles) and met with a tutor from Germany. She said she was leaving right away on holiday to Germany but referred me to another German woman at UCLA. She also said I should purchase a First Year College German textbook at the UCLA student bookstore, which I did.

I received no tutelage from this German tutor. She neither taught nor guided me in learning the language. I had decided I wanted to see a tutor to report on my progress for the structure this would provide. This is precisely what took place. Every two weeks I completed two chapters in the textbook, which included writing a brief essay after each chapter, and I reported to her on my progress. I paid her $20 each time. This was very healthy for me for another reason: it gave me something tangible and specific to work on during this very low period in my life when I had hit rock bottom. (In my case, with language.) Meanwhile I got a job working with small children as I also remembered my priest friend's words about having an experience in Germany and had decided to return to Europe to work in Germany. I saved money from my job to this end. So I was studying the language and working a job.

I obtained two addresses of farming communities in Germany and wrote a letter of inquiry to each one. From one of them, a bio-dynamic farming community in Schleswig-Holstein, I received a letter of welcome. The other one declined. I completed the First Year College German textbook in about six months and then read my first book in German. Then I flew to Frankfurt, stopping briefly on the East Coast on my way to see friends and family there. I was 19 ½ years old by this time.

I spent 4 ½ months on this visit to Germany, on the farm, in East and West Berlin (over Easter), with some time in Hamburg, which became my favorite German city. After 2 ½ months I was conversant in the language. When I left my spoken German was good. I also co-translated a medical paper for a German MD in Hamburg on prostate carcinoma for remuneration. This money just saw me through my stay as I had run out of funds.

Back in Los Angeles, I enrolled as a freshman at Pomona College. This was for September 1982. I was 20 years old. I took a placement exam and placed into fourth semester college German—the final lower division German course offered. I got an A. I got straight A's in all my German courses. Second semester freshman year I took a course on 19th century German poetry. Because of my love for the language and the beautiful poetry we read, I decided to major in German literature. I was later to compose poems of note in German. I became a poet and a writer.

After my sophomore year I took a year's leave of absence from college to study at the anthroposophical arts youth seminar in Stuttgart, Germany, where I had applied and been accepted. I had worked both summers after my freshman and sophomore years to pay for my trip to and from Germany as before, but also my tuition at the seminar. I was prepared in every way: humanly (by way of a relationship from which I gained necessary experience to be had in no other way), by my knowledge of German, and financially. I stood now ready to meet my future. Everything was in the German language. I attended this seminar 1984-1985 where I studied speech formation under the Swiss speech formationist Stefan Allenbach, and where also at this time I experienced my soul's spiritual awakening to Christ and therewith my higher I. This was during a morning course given by a French Christian Community priest (Gérard Klockenbring†) in German. As he spoke no English and I no French, our common language was German. I was 22 years old.

I studied Rudolf Steiner's *Theosophie* at the Jugendseminar when I began as a student of this thinking giant's intellectual work, and when my spiritual life took on deeper meaning. My spiritual knowledge has its wellspring in Stuttgart as I found the meaning of my life there. My work in speech formation in the German language proved crucial for my future vocation as a poet. The work I did there in speech translated naturally into my feeling for my Mother tongue, American English. My work as a sculptor saw its transformation at that time as well, under the direction of the German sculptor Manfred Welzel. The deepest relationship I have to the German language is in my heart that is truly religious. This warm, festive mood permeated my entire time at the Jugendseminar, while I experienced an internalization in my heart and soul just prior to my soul's awakening and personal meeting with the French priest. German is the deepest bearer of religious feeling in our era: the Anglo-Saxon Germanic. I was fortunate to learn German and to go to Germany at this crucial time in my life. More than good fortune, it is essential to my destiny. It was necessary in the deepest sense.

These significant experiences are on German soil in the German language. Whenever I speak with a native German, s/he believes I am a German, and when they learn I am an American they welcome me as one of their own family. Such warmth of heart I have encountered nowhere else. When I returned to Germany after two years of college in Los Angeles, I boarded the subway from the airport in Frankfurt to take the train. My first experience was when a young German woman offered me half of her sandwich—in German. As I accepted the sandwich thanking her, all of my German came back to me as if I had never left. To this day (I have not been back to Germany or Europe since my departure in 1985), whenever I strike up a conversation with a German here in Los Angeles, my German returns to me as though I'd never left. My German poetry differs from my American poems. Of course it must, because of language, but it has a real depth perhaps not achieved in my English poetry. My German poems 'come to me' in German. As with my English poems and most of my other creative work, I do not choose to compose a German poem; it chooses me. Thus it has an inspired character. The depth of my German poems is because of the speech sounds of the German language which I feel as in speech formation.

Later, I had other significant experiences in Los Angeles. So I left the place of my birth to know Christ, then returned for further learning and work.

The laws of reincarnation and karma apply to every human being identically, but are, as with each law, always specific in manifestation. When I knew the woman mentioned above who never left the Westside except very briefly, this was the summer 1994. We became very close friends. Ida once described meeting a man. At once they knew they were soul mates. She then told me they knew nothing would ever come of it as they both were married at the time. Ida was a Sun personality.

At the time I was convinced I had no soul mate. I had never experienced such a deep connection with any girl before. But in December 1997 I had a very brief encounter with a very sad girl. Immediately we saw one another, at the first moment, we both knew we were soul mates. This was a feeling that had nothing to do with chemistry or passion. It was within, and I saw it in her bright blue eyes. We were together about one week. Each day I wrote her love poems, and each day all that she wanted to do was to play Scrabble® with me, which we did for hours on end. This was in a hospital where patients were instructed to stay on the unit until recovery. Once however, at about midnight, at her initiation, we went AWOL. I bought my special friend candy and cigarettes at an all-night gas station store before we returned to the hospital and the unit. This was our date. I was reprimanded for going AWOL. When I explained it wasn't my idea, *she* was reprimanded. I felt very sorry for her, because she told me she slept little. I have never seen such a sad or beautiful girl in my life. Those eyes… I've never seen her again. Our relationship, brief to my experience as Alan Lindgren, was both deep and very close. It went back to at least one previous incarnation. She is a Saturnine.

I was born with other karmic relationships. With each of my parents I have always felt deeply in my heart, with my wonderful American Mother Margaret (Mars), and profoundly close with my Swedish father Arne† (Sun) from my earliest memory. He was an anthroposophist.

One very close one was with a very warm original, German girl (a Saturnine) in Europe. We met through the international Waldorf student movement. I visited her at her school in Hamburg. Several years later we both participated in a St. John's Tide ("Johanni") festival at the Christian Community in Hamburg. She gave me a Brothers' Grimm folk fairy tales book from Third Grade. In it, she wrote *König* ("King") and *Prinzessin* ("Princess") in large runic letters. I treasure that book. The last time I saw her was when I was attending the Jugendseminar. She took the train from Hamburg to Stuttgart to see me. We had a good visit.

I had close karmic relationships with several Americans who have since long gone on, with an Indian South African Christian Community priest (Walter Brecker†) in Los Angeles, several in Europe, one German priest in America (Diethart Jaenig†), and a number of anthroposophists and others from several European lands. My best friend (Sun), an American anthroposophist, that is a very strong karmic bond. The Englishman I described who is also an anthroposophist is my second best friend (Sun). With the French priest—that is my deepest relationship of all. All priest-pastors of the Christian Community are anthroposophists. The Christian Community priests I have karma with are all Sun destinies, likewise the anthroposophists mentioned. (Many of my karmic friends are karmically related to one another. This is typical.)

What distinguishes all of these relationships? It is in the feeling. This is what constitutes the closeness. It is possible and frequent for new karma to be formed. Whenever closeness is felt or suffered connecting human beings, the karma is brought from past earth-lives.

I had one strong karmic relationship with a housemate back in 2006-2007, which was unwanted by both of us. I say unwanted because there was extremely little sympathy, rather mostly antipathy. From my side, I could discover very little to love about the man. But I knew he was good and brave, highly disciplined and long-suffering, and at the same time I was cognizant to the fact it was Christ who connected us in the strongest possible manner. Although it was a painful tribulation for me, I affirmed our relationship as one that was to be cherished. I realized how much we both cared, if not for one other, then personally. I witnessed his mild goodness of heart, and generosity, with several Christ-Venus initiates, so I know Christ will always remember him. His soul is protected. Only karmic feeling holds such genuine and deep care.

One Choleric Saturnine woman, at least in her 70s, leads a Saturday writers' workshop I was privileged to attend on more than several occasions during the summer and autumn of 2012. Of every one I encountered at this group, I felt a genuine and close that is karmic connection only with her. I felt and still feel blessed by this. I was just 50 years old at the time. In these examples, reincarnation is apparent in the destinies of the people involved.

The karma described in this study is one of young souls—Saturnine, Sun, Mars, and Jupiter. Young souls are enthusiastic for the past and the present, warlike before or still at present. They know they are like children. Young soul karma is active and still formative. The karma of old souls—Moon, Venus, and Mercurial—appears differently. Old souls are contemplative, weary of the past, long for resolution, for Christ. They know they are old, if young in another way. I have had close friends who are old souls I cherished or whom I loved. However, I think they were not karmic relationships. I think often young souls connect with each other, and old souls have karma with one another. Old souls have had many more incarnations to form and suffer karma with one another—many thousands of years. Young souls feel close to those they know from fewer lifetimes, only several or more thousand years. I am aware of karmic relationships between old and young souls.

Santa Monica, California
September 26/28, 2011
Culver City, California
May 16-17/December 4
Los Angeles
October 26-27/30, 2014

Identity, Reincarnation, and Karma:
Needs and Choices for Our Journey

In her book *Orphans*: *Real and Imaginary* [1], Eileen Simpson shows us the sorrows and hopes of those who experience this human condition. Orphanhood is at once filled with tragedy and possibility. If there is one theme most essential in this excellent and informative volume, perhaps it is the significance of identity for the human being. Typically, orphans suffer a weak sense of identity. This is the uniquely human I, which name cannot reach my ears from outside if it to designate me. Only I can say "I" and mean me. We are tempted to believe environment is causal to the (in orphans often nearly absent) sense of identity, but because childhood is strongly karmic—our birth, family, and upbringing circumstances—we know it is actually the other way around.

The Sense of Identity and Present Experiences in Light of Past Lives

The sense of I or identity that is crucial for the human experience, the present and future, and individual and world progress, is determined by the destiny from which the eternal individuality learns and develops. What this means is our experiences in this lifetime are largely determined by what we did, thought, believed, endured, suffered, fought over, died for, lived for, and so forth in our previous earthly lives. They are therefore karmic; they follow the human, spiritual laws of the reincarnation of the spirit and the karma of the soul or the destiny, which is the bridge between the eternal individuality or human spirit and the physical body of heredity during earthly life.

We bring upon ourselves the karmic experiences, those we require for our development. The eternal individuality therefore knows what is to transpire karmically, which is on earth, before the soul is born; it knows that karma rules its earthly life. Where this may be undesirable or unwanted by the person undergoing the experiences, the spirit follows only spiritual laws with which it is in full accord. Our karma belongs to us and us alone. We are the creators of our karma. This becomes our destiny. Our perspective between death and rebirth is entirely different from that on earth. It is higher and oversees all things, which transpire on earth for the task of reincarnation. This is the inner path of experiences for development to perfection of the soul's earthly journey to Christ.

Orphanhood, Other Conditions of Want, Reincarnation, and Karma

We find among orphans frequently have had fewer and weaker karmic experiences, experiences, which are creative of karma, in previous earthly lives. Orphanhood is a condition required by the individuality as an experience and an opportunity to develop. This it shares in common with other intolerable karmic experiences, scarcity, deprivation, loss, all neglect, abuse, poverty, homelessness, hunger, disease, tragedy—all are part of a larger scenario; just as suffering, illness, and death are experiences a soul must know. The former conditions manifest in one incarnation.

Unwanted Conditions as Challenges/Suffering for Potential Realization

These conditions, entirely unwanted seen from an earthly perspective, are temporary. Things will look different in future incarnations according to potential realization from challenges or suffering. Therefore the soul must strive and endure or work and seek to find itself in self-discipline, the practice of virtues, and efforts for courage. It must begin with what it has, with what it has become, and work its way ahead with further karma creation or endure what it has created, while creating more karma to what it may yet, across lifetimes, become. These practices and efforts alone can bring the soul forward in inner progress. As Plato says, we should be compassionate with every one (as we are all) engaged in a soul-battle.

Physical as Well as Soul Needs for the Outer and Inner Human Being

The physical body also has requirements and needs. It houses the soul, which depends on the anchor of the body in which to work, carrying out daily tasks. In addition to meeting the soul needs of those who come to us looking for guidance, strength, courage, love, and affection—which means understanding, art as therapy, education, and genuine religious feeling (which is the heart of all compassion and concern)—a healthy diet, adequate exercise, sufficient rest and sleep, and medical attention are necessary for the striving individual. We meet the seeker and all those on their own, individual path, or who are looking for theirs, spiritually and practically both. This means provision for the outer and inner needs of human beings. Where the particular destiny as a group or many require similar care, the individual must always be taken into consideration for particular therapeutic needs. The initiate knows this.

Soul Development and the Sense of Identity Before Birth

A weak sense of identity is also found among non-orphans, not only half-orphans, who grow up with one parent, but who have both parents. In many such cases it is traceable to the family, to one or both parents, or to the main adult/s responsible for the child. Yet another human being born and raised in similar circumstances will have a sure or strong sense of I or identity.

This means the soul is developed before birth, signifying reincarnation. In cases with more than one child in a family with the same upbringing and educational opportunities (or absence), children exhibit entirely different characteristics, handicaps and gifts, faculties and capacities, talents, aptitudes and predispositions, interests and affinities, weaknesses and potentials, qualities, sense of identity—their actual physical bodies. All of this points to past earthly lives: reincarnation.

The spiritual individuality creates the form of the body together with lofty hierarchical, divine beings in the spiritual world before birth. This is to meet the soul's needs for inner development in the coming lifetime. This is deeply significant as the physical body is the instrument of the soul on which it 'plays its music'. The human countenance and body is but the physical expression of the spiritual Ego, which is eternal.

The Human Physical Body and the Sense of Identity

It is a fact that those with a weak sense of their I have different physical bodies than do those with a strong or sure sense of identity. It is the actual body that is taken hold of by the incarnating soul. Here we refer especially to the torso and limbs and hands and feet. Those with a weak sense of identity may have unusually large and rough or spindly hands and limbs, with excessively stout or skinny torsos in temperament exception or enhancement. Such an individual is often very handsome or beautiful but undifferentiated and with little inside. They may not be beautiful either, rather of wizened, crumpled, blank, or washed out face. The wrists and ankles may be weak and proportionately small. These seeming handicaps in the physical body are actually overcome on the incarnation of the spiritual man into the physical body taken hold of by the soul-with-spirit for its work on earth, a purpose of the imperfect or disabled physical body. The temperament/s always figure in the physical body, which is shaped by the etheric body of the child.

Those who have a sure or strong sense of themselves may also be handsome or beautiful, but then in a striking fashion, or they may show unusualness, even ugliness, behind which, however, a substantial and interesting soul and spirit is at work, visible in facial, hair, vocal, speech, hand, gesture, walk, and other human expression. As with their faces, their bodies, limbs, hands will be distinctive, individual. These are visible signs of the sense of I, of identity, here strong or sure, and healthy. It is the I which, taking hold of, keeps the body together, intact, healthy, and fit for life. The temperament/s are also determining.

The Physical Body: A Requirement for Our Karma

It is really a wonder each human being has a unique, individual physical body. This is required for our karma that is on earth. Our identity, which is individual, is related to but distinct from our planetary type or destiny, which is one of only seven. However, the planetary type can always be read in the biography *and is actually apparent in the physical body,*

unique it is. Thus our physical body and head/face is also individual. Our identity or soul-spirit-I is not our physical body and head/face, however *its expression* is physical. This is noted, with specific examples from real life, above. From our heads, faces-features, and limbs/hands/feet in this incarnation, we are creative of our heads, faces-features, and limbs/hands/feet for the next one. Thus we are not limited in our future development in the sense that we may direct the course of our future by our habits, choices, and intentions in this lifetime. We can *change our inborn habits (temperament), thereby developing the qualities and good aspects of the temperament opposite our main one. For temperament is inherently one-sided.* Like our temperament, our karma now comes from our past incarnation(s). It is allotted us from our past. Unlike our temperament/s, it rules our life. This is what we have: to work with, endure with, create our future karma with. But what we do and do not do with what we have, with our temperament and our karma, determines our progress and can regulate the course we take in future incarnations. Our work and endurance then is not only for the present, for our current incarnation. More than this, it is for our earth-life/lives to come. This is the significance of the knowledge of reincarnation for us.

Characteristics of Young Souls, Old Souls, and Identity

Those who are young souls who have a strong sense of identity (the realist destinies: Saturnine, Jupiter, Mars, Sun) are likely to make good choices because they are intent on what they are doing. They will be warm without losing warmth and, as such, will have substantial thoughts or insights into themselves, others, and/or various human and Nature experiences. They will relate to Nature and Nature- and human-inspired Art and have a wide range of emotional experiences. They understand symbols. Knowledge of science they have will be healthy and grounded in reality. They will show disinterest in/dislike of abstract and theoretical science. They experience reality as solely meaningful. Speculation they think little of. They seek humanity, Nature, and knowledge in which their humanity and divinity indwells. They will grasp what is real, what can be seen and handled. Abstraction threatens healthy experience; they will be healthy, grounded in reality; they want to gather more and more life-experience.

Those who are old souls who have a sure sense of identity (the idealist destinies: Venus, Mercurial, Moon) endure much more, are more inward and virtuous staying on their path, much truer than those with a weak sense of identity. They will be cool yet suffer a heart and, as such, enjoy beautiful ideas of a spiritual nature, the sciences, invention, the Arts of ideas, concepts. They also demonstrate real integrity of the I. This is the individual's identity. The importance of this cannot be overstressed as it is the strength or might of the individual soul and spirit without which they digress. They may or may not be scholars. They do not care for real or 'human' Art because it is not ideal or they cannot comprehend it. Their endeavors are ideal. They strive for simplicity, the Spirit, and perfection, though they be deep or complex; they experience reality as merely the plaything or symbol of the Spirit. They cannot bear reality; they love beauty and treasure their ideals, including spiritual magic. They take comfort in thoughts of God, Christ, or the Holy Spirit, which they love with childlike belief and innocence. In contrast to the realist destinies, which have a sure sense of identity, they long for the resolution of their age-old suffering by Christ. This must happen where all karma is formed: on earth.

Any one within one of the two groups—the old or the young souls—may exhibit the corresponding qualities and interests, but in the case of the weak sense of identity they will be more unhealthy/mentally unstable (old: Mercurial, Moon), or fleeting and thus not enduring (young: Saturnine, Jupiter, Mars). Venus (soul) and Sun (young) destinies both have a healthy sense of identity, which becomes stronger or surer over lifetimes. Unlike the other five planetary types (destinies) they do not progress quickly but surely, steadily, thoroughly. This is especially to be seen in work on the temperament, which is slow because it requires long-term, repeated, and faithful practices to change fundamental habits. Temperament work is deeply significant for inner development.

In both kinds of souls of weak sense of identity, the individual will experience greater inner disorientation and insecurity. In the case of the healthy, sure, or strong sense of I, the spiritual qualities and interests will be disciplined, fine, and noble (old souls: Mercurial, Moon); or original, unique, sincere, and qualitatively interesting (young souls: Saturnine, Jupiter, Mars). In both kinds of soul of strong or sure sense of identity, the human interests and qualities will be genuine and more distinctive.

It should be said that souls with conviction may have a strong sense of identity, and be genuine individuals, but they will be absolute in their views and thus limited in their ability to see themselves, others, life, and the world with openness. This is because their previous incarnation was in an oriental setting before, during, or just after the time of Christ when some Asian cultures were quite decadent and rejected the Earth. However, this need not stand between them and their spiritual aims (ideals, purposes) or hamper their dedication and devotion in any way. These souls may find the meaning and goal of existence in this earthly life or a future one. Likewise souls with a thoroughly European education may have a weaker sense of identity. It is only that they experienced Christendom (medieval Europe) with its cultural riches in their previous incarnation(s) when many individuals endured or thought much. However, these weaker souls were unable to derive much from these experiences, because they could endure or invest less in terms of soul and spirit, such that they have difficulty for independence or health in this incarnation. Often, however, this is not the case, because many of the former have a weak sense of identity and are not making it, or have not yet decided, while many of the latter either have, are close to, or are in the direction to attain life's meaning and goal. Finally, identity is an individual matter. (see The Source of Our Sense of Identity, below)

The Source of Our Sense of Identity, Present Qualities Found in Past Incarnations

What all this points to here in America is past earthly lives either of decadence, powerful but unhealthy spirituality, and rejection of the earth and the physical body in an oriental setting before, during, or just after the time of Christ (power of conviction who are often intelligent, sometimes well-educated individuals); or cultural experiences of inner refinement or richness, suffering creation and suffering, or real thought and feeling depth in European Christendom, when and where these realities were experienced and lived (a thoroughly European education). There are also other relationships of the power of conviction worldwide. These individuals, born in America and elsewhere, are often intelligent and may be well-educated.

Future Progress Depends on the Spirit-empowered Soul-I Taking Hold of the Physical Body: The Vital Role of Education for This Task

The future depends on the development of the sense of identity of numerous individuals where the spirit-empowered soul-I takes hold of the physical body. Then the individual is creative of and suffers karma to ever-increasing degrees of intensity, signifying progress. Education of the child is crucial for this task, especially in our time of childhood's fragile ecology. Waldorf education is ideal for the children because it nourishes the child's growing soul thereby strengthening and protecting its sense of identity right into the physical body for a fruitful adulthood, one fit for the tasks and demands of life.

Work on One's Temperament

Before puberty this is 'education as an art', meeting the needs of the child's temperament. This provides the ground on which the individual stands to weather the storms of life as an adult. Addressing the one-sidedness of the temperaments to develop the opposite qualities is the best thought-penetrated work an individual can perform as it directly serves to empower the sense of identity (I) and is intended by the adult, either the teacher in childhood or oneself in adulthood. Fostered by teachers and other adults with the children, this task can continue throughout life in adult self-education for essential progress. This is especially important in our society and time of many distractions.

Mental Qualities, Habits, and Virtues in the Seven Planets or Destinies

In high school education to meet the needs of the adolescent is not intelligence. It is the soul and the mind, sensible, ideal, and true. Education must address the mental qualities of the youth according to the destiny or planetary type. These qualities are essential for all progress as upon them rests the capacity to assign the appropriate tasks of individuals and peoples. Sound mental capacities/thinking qualities, content, good habits; and acting according to them with some self-discipline, and with patience, devotion, and love; is the byword. We note that the process is as significant if not more so than the arrival at the destination. Indeed, the destination cannot be reached without the journey on its way there (the process).

The Importance of the Sense of Identity, the Individuality, and Human Distinction

Our sense of identity or I is what makes us distinct from all others. It is the sense of our individuality that is individualized in us. Our individuality is our genius-nature or God-given Name. Like our souls, it is irreplaceable. Therefore to strengthen our soul-forces by empowering the I in the formation and suffering of karma in incarnations, and developing our individuality by good and positive habits and thought practices, which include those opposite our main temperament, are essential for our inner development, in this lifetime and for succeeding ones. Identity theft is an outer problem that concerns us as part of the system and that can be remedied. Loss of inner identity is a condition for which there is no cure. Nothing is more important for human beings than is one's Name or genius, the higher I that is our true identity that will incarnate in each one of us.

The sense of selfhood or identity is entirely individual. It has nothing to do with any group, family, temperament, race, nation, language, culture, or historical epoch, although it is developed in their context as in a civilization but in ever fresh and new relationships or settings over many lifetimes. These earthly experiences offer us possibilities for inner development to realize our potentials with the awakening of spiritual capacities.

The true sense of identity transcends the background of reincarnations to the essence of each one, the inner or higher Self, refined, pure, and good. Those who can perceive another human being are fully aware of the characteristics of the individual before them, including such aspects as the power of conviction or a thoroughly European education stemming from past incarnations. This leads us to the groups in country of birth, and to karma-necessary decisions or circumstances for immigration. Here we have the karmic relationships and individual connections of vocation that go back to preceding earthly lives. Previous karmic actions and sufferings make their contributions as well. Thus we have the individuality in every outer and inner aspect. All of these are keys to the destiny going back from the current to the very first incarnation. At the same time these gifted individuals see Christ at the table in the hall of each human soul in utter stillness and peace. It is this perception, which helps the individual on the path of life to realize their true potential. All of the factors contribute to this, but the essence remains untouched, as it were, the inner divine sun essence within. It is this quality that we will pay most attention to, the eternal individuality that reincarnates again and again for the opportunity to know Christ and therewith itself.

Education in Childhood, Youth, and Adulthood for the Attainment of Our Aims

Childhood is essential for the cradling of the growing soul of the child before exposure to the perils of society that include the connective and entertainment machine technologies and people who may traumatize it. Good human beings, simple toys, and quality school supplies are important for early and middle childhood education. Healthy nutrition, plenty of imaginative play, sleep, naps, warmth, and regular routine are crucial for small children; while the arts and music, the beauty of God's Creation and children's creativity, significant personalities outside the family (teacher and historical), and wise guidance to balance the inherently one-sided temperaments, are central for middle childhood.

In adolescence the young person easily gets lost in the crowd. The I or ego of the male young person is not properly anchored in his astral body (and therewith his physical body); that of the young girl is dissolved in hers. Hence independence of thought and distinction in the social life are essential for this age of aspiring youth. The ego or I incarnates into the lower sheathes (astral, etheric, physical bodies) in a seven-year process from the twenty-first to the twenty-eighth birthday. The importance of the sense of independence, freedom, and social distinction continues throughout adulthood for those who take up the most important education, adult self-education, which empowers the sense of identity, of the I, and grants those who find and go their own, individual path the surety to attain their aims in life. These aims are at once our living ideals, which is Christ, the inner light of human minds of spiritual purpose, and the genuine meaning of reality, which is Christ, the inner sun of human hearts of religious feeling. May we meet the future, which will find us, and may we do the work or endure the suffering to get there on the road of life that paves our way ahead. It is a fact that nothing can stand between those who aim to reach their inner goal and their goal. The future belongs to them and theirs.

Los Angeles
January 17
May 30, 2013
October 29, 2014
Culver City, California
May 13/15/17, 2014

1. Eileen Simpson, *Orphans*: *Real and Imaginary* (Grove Press: 1st edition, June 1987)

Journeys of the Human Soul

The human soul travels two journeys: one in earthly life (especially following its growth and maturation in childhood and adolescence in adulthood, ageing and dying in a physical body), the other in divine life (beginning with Christ at death and the spiritual beings in the planetary spheres and the world of the stars in eternity: from immortality to unborn). After death we take with us experiences only to be had on earth to the spiritual beings (the planetary spheres). So what happens—what we experience and feel, think and do not think, do and do not do—on earth is crucial for our life between death and rebirth and for future incarnations.

There are different earthly journeys a human soul undertakes. The first is universal, as it is shared in common by all of the destinies who choose to experience it, and it is one of seven possible according to the specific destiny or planetary type, both.

We note the connection between the divine life of the soul and spirit in the planetary spheres—with the spiritual beings—between death and rebirth, and earthly life as human beings, when the destiny—planetary type or soul-spirit part of us—traverses paths of human existence.

8888888888888888888888888888888888888888888888888888888888

The soul-spirit is to be distinguished from corporeality: from the body and gender, temperament, race, ethnicity, religion, nation, culture, and family of birth. It does not belong to the earth where it temporarily and spatially leads a mortal existence rather to 'the company of heaven', the Spiritual Homeland, Its 'places', processes, and beings: the so-called dead, the three hierarchies or nine angelic choirs or heavenly hosts, the holy Trinity.

The heavenly 'places' include the spiritual beings of the planetary spheres. We are each one of the seven planetary types or destinies, which means our eternal, soul-spirit part is configured with one of the seven spiritual individualities of our planetary system, as follows: Moon and the angels or sons of life or twilight; Mercury and the archangels or fire spirits; Venus and the archai or spirits of personality; Sun and the exusiai or elohim or spirits of form (creative of egos); Mars and the dynameis or spirits of movement; Jupiter and the kyriotetes or spirits of wisdom; Saturn and the thrones or spirits of will and imagination.

There are two still higher hierarchies that are in 'the world of the stars': the cherubim or spirits of the harmonies and inspiration; and the seraphim or spirits of love and intuition. The activity of conscience, which is the freest human activity, originated with the cherubim. In the seraphim the thoughts of God simultaneously become deeds. Additional to activities for human beings and evolution, the work of the seraphim is among the galaxies: a lofty task. Each one of three in each hierarchy (triad) or heavenly host has specific tasks; Christ runs in the middle through all of them up to His place in the holy Trinity above them all. Thus the nine heavenly hosts are the 'limbs of Christ'.

All of us 'wander through' all seven of the planetary spheres to the 'fixed stars' of the constellations of the zodiac and the galaxies (with the 'dead', the hierarchies, and the holy Trinity) after death and returning, in reverse, until rebirth. This is our spiritual journey in divine life.

****

Of course these planetary spheres and stars or spiritual beings do not have a location in the sense of a house on a street in a town or a city in a county in a state or a region in a country on a continent, or in the sense of the Earth entire or Sun or Moon as physical bodies in our solar system; that would be preposterous. Neither do we have physical bodies in the afterlife and pre-conception. They are neither spatial nor temporal.

The following is summarized from anthroposophy, the spiritual science of Rudolf Steiner. It is only the barest outline.

Spatial reality is limited by what is measurable: proximity/distance; physical dimension, weight, and movement. But spiritual beings can live in substance because substances are condensed out of spirit. This is impermanent, however. Actually, warmth-substance is one: spiritual-soul-physical, or was originally at the beginning of time. Our entire created planetary cosmos, which later became the solar system, consisted in this undifferentiated warmth-substance that was the sacrifice of the lofty thrones beings.

This was the very beginnings of time and of evolution when mankind's physical body and the mineral kingdom together at their earliest stage were warmth and thus our mineral-like existence at the planetary stage called Old Saturn in esotericism. After a rest period the next stage, called Old Sun, was when our physical body had developed further and we were endowed with an undeveloped etheric body. The plant kingdom and the insects had their beginnings at this stage. This was our plantlike existence. At this evolutionary stage the element was light-radiant air. After the next rest period came what is called Old Moon. Meanwhile our physical and etheric bodies had evolved further. Now we were endowed with our astral body in the element of fluid and tone; we were at one with the future animal kingdom. Old Moon was therefore our animal-like existence.

After much evolution of human-animals and animal-plants on Old Moon, when Sun and Moon repeatedly separated and rejoined alternatively, came the rest period followed by our Earth and actual human existence. But at this time the heavenly bodies of our present-day Earth, Moon, and Sun were one. Only later did the Sun separate from the Moon-Earth. On Moon-Earth human egos, the creation of the elohim or exusiai (see above), first incarnated into physical bodies, but these bodies were entirely different from ours today, and they were attached to the Earth. This was the beginnings of the human kingdom. Still later the Moon separated from the Earth because Earth-Moon had become too hard to support life for all but the strongest souls. Before this separation, all the other souls went out to the other planets until the conditions on Earth allowed them to return.

The evolution of the animals and, further, of the human being began when the animals made a great sacrifice in being shed from us that we might become more perfectly human. This took place in stages. First the saurians were shed (the dinosaurs); they died out. Next were the fishes, followed by the amphibians. At this point in evolution Man received iron into his blood. That is why the next and final kind of animals shed from Man—the mammals—are warm-blooded as are we. The last of the mammals shed by Man are the apes; that's why the apes most closely resemble us. We will redeem the animal kingdom by tremendous love in future, after all sickness is healed when peace will reign forevermore. Thus gradually, and in stages, our present-day solar system and the four earthly kingdoms evolved from this original warmth condition, but this required eons of time: the planetary stages or durations of evolution of Old Sun, Old Moon, and Earth, up to the present, and many more sacrifices of the lofty beings of the heavenly hosts, alternating with rest periods when these beings retreated from outer activity for a while.

In the present configuration of Sun, Moon, and Earth, evolution has continued, prehistory (mythology) has happened, and history has begun. Conditions on Earth were entirely different in times past. Earlier, after human bodies had developed much further, the brains of human beings were exterior organs of the head like tentacles that were eyes and ears at the same time. With these organs, exterior to the head, human beings oriented themselves in and perceived their environments. It was only later that the brain was enclosed in the head and the eyes and ears developed as they are today. The evolution of the human being—on

Earth alone—is thus very involved, requiring long periods of time. On Atlantis, prior to our present Epoch, the atmosphere was between air and water so that is was extremely moist. This enabled human beings to utilize a technology whereby they harnessed the power contained in plant seeds to fuel flying machines that was possible because the atmosphere was so thick. The great catastrophe—the Flood—occurred at the precipitation of this atmosphere that was semi-fluid, denser than air (forty days and forty nights). Solid matter is unique to our Earth.

****

The continued development of the human being depends on the individual. Like the artist, we must become co-Creators with God. Now we must make personal selfless sacrifices to 1.) help one another through perception and communication with dearest suffering, 2.) redeem the animal kingdom by great Divine love that we will develop, and 3.) spiritualize the mineral crust of the Earth, the hardest task, as this calls for the activity of the Divine Will, our seventh and highest member that we will develop much more slowly. Only by these sacrifices will we continue our development, helping the lower kingdoms in their evolution and the Earth. Evolution will continue after heaven and earth shall pass away and there is another rest period. This will be in three more planetary stages: Jupiter, Venus, and Vulcan. When heaven and earth pass away, matter will cease to exist.

On Jupiter, not to be confused with the present-day planet (it won't be physical; Jupiter's landscape will be ethereal, which we are already creating today with our thoughts; our cowardly ones will be the purples, blues, and greens of the valleys; and our courageous thoughts the reds, oranges, and yellows of the hills of Jupiter), we will be angels, the animal kingdom will have reached the human stage, the plant kingdom the animal stage, the minerals plants. On Venus, not to be confused with the present-day planet, we will be archangels, the animals angels, the plant kingdom human, the minerals animals. On Vulcan we will be archai, the animals archangels, the plants angels, the mineral kingdom human. The nine heavenly hosts above us will continue to evolve through further sacrifices. Following Vulcan, evolution and time will have run their course, and all will be an eternity of divine-blissful love-activity.

Christ united Himself with evolution by becoming human in Jesus of Nazareth that culminated with the Mystery of Golgotha—the crucifixion and resurrection. He is the Spirit of the Earth and of our hearts, if we have prepared a place for His inner birth. Thus the Christ Events with the Mystery of Golgotha of our present Earth stage are pivotal for all time and evolution, for it is the scene where the divine and the human become one, first in Christ Jesus, then—gradually—in human beings. When this process is complete, human beings shall resurrect. The other aspect is the Earth, which is dying and will also resurrect in spirit-life. Already beginning the first Easter Sunday, Christ resurrects every year on this morning everywhere in Nature. Then He is the cosmic Christ of the Sun, clouds, and stars until the Thirteen Holy Nights of Christmas and His birth in the Earth.

****

It is a task of human beings to create Christ's astral, etheric, and physical bodies for the future. Already today, we create His astral body-soul by our wonder and amazement at Nature, Art, our fellow human beings. This is how we are creating Christ's astral body, by our amazement and wonder. We create Christ's etheric body when we selflessly love one another. Each time we fight against one another we take away from His etheric body: pitting race against race, nation against nation, people against people, religion against religion; our divisive thoughts, words, and acts all take away from Christ's etheric body. Only through the beauty that is selfless love and sees only love, inclusive to each and all, all the groups, all men, women, and children, do we create His etheric body. We are creative of Christ's physical body only through the freest human activity: conscience. Through conscience-activity—not some preacherly morality in a customary or personal sense, rather divine conscience-activity but experienced in our inmost being—we will create Christ's physical body. It is only as numbers of individuals begin to say with ever-increasing certainty: *Not I, but Christ in me*, that this conscience-activity will become the potent force that will create Christ's physical body. This will be apparent only in future.

****

A good analogy to the condensation of the physical world, bodies, and matter from spirit is the snail shell or seashell that hardens or calcifies around the slug or sea animal (such as the clam). This shell is its temporary home. It solidifies from substance the animal exudes from its body to be left behind later on. So it is with the physical substance of plants, the physical bodies of animals, human beings, and the Earth— with all matter. We think of human and animal bones and teeth.

The physical planets and moons with their terrains and rocks that are devoid of life consist in such matter. The Earth is dying but is becoming a spiritual sun and shall resurrect when its material substance has died the death of matter. The beings, which formed and shaped these physical bodies, are not spatial or material just as the spirits of human beings are not spatial or material. But soul, soul-spirit, and spiritual beings remain in relationship with these heavenly bodies and with their orbits in particular.

****

When we 'explore space' and take rock samples from the Moon's and Mars's surfaces through the accomplishments of science and invention held in such high regard today, and really tremendous amounts of brainpower, we learn nothing about these beings but only about the chemical composition of dead matter. In short, we learn nothing but only about the material residue, that has long been dead, left behind by the sacrifices of the spiritual beings of the planetary spheres. Only the Earth and Her inhabitants remain alive. But here, too, science is only interested in the corpse, in what is dead, because science does not and cannot know life, soul, or spirit by analyzing what is material, physical, dead. The etheric Plant, the living ensouled Animal, and the living ensouled enspirited Human Being are beyond the limited scope of science, likewise the etheric Earth and Her great Soul and Spirit, which is Christ. Corpses, these are the objects of scientific study.

So science is also clueless when it comes to the interior of the Sun, which is negative space or pure love: the great Sun Spirit, Christ, Whose light shines in our daylight. Also, for example, our Moon is the physical body, which directs our attention to divine beings. Among these beings is foremost Yahweh, Who is one of the seven spiritual Egos of Christ, Which long ago left the Sun and took up His abode on the Moon so that not only negative influences would stream to Earth from this heavenly body, but also beneficial ones.

The other six spiritual Egos of Christ remain in the Sun: Christ, the great Light God (Zarathustra) or Sun-God illumines our world and warms our hearts by day in the radiant sunlight. The seven holy Rishis have the Moon sphere as their abode. The newly dead and the unborn are also at this station. As the secrets of heredity are in the divine Moon beings, the living bodies, reproduction, and growth of all plants, insects, animals (fish, amphibians, land animals, and birds), and people are under their influence. God works through the divine beings of the Moon.

The Moon exerts another power over the Earth from the Sun. This is in the strange cool moonbeams themselves. Where the Sun ordains the day and night and the four seasons of the year by Her regular, steadfast rhythms and warm-radiant light, the Moon's rhythms are cyclic, rapid, impulsive, determinant of the lunar period, the sexual activity of sea-life and animals, the heightening and decline of plant growth, and the fertilization of flowering plants. Effects are also experienced in human madness, the erratic behavior of restive mental patients, and crime, witnessed around the full Moon. Of all the heavenly bodies, the Moon is nearest Earth. Hence this influence is mighty indeed, affecting especially all fluidic bodies—the waters of the Earth and plants, the semi-fluid brain, and the liquid it floats in.

****

We should mention a special connection with Mars. The Mars sphere had long been a bad 'place' for human souls after death after the period spent in the Moon sphere. Because of the spiritual beings there, powerful disruptions take place there. The Buddha had fulfilled His earthly purpose after many incarnations as a bodhisattva. He could have gone on to the world of the stars, but He chose instead to go to the Mars sphere when human souls would have been prevented from further development because of coming materialism. So the Buddha made a great sacrifice by taking up His abode on Mars that corresponds to Christ's earthly sacrifice. Since the Mystery of Golgotha, Christ is the Spirit of the Earth. The Buddha made a great sacrifice in becoming the Spirit of Mars where He took up His abode. This was during the 15th century. At this time, after his lifetime as St. Francis and following a brief incarnation as a child, Francis of Assisi joined the Buddha on Mars. Since then every human being who wishes may become a meditant in his next earthly life. This is possible because all human souls spend time in the Mars sphere before rebirth. Francis is a pupil of the Buddha. He is way ahead of all the rest of us.

The influence of all the planets on the Earth is observable in the plant-life and even in the structures of mineral substances, visible in scientific experiment. Phenomenological or Goethean science examines phenomena using experiments and the senses that are carried out with even greater conscientiousness and attention to detail than the best material scientist. These scientific experiments are based on insights into phenomena that include a far greater range as they encompass life, soul, and spirit that are at work in and behind matter. They necessarily involve matter as matter and spirit are one in earthly reality. Unlike material science, Goethean science is idea-rich. Bio-dynamic agriculture utilizes a special calendar that has, not only the Moon phases, but the optimal times to sow and harvest particular crops of fruits, vegetables, and grains according to the influences of the planets. This includes Sun and Moon, and Mercury, Venus, Mars, Jupiter, and Saturn.

* *

Each of the seven heavenly bodies is associated with a metal: Sun and gold; Moon and silver; Venus and copper; Mercury and quicksilver (mercury); Mars and iron; Jupiter and tin; Saturn and lead. Gold is actually condensed sunlight, Silver condensed moonlight. These are physical facts. (Rudolf Steiner) But the Sun and the other planets also affect the Earth, Her life, animals, and human beings. This is apparent in the human body's organs.

We have mentioned the Moon and the brain. The brain is the most physical of the organs. The death-forces set in on the brain earliest: already at puberty, which signifies the capacity for clear, conceptual thinking. We also know that some people are cerebral without any intuition rather machine-like. The heart is the organ of the Sun and therefore the most spiritual of the organs. Feeling can be an organ of objective perception with fine sensitivity. Hence women are naturally more intuitive than are men; men have to work twice as hard for intuition than do women ('a woman's intuition'). (Men are more thinking and willing, women more thinking and feeling.) The lungs are the organs of Mercury, the kidneys of Venus, the gall bladder of Mars, the liver of Jupiter, the spleen of Saturn.

Further bodily relationships with the planets include the chest organization and the Sun, the sex region and the Moon, the abdomen and Mercury, between the region of the stomach and the region of the heart and Venus, the larynx and Mars, the forehead and Jupiter, the frontal lobes and Saturn. All of these relationships are at work in all human beings, but in those of each of the seven destinies or planetary types in the corresponding organs and places in the deepest, most intimate, or strongest manner. Importantly, they are revelatory of the destiny.

For example, in Mercurial personalities, the abdomen and lungs are foremost. The abdomen is the actual seat of knowledge. Not the head, but the abdomen is responsible for reasoning, acumen, logic. In Moon destinies the sexual region and the brain are foremost. This combination is behind great world-conceptions and the philosophies of these Moon souls, beautiful schools of thought, very fine, finely intuitive.

In Jupiter human beings, the forehead and the liver provide the key. These destinies are immersed in reality, reality that is spiritual-physical. They think in the present moment; their thinking is wise. In the Sun destinies the chest organization and the heart are central. Because of the deepest spiritual or esoteric nature of the human heart, Sun personalities think the really profound and ethical thoughts. They have big, powerful, religious hearts. They are formative of karma and thus important for all seven destinies. For destinies which realize their potential and carry out their task, the heart is essential. Without the essential heart-experiences nothing of any deeper meaning can be accomplished. Venus is under the influence of the Sun. Hence Venus has genuine religious feeling and suffers genuine religion. The Christ-Sun initiates are the modern-day saints, leaders, and educators; the Christ-Venus initiates the modern-day martyrs, mystics, and magicians.

There is an entire world of perspectives looking only at the animals, at the animal kingdom. This is ancient, going back to the Old Moon stage of evolution before our present Earth, of which we have written. Those who can perceive the past—the distant past reaching back to the beginnings of time, of evolution on Old Saturn, followed by Old Sun; they witness the origins of animals on Old Moon when they were one with the future humans.

There is also the moonsecret of the universe. Only Moon destinies know their Moon secret. The original, archetypal wisdom has to do with the unborn, the law of heredity, the divine beings of the Moon (destiny or karma), and with the spiritual self of every Moon destiny. As the Moon sphere is the last station before birth and the first station after death of a human being—the unborn and immortal states—understanding eternity provides the key to this secret wisdom of the Moon.

But it is not human beings who are Moon destinies who are gifted with dreams and connected with the so-called 'dead'. They are the Mars destinies, owing to their special heart qualities. Venus destinies are also gifted in their dreams. For those who are conscious (the martyrs), their dreams can reveal secrets, even regarding public figures.

✳✳

Although the destiny is our eternal, soul-spirit part, because we create and endure our karma on Earth, if we so choose, it cannot be viewed or studied apart from earthly life, from our human reincarnations. Thus, when we think of some one's destiny, we are looking at his/her earthly journey, at everything of significance in the person's life that contributes to her/his inner progress and development, and its resolution that also can take place only on Earth. This is our karma that is formed in past earth-lives and in the present one for future incarnations, seen in the biography. This becomes our story.

We have said at the beginning of this study there is one, universal journey in common with all who make it. This is seen, pictorially, in the Brothers Grimm folk fairytales. Rudolf Meyer wrote a book about this journey depicted in these tales entitled *Die Weisheit der deutschen Volksmärchen (The Wisdom of the German Folk Fairytales)*. However, there are seven different ways this journey is experienced, destiny (planetary type) depending. We have already given some indications regarding these seven destiny-determined experiences in our discussions, above.

88888888888888888888888888888888888888888888888888888888

Where the first part of this two-part study concerns our divine journey, our 'cosmic highway' between death and rebirth, this part will look at our journeying on Earth, into our earthly lives between birth and death and thus as mortals. Here we find, not only universality and the seven types (see above), but our own, individual path to Christ.

Here we are left entirely free. No one may choose for us. We may go backwards the easy way, or forwards the hard way. But there is no standing still. But taking the path that leads ahead is the only truly satisfying one. It brings with it trials and hardships, losses and suffering, endurance or work, but it is the only truly rewarding way. Progress happens. We learn and grow; we develop. We know it.

Our only guide on our path is our feeling: the feeling for the truth. But thinking—not the materialistic thougthts, but the spiritual thoughts, the anthroposophical thoughts—is a good preparation or training for sense-free, autonomous thinking when, through an intensification of thought, we penetrate into the inner place, within ourselves, where we seek the Thought-Center of the World, which center is Christ. This is His only true Name: the 'I AM' in our human I. Our human I is a hole, but in our true, higher I, Christ's 'I AM' awakens in our genius in our lower, human I. This is our angel, genius, or Name. The 'I AM' awakens the soul, not only the higher I, but the heart and mind(-soul).

Before we have entered this inner place in ourselves, we must already be spirit-seekers after Christ, but we do not know that it is Christ Whom we seek. We cannot know this, because without the conception of the living, spiritual Christ-Thought in our thinking in our I, that is also our perception of Him—His light—in the etheric realm, we can only know what has no life. And Christ *is* life. He is a living presence where we are gathered together in His Name, which is the 'I AM' in us, in our human I that we perceive in our human brethren and in nature-phenomena. The 'I AM' experience is thus one of the true communion of Man: *Awakening to the idea in reality is the true communion of humanity.* (Rudolf Steiner)

When we awaken to Christ in reality, He has entered time and space in us. Only in Man is this possible; the solution to Nature's questions must be sought in our own, inner being. We are human beings but spiritual, divine beings at the same time. Thus the divine lives in us in a drop of the divine sun essence in our hearts and souls. This drop is perfect; it is divine perfection in us: Christ. It is not the entire Christ sun essence; it is a drop, but it partakes of the whole; it has the qualities of the whole.

Where Christ (the real not shadowy Idea or Spirit or Truth or Divine Essence) is eternal, reality is spatial and temporal. Only when we awaken to the Eternal Idea (Christ) in reality (Time and Space) do we commune with our humanity. In this communion, we three are one: Christ and you and me. The second part can also be Nature or the lowest hierachy, for we provide the human aspect necessary for the communion of humanity. For in the spirit of Man and Man alone—in humanity—the perfect Idea (Truth, Christ, Divine Essence) awakens on Earth when we commune with Him in one another and in Nature.

****

There is, however, one other way we may commune with Him, and this is in the quiet of inner solitude in the selfless sacrifice of meditation when we are alone within our hearts with Sun of Christ. Therefore the inner practice of genuine meditation (as we have in those given by Rudolf Steiner), faithfully at the same time each day for years, will lead the meditant all the way to the Christ-Altar where, within ourselves, we awaken in Christ. This will be in the presence of Christ in a special, gifted human being. We have heard how this is possible: Because Francis of Assisi is a pupil of the Buddha on Mars, each one of us may be a meditant in earthly life. (see also my study *On Meditation, Human and Divine*, pages 389-391)

In the activity of meditation we turn inwards away from outer life. We are therefore entirely untouched by the outer world. There we approach the Christ-Altar that is within us in our hearts where we will commune with Christ. This daily practice strengthens us and grants us peace on our earthly journey as we wend our way on our path to and with Him.

Meditation-practice requires devotion and discipline, but if we do not love meditating and it becomes a duty for us then we accomplish nothing. Meditation is effective when we do so with devotion and self-discipline, but also with love. Meditation transcends our differences. There are different meditations, which Rudolf Steiner gave to different individuals according to their need (inner make-up), but a meditation can accompany *every* one who is on, or who is looking for, his own, individual path to Christ. This is our inner, earthly journey.

Other practices can also serve the life-traveler. These include curative eurythmy, speech formation, curative singing, curative painting (watercolor exercises), clay sculpture, and religious renewal (especially sacramental communion). *The Christian Community* is the movement for religious renewal. Private consultations with a priest/pastor of *The Christian Community* may also serve the journeyer. Anthroposophy may offer invaluable help, not only books, but in practice and with key individuals. Both priests/pastors and key anthroposophists have helped me on my journey to my soul's awakening and after.

Each person has to go her/his own path, but practices such as these can prove beneficial if not decisive.

We know their can be no world-progress without individual progress. Thus, if we wish to make a contribution to society, we must work on ourselves. These practices are beneficial for our own development, but they are also necessary for the whole of society. The two are actually one: the welfare of the human soul and of humanity, for humanity suffers in us, rejoices in us, dwells in us. In our small suffering and joys, in our hurt and pain, we are humanity. Therefore the welfare of each single soul is of immeasurable worth. If we help one other human being, then our life has not been in vain. We think of Anne Sullivan with Helen Keller. We require personal tending (Christ) in a time of illness.

****

Any and all initiative taken without external stimulus or motivation, but only from within, is essential. To the degree that I take initiative—of my own choice (although a guiding indication may be recognized and pursued in freedom)—and really follow through with self-discipline, and application and endurance or implementation, to that extent will I progress on my journey, path regardless. This may guide me for my karma. This may be my vocation. All vocation is karmic; we suffer it.

My good Swedish father Arne Lindgren began studying English with an Englishwoman in Sweden when he was eleven years old. That is a very young age to take such initiative. It served him well. He spent most of his 75-year life in Los Angeles where he met and married my Mother; they had two children. His English was better than most Americans.

It may seem to leave things open, but when we recognize the uniqueness of our path when once we find it, that it belongs to us according to our destiny and individuality and not to some one else, we see its necessity. The path of each one of us is singular, and each one must find and travel it. We will know it because of its personal meaning and genuineness.

****

What is genuine stands apart from all else. Think of a handmade piece of craftsmanship. Think of the work of a fine artist or sculptor. Think of an interesting building (architecture). Think of real acumen, logic. Think of reason and knowledge. Think of an original work of music. Think of a true poem. Think of memory. Think of deep feeling. Think of genuine thought. Think of human strength and sincere words. Think of wise gesture. Think of true love. Think of true beauty. Think of a wonderful head of hair. Think of original or hearty, struggling and suffering. Think of kind or hurting and wise with might but nice and friendly human beings. All these things are genuine. All of them have meaning to us; we cherish them.

****

Our path suits us perfectly. We must only find it. It demands neither too much nor too little from us, but the endurance or work must begin and continue steadily, for only those who are engaged in an inner soul battle make progress. Progress is inner, although the all-important work on the temperament can be quite physical. It is necessary for each one of us if we are to go forwards.

There are different stages in development, and the first stage is preparatory. But all future development that is progress depends entirely on this first stage, so whatever we endure or do in karma creation, suffering, and endurance is crucial for our entire future. Deep down we all know this in our feeling, in our hearts, for that is where karma is centered. And this center is essential for our past, present, and future. It is our feeling for the truth that is unmistakable, which is our true guide on our path, because feeling always tells the truth. Therefore our destiny is formed and resolved in the truth of human feeling in our karma on Earth. This happens over the course of many reincarnations or lifetimes, which is of the human spirit. This is our eternal individuality, which gathers our soul experiences during incarnations, the karmic experiences that become our destiny—for learning, for spiritual development.

We see the relationships: the body and heredity; the soul and karma (the destiny); the spirit and reincarnation. These are the three laws. The soul is the link or bridge between the spirit and the body in earthly life in reincarnations. This soul has a destiny it has created for itself that rules its life. The spirit takes karmic experiences from previous embodiments or reincarnations, and it thereby learns and develops according to spiritual laws and the destiny. Thus karma is necessary for all learning.

We are spiritually blind, deaf, mute, and ignorant before we awaken in Christ, but we know in our feeling and other sensing when we are headed in the right direction, what choices to make, what to avoid, what to welcome, what not to do, what to do. In key wise individuals we always feel His presence in our hearts and inner-outer environment. These individuals are there for us. They ever avail themselves to us, but they leave us entirely free to go to them or no. They recognize all forms of intelligence, and they also see through all human cleverness, talent, and wisdom we may possess to what is singular and genuine in us. Neither can they be misled; Christ—the 'I AM'—stands strong and immovable in them. They leave us entirely free.

****

Following the soul's spiritual awakening to Christ the individual embarks on a new path: one of the learning of Self-knowledge that is in full and wide-awake consciousness. The destiny's journey continues, but now it is entirely different because perception and thought are wakeful, autonomous, and living. Perception and thinking include, not only experiences by way of the senses and the brain, which are lifeless in quality and content, and which we retain, but also objective and sensitive feeling, and living (supra-sensory) perceptions and living (sense-free) thinking. This perception and this thinking are thus both objective, while we also observe the sensory world and the brain-bound thoughts, but with new objectivity, with sense-free thinking.

The road of knowing is not thinking; thinking directs the pupil or knower on the path of knowledge. Perception becomes knowledge. The feeling (the heart) becomes an objective organ of perceptive knowledge. To perceive is to know. We recall what was said regarding the soul's spiritual awakening to Christ (the true idea) in reality: Christ-knowledge or communion becomes Self-knowledge. This is our true, higher Self: the 'I AM' (Christ's only true Name) in our I; otherwise we are empty.

Penetration into the Thought-Center of the World proceeds in ever-intensifying thinking. There are no limits to knowledge (experience) but those we impose on ourselves. It depends on inwardness: deepening in knowledge-experience. Following a quite brief period of a few years' probation of the soul, which is very painful, the individual arrives at the spirit-threshold.

Ordinarily, this happens only at death when human existence and consciousness is left behind and spiritual dimensions are entered. But now the individual is empowered by Christ—the 'I AM' within his/her heart and soul—to cross over this threshold while fully conscious and awake in the physical body. On crossing the spirit-threshold the soul's thinking, feeling, and willing faculties become independent of one another such that they may be activated singly, in pairs, or all three simultaneously (but separately), granting the gifted person a new freedom. With this freedom of soul comes the will to love, and with spiritual love the purpose to serve humanity in selfless sacrifices with the vision of the heart, which is the spirit of freedom. This is the Christ-communion of which we have written. One crosses the spirit-threshold to spiritual dimensions and back again to physical reality at will. So begins the next part of the earthly journey of the destiny where it works itself out in the course of life. All who are so gifted know this. This is also the reality of divine or Christ-love, for some an experience of ever-deepening and heightening learning, for others Christianity is apparent and developed immediately.

Los Angeles
November 26/29
Revised and edited December 1-2, 2012
Further revised and edited May 16/19-20
October 29-30, 2014

Christ Need and Christ Help

The more willing we are, the more help we will receive, which means the closer we are to Christ. This closeness is internal in the sense that it is entirely inwards. It is not environmental, although the help comes in the person of a human being who occupies an outside physical space. This is clear, for two people cannot be in the same space at the same time. But the help does not occur spatially. It is within, in the heart and soul.

Where we are physically gathered together with an/other human being/s, the closeness is always an inner one. Hence we say, "We became so close." Or, "We were close from the first meeting." "We are soul mates; we both knew this the moment we first met." This has twofold meaning. First of all, the meeting or coming together is in the same place at the same time. Second, the closeness or being close is entirely within. "We have always been close, ever since we met at _____ 's home in _____ 2012."

But the closeness is not physical. To begin with it is felt as a physical presence, but we know we do not feel close to objects, such as rocks or cups, plates or spoons. Their presence is *only* physical. The physical presence of a human being can be much deeper. It is also one of soul and spirit.

This becomes clear when we consider one or both persons have died. If the connection is a karmic one, the closeness continues after death. What this means is we can be helped by (and help) another after her/his physical death. For death is a purely physical event. It has no meaning spiritually, except that the separation involved in dwelling in a physical body ceases to exist.

Death transcending overcomes all boundaries. There are no borders in the life between death and rebirth, neither is there separation any more.

This is the condition in the world of the stars. The so-called 'dead' are in the company of heaven, together with the holy Trinity, the hierarchies, heavenly hosts, or divine beings of God.

There are key people with whom this closeness takes on a deeper and stronger meaning. This is always felt. This is karmic. These individuals are Christ-human beings or helpers of Christ. They are the true servants of God. Where it is possible, and in many cases actual, for two persons, neither of whom is a Christ-human being, to be close to one another in heart and soul, then the connection is deeper. Then it penetrates into the core essence of the human heart.

After someone has received a drop of the spiritual sun essence (of Christ), their need for communion with Christ increases. Indeed, it must transpire, for the soul cannot live without it. This communion always involves at least three beings: the Christ Being; another human being, a discarnate soul (the so-called 'dead'), another being (such as an angelic being), or a nature-phenomenon; and one's own being. Hence it is a communion of souls with the Christ-Being. This can be sacramental (physical) or spiritual. For sacramental communion to occur, at least two human beings must be gathered together.

In sacramental communion, we partake of Christ's flesh and blood in the elements (the Bread and the Cup) in transubstantiation. This is what nourishes our souls, through our physical bodies in a process called the etherisation of the blood where Christ's blood flows in our veins (in our blood). The Christ-Spirit descends to earth in the elements. We are a part of the sacramental process as we bake the bread from the grain and crush the grapes into juice.

In spiritual communion, we are also joined together with Christ. This is a different process where we perceive Christ with our hearts and souls in another human being, in a nature-phenomenon, or with a discarnate being, such as a deceased loved one or an angelic being. It is also warm and felt in the heart, but it is the perception of Christ that is of essence.

Each time we experience the mystery of communion we are nourished and strengthened to continue on with our earthly journey until, once again, we are in the Spiritual Homeland (heaven), either during sleep or in the life between death and rebirth.

Willingness to receive help signifies need. If I do not want help in the depths of my soul, how can I find it? If I do not require something, intensity my efforts and need depending, how may I receive it? Only where there is genuine need may the help needed be granted.

God sees each human being according to his/her need. God meets human need through His workers that is servants. Then, in an encounter with a servant of God (a Christ-human being), some one needs the help of Christ (s/he wants Christ's help), Christ gives the needy person the help they seek or ask for, because the servant knows this.

How does the servant of Christ know when some one needs that is wants the help of Christ? Because such a servant stands in the world as a Christ-tree stands in a forest of trees. The person who needs that is wants help will always go to the servant who is standing there. The helper of Christ makes her/himself available to all those who seek His help, all who are in need, every one who wants the help of Christ. S/he senses the seeker at once, because the seeker makes him/herself unmistakably known. These are often through mutual human beings. One connection leads to another by way of mention, for example. Or the helper of Christ becomes aware of a karmic connection when the seeker appears at a lecture or comes to her/him in another context. Ever ready, the helper of Christ avails him/herself of all who are in need. Indeed, this is the main task of the helper of Christ, serving Him in human souls in need of Christ.

Here, there is no compulsion. Here, we know our friend is true. However great is our friend, s/he serves us in our deep need of Christ. Indeed the greater the servant of Christ, the more help s/he offers. Those who have little or no need for the help of Christ have little or nothing. They have no purpose in life. There, the servant can do nothing. It matters not what the servant personally wants. It matters only to serve Christ in all those human beings who are looking for help. Again, this means they are in need of Christ's help.

There is no time to waste. Time is precious. Our time on earth is precious. What makes our time on earth precious? All those times and places where we gather together in Christ's Name that is receive the help of Christ.

We receive the help of Christ in the same measure we are in need of it, which is the measure in which we want it. In matters of soul, *need and help are equal.* The more I want something, the closer I come to it. The more I want Christ, need Christ, the more He comes to me, finds me. He finds me in the persons of the servants of Christ. The servants of Christ need Christ as well, but in the persons of immature souls. Thus karmic relationships are formed where both human beings receive the help they require.

If I want something very badly, I must necessarily experience it. This deep wanting in me is my need. This need is for Christ, though I know His Name not. This wanting of mine is my need for Him. If I want only a little, then my need is only a little. Then I will be helped only a little. If my wanting is greater, then my need is greater. Then I will be helped much more. If my wanting is very great, then my need is very great, and I will receive a great deal of help.

Those who want that is need Christ's help very badly, they are the seekers after Christ. They actively seek Christ's help. They may not know this, but that is of no account. They do know they want something very badly. If they do not have the word that is the name for this, then they are not yet conscious of Christ. But they know they want that is need Him, because they can feel this, and their wanting becomes everything they are doing.

The seekers include those who know Christ. Indeed they depend on Christ in karma in order to live, and in large measure. But all seekers, and all those who need help that is want help who are not yet seekers, receive the help of Christ.

The seekers are willing to suffer much more. Seeking help always entails trials and ordeals. But they who are the seekers are willing, because they want the help of Christ so much that the suffering becomes very dear to them.

Seeking is the only truly rewarding and satisfying life. My efforts or need is met by help in the same measure as my seeking Christ.

Here is the last stanza of a poem I composed in 2004 entitled "Cupid's Bow" that describes the equality of need and help:

Sun, Thou Christ, dost bide with us
Though we many, numerous
Each receives his portion be
For his own humanity.

Alan Lindgren
Santa Monica, California
July 23, 2011
Los Angeles
October 30, 2014

Sculpted forms and colors painted
I am with them well-acquainted
But I know that not alone
Are they inner in me home
No within me are the same
Powers creative of my name
I can see the hallowed Thou
Love is smiling on my brow
Thou and I are only One
Eternity of Nature's Sun.

a free verse translation
composed by Alan Lindgren
from a German poem by Christian Morgenstern

October 27, 2014

Wonder

What a wonder wills in me
Rhythms pulsing poetry
Sounds of speech like song inspire
Words of languages in choir.

If you wonder who I am
Speak my poetry again
Find my rhythms, feel my words
Hear my vowels, those little birds!

October 27, 2014

Finding autumn mountains
Forests surrounding lakes
Fog the woods
Green the firs' long-needled branches
A lumberjack
In solitude wandering with axe
Finds a tall evergreen
Falls it with few mighty swings

Winter snows blanket the world
Lakes frozen hard
Snowflakes fall softly
Decking house and tree
With white wonder

Springtime mornings
Rising sun melts freezing waters
Winter begins to flow in streams
Trees bud
Small birds sing merrily
My heart gladdens to music
Of Mother Nature's spring

Warmth of green summers
Sunshine-imbued out-breath of air
Lulls lazily all life
To daydreams 'til evenings
Begin to cool into balmy nights of moon and stars.

November 2/4, 2014

Tender

A mountain stood
Massive there
Impenetrable as stone and cliff

I knew when
My soul healed
I shone, my higher Self in me
Through my mind free
Remaining strong

But warm, tender, my dear heart
I inwardly
Give and receive
Pure heart-feeling
I found, in me.

November 19, 2014

Family

I found in humankind my mind
Within my God, in me He signed
I felt within my heart revere
The sunlight of the day so clear

If you would understand a pearl
Return from visiting the world
To hearth and home find warmth again
Once more the family of Man.

Alan Lindgren
Los Angeles
November 23, 2014

About the Author

Alan Lindgren was born in Encino, California in 1962. He is a poet by vocation, and a gifted fiction and non-fiction writer as well. He has forty-eight books published 1987 and 1997–2014. Of his 1,500 poems over 1000 are published. His tales and stories are published. His five biographies and an autobiography are published. Over 200 of his well over 300 articles and essays have seen publication. He is a playwright with four plays published and the published librettist to an operetta.

Mr. Lindgren's fiction, articles, and poetry have appeared in *Biodynamics*, a publication of the *Bio-Dynamic Farming and Gardening Association, Inc.*, *The Correspondence*, newsletter of the Central Region of the Anthroposophical Society in America, and Highland Hall Waldorf School's newsletter *Rhythms*. His work has been used in an anthroposophical studies-in-English program and displayed at the Chicago Seminary of the Christian Community and a Christian Community church for students, members, and others.

He is a lyric poet. He has composed poetry since 1986, written fiction 1987/1993 on, non-fiction 2001 on, biography and autobiography in 2005/2006. He wrote his plays in 2010 and operetta libretto in 2012. He painted a series of phthalo blue watercolors entitled *Study in Blue* in 1999. After studying classical piano for ten years, Mr. Lindgren played as a *virtuoso* in May of 1987. One day before his twenty-third birthday, on August 4, 1985, he gave the *a cappella* solo *Were You There?*

1982-1984; 1985-1986 Mr. Lindgren majored in German literature at Pomona College where he also studied sculpture, working primarily in *California alabaster*. His sculpture has appeared in three exhibitions. In 1984-1985 he attended the Freies Jugendseminar Stuttgart in Stuttgart, Germany, an anthroposophical arts youth seminar in the German language where he studied speech formation, eurythmy, clay sculpture, and other subjects. Some of his sculptures are perfect works of art. He has eurythmy abilities. He is a student of the work of Rudolf Steiner.

In 1982 Mr. Lindgren worked on the bio-dynamic farm Buschberghof in Schleswig-Holstein, Germany. In 1981-1982 he studied German privately. Through his private and college studies, and his experiences in

About the Author

Germany, he achieved proficiency in the language. Some of his poems of note are in German, his favorite language.

As a child and youth, Mr. Lindgren attended Waldorf Schools (Highland Hall in Northridge, California, October 1973-1980; Green Meadow Waldorf School in Spring Valley, NY, autumn 1979). His Waldorf education is essential to his life. In 1971-1972 he lived with his family in Tunis, Tunisia, North Africa.

He has had a variety of work experiences including dish washing, waiting on tables, clerking in a drugstore, assistant teaching of small children on four occasions, gardening, student grounds work, work as a farmhand, a handyman, in a hardware store, secretarial work, and production line work in a warehouse. He has tutored math and English. He is conversant in Spanish. He has done translation work from German into English.

Alongside writing, his greatest pleasures include walking, reading German, American, and English literature (particularly anthroposophy, the classics, and poetry), and playing and listening to live classical music. He has sung in eight choirs and enjoyed singing since the Fourth Grade. He is a first tenor with a sweet voice. His favorite music is German baroque religious—especially J. S. Bach—and all folk music.

Mr. Lindgren loves people of all ages. The warm and beautiful sun; the small birds, playful squirrels, friendly dogs, and little cats; the green, blue, purple, and white valleys, hills, and mountains; the bright radiant clouds and sunlight; the colorful blossoms; and the wondrous ocean, moon, and stars, speak to the poet in him. He has a special relationship to the realm of light and color. This is evinced in his love of flowers, the play of light, shadow, and color in the heavens, and painting.

He is a "child of anthroposophy and of the Christian Community." His dearest friends are anthroposophists and priest-pastors. His father Arne Lindgren (1918-1994) was an anthroposophist from Sweden.

Mr. Lindgren lives and works in Los Angeles. His dear Mother lives nearby so that they can visit often.

www.ingramcontent.com/pod-product-compliance
Lightning Source LLC
Chambersburg PA
CBHW020244030726

47499CB00001B/47